T0163573

Mothers on Trial

··

THE BATTLE FOR CHILDREN AND CUSTODY

··

Revised and Updated Second Edition

PHYLLIS CHESLER

Lawrence Hill Books

Library of Congress Cataloging-in-Publication Data

Chesler, Phyllis.

  Mothers on trial : the battle for children and custody / Phyllis Chesler. — Rev. and updated 2nd ed.

    p. cm.

  Includes bibliographical references and index.

  ISBN 978-1-55652-999-3 (pbk.)

  1. Custody of children—United States. 2. Mothers—Legal status, laws, etc.—United States. I. Title.

  KF547.C465 2011

  346.7301'73—dc22

                    2011005769

Cover and interior design: Sarah Olson
Cover photograph: © Andrew Davis/Trevillion Images

Second edition
Published by Lawrence Hill Books
An imprint of Chicago Review Press, Incorporated
814 North Franklin Street
Chicago, Illinois 60610
ISBN 978-1-55652-999-3
Printed in the United States of America
5 4 3 2 1

Contents

··············

Acknowledgments

··············

I am grateful to my literary agents—Jane Dystel, Miriam Goderich, Chasya Milgrom, and Stephanie DeVita—for connecting me with Chicago Review Press/Lawrence Hill Books. I am grateful to my editor at Lawrence Hill, Sue Betz, and my copyeditor, Kelly Wilson, who both believed in this work and helped me improve it.

I wish to thank the lawyers who assisted me in my review of contemporary legal trends, especially Alisa Greenstein and Teresa Schiller. I am especially grateful to Marcia Pappas, president of NOW–New York State, and to Dr. Mo Therese Hannah for distributing my questionnaires, which in turn led to many in-depth interviews.

I would also like to acknowledge the very efficient work of my assistant, Nathan Bloom, who made a very difficult task less so, and the valuable and faithful research assistance of Fern Sidman. I am filled with gratitude for the ongoing philanthropic and visionary support of my work by Cornelia Foster.

Above all, I would like to thank the custodially embattled mothers who shared their stories and their documentation with me. They showed me once again how strong and courageous mothers can be, even as they undergo the most profound siege.

New Introduction to the 2011 Lawrence Hill Books Edition

....

This is a book that cried out to be written. I first heard that cry in the mid-1970s and, after years of research, published the first edition of *Mothers on Trial: The Battle for Children and Custody* in 1986. At the time, the book created a firestorm and was widely, if controversially, received.

In the last twenty-five years, there have been some improvements, but matters have decidedly worsened. The book you are holding has been revised and updated and brought into the twenty-first century.

Myths about custody still abound. Most people still believe that the courts favor mothers over fathers—who are discriminated against because they are men—and that this is how it's always been.

This is not true.

For more than five thousand years, men—fathers—were legally *entitled* to sole custody of their children. Women—mothers—were *obliged* to bear, rear, and economically support children. No mother was ever legally entitled to custody of her own child.

During the nineteenth century, pro-child crusaders gradually convinced the state that young children required maternal "tenderness"—but only if their mothers were white, married, Christian, and moral. The children of African slaves, of Native American Indians, of immigrant, impoverished, sick, or "immoral" parents—all were untenderly appropriated by slave owners and by the state. They were clapped into orphanages, workhouses, and reformatories or farmed out into apprenticeships for "their own good."

By the turn of the century, a custodially challenged American mother enjoyed an equal right to custody in only nine states and the District of Columbia—and only if a state judge found her morally and economically worthy of motherhood. Until the 1920s, no American mother was entitled to any child support. Since then, few have received any.

The maternal presumption was never interpreted as a maternal right. The maternal presumption has always been viewed as secondary to the child's "best interests"—as determined by a judge. This "best interest" was always seen as synonymous with "paternal rights."

The contemporary fathers' rights (or fathers' supremacist) movement, which has been wildly successful in instituting joint custody and false concepts such as "parental alienation syndrome," is also a throwback to the darkest days of patriarchy. It is not the modern, feminist, progressive movement it claims to be. Individual men may indeed be good fathers, and, like good mothers, they too may encounter discrimination and injustice in the court system. What I am talking about here is an *organized* political, educational, and legal movement against motherhood that has turned the clock back.

This book is about what it means to be a "good enough" mother and about the trials such mothers endure when they are custodially challenged. This book is not about happy marriages or happy divorces—it is about marriages and divorces that erupt into wild and bitter custody battles.

By now, many books have been written about the role of caring and responsible fathers, about male longings for a child, and about a child's need for fathering. This book clarifies the difference between how a "good enough" mother mothers and a "good enough" father fathers. It clarifies the difference between male custodial *rights* and female custodial *obligations*.

Since *Mothers on Trial* was first published in 1986, thousands of mothers have called or written. "I'm in your book," they say. "It's as if you knew my story personally." "You showed me that it's not just happening to me, that it's not my fault." And, *"Can you help me save my children?"*

In the first edition of *Mothers on Trial*, I challenged the myth that fit mothers always win custody—indeed, I found that when fathers fight, they win custody 70 percent of the time, whether or not they have been absent or violent. Since then, other studies, including ten state supreme court reports on gender bias in the courts, have appeared that support most of what I say. (The Massachusetts report actually confirms my statistic of 70 percent.[1])

Although the majority of custodial parents are usually mothers, this doesn't mean that mothers have *won* their children in a battle. Rather, mothers often retain custody when fathers choose not to fight for it. Those fathers who fight tend to win custody, not because mothers are unfit or because fathers have been the primary caretakers of their children but because mothers are women and are held to a much higher standard of parenting.

Many judges also assume that the father who fights for custody is rare and therefore should be rewarded for loving his children, or they assume that something is wrong with the mother. What may be wrong with the mother is that she and her children are being systematically impoverished, psychologically and legally harassed, and physically battered by the very father who is fighting for custody.

Today more and more mothers, as well as the leadership of the shelter movement for battered women, have realized that battered women risk losing custody if they seek child support or attempt to limit visitation. Incredibly, mothers also risk losing custody if they accuse fathers of physically or sexually abusing them or their children—*even or especially if these allegations are supported by experts.*

An ideal father is expected to legally acknowledge and economically support his children. Fathers who do anything more for their children are often seen as "better" than mothers, who are, after all, supposed to do everything.

The ideal of fatherhood is sacred. As such, it protects each father from the consequences of his actions. The ideal of motherhood is sacred, too. It exposes all mothers as imperfect. No human mother can embody the maternal ideal perfectly enough.

Given so many double standards for fit mothering and fathering and so many anti-mother biases, I wanted to know: Could a "good enough" mother lose custody of a child to a relatively uninvolved or abusive father? How often could this happen?

I first interviewed sixty mothers who had been their children's primary caregivers, were demographically similar to the majority of divorced white mothers in America, and had been custodially challenged in each geographical region of the United States and Canada.*

On the basis of these interviews I was able to study how often "good enough" mothers can lose custody *when their ex-husbands challenge them.* I

---

* I also interviewed fifty mothers who were African, Asian, Hispanic, and Native American. Some—but not all—are part of this first study. They are very much a part of this book.

was able to study why "good enough" mothers lose custody battles and how having to battle for custody affects them.

On the basis of these interviews and on the basis of additional interviews with fifty-five custodially embattled fathers, I was able to study the kinds of husbands and fathers who battled for custody, their motives for battling, and how and why they won or lost. I was also able to study the extent to which the custodially triumphant father encouraged or allowed the losing mother access to her children afterward.

To repeat: Seventy percent of my "good enough" mothers lost custody of their children.

Today the same experts who once tyrannized women with their advice about the importance of the mother-child bond appear, in the context of custody battles, ready to ignore it or refer to it, if at all, as of only temporary importance. They view the mother-child bond as expendable if it is less than ideal or another woman is available. Perfectly fit mothers are viewed as interchangeable with a paternal grandmother or a second wife.

In 1975 New York judge Guy Ribaudo awarded sole custody of two children to their father, Dr. Lee Salk. Their mother, Kersten Salk, was not accused of being an "unfit" mother. It was clear that Kersten, not Lee, had reared their children from birth "without the aid of a governess" and that Lee would probably require the aid of a "third party" housekeeper-governess were he to gain sole custody. The judge used an "affirmative standard" to decide which parent was "better fit" to guide the "development of the children and their future." Kersten Salk's full-time housekeeping and mothering were discounted in favor of Lee Salk's psychological expertise and "intellectually exciting" lifestyle. Lee was widely quoted as saying the following: "Fathers should have equal rights with mothers in custody cases and more and more fathers are getting custody. . . . The decision in *Salk v. Salk* will touch every child in America in some way. It will also give more fathers the 'incentive' to seek custody of their children."[2]

This case swept through public consciousness; it was an ominous warning, a reminder that children are only on loan to "good enough" mothers. They could be recalled by their more intellectually and economically solvent fathers.

Although mothers still received no wages for their work at home and far less than equal pay for equal work outside the home, and although most fathers had yet to assume an equal share of home and child care, divorced fathers began to campaign for equal rights to sole custody, alimony, and child support and for mandatory joint custody.

Fathers' rights activists—both men and women—picketed my lectures, threatened lawsuits, and shouted at me on television. "Admit it. Ex-wives destroy men economically. They deprive fathers of visitation and brainwash the children against them. Fathers should have rights to alimony and child support. Joint custody should be mandatory. We've already convinced legislators and lawyers, judges and social workers, psychiatrists and journalists to see it our way."

Indeed, as we shall see, they have.

By 1991, more than forty states had shared-parenting statutes in which joint custody was either an option or preference, and most other states had recognized the concept of joint custody in case law.

The mothers began to find me. Would I testify on their behalf? Marta consulted me as a therapist. She said she was "depressed" and "wanted to kill herself." Weeping, she told me, "For fifteen years my children were my whole life. I did everything for them myself. Six months ago a judge gave my husband exclusive custody of our children. How could this nightmare ever happen? At first, I thought they'd come back to me on their own. But they haven't. Why should they? I have a small one-bedroom apartment. Their father was allowed to keep our five-bedroom house. He gives them complete freedom and the use of their own credit cards. I work as a salesgirl for very little money. Is this a reason to go on living?"

Carol, a complete stranger, asked me for money. "My husband kidnapped our six-year-old son two months ago. It's what they call a 'legal' kidnapping. We're only separated, not divorced. I need money to hire a detective to find them. I need money to hire a lawyer once they're found. I only have six hundred dollars in the bank. And I'm four months pregnant."

Rachel, also a stranger, mailed me a description of her custody battle. She entitled it *A Case of Matricide in an American Courtroom*. Rachel had a "nervous breakdown" after she lost her battle for child support, custody, and maternal visitation.

In 1977, when I myself was six months pregnant, I decided to study women and custody of children. The theme had claimed me.

Over the next eight years, I formally interviewed more than three hundred mothers, fathers, children, and custody experts in the United States and Canada and in sixty-five countries around the world. On the basis of these interviews, I conducted three original studies and six original surveys for the 1986 edition of this book. I wanted to understand why we take custodial mothers for granted but heroize custodial fathers, why we sympathize with noncustodial fathers but condemn noncustodial mothers, and why we grant noncustodial fathers the right to feel angry or sad but deny noncustodial mothers similar emotional "rights." I also wanted to compare what noncustodial mothers and fathers actually *do* and contrast it with how they perceive themselves and are perceived.

Must custodially embattled mothers be viewed only as victims? Can such mothers also be viewed as philosophical and spiritual warriors and heroes? Gradually I came to view them as such. Under siege, "good enough" mothers remained connected to their children in nurturant and nonviolent ways. They resisted the temptation to use violent means to obtain custody of their children. This is one of the reasons they lost custody. But they never disconnected—not even from children whom they never saw again.

THE 2011 UPDATE

What's changed since I first started researching and writing about custody battles?

Documented domestic violence does get factored in somewhat more than before. Where real assets exist, judges have the power to award more of them to mothers and children. Fewer mothers and fathers automatically lose custody or visitation because they are gay or because they have high-powered careers. However, certain injustices (crimes, really) that I first began tracking in the late 1970s have now gotten much worse. For example, battered women are losing custody to their batterers in record numbers. Children are being successfully brainwashed by fathers, but many mothers are being falsely accused of brainwashing. Worse: Children who mandated reporters—physicians, nurses, or teachers—report as having been sexually abused by their fathers are usually given to those very fathers. The mothers of these children are almost always viewed as having "coached" or "alienated" the children and, on this basis alone, are seen as "unfit" mothers.

I understand that this sounds unbelievable. But it is still true. The mothers of raped children, who are also described as "protective" mothers, are seen as guilty of "parental alienation syndrome." The fact that this concept, first pioneered by Dr. Richard Gardner and widely endorsed by fathers' rights groups, has been dismissed as junk science does not seem to matter. Most guardians ad litem, parenting counselors, mediators, lawyers, mental health professionals, and judges still act as if this syndrome were real and mainly find mothers, not fathers, guilty in this regard. In 2010 the American Psychiatric Association was still fighting to include a new disorder in the *Diagnostic and Statistical Manual of Mental Disorders*: the parental alienation disorder, to replace the debunked parental alienation syndrome.

In 2009 and 2010 more than fifty mothers from twenty-one U.S. states* and a number of foreign countries all shared their stories with me. Their cases took place between the late 1980s and 2010. Some cases are still ongoing.

In some instances, I spoke with the mothers in person or at length on the phone. Some mothers filled out questionnaires, but many also sent additional narratives and documentation. Some mothers sent me eloquent, beautifully written, full-length memoirs. Some wrote pithy but equally heartbreaking accounts of their marriages and custody battles.†

Custody battles can take a very long time. They range from only several years to more than fifteen or twenty. They may have profound legal, economic, social, psychological, and even medical consequences for years afterward, perhaps forever.

Going through a custody battle is like going through a war. One does not emerge unscathed. Yes, one may learn important lessons, but one may also be left broken and incapable of trusting others, including our so-called justice system, ever again.

With a few exceptions, most of my 2010 mother-interviewees said that the system was "corrupt" and that lawyers and judges don't care about "justice," are "very biased," or can be "bought and sold." These mothers said that social workers, mental health professionals, guardians ad litem, and parent coordinators—especially if they were women—actively "disliked" and were "cruel and hostile" to them as *women*. (Perhaps they expected women

---

* The American cases took place in Alaska, California, Colorado, Florida, Georgia, Hawaii, Illinois, Iowa, Kansas, Maryland, Missouri, New Jersey, New York, Ohio, Oklahoma, Pennsylvania, Texas, Vermont, Virginia, Wisconsin, and Washington.

† In most instances I have changed the names of my mother-interviewees and their children. I have also renamed some, but not all, of any experts involved in a particular case. When a mother requested it, I changed the name of the state where her custody battle took place.

to be more compassionate toward other women. In this, they were sadly mistaken).

Also, many mothers found that female professionals were often completely taken in by charming, sociopathic men ("parasites," "smother-fathers"), dangerously violent men, and men who sexually abused their children.

Perhaps the mothers who sent me their stories were married to uniquely terrible men who used the court system to make their lives a living hell; perhaps mothers who did not write to me had the good fortune to have been married to and divorced from far nicer men.

Good fathers definitely exist. Some fathers move heaven and earth to rescue their children from a genuinely mentally ill mother but do not try to alienate the children from her. If the mother has been the primary caretaker, some fathers give up custody, pay a decent amount of child support (and continue to do so), and work out a relationship with their children based on what's good for both the children and their mother. These men exist. They do not launch custody battles from hell.

And good fathers are also discriminated against in a variety of ways in the courtroom. For example, mothers who are independently wealthy or who come from powerful families can and do custodially persecute good-enough fathers. That is the subject of another book. And, when fathers do assume primary-caretaker obligations, traditional judges may view them unfairly as "sissies" or "losers." Liberal judges will award them custody in a heartbeat.

For this 2011 edition, I also reviewed hundreds of legal decisions, which I obtained through LexisNexis and which all commenced and/or were resolved in the last quarter century. I interviewed lawyers and judges. I clipped articles about custody battles that appeared in the media from 1990 to 2010. Some were celebrity cases; others concerned high-profile international kidnapping cases; some were about one spouse's murder of the other during the course of a custody battle.

When I was researching the 1986 edition of *Mothers on Trial*, joint custody was a totally new idea. Now, as I've previously noted, "shared parenting" or joint custody (defined in a variety of ways) is the preferred norm. Joint custody is seen as fair, progressive, feminist, and in the child's best interest—even though a number of recent studies have shown that under certain conditions joint custody may be harmful to the children involved. Other studies conclude that we cannot prove that a particular custodial arrangement is either helpful or harmful to children.

For example, according to a 1989 study, "a link was consistently found between frequency of visitation/transitions between parents and [child] maladjustment." The study also found that "children shuffled more frequently between parents were more exposed to and involved in parental conflict and aggression and were more often perceived by both parents as being depressed, withdrawn, uncommunicative, and/or aggressive."[3]

A 2003 study found that "alternating custody"—for example, week on, week off—"was associated with 'disorganized attachment' in 60 percent of infants under 18 months. Older children and adults who had endured this arrangement as youngsters exhibited what the researcher described as 'alarming levels of emotional insecurity and poor ability to regulate strong emotion.'"[4] Nevertheless, from the 1980s on, the entire national court system and its various helpers believed that joint custody was the preferred way to go.

As we shall see, joint custody research in the twenty-first century is a minefield of dangerous biases, conflicting conclusions,[5] and outright lies.

THE VIEW FROM THE BENCH

While lawyers and judges are quick to say that joint custody should not apply where there is domestic violence and incest, they are often the ones who do not believe that domestic violence and incest exist all that much. And, although lawyers and judges also say that joint custody may not work in "high-conflict divorces," that does not mean that they still don't encourage or even order it.

From their point of view, if everyone walks away with something, there is less likelihood that their decision will be appealed or that the case will continue to stall. One judge said, "Maybe this will actually force these warring parties to grow up and learn to compromise for the sake of their children."

Thus, the role of "parenting coordinators" and guardians ad litem has increased considerably. Many mothers view them as impoverishing agents because they are ordered to pay for their services.

Talk to some good judges—those who are hardworking, experienced, and not corrupt—and you will find that their concerns are far different from those who consume the mothers who appear before them. Judicial concerns are not those of the plaintiffs or defendants. What you will hear is about how important it is to move the cases along, how huge the backlog always is, and how impossible it is to spend too much time on any one case. Judges are annoyed, even contemptuous, when rich people can afford to pay for a long, drawn-out trial. They understand that the working poor have no such luxury, and, at both conscious and unconscious levels, the judges may resent this disparity and despair over the arrogance of the rich. One judge said, "Rich people fight over everything. Even if they don't need it, they will prolong the case in order to 'win.' It can be a second boat, a third home, a million dollar piece of art over another. They are spoiled children and I only pity their real children."

Talk to judges and listen to them speak, and you will realize that judges do not feel responsible for the perpetual logjams that frustrate, enrage, and impoverish mothers. In fact, judges feel that they too are victims of a system that does not pay them that well. They feel it does not allot resources for the necessary number of judges. The system is beyond bursting at the seams. In addition, the matrimonial bench is utterly devalued because it concerns "families," "mothers," and "children," all of whom are not high on the priority totem pole.

Most judges are overworked and underpaid compared to what the lawyers who appear before them are paid. Judges are not given the proper time to really hear a case. They are forced into forcing plaintiffs and defendants to accept limited, far-from-perfect settlements, because that will close the case and get it off the judge's roster. They opt for hard-and-fast compromises in the interest of moving a case along.

From the point of view of a "protective" mother whose child is being molested, there can be no compromise. Allowing a pedophile father or a domestically violent husband to have access to his former spouse or child endangers both mother and child. Such mothers protest. They will not play ball. Their relationship to their children is not a corporate-like entity. It is "all or nothing" as far as they are concerned. They resist for as long as their money holds out—and then they go pro se.

Their resistance to compromise is viewed as proof of "narcissism" or "mental instability." The mother who insists on not compromising is also viewed as annoying, difficult, impossible, unrealistic, and perhaps even dangerous to the smooth functioning of an already overburdened system.

Unless she has unlimited funds, it will cost her lawyer hundreds of thousands—maybe even millions—of dollars to fight for an *uncompromised* settlement. Some mothers fully expect their lawyers to do so, and when lawyers cannot, or refuse to do so, a mother will often turn on them and sue them for malpractice. "Protective" mothers view a lawyer who needs to make a living as a traitor and a sellout.

Mothers do not understand how to divide a baby in half or share parenting with an absent, neglectful, or abusive father. Judges do not see it as dividing the baby in half at all. One judge pointed out, very reasonably, that in order to keep the nonprimary caretaker involved in a nonembittered way, the judge must give him or her some things to do.

"But what if this father has never taken any responsibility and does not know what he is doing?" I asked.

"All the more reason to bring him in. It can't be good for a child to have no contact with the nonprimary-caretaker parent."

Please note the careful, automatically gender-neutral language that one might initially view as a feminist step forward. And it is—except that such language usually "disappears" the much harder work that mothers (primary caretakers) have undertaken, the higher standards to which they are held, and the nonprimary caretaker's failure to take primary-caretaking responsibility during the marriage, not just after the divorce.

The judge continued. "Why punish a child because their nonprimary-caretaker parent did not function as a caretaker in the past? As the child grows, nonprimary-caretaker parents can offer the child different opportunities."

The judge was right, and yet she was absolutely committed to the following myths: (1) sane, good parents are ultimately going to do whatever's in their child's best interests; (2) all divorcing and custody-battling parents are equally crazy and have to be forced into better behavior; (3) mothers routinely allege battering falsely; (4) mothers are crazier and more difficult to deal with than fathers; and (5) mothers, not fathers, tend to "alienate" the child from the other parent.

These are all myths.

Myth 1: Are divorcing parents really "reasonable grown-ups"? Many parents are far from ideal, even far from adequate. What is known as a "high-conflict" divorce does not involve parents who have their child's best interests at heart. They are often more concerned with their own interests.

Myth 2: Sometimes a father is a charming sociopath. Just as we have no way of distinguishing rapists from non-rapists, we have no easy way to "spot" a pedophile, a parasite, or a wife beater. Sometimes a mother is genuinely sadistic, abusive, or bipolar. This is more quickly spotted, diagnosed, or even assumed by laypeople in the court system. Thus, if a mother has been losing sleep over the possibility of losing her children and/or is exhibiting the normal human response to being battered or terrorized at home, she may also be stigmatized by the belief that women are naturally "crazy" and "impossible."

Myth 3: Most mothers do not allege battering falsely. Some, a minority, do.

Myth 4: Mothers are not necessarily "crazier" than fathers; some are. However, facing the end of a marriage, the probable poverty it may entail, plus a possible custody loss, is a far greater stressor for mothers than for fathers. It does make them highly nervous, vigilant, overly demanding, unrealistic, and prone to engaging in self-sabotaging tactics. Men tend to recoup more quickly; women don't.

Many fathers, on the other hand, are more capable of treating a custody battle as just one more businesslike venture. This style is more compatible with what lawyers and judges need. Thus, even if the father is a secret drunk or drug addict, an embezzler, an active philanderer, and a whoremonger and/or treats his wife and children coldly, sadistically, and abusively, these facts will not necessarily come into play in a custody battle.

Myth 5: According to most research and statistical data and my own interviews, it is mainly fathers who brainwash and kidnap children, not mothers. Fathers falsely claim "parental alienation" when it is not true; yet they are believed. Mothers claim brainwashing when it is true, but they are not often believed.

I do not view matrimonial lawyers as the main or sole problem. True—some lawyers are grossly incompetent and fail their female clients in every way: by misadvising them, sleeping with them, and prolonging their cases unnecessarily for monetary reasons. But it is also true that many lawyers serve their female (and male) clients effectively, even nobly.

Lawyers do not cause men to impoverish, batter, or abuse their wives and children; lawyers themselves are often hobbled by a system of laws and by a courtroom pace that is glacial. One cannot blame lawyers because it is enormously expensive to wage a high-conflict divorce. Some women expect their lawyers to actually *pay* for their divorces and feel betrayed when lawyers will not or cannot do so. With some exceptions, our government will not and cannot subsidize the cost of high-conflict divorces for the parent, usually the mother, who is without resources in a country where money does buy one's chance to obtain justice, however imperfect.

Custody cases are also very stressful and difficult for the judges involved, many of whom try very hard to do the right thing. The law is not able to cure sociopaths or psychopaths; sometimes compromising with the devil is, unbelievably, the only possible solution. A judge might only be able to "save" one child—not all three. A judge might be able to save a child from the probable horrors of state care by allowing custody to remain with one far-from-perfect parent.

Having said this, I would like to stress that both judges and lawyers, as well as the entire courtroom cast of characters (guardians ad litem, parenting coordinators, mental health experts, social workers, state agency employees, and the police) have acted in tragically anti-mother and anti-child ways. While feminist progress led to more women on the bench and to more female attorneys, many female professionals have shown very hard hearts toward the mothers whose fates are in their hands. So have their male counterparts.

For this 2011 edition of *Mothers on Trial*, I have given honorable discharges to six previous chapters, although I've preserved some of the material throughout the book. I've also added eight new chapters in addition to this introduction. The new chapters include "Court-Enabled Incest in the 1980s and 1990s," "Court-Enabled Incest in the Twenty-First Century," "Legal Torture from 1986 to 2010," "The Fathers' Supremacist Movement from the 1980s to 2010," "Contemporary Legal Trends, Part I," "Contemporary Legal Trends, Part II," "What to Expect When You're Expecting a Divorce: A Private Consultation with Divorce Lawyer Susan L. Bender," and a section of resources.

Immediately after first publishing this book, I coordinated a Senate briefing in Washington, D.C., that was attended by some hand-selected custodially embattled mothers, as well as then Congress, now Senate members Barbara Boxer and Chuck Schumer. Together with the National Organization for Women of New York State, I also coordinated a national speak-out about women's losing custody of children, which took place in New York City in the spring of 1986. Hundreds of mothers traveled from around the country to "speak out," and many legislators, judges, and lawyers also participated in panels. I videotaped this event but, as yet, have not made these precious videos available to the public. I also appeared on network television programs together with "my mothers," where we all said amazing things and were fairly well received. Women began organizing similar speak-outs elsewhere; I spoke at several in the United States and Canada the following year.

In 1984 a new nonprofit organization, ACES (the Association for Children for Enforcement of Support), was launched. It now has forty thousand members and one hundred sixty-five chapters in forty-five states.[6]

In 1988 Monica Getz founded the New York–based National Coalition for Family Justice, which offers ongoing support groups for divorcing and custodially embattled mothers. Their mission statement reads in part as follows: "To identify problems and advocate for systemic changes in the divorce and family court systems in order to make them fair, user friendly, accountable, and affordable; to provide victims and children involved in domestic violence situations with crisis intervention, information, support, legal access, and advocacy." They do not provide pro bono lawyers. But, in conjunction with the National Organization for Women in New York State, they have hosted important hearings and conferences.[7]

In the mid- to late 1980s "protective" and custodially embattled mothers also began running away from husbands who were sexually assaulting their child or children. Such mothers were almost all captured and jailed and lost custody of the children they were trying to protect. See chapter 4, which outlines my own original study; chapter 14, where I write about the underground for such mothers and my involvement in it; and chapter 15, "Court-Enabled Incest in the Twenty-First Century."

By the early twenty-first century, custodially embattled mothers, including battered and "protective" mothers, had begun to form organizations that now meet annually and monthly. In 2003 Dr. Mo Therese Hannah began a new organization, and in 2010 Dr. Hannah coordinated and hosted the *seventh* national Battered Mothers Custody Conference. More than five hundred women travel from around the country each year to attend it. In 2010 they began a quilt project, *Children Taken by the Family Courts*, which is modeled after the AIDS quilt. They have asked mothers who have legally lost their children to provide a commemoration panel. Dr. Hannah has also published a book, *Domestic Violence, Abuse, and Child Custody: Legal Strategies and Policy Issues*.[8]

In addition, many mothers throughout the Western world have created listserv groups and websites in which they tell (and keep updating) their own outrageous and heartbreaking stories in the hope that this information might help other women. Some ex-wives have become divorce coaches. (I recently interviewed two very impressive such coaches in New York: Margery Rubin, the author of *What Your Divorce Lawyer May Not Tell You*,[9] and Kim Lurie, the president of the Alliance to Restore Integrity in Divorce.[10])

Some mothers (including those whose interviews are contained in this book) became matrimonial lawyers and mental health professionals dedicated to helping mothers and children. Some researchers have tried to document ongoing injustices in terms of custody in family court. For example, in 2004 Renee Beeker launched the National Family Court Watch Project, which trained and sent volunteers into family court in California, Massachusetts, Michigan, New York, and Rhode Island between 2004 and 2009. Preliminary findings document a worrisome pattern of irrationality, contempt, prejudice, and a lack of evenhandedness on the part of judges and lawyers. In Beeker's view, "Family Court has become a dangerous place for women and children."[11]

Yes, custodially battered mothers whose children are being sexually abused have organized more visibly than mothers who have "merely" been impoverished and legally tormented and who must also share custody of their children with men who hate them as ex-wives and do not respect them as mothers.

On Mother's Day 2010, a peaceful, silent vigil was held at the White House. In the somber spirit of the U.S. suffragettes, American mothers—along with the Argentine Mothers of the Disappeared, Turkey's Saturday Mothers, the German Rose Street Women, and the Liberian women who stopped a civil war—gathered at the White House to "ask our President to meet with us and to help stop the systematic removal and oppression of our children by family court."

The participating mothers carried the following signs:

CHILDREN ARE TAKEN FROM SAFE MOTHERS AND FORCED TO LIVE
    WITH ABUSERS. WHY?

I GAVE BIRTH TO A BELOVED DAUGHTER. HER BATTERER HAS
    CUSTODY.

I GAVE BIRTH TO A CHERISHED SON. HIS IDENTIFIED MOLESTER HAS
    CUSTODY.

I GAVE BIRTH TO THREE PRECIOUS CHILDREN. OUR VIOLATOR HAS
    CUSTODY.

I FEAR JUDICIAL RETALIATION. WHAT COUNTRY *IS* THIS?

MR. PRESIDENT, PLEASE STOP THE CHILDREN'S SUFFERING.

1

A Historical Overview

. . . .

By the laws of England, the custody of all legitimate children from the hour of their birth belongs to the father. If circumstances, however urgent, should drive the mother from his roof, not only may she be prevented from tending upon the children in the extremity of sickness, but she may be denied the sight of them; and, if she should obtain possession of them, by whatever means, [she] may be compelled by the writ of habeas corpus to resign them to her husband or to his agents without condition—without hope. Let it not be supposed that this law is one which is rarely brought into operation. The instances in which it is brought before the public cognizance may be few, but [it] is ever in the background of domestic tyranny, and is felt by those who suffer in silence.

—Master Sergeant Talfourd, 1837

We true, natural women cannot live without our children. We had rather die than have them torn from us as your laws allow them to be. Spirit wrongs are the keenest wounds that can be inflicted upon women. When woman is brought before our man courts, and our man juries, and has no marks of violence upon her person, it is hard to realize that her whole physical system may be writhing in agony from spirit wrongs, such as can only be understood by her peers. Spiritual, sensitive women suffer on in silent anguish without appeal, until death. Kindly liberate her from her prisonhouse of unappreciated suffering.

—Elizabeth Parsons Ware Packard, 1864

In 1818 Harriet Brent Jacobs was born into slavery in North Carolina. Her "kind mistress" taught her how to read and then bequeathed her to Dr. James Norcom.[1]

Norcom, who was fifty-two years old, sexually harassed the twelve-year-old Harriet. He threatened to rape, sell, or kill her for resisting his advances. Mrs. Norcom persecuted Harriet for "attracting" her husband's attention.[2]

When Harriet was fifteen, she fell in love with a "colored carpenter and free-born man." She asked for permission to marry. Norcom threatened to whip her and shoot her "lover" on sight. Harriet's grandmother then sent a friend to advise her.

Samuel Tredwell Sawyer, the "friend," was a white man, a past member of the North Carolina legislature, and a future U.S. congressman. Within a year, Harriet gave birth to Sawyer's son, Joseph.

Harriet's "grim tormentor," Norcom, "[pitched] her down a flight of stairs" and "[cut] her hair very close to her head, storming and swearing all the time." Harriet had a second child, Louisa, by Sawyer. Norcom threatened to sell both her children if she saw Sawyer again while continuing to spurn him.

Children were a woman's joy and only consolation. But a slave mother's joy belonged to her master. Norcom fathered eleven slave children and sold every one to "spare" Mrs. Norcom's feelings and profit from his own "licentiousness." What would prevent Norcom from selling all of Harriet's children once she became pregnant by him?

Ah, if Harriet didn't exist, Norcom would not hold her children hostage. *Harriet escaped.* Norcom imprisoned her children and then sold them to a speculator whom Sawyer had secretly sent.

In hiding, Harriet rejoiced. Her children—*her* children—would be free. Sawyer then sent Joseph and Louisa to live with their great-grandmother. Harriet fled her hiding place and walked through the dreaded "snaky swamp." From there she went swiftly to her grandmother's house and up into a dark and "airless" space, which measured seven by nine feet, beneath the roof.

For seven years Harriet was entombed here. She could never stand up or walk around. All summer she was aflame with red insect bites; in winter she developed frostbite. Harriet bored a peephole through which, sight unseen, she saw but could not touch or talk to her children.

On one of these sale days, I saw a mother lead seven children to the auction block. She knew that some of them would be taken from her: but they took *all*. The children were sold to a slave-trader, and their mother was bought by a man in her own town. Before night her children were all far away. She begged the trader to tell her where he intended to take them: this he refused to do. How could he, when he knew he would sell them, one by one, wherever he could command the highest price? *I* met that mother in the street, and her wild, haggard face lives to-day in my mind. She wrung her hands in anguish, and exclaimed, "Gone! All gone! Why don't God kill me?" I had no words wherewith to comfort her.[3]

Sawyer, newly married, offered to send Louisa to live with his relatives "up North," out of Norcom's scheming reach. After six long months, a letter arrived from "Brooklyn, Long Island," praising Louisa as a good "waiting maid" to her cousin. Had Sawyer sent his daughter north as a slave? Had Harriet's entombment been in vain?

Harriet had to know. She escaped north by ship. At first Harriet didn't recognize Louisa—she was so shabbily dressed and so obviously "unattended" to. At nine, Louisa was still illiterate. Harriet immediately found work as a domestic. She bought Louisa shoes and clothes and paid for her to see a doctor.

Harriet's experience at the hands of both her master and mistress was echoed in *Autobiography of a Female Slave*, written by ex-slave Mattie Griffiths:

I once saw a white lady, of refinement, sitting on the portico of her own house, with her youngest born, a babe of some seven months, dallying on her knee, and she is toying with the pretty gold threads of his silken hair, whilst her husband was in the kitchen, with a whip in his hand, severely lashing a negro woman, whom he had sold to the trader—lashing her because she refused to go cheerfully and leave her infant behind. The poor wretch, as a last recourse, fled to her mistress, and, on her knees, begged to have her child. "Oh, mistress," cried the frantic black woman, "ask master to let me take my baby with me." What think you was the answer of this white mother? "Go away, you impudent wretch, you don't deserve to have your child. It will be better off away from you!" Aye, this was the answer accompanied [by] a derisive sneer, [that] she gave to the heart-stricken black mother.[4]

Harriet lived in terror of Norcom's "bounty hunters." Warned of her imminent capture, Harriet fled New York for Boston. She took Louisa with her. Once settled, Harriet sent for Joseph, who arrived one morning out of breath, "having run all the way."

For the first time in nine years, Harriet and her children lived together in broad daylight. Harriet sewed; Louisa studied; Joseph learned a trade. On June 21, 1853, under a pseudonym, Harriet published an article in the *New York Tribune* about the separation of children from their slave mothers.[5]

Again Mattie Griffiths confirmed this grim but common reality:

A tall, hard-looking man came up to me, very roughly seized my arm, bade me open my mouth; examined my teeth, felt my limbs; made me run a few yards; ordered me to jump; and being well satisfied with my activity, said to Master Edward, "I will take her." After a while, my mother came up to me. Her whole frame was distorted with pain. She walked toward me a few steps, then stopped, and suddenly shaking her head, exclaimed, "No, no, I can't do it. Here, Kitty," she said to an old negro woman, who stood near, "you break it to her. I can't do it. No, it will drive me mad. Oh, heaven. That I was ever born to see this day." Then rocking her body back and forth in a transport of agony, she gave full vent to her feelings in a long, loud, piteous wail. . . . Why, I remember that when master sold the gray mare, the colt went also. Who could, who would, who dared separate the parent from her offspring?[6]

Harriet's pursuers were now willing to sell her. In 1855, when Harriet was thirty-seven years old, her friend and employer, Mrs. Willis, bought her for three hundred dollars. She wrote, "Those words struck me like a blow. So I was sold at last! A human being sold in the free city of New York! The bill of sale is on record, and future generations will learn from it that women were articles of traffic in New York, late in the nineteenth century of Christian religion. I well know the value of a bit of paper; but much as I love freedom, I do not like to look upon it."[7]

As a mother, Harriet longed for "marriage" and a "home made sacred by protecting law." She says so over and over again in her remarkable autobiography, *Incidents in the Life of a Slave Girl*.[8]

Harriet Brent Jacobs was right. She was also wrong. Laws do not keep mothers and children together. The whitest and most married of Christian mothers has no legal right to her husband's children. By law, children "belong" to their fathers.

·····

In 1816 Reverend Ware's only daughter, Elizabeth, was born in Massachusetts. Elizabeth was "blest" with modesty, religious fervor, and "a liberal education." In 1839 Elizabeth married the Reverend Theophilus Packard, who was fourteen years her senior. They moved to Illinois, where Elizabeth gave birth to six children in sixteen years. She ran the household, cared for her beloved children, helped Theophilus write his sermons, raised church funds, and "ministered" to her husband's congregation.[9]

Theophilus Packard was "sluggish" and "[clung] serf-like to the old paths, as with a death grasp." Elizabeth had a more "active" and "progressive temperament." The "dull" and "crafty" Theophilus seized upon Elizabeth's belief in a "free and open-minded discussion of original sin" as proof that she was "insane."

In 1860 when their youngest child was eighteen months old, Theophilus had Elizabeth "forcibly" removed to the insane asylum in Jacksonville. Dr. Andrew McFarland, the asylum director, confiscated Elizabeth's clothes, books, and writing paper. He sexually harassed her, threatened to kill her, threw her into solitary confinement, and imprisoned her on the asylum's "worst ward."

Elizabeth Packard ministered to her sisters in bondage. She washed them, comforted them, prayed with them, and tried to shield them from beatings and from suicide. After three and a half years, Elizabeth finally convinced the asylum trustees that she was lucid and God-fearing. They released her.

Theophilus forbade Elizabeth to return home or to see or speak with their children. Elizabeth decided that she had to return to her husband's legal "protection." She could not see her children if she remained apart from Theophilus. Elizabeth was right. American courts followed British law. Thus, for example, in 1857 in New York State an abusive husband was granted sole custody of his infant child. The decision reads as follows:

> Mr. Rhoades has been wanting in respectful and kind attentions to his wife, and has often used harsh, profane, and vituperative expressions to her and to others concerning her, but he has been guilty of no such misconduct as would justify the wife in a separation. The only

difficulty arises from their child being of tender age, and deriving sustenance, in part from the breasts of the mother. But upon the evidence,
I think these circumstances form no obstacle to the father's right. [The
child] was placed by the father with a competent person, [and has]
been doing well and growing fleshy. Therefore, on the undisputed facts
of the case the father [has] the legal right to the custody of the child.[10]

Our hero Elizabeth arrived home one snowy November morning.
Theophilus did not bother to conceal his hostility. Elizabeth embraced her
children. She did not raise the subject of her psychiatric imprisonment. She
had returned to "resume her domestic duties."

Theophilus forbade Elizabeth to heat water on the stove or to hire anyone
to help her clean the house. Elizabeth scoured the house by herself with cold
water. Theophilus intercepted Elizabeth's mail. He forbade her to leave the
house. Then he locked her in her bedroom both day and night.[11]

After six weeks, Elizabeth smuggled out a note. Friends took it to a judge,
who issued a writ of habeas corpus for her. Before Theophilus could act on
his plan to psychiatrically imprison Elizabeth again, he had to first prove to
a jury that she was "insane."

In 1864 a jury of twelve men "acquitted" Elizabeth of insanity. She
returned to her husband's custody only to discover that Theophilus had
mortgaged her dowry-bought house and fled to Massachusetts with their
children. Elizabeth was alone and destitute. She had no legal right to her
dowry or her children.

Her fate was echoed by that of Catherine (Mrs. Charles) Dickens, who
resided in London. Professor and author Phyllis Rose writes,

Mrs. Charles [Catherine] Dickens was to have a settlement. Her own
house, and her eldest son, Charley, would live with her. But all the
other [nine] children were to stay with Dickens. They could visit their
mother if they chose to, but Dickens did not encourage them to—
in fact, quite the opposite. Dickens did not make his children choose
between himself and their mother. He simply assumed that, as the law
allowed, they would stay with him. And [for twenty years] so they did.
They were happy to. He was dynamic, funny, famous, charismatic,
and powerful. . . . When their son Walter died suddenly in 1864, Dickens did not even send her a note. When Dickens himself died, no one
troubled to invite her to the funeral.[12]

From 1864 on, Elizabeth Parsons Ware Packard supported herself by selling copies of her autobiography, entitled *Modern Persecution, or Insane Asylums Unveiled* (volume 1) and *Modern Persecution, or Married Woman's Liabilities* (volume 2). She also drafted many bills on behalf of imprisoned mental patients and married women.

Packard "beseeched" her "brothers" in the state legislature to grant their wives a "junior partnership" in the "firm of marriage." She viewed married women as "legally a non-entity" and "therefore an American slave." What she wanted was "protection in the union" and "protection from the cause of divorce."[13]

Elizabeth prepared to battle for custody of her youngest children in Massachusetts. Theophilus gave the children to her voluntarily "rather than have [Elizabeth] come into possession of them by the Court's decision." On July 3, 1869, after a nine-year separation, Elizabeth "worship[ped] and br[oke] bread" with all her children "as one family unit." She rejoiced and said, "It is for you, my jewels, I have lived—it is for you I have suffered the agonies of Gethsemane's Garden—it is for you I have hung on the cross of crucifixion; and been entombed three years in a living cemetery; and oh! it is for your sakes I hope to rise again. Children dear, when all the world forsook me and fled, you alone were true to the mother who bore you. . . . Thy Father, God, will not disinherit thee for loving thy mother."[14]

In 1860, the year Elizabeth Packard was psychiatrically imprisoned, Susan B. Anthony was visiting her friend Lydia Mott in Albany, New York. A disheveled and sobbing woman was admitted to the parlor. She was Mrs. Phelps, the wife of a Massachusetts state senator and the sister of a U.S. senator. "Please, won't you help me? No one else will. I am a wife and mother. When I finally confronted my husband with proof of his adulteries, he beat me and had me put away in an Insane Asylum. My brother had me freed, but could not obtain permission for me to see my children. Yesterday, after a year, I was allowed to visit one child. I fled the state with her immediately. And now I am a fugitive."[15]

Anthony agreed to help Mrs. Phelps. She escorted her to New York City and obtained refuge for her there.[16] State Senator Phelps threatened to have Anthony arrested during one of her public lectures. He also enlisted Anthony's two most cherished abolitionist comrades, Garrison and Phillips, in his campaign against her.[17]

Anthony's comrades strongly believed that her action endangered the "woman's rights movement and the anti-slavery cause." Anthony disagreed with them. She said, "Don't you break the law every time you help a slave to Canada? Well the law which gives the father the sole ownership of the children is just as wicked and I'll break it just as quickly. You would die before you would deliver a slave to his master and I will die before I will give up the child to its father."[18]

Phelps hounded Anthony for more than a year. She remained firm. Finally, he hired detectives to locate his missing child. One Sunday morning, on her way to church, the young Miss Phelps was kidnapped on the street and "legally" returned to her father.

There is a long (and largely forgotten) history of feminist agitation on behalf of maternal custody. For example, in 1852,

> As women's rights campaigner Clarina I. Howard Nichols traveled from Vermont to Massachusetts, an elderly man and a sheriff boarded her train and tried to seize the youngest children of a female passenger. Nichols immediately stood up and told the startled passengers: "It means, my friends, that a woman has no legal right to her own babies; that the law-givers of this Christian country (!) have given the custody of the babies to the father, drunken or sober, and he may send the sheriff . . . to arrest and rob her of her little ones!" Learning that the husband had transferred his custody rights to his own father, Nichols quickly explained that a recent Massachusetts court decision held that only a father could take children away from their mother. The passengers then threw the pair out.[19]

In 1869, the year Elizabeth Packard was reunited with her children, the well-known journalist Albert D. Richardson was shot and killed by Daniel McFarland. Richardson had been "attentive" to McFarland's *divorced* wife; he married her on his death bed. The new Mrs. Richardson was seen as the "villain," although her divorce was granted because of McFarland's "brutality and instability." The court acquitted McFarland of murder on the grounds of "temporary insanity" and gave him custody of his twelve-year-old son. Susan B. Anthony and Elizabeth Cady Stanton called a protest meeting. Two thousand people attended it. Stanton said the following:

> As I sat alone late one night and read the story of Abby Sage Richardson, the fugitive wife, I tried to weigh the mountain of sorrow that had rolled

over that poor woman's soul, through these long years of hopeless agony ... and the unjust decision setting a madman free to keep that poor broken hearted woman in fear for her life as long as he lives. . . . Although by the revised statutes of this state the mother is the equal guardian of her child to-day, yet in the late trial we have the anomaly of a criminal, acquitted on the ground of insanity, walking out of court with his child by his hand, its natural protector, while the mother of sound mind capable of supporting it, is denied the custody of its person.[20]

Did Elizabeth Packard believe that a divorced woman was entitled to "joint guardianship" of her children? Did she include "adulteresses" or "free thinkers" in her pleas for the rights of married women?[21]

In 1837 in England, Master Sergeant Talfourd presented an eloquent brief on behalf of maternal *visitation*—but for virtuous wives only. Talfourd did not want to "alter the laws" of the Father Right but to "mitigate" the mother's lot and provide "intervals in which forsaken nature may be cheered and waning strength repaired." Adulterous mothers were beyond the pale of Talfourd's mercy. They—and "immoral" women in general—were to be "deprived of both custody and access."[22]

In 1795 Frances "Fanny" Wright was born to wealthy Scottish parents. In 1825 Fanny established a commune in Tennessee to educate emancipated slaves. In 1828 she became the first nonpreacher woman to lecture in public in the United States.[23]

In 1830 Fanny quietly left America. Early in 1831 she gave birth to her (and William S. Phiquepal D'Arusmont's) daughter, Sylva, in Paris. Fanny was a brilliant, accomplished, and independently wealthy woman. She was the friend and confidante of the Marquis de Lafayette, Jeremy Bentham, and Robert Owen—and yet she married Phiquepal, a "handsome" person of "no genuine distinction of either intellect or spirit," who was sixteen years her senior, in order to protect her child from "stigma."

By 1836 Fanny Wright and William S. Phiquepal were seriously "estranged"; by 1838 Phiquepal had taken Sylva to Cincinnati, leaving Fanny alone and very ill in New York. Phiquepal then began his legal appropriation of Fanny's fortune.[24]

In 1848 Fanny capitulated and granted Phiquepal her inheritance and property. He promptly announced that he and Sylva were "independent of her, and [can] do without her." He put Fanny on a small "allowance."

In an attempt to recover some part of her estate, Fanny filed for divorce in 1850. She claimed that Phiquepal married her for her money and "alienated their daughter's affections"; Phiquepal retaliated with an open letter to the newspapers. He wrote, "Your life was essentially an external life. You loved virtue deeply, but you loved grandeur and glory [even more]. Your husband and child ranked only as mere appendages to your personal existence. [I] imposed on [myself] the sacrifice of attending your lectures but could not impose it on [my] child. Sylva's education has been the main object of [my] life, while [you] have often interrupted that education by the life [you] led traveling from one land to another."[25]

In 1851 Fanny was granted a divorce as an "abandoned" wife. Part of her fortune was restored to her. However, she lost Sylva forever.

Fanny's hopes for her daughter were never realized. Though she was in Cincinnati at the time, Sylva did not see her mother in her last illness. Sylva became an ardent Christian. In 1874 she testified before a congressional committee against female suffrage. "As the daughter of Frances Wright, whom the Female Suffragists are pleased to consider as having opened the door to their pretensions," Sylva begged the Speaker and the members of the House committee "to shut it forever, from the strongest convictions that they can only bring misery and degradation upon the whole sex, and thereby wreck human happiness in America!"

No matter how educated or well connected a woman was in the nineteenth century, no matter how good a mother she may have been, custody belonged to the father. Perhaps matters were better for mothers in post-Enlightenment and post-Revolutionary France? *Mais non.*

For example, the writer George Sand, christened Amandine Aurore Lucie Dupin, was born in 1804. In 1822, a year after inheriting a small fortune, she married Baron Casimir Dudevant. Sand gave birth to a son, Maurice, and a daughter, Solange. In 1831 George left Casimir, who was a cruel and openly adulterous husband. The following year Sand began an affair with Alfred de Musset. In 1835, after Casimir threatened her with a gun and began his legal appropriation of her fortune and property, Sand sued for a legal separation. In 1836 the jury was divided, so Sand settled out of court, giving Casimir half her fortune and her Paris townhouse. In 1837 Casimir attempted to kidnap Maurice, though he despised him and considered him to be too "feminine." Sand managed to spirit Maurice away to safety, but then Casimir kidnapped Solange, whom he addressed contemptuously as "a harlot's daughter." Sand discovered where Solange was hidden and had Casimir's hiding place surrounded with armed policemen.

According to Sand's autobiography and biographies written about her,[26] this was what happened next. "Trying to look calm, [Casimir] came to the door and politely invited his former spouse to step inside, an honor she no less courteously declined. Solange was brought out and entrusted to her mother 'like a princess at the limit between two states.' Casimir vowed that he would get Maurice back 'by authority and justice.'"

Sand was terrified. What if Casimir were successful? Exhausted, unable to write, she borrowed ten thousand francs, which she would use to sail to America with her children if Casimir were to gain custody.

Her fears were realistic.

What if a mother were an educated woman whose close friend were Britain's prime minister? Would the right connections help such a mother gain custody of her children?

In 1836 head-turning British socialite and author[27] Caroline Norton left her husband, the barrister and member of Parliament George Chapple Norton. She managed to get by on her earnings as a writer, but her husband convinced a court that those earnings belonged to him. Giving him a taste of his own medicine, she ran up bills in her husband's name.[28] Her debts belonged to him too.

Shortly after their separation, he kidnapped their three sons and hid them with relatives in Scotland.[29] According to British law at the time, they were his property, and there was little she could do. She sought a divorce, but he blocked her attempts.[30] He accused her of having an affair with Lord Melbourne, her close friend who was also the prime minister.[31] Caroline's reputation was permanently tarnished.

In a letter to Lord Holland, Lord Melbourne wrote that "the fact is he (Norton) is a stupid brute, and she had not temper nor dissimulation enough to enable her to manage him." Nevertheless, he urged Caroline to return to her husband, arguing that "a woman should never part from her husband whilst she can remain with him."[32]

These tribulations left Caroline bitterly conscious of the inferior legal status of married women and led her to publicly condemn the laws regarding divorce and child custody. In 1839, in large measure because of Caroline Norton's intense campaigning, Parliament passed the Custody of Infants Act, which granted mothers limited custodial rights over minor children.[33]

Caroline finally entered into a separation agreement with her husband, which allowed her the right to see and nurse her dying son.[34]

When Parliament debated the subject of divorce reform in 1855, Caroline submitted to the members a detailed account of her own marriage and described the difficulties that British women faced.[35]

> An English wife may not leave her husband's house. Not only can he sue her for restitution of "conjugal rights," but he has a right to enter the house of any friend or relation with whom she may take refuge . . . and carry her away by force. . . . If her husband take proceedings for a divorce, she is not, in the first instance, allowed to defend herself. . . . She is not represented by attorney, nor permitted to be considered a party to the suit between him and her supposed lover, for "damages." If an English wife be guilty of infidelity, her husband can divorce her so as to marry again; but she cannot divorce the husband, a vinculo, however profligate he may be. . . . Those dear children, the loss of whose pattering steps and sweet occasional voices made the silence of [my] new home intolerable as the anguish of death . . . what I suffered respecting those children, God knows . . . under the evil law which suffered any man, for vengeance or for interest, to take baby children from the mother. . . . I exist and I suffer; but the law denies my existence.[36]

In 1857, thanks to Caroline Norton's efforts, Parliament passed the Matrimonial Causes Act, which allowed married women to inherit property and take their grievances to court.[37]

Did the new ruling apply to "uppity" women whose ideas offended those in power? Probably not.

In 1873 in England, Annie Besant, the writer and publisher, separated from her husband, Vicar Frank Besant. In a deed of separation, Frank gave Annie custody of their three-year-old daughter, Mabel. Annie continued to mother and to publish books and pamphlets, including those on atheism and birth control.[38] In 1877 the government charged Annie Besant with "obscenity" for publishing a fifty-year-old pamphlet about birth control. The charges against her were ultimately dropped, but the pamphlet was banned. Reverend Besant then petitioned the court for custody of his daughter. The judge acknowledged that Annie was a good mother. "Mrs. Besant has been kind and affectionate in her conduct and behaviour towards the child, and has taken the greatest possible care of her. I have no doubt she entertains that sincere affection for the child which a mother should always feel."

The judge nevertheless ordered Mabel into her father's custody. He reasoned that Annie's public affiliation with unpopular or minority opinions would "cut her off from social intercourse[39] with the great majority of her sex. [It would not] be beneficial for any young girl to be brought up by such a woman."[40]

On appeal, Annie Besant reminded the court that every British subject was guaranteed the right to advocate their opinions and that *legally* she was her daughter's "father"—that is, her husband had given her contractual custody.

The judge reminded Besant that, as a mother, she could never have the same rights as a father. "No such substitution or delegation is possible by our law," he asserted. "Any child who is not under her father's control is (automatically) a ward of the court. No ward of a Christian court can remain under the guardianship and control of a person who professes and teaches and promulgates [such] religious, or anti-religious, opinions."[41]

Surely such a draconian punishment applied only to commoners, not to royal personages? Not so.

In *A Midsummer Night's Dream*, Shakespeare depicts a custody battle between Oberon, the fairy king, and Titania, the fairy queen. Titania's custodial interest in the orphaned child is "maternal"; Oberon's is "paternal."

> **Puck:** Take heed the queen [Titania] come not within his sight;
> For Oberon is passing fell and wrath,
> Because that she as her attendant hath
> A lovely boy, stol'n from an Indian King;
> She never had so sweet a changeling;
> And jealous Oberon would have the child
> Knight of his train, to trace the forests wild;
> But she, perforce, witholds the loved boy,
> Crowns him with flowers, and makes him all her joy. . . .
>
> **Oberon:** Why should Titania cross her Oberon?
> I do but beg a little changeling boy to be my henchman.
>
> **Titania:** Set your heart at rest;
> The fairy land buys not the child of me.
> His mother was a votaress of my order;
> But she, being mortal, of that boy did die;

And for her sake do I rear up her boy,
And for her sake I will not part with him.[42]

Titania is no Christian queen. If she were, she would not quarrel with her husband the king, certainly not over a child. Royal children—and, for that matter, any child claimed by a king—belong to him and not to any queen.[43]

With some exceptions, the majority of Europe's Christian queens were breeders, not rulers. As *mothers*, queens were not entitled to anymore authority over their children than that enjoyed by the king and his family. Queens rarely took lovers; if they did, they rarely had or acknowledged their illegitimate children as such.

In the twelfth century, Queen Eleanor of Acquitaine divorced King Louis VII of France. Their children remained behind as "the property of the French Crown." Eleanor remarried King Henry II of England and gave birth to seven more children. When Eleanor's oldest sons rebelled against Henry, Eleanor supported them. King Henry reconciled with his sons but placed Eleanor under house arrest for fifteen years (1173–1189). Henry allowed Eleanor to see her children, then seven, eight, and twelve years old, and her grandchildren only "on occasion."[44]

In the sixteenth century, Queen Elizabeth I of England had no children and no consort. She was as directly involved in decisions of war and peace as any monarch had been. Interestingly enough, Elizabeth herself was the daughter of Anne Boleyn, one of the wives whom her father, King Henry VIII, had beheaded. According to one biographer, Queen Elizabeth never mentioned her mother directly, nor did she ever openly condemn her father for her own motherless childhood.[45]

In the seventeenth century, Anne Pierrepont, daughter of the Marquis of Dorchester, married John Lord Roos. The bridegroom was an impotent alcoholic and a gambler. Anne left and became pregnant without him. Her mother-in-law, the Countess of Rutland, had Anne imprisoned until she gave birth. Anne's son was baptized Ignoto and taken away from her immediately. According to Antonia Fraser, "At first Lord Roos hung on to custody of the boy saying that 'although the child is not of my begetting, so long as the law reputes it mine, I must and shall keep it.' But this, it is clear, was merely a manoeuvre in order to induce from Lady Anne a confession of the truth. Once Lady Anne had admitted her [adultery and a divorce was granted], then she could have the child and do what she liked with it."[46]

In 1729 in Stettin, Pomerania, Princess Johanna Elizabeth—the wife of Christian Augustus, the Prince of Anhalt-Zerbst—gave birth. The child, baptized Sophie, seldom saw her father and was "merely tolerated and often violently repulsed" by her mother, who subsequently gave birth to a son "whom she passionately love[d]."[47]

In 1744 when Sophie was fifteen, Empress Elizabeth summoned her to the court of St. Petersburg to become engaged to Peter, Elizabeth's nephew and the heir to the Russian throne. Sophie found the nobles "illiterate," the intrigue "intricate," and her fiance "childish" and perhaps insane.

Sophie married the Grand Duke Peter in 1745. He spent "all his time playing soldiers in his room with his valets, performing military exercises and changing uniforms twenty times a day." Empress Elizabeth "befriend[ed]" and "persecute[d]" Sophie; Peter neglected, bored, and abused her.[48]

In 1752, despite Peter's succession of mistresses, he had yet to consummate his marriage. Sophie was urged to provide Peter with an heir. Her choice was Count Sergei Saltikov, a member of the old Russian nobility, a "vain" and "ambitious" man.[49]

Sophie became pregnant in 1754. On September 20, 1754, after a "very hard labor," she gave birth to a son. The newborn was swaddled and immediately taken to Empress Elizabeth. In her own handwriting, Sophie described her royal childbed:

> I had sweated abundantly, and I begged Mme. Vladislavov to change my linen and put me back into my own bed; she said she dared not do that. She sent several times for the midwife but the latter did not come. I asked for water and got the same response. . . . I had been in tears ever since the birth had taken place, particularly because I had been so cruelly abandoned, lying in discomfort after a long and painful labour, with nobody daring to carry me back to my bed. I was too weak to drag myself there. Four hours later, Mme. Shuvalov left the room and went to fetch the midwife, for the Empress had been so busy with the child that she would not let the midwife leave her for an instant.[50]

The empress did not permit Sophie to see her son at all. Sophie fell ill. She spent the "whole winter" in a "miserable little narrow room, about five to six feet long and four across." After forty days of "confinement," Sophie saw her son for the first time. The moment "the prayers were over the Empress had him carried away and herself departed."[51]

Sophie was next allowed to see her son at Easter, seven months later. In 1758 she became pregnant again. In December of that year she gave birth to a daughter, Anna Petrovna, who was also appropriated by the empress. Again, Sophie was "abandoned like a miserable creature."

Sophie was allowed to have a lover and her own political confidantes—as long as the empress was allowed to spy on her and to exile her friends regularly. Sophie was only allowed to see her children sometimes.

Empress Elizabeth died on Christmas Day, 1761. By the spring of 1762 Czar Peter was publicly threatening to kill Sophie and their eight-year-old son, Paul.

Sophie, wearing an officer's uniform, her "hair flying in the wind," rode at the head of twenty thousand soldiers to arrest the czar. Peter formally abdicated. On July 6, 1762, while in custody, Peter was "accidentally" killed in a fight—or died of a "haemorrhoidal colic, with brain complications."[52]

Sophie—better known as Catherine the Great of Russia—reigned for thirty-four years until her death in 1796. In her memoir, Catherine wrote that "for eighteen years, (the period of my married life) I have led a life which would have rendered ten other women mad and twenty others in my place would have died of a broken heart."[53]

Was motherhood more of a curse than a blessing for those mothers who happened to be queens? Were queens more savagely separated from their children than poor, uneducated, nonroyal mothers are? Douglas Rendleman explains that "in 1562, [the English] Parliament passed the Statutes of Artificers which provided that the children of pauper parents were to be involuntarily separated from their parents and apprenticed to others [until they reached full age]. As of 1601, the Poor Law act established forced labor for the able bodied and cash relief for those unable to work. There was no need to justify legislation which controlled the labor of the lower classes, even at the expense of their family solidarity."[54]

Were things better for mothers in the New World?

In colonial America, it was a capital crime for a wife or a slave to defend herself against a violent husband or master.[55] Female nonmarital sexual activity was either severely punished or treated as a capital crime.

A white colonial woman who gave birth to a black or mulatto child out of wedlock was sold into slavery together with her racially mixed child.[56] When an unmarried white woman was seduced, raped, or impregnated by her male employer, she either lost custody of her bastard or was forced into additional years of service.

The laws made indentured servants' pregnancies worth their masters' while, and so many unscrupulous masters bound their servants to additional years by rape.[57]

In the seventeenth century, most of the unmarried mothers were bound servants who paid dearly for their indiscretions. The woman was heavily fined, and if no one would come forward to pay the fine for her, she was whipped. Furthermore, she served an extra twelve to twenty-four months to repay her master for the "trouble of his house," which was the lost labor and the maintenance of the child if it lived.[58]

If a mother wished to avoid such punishment, she would have to end or conceal her pregnancy or, like Nathaniel Hawthorne's *Scarlet Letter* hero, Hester Prynne, live with the letter *A* emblazoned upon her breast.[59]

"Infanticide"—which ranged from the use of birth control and abortion to the accidental or purposeful murder of a newborn—was viewed as a special "female" crime. Such crimes were more severely punished than (white) male homicide, wife murder, or political insurrection. Concealing the death of a bastard became a capital offense in England and the Virginia colony in 1624 and in Massachusetts in 1692.[60]

In the colonies, many fathers died young. Wives tended to outlive them, but they themselves often died in childbirth. Kinship networks were nonexistent or very fragile. Something had to be done for the orphans and bastards. Colonial orphans were usually apprenticed out. They were dependent on neighbors, friends, or surviving relatives to save their lives—or their inheritances—from an "evil" executor or stepfather. In 1678 in Maryland, William Watts died, leaving three motherless boys under the age of eight. Their executor, a merchant, apprenticed them to an overseer who "'putts them to hard Labour Equal to any servant or Slave & keeps them without clothes,' allowed them scanty food, and permitted them to be 'saddly beaten & abused by ye overseer as tyed up by the hands & whipt.'"[61]

As potentially abusive as the apprenticeship system was, it was better than life on the streets or in the poorhouse. The poorhouse was filled with "rogues, vagabonds, idlers, drunkards, brawlers and the hopeless." It was "the deathhouse of the pauper sick, the winter home of the diseased vagrant, the last refuge of the broken down prostitute, the asylum for the insane, the lying-in hospital both for the feebleminded members and also for the poor unfortunate girl, the victim partly of ignorance and partly of lust, and perhaps saddest of all, the home of some independent, high-spirited persons whom misfortune or filial irreverence in his declining days left with only such a place in which to close his eyes in the last long sleep."[62]

Impoverished widows usually apprenticed their children. When they remarried, they petitioned for the return of their children, who were then at the legal mercy of their new stepfathers. Some colonial second husbands were unable or unwilling to support stepchildren; some were only too happy to do so.[63] Stepfathers were notorious for appropriating stepchildren's inheritances. For such reasons, some colonial fathers tried to ensure their children's inheritance (if one existed) by bequeathing it—as well as custody—to their wives.[64]

In 1772 in New England, Mary Jones was convicted of stealing bread to feed her two children. She was hanged.[65] Since female sexuality *and* poverty were viewed as crimes, most women got married, remarried, and stayed married, even to violent or adulterous husbands who squandered their dowries, appropriated their wages, and neglected or abandoned them and their children.[66]

The king and the state had very little hold over what a wealthy father did (or did not do) for his children. A wealthy father could neglect and abuse his children—as long as he still supported them. Such a father could only be stopped by *his* own father or by the child's maternal *grandfather*—and then only if the grandfather was both willing and able to economically support the child.[67]

In the United States, the child of a poor or impoverished father belonged to the state or to whoever was best able to support her. In 1796 Mr. Nichols of Connecticut became the first American father to judicially lose custody of his child. Mr. Nichols had "very little property, no house," and he also possessed a "very irregular temper." The court awarded custody of the Nichols child not to her mother but to her wealthy "maternal grandfather."[68]

In 1839 a Pennsylvania mother committed her "morally unmanageable" daughter to a state house of refuge. The girl's father sought her release, arguing that commitment without a trial was unconstitutional. The court denied his petition. For the first time, it claimed that as the paternal guardian to the community (*parens patriae*), the state had the right under certain circumstances to determine custody and that such a right was based on—but superseded—the custodial rights of an individual father.[69]

In 1879 Mr. and Mrs. Ackley's Kansas crop failed, and both Ackleys fell ill. They and their seven-year-old son were sent to the county poor farm.

Mr. Ackley recovered his health, found employment, and tried to reunite his family. However, the state had already apprenticed Ackley's now eight-year-old son for ten years to a Mr. Tinker.

Upon Ackley's petition for his son, the court found the apprenticeship immune. If the county were expending funds for relief, the child was a county charge, and the superintendent of the poor farm was able to apprentice the child without the knowledge or consent of his parents.[70]

In 1899 the Hulls, a family of Connecticut farmers, "came on hard times" and "required public aid for medicine." The state removed five of the six Hull children to an almshouse and "forcibly removed" their parents to another almshouse. When petitioned to release and reunite the Hulls, the court stated that "no constitutional right was violated by the proceedings in controversy. Town paupers belong to a dependent class. The law assigned them a certain status. This entitles them to public aid, and subjects them, in a corresponding degree, to public control. (So much for the families' home, their children, and their freedom to come and go as they pleased.)"[71]

Racially despised parents were still custodially endangered (rather than protected) by the state. For example, when emancipation was imminent, many slave owners drew up apprenticeship agreements binding young slaves to them for long terms of service. In Maryland on November 1, 1864, one day after the slaves were freed, "wagonloads of black children were brought to orphan's courts throughout the state to be apprenticed to their former owners. So many children were bound out without their parents' consent that General Lew Wallace, ranking Union officer in the State, offered to intervene in their behalf. He and his aides were besieged with appeals from mothers, fathers and grandmothers."[72]

By the 1890s the American state had killed or displaced most of its Native American Indian population. Survivors were imprisoned on reservations, and their children were often taken from them and sent to boarding schools and private households for training in Christian obedience and agricultural, domestic, and industrial servitude.

As we have seen, the state already had the legal right to appropriate the children of the poor. Now, under the influence of "child savers," the state gradually began to justify its child stealing as in the "best interests" of the child. Many child crusaders were genuinely horrified by child abuse among the immigrant poor. As white, Protestant, middle-class, conservative, and culturally ethnocentric Americans, they were also horrified by the influx of Catholic, Italian, and Eastern European immigrants.[73]

Child savers scorned unwed, impoverished, or working mothers. They had very fixed ideas about "proper" sex and class role behavior. Their motives were as mixed as their ultimate results.[74] Child savers and the state removed children from their impoverished city parents and placed them with "respectable" farmers in the country. The children of impoverished immigrants were also placed in orphanages, state poorhouses, training schools, and reformatories where they were treated very harshly, routinely punished, and sometimes tortured.[75]

To some extent, the state appropriation of *abused* children was a genuine act of Christian mercy. Poor children *were* starving and dying. Some were forced to beg, steal, pimp, and prostitute themselves at extremely young ages. Some poor children were also beaten, raped, murdered, and abandoned by their parents, stepparents, and other adults. Oscar Dudley tells the story of Max Gilman, an eleven-year-old boy

> who was beaten to death by his step-father August Hetzke, in February 1888. The boy's mother died in June 1887; and from that time the brutal parent beat and starved the unhappy boy for months. A witness named Haartze heard sounds of a whipping and plaintive cries of "Papa" at eleven o'clock at night, and then a heavy fall as of a body hurled on the floor. At seven in the morning the beating renewed, and then, with a refinement of hypocrisy, the wretch bade the boy to "get his bible and read the commandments." In the afternoon he was dead.[76]

·····

Abused nineteenth-century children also had well-to-do Caucasian fathers. However, how could the state remove such children from their economically solvent fathers without dislodging the principle of a father's or the state's own absolute right to custody or providing similar redress for abused wives?

Were judges prepared to deprive an economically solvent father of custody in order to "save" a child? Judges rarely faced this decision. When they did, they attempted to "save" the child through clever, commonsense solutions and without establishing dangerous judicial precedents. The state was willing to view child abuse as a poor man's—not a rich man's—crime. The state was unwilling to view its own separation of a child from his or her family as a crime at all, nor was the state anxious to condemn *itself* for apprenticing children to criminally abusive masters. As late as 1894, a state overseer (but not the apprenticeship system) in Pennsylvania was prosecuted for "indenturing a seven-year-old pauper child for fourteen years to a cruel farmer. The overseer was warned before and after the indenture, and visited the farmer, but reported that the boy was not maltreated. The boy died of starvation and overwork after a few months."

By the end of the nineteenth century, an all-male judicial patriarchy had effectively usurped the absolute custodial rights of impoverished, racially despised, and excessively abusive fathers. Sometimes a judge even awarded an impoverished or abusive father's child to a maternal surrogate—if she was already supporting the child economically.[77] Incredible as it may seem, *biological* mothers had fewer custodial rights than token mother-surrogates did. Certainly no mother had custodial rights equal or superior to those already enjoyed by fathers and/or the state.[78]

Biological and adoptive mothers are *women*. The legal concept of parental rights was interpreted by men, for men—and against women. The concept of parental rights for mothers simply did not exist. According to legal historian Michael Grossberg, "[The systematic] decline of paternal rights did not automatically increase maternal ones. On the contrary, the law reduced the rights of parenthood itself. Judges often biased custody determinations toward mothers. Yet they were so rooted in judicial sexual biases, that mothers could claim that preference only when they conformed to the bench's idea of womanhood. The newly instituted maternal preference remained a discretionary policy, not a statutory prerogative. As a result, it could be easily revoked any time a mother did not meet the standards of maternal conduct decreed by judicial patriarchs."[79]

The nineteenth-century judicial concept of moral motherhood had not changed since colonial times. Female "immorality" still consisted of displeasing or divorcing a husband (even an abusive one), committing adultery, engaging in any independent economic or intellectual activity, preaching or practicing birth control or abortion, bearing an illegitimate child, and engaging in nonmarital fornication or prostitution.[80]

The same state judge, legislator, or social worker who thought nothing of separating a child from his impoverished father felt even more righteous about separating him from an impoverished or "immoral" *mother*. The state was not interested in redeeming "immoral" mothers—not even for the sake of their maternally needy children. The state was interested in punishing "immoral" women and turning the situation to state (and private) economic advantage.

In 1856 the nation's first reform school for girls was founded in Lancaster, Massachusetts. The majority of Lancaster's earliest inmates were poor Irish Catholic immigrants.[81] Some girls had been abandoned or turned over to the state by their families; some were the victims of incest and child abuse; some were sentenced to Lancaster for past—and to prevent future—fornication or prostitution.[82]

In 1858 Hannah K., "a pretty little girl" of eleven, was brought to Lancaster by her father because she was a "chronic masturbator." He and his invalid wife had not been able to "restrain her," not even by "tying her hands all night." The Lancaster matron quickly discovered that Hannah suffered from a chronic rash (erysipelas) and that she was to be "pitied" and treated "medically, and with kindness." The matron went on: "Nevertheless [Hannah] was allowed to remain [at Lancaster] as a dependent of the state for eight more years. She was then indentured under the supervision of the state for another two years. Her continued incarceration may have been due to the sympathy of the authorities; it may have also been a result of their fear of what might befall a poor girl from a disrupted home. In the trustees' eyes, she was still considered potentially deviant."[83]

The state "saved" Hannah by training and indenturing her as a domestic servant. There was always a shortage of desirable female servants, and female "redemption" meant service to a family. In 1869 the Lancaster trustees explained why. "[We think] domestic service is better and safer for [girls] than a trade, because housework in a private family is the only life that affords them sufficient protection after they leave the school. Allowing a girl to board, and work in a shop or factory, gives a freedom which they would too often abuse."[84]

Never at a loss for new ideological ways of blaming the victim and profiting from her victimization, the state then decided that *all* female sexual activity was proof of genetic imbecility or feeblemindedness. "Imbeciles" would not miss their children, and their children would be better off without them.[85] Thus sexually active poor girls and women who were perhaps seduced or even raped were treated as criminals or imbeciles and often institutionalized. Their children were automatically taken from them. For example, at the beginning of the twentieth century,

> Beulah S. had been deserted by her parents as an infant and left to the mercy of the state. At age fourteen she mothered an illegitimate child and afterward was sent to Lancaster for theft and incorrigibility. . . .

When she was twenty-six, Dr. Fernald described her as having "keen sexual propensities." Accordingly, Fernald labeled her a "moral imbecile" and consigned her to the custodial department of the institute.

Mary R. entered Lancaster reportedly as unchaste and "diseased." Her Lancaster records report her as "of average intellect." . . . The Lancaster officials did not express great surprise that Mary, after five placements in four years, had an illegitimate child. Although Mary was reportedly a good mother, the baby was sent away from its mother and placed in the infants' asylum.[86]

By the beginning of the twentieth century, an American mother enjoyed the right to custody only in nine states and in the District of Columbia—and only if a state judge found her morally and economically worthy of motherhood.[87]

2

A Contemporary Overview

....

In the twentieth century in the Midwest and New England, Catherine, Nora, and Adele each were custodially challenged by their physician husbands. These mothers had been married for an average of sixteen years. Among them, they had mothered eleven children in loving and highly traditional ways. Catherine and Adele were full-time, stay-at-home mothers. Nora was also a full-time mother with a scientific career.

Adele was a wife and mother for fourteen years. She initiated a divorce reluctantly—only after she became convinced that her husband would never give up his mistress and would never spend enough "family time" at home.

> **Adele:** We lived in a very large house. I had a housekeeper three times a week during the day when the children were infants. The housekeeper did the laundry and cleaning. I did most of the cooking and all of the child care. The housekeeper left about four o'clock each day. At the trial, my ex-husband said I had a maid and did nothing but sleep. He said I couldn't even keep the closets as super neat as he wanted and that I never managed to cook the way his mother cooked.
>
> **A Fit Mother:** *Does not need a housekeeper, does not sleep, keeps the closets neat, and cooks the way her husband's mother did.*
>
> **Adele:** My ex-husband's psychiatrist friend was one of his expert court witnesses. The psychiatrist said that I was an

"awkward mother" who "tried too hard" and was too tense because I wasn't "biologically secure." I was an adoptive mother. That hurt terribly.

A Fit Mother: *Is a biological mother. Adoptive fathers are more fit than adoptive mothers.*

Adele: I was also accused of being a flaky artist. The judge was told that I couldn't support my children on what I could earn and that I would probably bring other flaky artists into the home and give my children "wrong ideas."

A Fit Mother: *Is not an artist and has no artist friends. If she is an artist, she earns as much as a physician does.*

Adele: It's like the old Solomon story. The true mother lets go. When my children were with me, their father pulled them to pieces. Now that they're with him, I won't pull them to pieces. I won't say, "Your Dad's no good" or "I need you." If they complain to me about their father, I say, "Yes, I know he's difficult. I know he's got a bad temper, but you've got to work it out."

A Fit Mother: *Is a psychologist, philosopher, and saint, for which she gets no credit.*

After ten years of enforced marital celibacy, Catherine had a love affair. Catherine's husband immediately moved for both divorce and custody. Catherine began the first full-time job of her life a year before her trial.

Catherine: I did everything for my children by myself. I didn't want any babysitter or housekeeper to come between me and my children. When they were in school plays, I sewed their costumes myself, by hand. I made all sorts of fantastic decorations for every children's party. I loved every minute of it. The judge refused to listen to any of this.

A Fit Mother: *Does not rest on her laurels.*

Catherine: I had inherited a great deal of money. However, my husband controlled all my money. He refused to sign it over to me, especially after our separation. I was able to earn only the minimum wage. My husband told the judge that I couldn't afford to support the children. Only he could.

A Fit Mother: *Does not work for the minimum wage and is not entitled to her own inheritance.*

Catherine: I took a job from nine to five. I couldn't get home till six-thirty at night. I shopped on the weekends and made spaghetti sauce, beef stew, casseroles—dishes that could be heated up at night. Six months before the trial, my husband started arriving home at five-thirty. He refused to heat anything up or wait until I got there. He'd be gone with the children by the time I got home. How could I be a good mother, he asked the judge, if I came home long after he did at night.

A Fit Mother: *Always arrives home before her husband.*

Catherine: They said that an adulteress really couldn't care about her children. Two of my husband's witnesses, a priest and a psychiatrist, said that something was wrong with me because I had committed adultery—especially since my husband hadn't.

A Fit Mother: *Remains celibate if she has to, even for ten years. She never commits adultery, especially when her husband doesn't.*

Catherine: My youngest children started questioning me. Why didn't I love them anymore? Why did I have to work? Why did I insist on hurting their father? Didn't I understand how hurt and angry he was? I said nothing to them. I didn't feel it was right to involve them in our adult problems.

A Fit Mother: *Never works and never angers or hurts her husband. She never burdens her children with her side of the story, and she gets no credit for this.*

Catherine: The judge was very impressed by my husband's medical credentials. He treated him with a lot of respect. I was "just a mother" who couldn't earn enough money on her own. I was also an adulteress.

A Fit Mother: *Is a married physician who really doesn't need to work—except at a high-paying job with very flexible hours.*

After years of marital discord, Nora initiated a divorce. Her husband tried to kill her, kidnapped their two youngest children, fought for custody, and "on principle" refused to pay any child support or divide up their marital assets.

Nora: My ex-husband used to boast about how efficient I was as a mother and as a scientist. Yet his lawyer kept asking the judge how I could possibly be a single mother and also have a full-time career. They claimed that as hard as I worked, I still couldn't earn as much as my ex-husband did.

A Fit Mother: *Is married and does not have a career. She spends all her time with her children. If she is divorced, she must support her children on inherited wealth.*

Nora: I believe in respecting my children's judgment. I believe in letting them learn from their mistakes. This became proof of my unfitness. Someone testified that she'd seen one of my sons improperly dressed on a cool day. Yes, he refused to put on a jacket. I wanted him to learn from his own mistake.

A Fit Mother: *Forces her children to wear jackets in cool weather. She must not let her children make their own decisions, nor can she afford to respect their judgments.*

Nora: My ex-husband now believes that I'm a very wicked mother because I left him. He doesn't think he is a wicked father because he tried to kill me or kidnapped the children.

A Fit Mother: *Never leaves her husband—no matter what.*

Nora: The judge sent me to a psychiatrist, who described me as paranoid about my ex-husband—and overly suspicious of psychiatry! The psychiatric report described my husband's choking me and kidnapping the children as a singular episode. The psychiatrist doesn't think my ex-husband represents a threat to anyone but me, and then only because I "provoke" him. The psychiatrist said that my fear of my ex-husband and my refusal to forgive him will stunt the children's normal emotional development. He therefore recommended that the children live with their father.

A Fit Mother: *Never has to see a psychiatrist.*

Question: *Is a father who murders his wife still entitled to legal custody of his children?*

Answer: *Yes.*

Question: *Is a divorced mother who lives with a man out of wedlock still entitled to legal custody of her children?*

Answer: *No.*

In Illinois, Lonnie Abdullah bludgeoned his wife, Anna, to death with a large kitchen knife. Mr. Abdullah was found guilty of first-degree murder and imprisoned for sixty years. The state moved to have his three-year-old son legally adopted. The imprisoned father contested the proposed termination of his parental rights. The Illinois Supreme Court decided that a murder conviction was not sufficient reason to automatically deprive Mr. Abdullah of his paternal rights. The dissenting judge noted that "where a person murders his wife, thus depriving his child of a parent, the State should not be compelled to obtain that person's consent before it may place the child for adoption. By murdering the child's mother, the respondent has demonstrated his disregard for the child's best interests."[1]

This judge contrasted the court's *Abdullah* decision with its decision in the *Jarrett* case. Jacqueline Jarrett, a divorced mother of three children, lost custody of her children because she had a live-in boyfriend. She appealed this decision. The appellate court returned custody to her, noting that "[Mrs. Jarrett] is a kind, affectionate mother. She had not neglected her children in any way as a result of the relationship. The schooling and religious training of the girls was being attended to. . . . It is evident that Jacqueline Jarrett, Wayne Hammon [her live-in boyfriend] and the three children function as a family unit."[2]

Jacqueline Jarrett lost custody in the Illinois Supreme Court. The *Abdullah* court decided that Jacqueline's "non-marital relationship *in and of itself* was harmful to the children."[3]

Question: *Can an immigrant, unwed, and impoverished mother lose custody of her child because she is these things?*

Answer: *Yes.*

Christina Landaverde fled her native El Salvador. Like so many immigrants before her, she arrived in the United States destitute, pregnant, and with a "poor" knowledge of English. Social workers persuaded Christina to part "temporarily" from her newborn son, Mauricio. "The document [Christina] signed . . . contains the following unequivocal clause: 'I understand that this declaration is not a consent to adoption and that in signing this document I retain rights to the custody, control, earnings and support of said child.' All the lawyers and social workers assured her that she was not giving away her baby and was reserving her option to change her mind."[4]

Within three weeks, Christina wanted her son back. She was three weeks too late. The social workers had already found Mauricio a "real" family: a white married American couple, both of whom spoke English perfectly and neither of whom worked as a "domestic."

For three years, Christina Landaverde waged a heroic and lonely war for custody of her son. The court confirmed that Christina had not surrendered, abandoned, or persistently neglected Mauricio. She had not been an unfit mother. On the contrary. "This mother has ever been very devoted, dedicated to the struggle to regain her child—overcoming her lack of language and her paucity of funds, by her trek across America, by her persistent visits to the child, as well as by her legal efforts. . . . [It is] difficult to avoid measuring the relationship of parent and child by our own North American standards of culture, language and nature of family constellation."[5]

However, a New York court sadly and with regret denied Christina custody of her son. The court viewed Mauricio's "future welfare" as more important than his natural mother's right to custody. Theoretically, Christina could be deported back to El Salvador—a country declared "unsafe." Christina still worked as a domestic; she was still unmarried. Mauricio's best interests were judicially perceived as better served by remaining in a "stable, devoted, two-parent home."[6]

> **Question:** *Can a native-born American lose custody because she lives on welfare?*
> **Answer:** *Yes.*

Linda Gould, a divorced Wisconsin mother, lost custody of her seven-year-old daughter, Kimberly, because as a stay-at-home welfare mother she "earned" six times less than her ex-husband, Steven, an engineer. Steven was also perceived as an "achiever." Linda was perceived as an "unemployed high school graduate."

Despite the fact that Linda was seen as a good mother and that her daughter wanted to remain with her, the court felt that Kimberly's father could provide her with "enhanced opportunities for academic achievement, social stimulation, and formal religious instruction."[7]

Question: *Can a native-born mother who works (and isn't on welfare) lose custody because she earns less money than her husband?*
Answer: *Yes.*

Audrey E. Porter, a North Dakota mother, lost custody of her three children because she earned too little money as a part-time waitress at night. In order to earn what she could, Audrey had to leave her children with a babysitter. She preferred to be there during the day when the children arrived home from school—but she was willing to work days doing housework. The court nevertheless awarded the children to their father, Thomas, an air force captain.

On appeal, the mother argued that it was unfair for her to lose her children because she chose to stay home with them, foregoing career opportunities. But the court, in a cruel twist of customary logic, stated that it would not be more fair to deprive the father of custody because he did not stay home during the day, as "both care and support are important."[8]

Shirley Anne Dempsey, a Michigan mother, lost custody of her children because of her low earnings. Mrs. Dempsey had been her children's only domestically active parent. In fact, Shirley Anne initiated the divorce because her husband had no interest in family life.

The father, who was a hard earner and hard worker, frequently missed dinner with the family, worked long hours, and spent his leisure time bowling and going on snowmobile trips without the family. The trial court judge, in reserving a ruling on the mother's obligation to pay child support, suggested that she might fulfill this obligation by serving as the children's regular babysitter![9]

Question: *Can a "career" mother lose custody because she works and isn't poor?*
Answer: *Yes.*

Divorced Michigan mother Esther Gulyas lost custody of her six-year-old daughter because she worked "forty to fifty hours per week (during the tax season), and ten to thirty hours per week at other times." Esther was forced to rely on "day care." For these reasons (her "career" and her reliance on "day care"), the judge awarded custody of the girl to her father—who had never assumed any child-care responsibility and who, unlike his ex-wife, could not leave work at midday.[10]

A Kansas mother, Kathleen V. Simmons, lost custody to her ex-husband for similar reasons. Mr. Simmons was the "millionaire president of an oil company." When Kathleen appealed, the court found that "[Mrs. Simmons's] business and social interests, after the divorce, had priority over her concerns for her children. [The husband], on the other hand, had remarried and he and his wife were willing and able to offer the children a more stable home environment."[11]

A Chicago mother, Mildred R. Milovich, lost custody of her children. This decision was upheld on appeal. While neither parent "emerged as a monster or a saint," Mildred had presumably committed adultery, had to travel some of the time as part of her job, and was presumably less "affectionate" than her former husband to the children she had mothered.

Mildred's ex-husband, Peter, had presumably not committed adultery (but he was accused of hitting his daughter). He worked full-time for the Chicago Housing Authority—but he never had to travel out of town.

Judge Charles J. Grupp noted that Mildred "is entitled to pursue her own career, but that her children were entitled to a stable environment." Peter got custody and possession of the marital home.[12]

Louisiana judge Melvin Duran awarded custody of a four-year-old girl with cerebral palsy to her father, a physician, because her mother, Margaret Gaines Bezou, was a lawyer. The judge derided Mrs. Bezou for being

> interested first and foremost in herself and in furthering her own career. . . . She gives no promise of putting an end to her career ambitions. [Mrs. Bezou has shown no signs of being] willing to sacrifice advancement of her career [for the youngest child's benefit]. This woman would move with her two daughters to American Samoa if a better job opportunity opens up.
>
> The handicapped girl has been "cursed" with two ambitious parents, especially a mother who wants to be a lawyer more than she wants to be a mother. . . . Gabrielle's illness indicated that "the Lord tried to give this mother a message to 'settle down'" but Mrs. Bezou refused to listen.[13]

Question: *Can a divorced, remarried, stay-at-home mother without a career lose custody of her child—if her political activities offend her ex-husband and the state?*

Answer: *Yes.*

Tina married Ted Fishman, a nuclear physicist, subsequently employed by the Lockheed Missile and Space Company. Tina gave birth and was a devoted mother to her daughter, Riva. She was also a supporter of "revolutionary communism." The couple divorced; Tina remarried and retained custody of Riva for the next seven years.[14]

While Riva was visiting her father for the summer, Tina participated in a demonstration in front of the White House. She was arrested, indicted, immediately released on bail, and eventually acquitted. Ted seized this opportunity to convince California Commissioner James Browning that Tina's activities constituted an emergency in terms of Riva's life.

Browning decided that Riva was "unquestionably well cared for but that her mother's passion for politics" specifically constituted neglect. Browning transferred custody to Ted.[15] For eighteen months Ted refused to let Riva see her mother. Tina and John Stevenson, her husband of seven years, fought Browning's emergency order in California, Indiana, and Illinois. Two years later, California judge Gerald Ragan overturned Browning's initial emergency order. He still refused to return Riva to her mother. Judge Ragan contrasted Ted's "stable, safe, religious and orderly home" with Tina's *character*, which he found "totally absorbed by a fanatical obsession with a political cause which has blinded her to the true needs of a ten to twelve year old."[16]

Because Riva *had* been brainwashed against her mother, Judge Ragan felt the girl needed more time *with her father* to get used to the idea of returning to her mother. Ragan therefore extended paternal custody for another six months and allowed Tina five days of maternal visitation. Thus Tina Fishman lost custody of her daughter for the third time. Tina said, "The whole message the court is giving is if a woman is political she's unfit to be a mother. My case is being used as a forum by conservative government machinery to punish me for my political activities."[17]

Question: *Can an apolitical "career" mother lose custody of her children because her husband and a judge find the confessions in her private diary offensive?*

Answer: *Yes.*

After twelve years of an increasingly "tense and troubled" marriage, a "professional" couple (*Anonymous v. Anonymous*) separated. The mother accepted a one-year appointment at the University of West Virginia. Her husband forbade her to take their children along. She obtained an agreement in writing that her "leaving would not constitute either an abandonment or desertion of her husband and three children, all under ten." She visited her children for "long weekends" every three weeks and saw them on holidays.

In the summer, the anonymous mother returned home. Marital discord continued. For the next year the father, a well-paid astrophysicist in the space industry, kept a careful record of exactly how many weekends he spent alone with the children (twenty-eight), compared to his wife's fourteen. He recorded the number of hours she spent in the library working on her dissertation and how often she complained about or refused outright to cook and clean.

The anonymous father then "accidentally discovered a diary written by the mother." He read it, moved out, and sued for divorce and sole custody. "In the best interests" of the child, the judge, Willens, admitted this diary as evidence against the mother.

Judge Willens was shocked by what it contained, although he carefully stated that he was not against "career mothers," nor did he think that marital unhappiness was immoral.

The mother's handwriting states that she "dislikes housework"; yearns for a "housekeeper" to "free her from the obligations of parenting"; has on occasion lost her temper and her patience with her children, who "crowd around her like animals, like maggots"; has been in a "panic" over this situation; has "experimented" with marijuana; and has engaged in at least twenty episodes of adultery with both men and women while in West Virginia.

Judge Willens confronts the anonymous mother with her "selfishness" and "self-indulgence"—all based on her diary. The mother denies that what she has written expresses the whole "truth" of the matter. Willens decides that

> [she has also] chosen to perjure herself, amounting to a double jeopardy, self-imposed. Her love affairs with other women are her own business and do not enter into the court's deliberations. Neither does the fact that she was involved in heterosexual relationships suggest any moral turpitude. However the large number of these adulterous liaisons; the desperate quality of the relationships . . . together with

her involvement with drugs . . . reflect poor judgment. . . . Concerning the right of a mother to live her own lifestyle, "this is her prerogative, but it must yield to the best interest and welfare of the child." Obviously, the same rule would apply to a father.[18]

Judge Willens admits that both parents have been "fit." However, he awarded sole custody of all three children to their anonymous father, the more "fit" parent—one who was already engaged to marry a schoolteacher and "prepared to care for the children every day after 3:30 in the afternoon."

Question: *Can a wealthy, apolitical, noncareer, stay-at-home mother lose custody of her child because, like her husband, she commits adultery?*
Answer: *Yes.*

Roxanne Pulitzer lost custody of her twin five-year-old sons to her husband, Herbert. She lost her appeal. Roxanne's reliance on a governess and housekeeper whom she, not Herbert, supervised, wasn't at issue, as it once was in the more notorious Vanderbilt custody case.[19]

The presiding judge found Herbert Pulitzer's admitted "flagrant adulteries" irrelevant. The Florida judge castigated Roxanne for *her* "flagrant adulteries." His opinion was as follows: "This court finds that the wife's gross moral misconduct involved more than isolated discreet acts of adultery. She openly engaged in a continuous adulterous relationship with her male paramour. The marriage union is the very bedrock upon which our society is built. Flagrant acts of adultery and other gross marital misconduct demean the sanctity of the marriage and family unit and will not be tolerated."[20]

For her sins, Roxanne lost custody of her children and access to her home and "life-style." She was given limited rather than liberal visitation and was ordered to start "job-hunting."

Throughout the twentieth century, fathers continued to commit adultery and to engage in post-divorce sexual activities without experiencing their sexuality as a custodially or an economically punishable offense.[21] Throughout the twentieth century, mothers, like fathers, continued to commit adultery. Despite the alleged existence of a maternal presumption, "good enough" adulterous mothers continued to risk losing custody for this reason.

For example, in New York, Ethel Bunim was sued for divorce and custody by her physician husband on the grounds of adultery. The dissenting judge described Ethel as a "good and devoted mother; her indiscretions were unknown to the children; she was deeply concerned with their welfare; and for their part, the children returned her affection with attachment that was in the language of the trial court 'almost Biblical' in its intensity. . . . [The father is] inordinately preoccupied with his professional duties; that as a result, he gave little of his time or of himself to the children; and that not infrequently he treated them brusquely, impatiently and even intemperately."

Ethel nevertheless lost custody of all her children. Despite her daughters' "passionate and intense attachment" to her, the court was deeply offended by her "belief that she had done 'nothing wrong.'" The "belief in the propriety of indulgence, by a dissatisfied wife such as herself, in extramarital sex experimentation [is unforgivable]. Our society is based on the absolute fundamental proposition that: Marriage [creates] the most important relationship in life, [and] has more to do with the morals and civilization of a people than any other institution."[22]

Some twentieth-century women who committed adultery *had* been able to win custody of their children, but they were able to do so for reasons having little to do with their natural or earned rights as mothers. For example, a woman could sometimes retain custody if she genuinely repented her *single* lapse from virtue, if she returned home to live with her parents, if she could support her children on her own or with help from her father, if her ex-husband could not support his children, and if her ex-husband had no more money than the convicted woman did.

In Arizona, after reading his wife's diary and realizing that she had had an affair during his military absence, William Henry Grimditch Jr. sued for sole custody of his children. Gioia Grimditch came from a well-to-do family and had been supporting her children from her own family funds. The judge viewed Mr. Grimditch as a "cold" husband who "abandoned his wife [in the hospital] with a badly broken body, immobilized by several casts after a car accident in which he was the driver. He returned only after a month to show her her diary, and to announce that he was taking the children."[23]

The judge awarded Gioia custody because she was a "fit" mother, had already suffered, and was now planning to live with her wealthy and socially prominent father. The judge might not have allowed her custody of "older" children. According to the court, "the same immoral conduct in the mother of older children might deprive her of custody since older children are more impressionable."[24]

What if a married mother not only commits adultery but gets pregnant and gives birth to a child that is not her husband's? In 1943 Ruth Taylor Blain, an Arkansas schoolteacher, was sued by her ex-husband for custody of their "legitimate" daughter on the grounds of adultery, which had resulted in the birth of a second and "illegitimate" child. (Blain had deserted and divorced Ruth and was himself remarried by the time of this "illegitimate" birth.)

Ruth was allowed to retain custody of her "legitimate" daughter for a number of reasons. The presiding judge was convinced that she had been guilty of only one "lapse from virtue" and that she had "genuinely reformed." He noted that the ex–Mrs. Blain attended church regularly and had regained the respect of her "community," many members of which testified on her behalf. Her own family took her back. She was also supporting both her "legitimate" and "illegitimate" children with no help from either of their fathers.[25]

What if Ruth had no family to take her in? What if she had to live on welfare or work for minimum wage? What if she and Mr. Blain were white—but her lover wasn't?

> **Question:** *Can a divorced mother lose custody of one child because she gives birth to another (illegitimate) child of the "wrong" color?*
>
> **Answer:** *Yes.*

Kathleen Blackburn, a divorced white mother, lost custody of her four-year-old white son, Nicholas, for the third time after giving birth to a half-black "illegitimate" daughter. The Blackburns had divorced. Mr. Blackburn remarried and won sole custody of Nicholas after charging Kathleen with "lewd" and socially tabooed behavior. Superior Court Judge W. C. Hawkins awarded custody to the boy's paternal grandmother, "commenting later that the Southeast Georgia town of Millen was not ready for that kind of integration. [He denied] that race influenced his ruling."

Kathleen Blackburn appealed this decision and won custody of Nicholas in the Georgia Supreme Court, which, however, noted that "the defendant's extramarital relationship resulting in the birth of an illegitimate child should [not] be condoned. It would be unrealistic to ignore the fact that society may stigmatize Nicholas [the boy] because his sibling is illegitimate."[26] Within a year, the Georgia Court of Appeals upheld Judge Hawkins's original decision. They noted that since her divorce, Kathleen had had an abortion as well as an illegitimate child. Kathleen noted that "attempts to take Nicholas away from [me are] racially motivated since no one tried to gain custody of [my] racially mixed daughter."[27]

> **Question:** *Can a divorced lesbian mother lose custody because she is a lesbian?*
>
> **Answer:** *Yes—unless she refrains from lesbian activities.*

In Washington State, two ex-husbands "ganged up" on their ex-wives, Sandra Schuster and Madeleine Isaacson. Both mothers had previously been awarded custody of their children—provided they did not live together. The two women therefore took apartments across the hall from each other.

When both Mr. Schuster and Mr. Isaacson remarried, they petitioned the court to modify its custody decision on the ground of "changed circumstances." Sandra and Madeleine had begun to "stigmatize" their children by being openly gay; they had even made a film entitled *Sandy and Madeleine's Family*. Also, since both husbands had remarried, they could now provide their children with a two-headed heterosexual household. The Washington State Supreme Court upheld maternal custody in both cases—provided the women continued to live apart.[28]

A California lesbian mother lost custody because she insisted on her right to engage in lesbian activities—"in the best interests" of her children. She described her children's relationship with her co-mother and lover as "mature and sensitive." She said, "My lover takes my son to Cub Scout meetings. We have a warm and stable family life. She takes him to those games much as an aunt, or a grandmother, or a mother might."[29]

The judge insisted that the female lover was acting out the "butch," or male, role and that *this* was confusing and dangerous for a boy in need of a *male* father figure.

> **Question:** *Is life with a lesbian mother worse than life in a state institution?*
>
> **Answer:** *Yes.*

In California, the mother of four children was arrested and released for possession of a small amount of marijuana. As the state bureaucracy began to return her children to her from various state institutions, her lesbianism was "discovered." No one was challenging this mother for custody of her children. However, the state was upset that her children *knew* she was a lesbian and that she refused to repent of it.

The court didn't argue that her lesbianism *had* had a negative effect on her children. Instead, the court removed her children to a state institution to protect them against any potential *future* emotional problems. For some reason, the state allowed her to retain custody of her sons—but not of her daughters.[30]

Question: *In a contest, is a sperm donor ever entitled to his paternal rights over the single mother's objection?*

Answer: *Yes—especially if the mother is a welfare-dependent lesbian and the sperm donor says he is willing to reimburse the state partially.*

In California, a woman collected sperm in a jar from a "politically sympathetic" homosexual. She inseminated herself with a turkey baster and gave birth to a son. In order to be a stay-at-home mother, she gave up her full-time job, worked part-time, and received partial welfare payments. When her son was eighteen months old, she and he accidentally met the sperm donor on the street. According to San Francisco attorney Donna Hitchens,

The sperm donor was suddenly taken with the idea of having a real son. He hired a lawyer and sued to be recognized as the "father" and to obtain visitation rights. The mother didn't want to share her child with a man, who was essentially a stranger—and who by now was actively hostile to her. The sperm donor pursued the matter in court. Once the District Attorney and the judge understood that she was a lesbian mother on welfare; and that he was willing to reimburse the state by about $100.00 a month, the judge ordered visitation to commence immediately for one day each week. This sperm donor was then in a position to get custody—if he ever wanted it.[31]

Question: *What happens when a battered mother kills her husband in self-defense?*

Answer: *If she is not sexually active and she is lucky, she will be separated from her children and imprisoned for life as "insane."*

When battered mothers kill their violent husbands, boyfriends, or ex-husbands in self-defense, they are usually imprisoned without bail and given maximum sentences. Acquittals, although newsworthy, are rare.[32]

In Wisconsin, just after Francine Hughes had set fire to her husband's bed in Michigan, Jennifer Patri shot her husband to death, buried the body, and set the house on fire. Jennifer was a Sunday-school teacher, PTA president, and a hardworking farm wife. Her husband, Robert Patri, was violent, alcoholic, and adulterous. He had also sexually molested both Jennifer and their twelve-year-old daughter. Jennifer shot Robert when, "armed with a butcher knife" and "threatening to shut [Jennifer's] mouth once and for all," he came to demand his visitation rights.

The press portrayed Jennifer as a woman who "battered back" and as a wife who shot her husband in the back and still "enjoyed a total victory in the courtroom." Jennifer was sentenced to ten years in prison. After a year, she was also convicted for arson.

Defense psychiatrists testified that indeed Patri had been temporarily insane when she set the fire after the shooting, but the jury went the experts one better. They decided that she was still insane and should be transferred from prison to a state mental hospital. And there Jennifer Patri remains, having won—in the words of Ann Jones, author of *Women Who Kill*—"a complete and total victory."[33]

> **Question:** *What happens when a sexually active mother is accused of infanticide?*
>
> **Answer:** *She will be tried and convicted for her sexual activities. These crimes are viewed as interchangeable.*

Any mother capable of leaving her husband and engaging in "promiscuous adultery" is probably capable of "anything"—including the murder of her own children.

On July 15, 1965, Alice Crimmins, a New York "working-class housewife," called the police to report that her children were missing. The first detective assigned to her case, the prosecuting attorneys, the jury, the judge, and the press all viewed Alice as a "bitch," a "tramp," and a "swinger" who "deserved to die."[34]

Alice was guilty of having boyfriends—*and not being ashamed of it.* Although Eddie Crimmins, the children's father, admitted that he "exposed himself to little girls in the park" and "hid in the basement under [Alice's] bedroom to listen to her have sex with other men," he was never viewed as capable of killing his children. Nor was he investigated.[35]

Once the children's bodies were found, Alice was arrested and held without bail. On the basis of flimsy, inconclusive, and strongly contested evidence, twelve male jurors found Alice guilty of first-degree murder in the case of her son and manslaughter in the case of her daughter. The judge sentenced Alice to life imprisonment on the murder charge and five to twenty years for manslaughter.

For the next twelve years Alice was either in prison, working on an appeal, on trial, being psychiatrically examined by the state, or being "lewdly" examined by the press. She was not seen—or comforted—as a mother whose children had been kidnapped and murdered. Alice addressed the prosecuting attorney in this way: "Anything you people have done to me in the past, anything you are doing to me now, and anything you may do to me in the future can't be worse than what was done to me six years ago when my children were taken from me and killed. And I just hope and pray the world will see all your lying and scheming against me. And I just hope and pray to have the chance to put you all down some day for what you are."[36]

> **Question:** *What is going on?*
> **Answer:** *Patriarchal law is going on.*

In chapter 1, we saw that perfectly good mothers—because they were women—routinely lost custody. We also saw that women were historically punished for fornication, adultery, and having "illegitimate" babies. They were also punished for using birth control, having abortions, concealing the deaths of "bastards," committing infanticide, and committing "husband murders." These are the quintessential female crimes under patriarchy. They are often seen as interrelated. Why?

If a husband doesn't maintain a twenty-four-hour guard, how can he be sure his (disobedient) wife's children are really "his," not another man's? How can he be sure that her every pregnancy results in the birth of "his" child? How can a disobedient woman ever be trusted alone with children?

Any woman capable of breaking patriarchal law—sexually, reproductively, theologically, or economically—may also be *capable* of infanticide. Her *capacity* is unforgivable. The fear of the disobedient woman is the fear of the unwed mother, the fear of the spurned wife turned rebel, the fear of the witch, and the fear of Medea.[37]

Who is Medea? In Greek mythology, Medea is the granddaughter of the sun god Helias. She is an Asian princess, a dusky "barbarian," a powerful priestess.

Medea, strange to say, "falls in love" with Jason, a Greek adventurer. Medea marries him and betrays her blood ties and homeland to aid him in his quest for the Golden Fleece.[38] Years later, Jason abandons Medea, the "aging" dark-skinned refugee. He is about to marry King Creon's daughter, the young and "yellow-haired" Princess Glauce.

Jason's marriage is not an affair of the heart; it is a political decision. Strictly speaking, Jason is not *romantically* betraying Medea, but he is legally "demoting" her to the status of a prostitute or concubine. He is consigning both her and their sons to poverty, ostracism, and exile.[39]

Jason informs Medea that her banishment is her own fault. King Creon is afraid of her "cleverness," her "evil arts," her "anger," her "stubborn temper," and her "loose talking." According to Jason, Medea should consider herself "lucky that exile is her [only] punishment."

Jason defends his marriage to Glauce as a "clever move" and in Medea's "best interest." Marriage to Glauce will make him a powerful Corinthian citizen. He will father more children. This will "benefit" Medea's children. They will be the half-brothers of princes. Jason asks Medea the following:

Do you think this is a bad plan?
You wouldn't if the love question hadn't upset you.
But you women have got into such a state of mind
That, if your life at night is good, you think you have
Everything; but, if in that quarter things go wrong,
You will consider your best and truest interests
Most hateful. It would have been better far for man
To have got their children in some other way, and woman
Not to have existed. Then life would have been good.[40]

Despite everything she knows and despite who she is, Medea has forgotten herself for the sake of love. She has used her powers to help one man—her husband. Medea has never committed adultery, nor has she ever disobeyed Jason. She has happily counted her children as "his." Medea's love-humbled behavior is what accounts for her tragic downfall.

By contrast, Jason has been an absent father and faithless husband. He is a spoiled and foolish man-child. Jason has used Medea as if she were a powerless Greek wife. Without pity, he is ready to move on. Jason under-estimates both Medea and her power. This is what accounts for his tragic downfall.

Medea's "heart is broken"; she wants to "die"; she is "finished." She has loved a man not worthy of her, a "civilized" man who neither loves nor hon-ors her as the mother of his children. Jason is guilty of "the worst of all human diseases, shamelessness."

Medea calls the *women* of Corinth together. She orders them to "stay and watch how the barbarian woman endures betrayal." She will destroy the "upstart" Jason. He is not worthy of immortality—that is, of children who are no more to him than property.[41] Medea will also destroy her "enemies"—the mighty King Creon and Glauce, Jason's child bride. She tells the women of Corinth that it is not "bearable to be mocked by enemies."

> You there! You thought me soft and
> submissive like a common woman—who takes a
> blow
> And cries a little, and she wipes her face
> And runs about the housework, loving her master? I
> am not such a woman. . . .
> I shall not die perhaps
> As a pigeon dies. Not like an innocent lamb, that feels
> a hand and looks up from the knife
> To the man's face and dies.[42]

Medea turns Jason's inability to feel her pain against him. She asks Jason to "forgive" her and to "beg Creon that the children not be banished." She will give them up and go into exile without them. Jason, fool that he is, actu-ally thinks this is a good plan.

From this point on, Medea cannot compromise with tragedy. She sends her sons to the palace bearing wedding presents for Glauce: a dress and a diadem. Glauce can't resist trying on Medea's golden finery. She and her kingly father are consumed in Medea's poisoned flames. Corinth is in com-motion. Jason rushes in to save his sons; Medea greets him in a "chariot drawn by dragons." She tells Jason that his sons are dead; their bodies are in the chariot with her.

Jason begins to "suffer"—that is, to feel self-pity. He is destroyed. He is childless. Jason calls Medea a "hateful" and "loathsome" thing. She is a "wicked mother, an evil monster, not a woman." Jason is correct. Medea is no ordinary woman. She is not even an ordinary queen. She is half goddess and a powerful priestess (a witch). She speaks the language of power. That is why she is capable of destroying, by any means necessary, those who betray her will, her love, or her honor. She tells Jason that

> You had love and betrayed it: now of all men
> You are utterly the most miserable. As I of women.
> But I, as woman, despised, a foreigner, alone
> Against *you* and the might of Corinth
> Have met you, throat for throat, evil for evil, vengeance
> for vengeance.[43]

What choices does Medea, the mother, have? Can she protect her sons in exile, as she

> Wander[s] with fear and famine
> for guide and driver, through all the wild winter
> storms
> And the rage of the sun; and beg[s] a bread-crust and [is]
> derided; pelted with stones in the villages,
> Held a little lower than the scavenger dogs, kicked,
> scorned and slaved?[44]

Can Medea the mother protect her sons by killing herself or Jason? Can she protect them by giving them up, never seeing them again, or leaving them behind "in a country that hates her, to be the prey of [her] enemies' insolence?"[45]

Can Medea the mother protect her sons from being killed once *she* has killed Glauce and Creon? And if Medea can save her sons and is willing to live with them as hunted fugitives in poverty, can she bear to remain the mother of Jason's sons?

> Am I to look in my son's eyes
> And see Jason forever? How could I endure the end
> less defilement, those lives
> that mix Jason and me?[46]

But how can Medea kill her own children? (They are not hers; they "belong" to their father.) But they are *her* children, too. She alone has given birth to and reared them; she alone loves them.

> I cannot bear to do it. I renounce my plans. . . .
> Why should I hurt their father with the pain
> They feel, and suffer twice as much of pain myself?
> I wish you happiness, but not here in this world.
> What is here your father took. Oh, how good to hold you!
> How delicate the skin, how sweet the breath of children!
> Go, go! I am no longer able, no longer
> To look upon you. I am overcome by sorrow. . . .
> Oh, come my hand, poor wretched hand, and take the sword. . . .
> And do not be a coward, do not think of them.
> How sweet they are, and how you are their mother. . . .
> Afterward weep; for even though you will kill them,
> They were very dear—Oh, I am an unhappy woman![47]

Medea is neither an "unfit" mother nor deranged—that is, unaware of what she is doing. Medea the mother does not want to kill her sons. Medea the pagan priestess, Medea the matriarchal queen, and Medea the goddess all say they are determined to do so.[48] And, by the way, Medea may not have killed her sons. She wrestles with her own ambivalence; she takes them—or their bodies—away with her when she flies away.

On the other hand, Medea's murder of Jason's children—and of those "enemies" that would crush both her and them—constitutes a stunning insurrection against patriarchal husband rule.[49] Or is it an act of madness?

In Medea's time—at least, in Euripides' time—only fathers, never mothers, had the legal right to kill their "own" children. Men, not women, had the right to revenge themselves against their enemies and fight wars of honor.[50]

How many wives dare to speak of their "honor" or have the power to revenge its loss? How many mothers *abandon* (no less kill) their children to protest maternal impoverishment and betrayal? How many mothers kill their children to avoid having to serve a child who looks like, "belongs" to, and admires the very man who has abandoned or betrayed her?

What is the play *Medea* telling men to do? Perhaps it is telling men not to dishonor or divorce their wives. Perhaps it is telling men to mistrust their wives from the beginning and treat them harshly—lest they are destroyed by them.

What is the play *Medea* telling women to do? Perhaps it is telling women not to fall in love with shameless adventurers, not to marry them, or not to tell them who their children are—lest they one day find themselves in Medea's tragic position.

The crime of maternal infanticide has long been associated with Medea in the patriarchal imagination. Medea's crime is one of essential being. Medea is a proud and powerful woman. Her sacred power has been forbidden, debased, condemned—and eroticized as a sexual crime.

The *idea* of Medea threatens men's trust in their wives. The *idea* of Medea therefore threatens all women's highly circumscribed access to a (man's) child. This may be why disobedient women are always first condemned by other women.

Who, then, is really an unfit mother? Can a mother be as fit as Medea and still kill her children? Would she have to be insane to do so or, like Medea, powerful when crossed?

Who, then, is really an unfit father? Can a father be as unfit as Jason and still hope to keep his children? How fit and how sane is the father willing to send his children and their mother into exile or to separate his children from their mother forever?

3

What Is a "Fit" Mother or Father? An "Unfit" Mother or Father? Who Decides?

....

Who ever saw a human being that would not abuse unlimited power? Base and ignoble must that man be who, let the provocation be what it may, would strike a woman: but he who would lacerate a trembling child is unworthy of the name of man. A mother's love can be no protection to a child. It is folly to talk of a mother moulding the character of her son, when all mankind, backed up by law and public sentiment, conspire to destroy her influence.

—Elizabeth Cady Stanton

While maternal devotion may be perfectly genuine, this, in fact, is rarely the case. Maternity is usually a strange mixture of narcissism, altruism, idle daydreaming, sincerity, bad faith, devotion and cynicism. The great danger which threatens the infant in our culture [is that its] mother is almost always a discontented woman.

—Simone de Beauvoir

What are our standards for parental fitness? Who determines such standards? Are they the same for both mothers and fathers and for all classes and races? Judith Arcana, in *Every Mother's Son*, describes the "idealized mother [as] a woman who is boundlessly giving and endlessly available. She is truly present to her son. The idealized father is practically invisible; he is almost never available, rarely giving; his sparse favor and scarce presence to his son become miraculous and precious when they do appear. He is like the unknowable Judaeo-Christian father-god, who is the epitome of this idea."[1]

Mothers are expected to perform a series of visible and invisible tasks, all of which are never ending. Mothers are not allowed to fail any of these obligations. The ideal of motherhood is sacred; it exposes all mothers as imperfect.

Fathers are expected to perform a limited number of tasks. They are also allowed to fail some or all of these obligations. In addition, fathers who do *anything* for children are often experienced and perceived as "better" than mothers, who are supposed to do everything. The ideal of fatherhood is also sacred; it protects each father from the consequences of his actions.

Father-starved and father-wounded sons (and daughters) rarely remember, confront, or publicly expose their absent or abusive fathers. Arcana also notes that

> we mothers watch our young boys go from expecting to be cherished and nurtured by their fathers to the sullen and bitter understanding that dad will not come across. And then, so powerful is society's sanction of that "ideal" paternal behavior, we see our sons come to an acceptance so complete that they will defend their fathers even against the criticism and anger they've expressed themselves. And all along, the boy will not—or cannot—confront his father. Young sons will not push their fathers the way they'll push their mothers—they learn early that dad's affection, such as it is, is tenuous and conditional. Most boys understand all this before they are 12 or 13 years old.[2]

When a father fails his paternal obligations, we don't necessarily view him as an example of *all* fathers, nor do we automatically hold other fathers "accountable" for one father's failure. We may be horrified when a father abuses or kills his child, but we first view him as the *exception* among fathers.

Or we make excuses for him. He didn't mean to hit, molest, rape, hurt, maim, or kill his child. He is a man. Men are violent and don't know their own strength.

Or we blame his wife. Perhaps she "drove" him to it. How could any mother leave her child alone with such a man? Where was she when her child was being hit, molested, raped, hurt, maimed, or killed?[3]

When a mother does irresponsibly abandon or savagely abuse her child, we are truly stunned and terrified. How could a *mother* of the human race "act like a man"? How could both biology and culture fail to ensure maternal pacifism under stress?

When one mother neglects or abuses her child, we tend to hold *all* mothers accountable for her failure. One mother's "crime" forces all mothers to prove—to themselves and to everyone else—how unlike Medea they are and how like the Virgin Mary they are.

After reading several news accounts of maternal suicide and infanticide, I read about a mother who failed in her double suicide attempt. She succeeded in killing her child but failed to kill herself. Plunging headlong out the window, she "merely" broke every major bone in her body instead.

I wanted to visit her in her hospital bed. After many phone calls, I was made to understand that her own mother refused to see her and that her husband had vowed never to speak to her again. Women who knew her and her husband tried to dissuade me from seeing her. Women said, "Don't make a heroine out of her. She's a real sickie. You wouldn't have liked her. None of us did. She's broken her husband's heart. He's a wonderful man." Others said, "Her husband was about to leave her. She knew that her son would follow his father, sooner rather than later. The bitch just couldn't let go. Why didn't she die instead of her son?"

Voices without mercy; voices determined that no one comfort her on her cross. This mother was viewed not as human, or even as psychiatrically ill, but as an evil monster, a "loathsome thing," a "Medea."

I am always amazed that Medea's knife, unseen onstage, looms so much larger in our collective memories than Agamemnon's knife, with which he kills his daughter, Iphigenia, or Laius's mountaintop exposure of his newborn son, Oedipus. The infanticidal fathers apparently leave no bloody footprint, no haunting shadow.[4]

Are contemporary mothers and fathers as abusive to their children as parents presumably once were in the past? Historians have described medieval European and colonial American children as essentially their family's "servants." A girl was her mother or stepmother's domestic servant and her father's companion and nurse; a boy was his father or stepfather's agricultural servant. Both boys and girls were often apprenticed out at young ages. Their wages belonged to their fathers.[5]

According to psychoanalyst Alice Miller, child rearing in the West was a form of "poisonous pedagogy." Harsh parental punishment was defended for its being "for the child's own good":

> A sophisticated repertory of arguments was developed to prove the necessity of corporal punishment for the child's own good. In the eighteenth century, one still spoke of [children] as "faithful subjects" . . . child rearing manuals teach us that: "Adults are the masters (not the servants) of the dependent child; they determine in godlike fashion what is right and what is wrong; the child is held responsible for their anger; the parents must always be shielded; the child's life-affirming feelings pose a threat to the autocratic adult; the child's will must be 'broken' as soon as possible; all this must happen at a very early age, so the child 'won't notice' and will therefore not be able to expose the adults."[6]

In Puritan New England, child rearing was synonymous with "breaking" a child's (sinful) "will":

> Every child was thought to come into the world with inherent tendencies to "stubbornness, and stoutness of mind": these must be "beaten down" at all costs. One aspect of such tendencies was the willful expression of anger which was, by Puritan reckoning, the most dangerous and damnable of human affects. Children must therefore be trained to compliance, to submission, to "peace." To effect such training, drastic means were sometimes needed. Puritan parents were not inclined to spare the rod; but more important than physical coercion was the regular resort to shaming.[7]

Mothers worked hard and had little "child-centered" time to spend alone with each child. Although mothers (or women) were exclusively responsible for birthing and rearing children, they were not considered "expert" in this area. "Students of child-rearing literature in England and America tell us that in the 16th and 17th centuries the father was depicted as the important figure in the rearing of children, as well as being the ultimate authority in familial matters. In fact, most of the manuals of these centuries directed advice to fathers."[8]

In the mid- to late eighteenth century, male experts began to address mothers directly. Formerly viewed as vain and without souls, mothers were now viewed as their children's moral guardians.[9]

Mothers of the middle class were encouraged to experience biological motherhood as the source of their greatest pride and joy. The influential Jean-Jacques Rousseau viewed motherhood as a personal religious calling:

> The true mother, far from being a woman of the world, is as much a recluse in her home as the nun is in her cloister. . . . [A good mother] will not be willful, proud, energetic or self-centered. In no event should she become angry or show the slightest impatience . . . she must be taught, while still very young, to be vigilant and hard-working, accustomed at an early age to all sorts of constraints so that she costs [her husband] nothing and learns to submit all her caprices to the will of others. . . . She serves as liaison between [the children] and the father, she alone makes him love them.[10]

Throughout the nineteenth century, male experts continued to urge women into motherhood as a religious calling. However, these experts insisted that "instinctive" (emotional, "soft") maternality was harmful to children. They advised mothers to behave in more "manly" ways.[11]

By the twentieth century, male experts told mothers to give up breast-feeding, to feed their infants only at rigid intervals, not to pick up their crying babies, and to toilet train them as soon as possible.[12]

Some male experts advised mothers to "bond" with their infants immediately at birth. According to these experts, if mothers didn't "bond" with or didn't "let go" of children perfectly enough, they doomed them to "neurosis."[13] According to psychiatrist Ann Dally, mothers were tyrannized into believing that it was "dangerous" to leave their children "even for an hour."[14]

We do not know how many women actually succumbed to the tyranny of the male experts. Enslaved or impoverished mothers did not have the time, the literacy, or the resources to act on scientific opinion; wealthy and royal mothers continued to delegate their maternal responsibilities. (Perhaps some royal and impoverished mothers felt guilty about this.) Middle-class mothers were in a position to be most easily tempted by expert promises.[15]

The church fathers always assured mothers that they were important and irreplaceable. They also tried to convince men that it was anti-God and anti-church to divorce their wives or abandon their children.

The scientific fathers shared these churchly beliefs. However, they also promised mothers "control" over the outcome of their maternal labors and over children at home in lieu of "control" over armies, parliaments, churches, or banks.[16]

What about fathers? Did they matter at all beyond their legal acknowledgment of sperm and economic support of families? Did it affect children badly, or at all, if fathers were absent, distant, or tyrannical? What is a "good" or a "good enough" father?

According to our state and church fathers, a "good" father is someone who legally acknowledges, economically supports, and teaches his children to obey the laws of state and church. The scientific fathers failed to consider the paternal role. When pressed, one twentieth-century expert said, "The first positive virtue of the father is to permit his wife to be a good mother. In the child's eyes the father embodies the law, strength, the ideal, and the outside world, while the mother symbolizes the home and household. . . . The only thing one can usefully demand of the father is to be alive and stay alive during his children's early years."[17]

Some scientific fathers went to great lengths to deny the existence of "bad" fathers. Psychoanalysts, for example, were actually more eloquent about the rivalrous impulses of sons than about the murderous deeds of fathers.[18] Most psychoanalysts rarely paid attention to real-world "facts" or held real fathers responsible for anything they did—or failed to do.[19]

Psychoanalysts and other, more popular child-development experts failed to acknowledge their own expert fathering as "responsible" for an increase in maternal guilt and for turning mother blaming into a "science." For example, the phrase *maternal deprivation* terrorized countless mothers in the twentieth century. A woman who "maternally deprived" her child was a "bad" mother. Dr. John Bowlby first used this phrase in 1951 to describe what happened to children whose state father had institutionalized them.

Bowlby did not condemn the state father for "depriving" his institutionalized children, nor did he (or his popularizers) hold the state responsible for the crimes such children might commit in the future. The sins of the state fathers were used to control maternal behavior. The specter of "maternally deprived" children kept mothers guilty and sleepless. (State orphanage employees and members of Parliament slept quite soundly.)

Popular accounts of child abuse invariably focus on the "sensational" episode as opposed to the more entrenched forms of child abuse. A male homosexual child molester makes ready headline copy; his more numerous male heterosexual counterparts remain invisible.

A single school or a large church involved in the sexual abuse of children becomes a scandal; the high incidence of male heterosexual abuse of female children, including paternal incest, is denied or minimized.

What exactly is child abuse? Is *physical* child abuse increasing in America? Most incidents of physical child abuse are probably never reported. Nevertheless, the National Center on Child Abuse and Neglect reports a "dramatic increase" in child abuse.[20]

Naomi Feigelson Chase found that, historically, "serious" child abuse was either underreported or atypical.[21] Chase and Leontine Young attempt to distinguish between severe physical neglect—lack of adequate or regular feeding—and moderate neglect, which includes lack of cleanliness, lack of adequate clothing, and failure to provide medical care.[22]

They also point out that physical neglect is not the same as physical abuse, which, in turn, may be either moderate or severe. According to Young, the prolonged physical and psychological abuse of children constitutes a category all its own, as does child murder: "Severe [physical] abuse is consistent beating that leaves visible results. Moderate abuse occurs when parents beat children under stress or when drunk. [Those in the] severe category are unable to be helped. The abusing parents' hallmark is deliberate, calculated, consistent punishing without cause or purpose."[23]

In 1978 Dr. David Gil analyzed the thirteen thousand *reported* cases of physical child abuse in the United States. Of these, 3 percent were fatal; less than 5 percent "led to permanent damage"; 53 percent (6,890 cases) were not serious; 90 percent "were expected to leave no lasting physical effects."[24]

These studies of reported child abuse were almost *always* correlated with extreme poverty, severely "deprived" parental childhoods, mental illness, overburdened and isolated single motherhood, and unrelieved or profound stress.[25]

In view of the high incidence of and extraordinary stress associated with single motherhood and the great amount of time mothers have to spend with children, it is significant that both Gil and Chase found no evidence that mothers "abuse" their children any more than fathers (or boyfriends) do. On the contrary. According to Chase, "a mother or stepmother was the abuser in 50 percent of the incidents and the father or stepfather in about 40 percent. Others were caretakers, siblings, or unrelated perpetrators.

However, since almost a third of the homes were headed by females, fathers had a higher involvement rate than mothers. Two-thirds of the incidents in the homes where fathers or stepfathers were present were committed by the father or stepfathers; while in homes with mothers or stepmothers, the mothers and stepmothers were perpetrators in less than half the incidents that took place."[26]

Researchers studied pregnant mothers who were potentially "high-risk" physical child abusers. All these mothers were young, poor, unwed, and going through with unplanned *and* unwanted pregnancies. The study found that, as expected, one-quarter of the children was abused *psychologically.* The researchers explained this abuse in terms of the mothers: they had received no "maternal nurturance" in childhood. The psychologically abusive mothers "don't know how to be nurturing. Instead of giving to the child, they look to the child to satisfy their own needs for nurturance and love, and the child cannot provide."[27]

This study actually shows that 75 percent of "high-risk" mothers do not psychologically or physically abuse their children and that "high-risk" mothers need emotional as well as economic support in order to mother properly. The study focuses on maternal, not on paternal, abuse.

Researchers have no control over how their work is viewed or used. This study (and others like it) are used to "indict" mothers in the public imagination, to incite middle-class or married mothers to paroxysms of time-consuming guilt, and to justify the state's custodial or reproductive punishment of poor, unwed mothers.[28]

Mothers do not *physically* or sexually abuse, abandon, or neglect their children as often as fathers do. Several statistically sophisticated studies have confirmed that it is mainly men—fathers, grandfathers, stepfathers, boyfriends, older brothers, uncles, and male strangers—who physically and sexually abuse both mothers and children.

How many fathers and adult men beat or rape mothers? No one really knows. Research suggests that anywhere from 15 to 50 percent of all mothers in America are physically battered and/or raped by their husbands or live-in boyfriends.[29]

Some studies (and common sense) suggest that wife beaters also tend to abuse their children physically, sexually, and psychologically. The sons of wife beaters often become wife beaters; their daughters often become battered wives.[30]

How many fathers sexually abuse their own genetic or legal children and grandchildren? No one really knows, though a number of first-person and clinical accounts about paternal incest have been published and publicized.[31]

In the past, according to incest researchers, two to five million American women were paternally raped as children; one in every seven[32] or one in every five American children was the victim of paternal incest or of male sexual abuse;[33] 19 percent of all American women (one in six) and 9 percent of American men were sexually victimized as children.[34] Other studies have shown that perhaps 20–25 percent of American girls were sexually abused in childhood[35] and that 30–50 percent of their abusers were male members of their own family.[36]

It is my impression that the majority of unfit mothers do not kill, torture, maim, rape, or abandon their children outright. The majority of unfit mothers seem *physically to neglect* and *psychologically to abuse* their children.

Mothers do spend more time with children than fathers do. Mothers also turn up in emergency rooms alone with battered children. The sight of a mother accompanying a child with a broken arm or a suspicious burn is sickening and impossible to forget.

We do not ask, "Why is she here alone?" or "Where is the child's father or other adult member of his family?" We do not comment, "Maybe the father (or a man) actually beat this child, and she's confessing in his place," or "Perhaps the absence of a supportive husband 'drove' her to it."[37]

Still, it is my impression that when an unfit mother does physically abuse her child, she may do so less forcefully, less often, and less fatally than her paternal counterpart. (There are many exceptions among drug-addicted and mentally ill mothers.)

Physically neglectful or physically violent mothers are more closely and critically scrutinized than physically abusive fathers are. Such mothers have also often internalized certain maternal ideals. Whether they achieve or fail them, they are aware of, and often guilty about, their imperfect or failed maternal performance.

Clearly, children are equally endangered by equally physically violent parents whether they are mothers or fathers. However, women in general are more rigidly socialized into nonviolent maternal behavior *under stress* than men are.

Female socialization, the experience of pregnancy and childbirth, maternal practice, and the social "watchdogging" of mothers all tend to reinforce maternal physical nonviolence. Children tend to be *physically* safer with most mothers most of the time. Sara Ruddick observed that most mothers are (objectively) "powerless" women who find themselves

> embattled with weak creatures whose wills are unpredictable and resistant, whose bodies [they] could quite literally destroy, whose psyches are at [their] mercy. . . . *I can think of no other situation in which someone with the resentments of social powerlessness, under enormous pressures of time and anger, faces a recalcitrant but helpless combatant with so much restraint* [author's italics]. It is also clear that physical and psychological violence is a temptation of maternal practice and a fairly common occurrence.
>
> *What is remarkable is that in a daily way mothers make so much peace instead of fighting, and then when peace fails, conduct so many battles without resorting to violence* [author's italics]. I don't want to trumpet a virtue but to point to a fact: that non-violence is a constitutive principle of maternal thinking, and that mothers honor it not in the breach, but in their daily practice, despite objective temptations to violence.[38]

Children are potentially more *physically* endangered by fathers, whose socialization as men has predisposed them to flight or physical violence under stress and has forced them into a fierce dependence upon obedience from wives and children. Fathers, as men, are not closely "watchdogged" within the house; in a father-idealizing and father-absent culture, they are romanticized by children. (This dynamic allows children to deny paternal violence against them or to blame themselves when it happens.)

Both nature and culture have prepared women to mother in *physically* nonviolent ways under very oppressive conditions. Some observers romanticize the female ability to do this; others lament it as a virtue by default. Most mothers are usually able to absorb frustration, humiliation, unemployment, poverty, celibacy, and extreme loneliness without abandoning, seriously abusing, or murdering their children. As such, mothers as a group are rearing their children *as well as can be expected of the human race to date.*

Does a child *physically* need his or her father or father figure during pregnancy or childbirth, during infancy, or at some point later in childhood? Common sense and personal experience confirm that men and women do not have the same physical relationship to children.

It is crucial to remember that many children grow up without any fathers or father figures. Studies suggest that such children are no different from children with fathers—if severe impoverishment is not confused with paternal absence. Perhaps few children are *physically* fathered whether they live with fathers or not.[39]

It is also clear that fathers have an effect on children whether they are absent or present, that fathers may influence a child directly or indirectly, and that paternal influence can be "advantageous, disadvantageous, or neutral."[40]

A number of feminist theorists and researchers have written about the psychological importance of "fathering" and about men's potential ability to "nurture." Such researchers have tried to show that a "good "father is potentially as good as (or similar to) a "good mother."[41]

These studies have essentially shown that white, middle-class, well-educated fathers can, under experimental conditions, "bond" with infants and can perform many of the physical and emotional tasks of "maternal nurturance."[42]

However, studies also show that "good enough" fathers tend to spend radically less time with infants, toddlers, preadolescents, and teenagers than mothers do; that fathers tend to "play" with children rather than physically to "service" them; and that fathers tend to "mother" children for comparatively short periods of time.[43]

In real life, some (married) fathers are indeed physically "nurturant" to their children. However, unlike most nurturant mothers, such fathers are unwilling or unable to "nurture" children all day, every day, for all the years of each child's childhood.

Fathers do not get pregnant. They do not give birth to, breast-feed, or routinely take care of newborn infants.[44] Traditional fathers and mothers do not view these tasks as men's province.[45]

Researchers have found that "good enough" fathers are not able or willing to do what "good enough" mothers must do *physically* in related areas in order to maintain family life. For example, past studies confirmed that American wives did 70 percent of the housework, whether they were employed outside the home or not.[46]

In their study of American couples, Drs. Philip Blumstein and Pepper Schwartz found that married men had such an intense aversion to housework that when wives insisted they do it, intense acrimony and a greater probability of divorce resulted.[47]

Even if a "good enough" father is unemployed, he does much less housework (and child care) than a wife who is a full-time employee outside the home. One of my interviewees said, "My ex-husband was once unemployed for about a year. I taught full time and rushed home at three, collected the kids, shopped, and cooked dinner. I was very tired by the time I put the kids to bed and finished the dishes. I begged him to cook dinner. He refused. After much battling he agreed to cook every Friday night. He finally cooked dinner about twice a month. We all had to praise him and eat everything. I had to clear the table and do the dishes. Everyone said I had to be very understanding because he wasn't employed."

Of course, a father may be able to earn more money or physically lift more weight than a mother can. Such (innate and cultural) abilities may have nothing to do with satisfying the daily physical needs of children directly or with satisfying these needs in a physically nonviolent way, especially at times of parental stress.

Is physical punishment always a form of child abuse? Is a slap the equivalent of a broken arm? Is *physical* abuse the most serious form of child abuse? Is a child who is made to feel "unloved" or "unworthy" more severely abused than a child who is physically punished?

What do we know about psychological mothering and fathering? "Good enough" fathers may be *psychologically* cold, cruel, demanding, rivalrous, ambivalent, smothering, and abusive toward their sons and *psychologically* seductive and incestuous toward their daughters. A "good enough" father may also be infinitely more psychologically patient, understanding, relaxed, and generous to his children (especially to a daughter) than a mother may be.[48]

"Good enough" mothers may be *psychologically* cold, cruel, demanding, rivalrous, ambivalent, smothering, and abusive toward their daughters (and to a lesser extent toward their sons). They may also be either more positively—or negatively—"maternal" toward their children than a father may be.[49]

Drs. Joseph Goldstein, Anna Freud, and Albert J. Solnit have noted that the "best" parent-child relationship is both "positive" and "negative"; that it "fluctuates" over time; that "wanted" children may be "excessively valued" to their detriment; and that "good" parents cannot guarantee ideal child development even when they are their child's *psychological* parents—that is, present and active in daily and physically caring ways.[50]

Most parents do not view the psychological abuse of children as an epidemic with "devastating" consequences. According to psychoanalyst Alice

Miller, most parents unthinkingly "murder their children's souls." Parents suppress their children's "vital spontaneity" by the "laying of traps, duplicity, subterfuge, manipulation, 'scare' tactics, withdrawal of love, isolation, distrust, by humiliating and disgracing the child, scorn, ridicule, and coercion even to the point of torture. The former practice of physically maiming, exploiting, and abusing children seems to have been gradually replaced in modern times by a form of mental cruelty that is masked by the honorific term child-rearing."[51]

Miller may or may not be right. However, she rarely distinguishes between paternal and maternal behavior. She merges what mothers and fathers do (and don't do) into "parental" behavior. Also, Miller's psychologically high standards, while admirable, are rarely applied to fathers—or to mothers of all classes and races.

Unless or until we (and the "experts") are prepared emotionally to judge all parents by the same standard, several conclusions are in order about how most mothers and fathers behave today.

Mental health experts, like the rest of us, tend to blame mothers, not fathers, for any problems a child may have; to praise fathers, but not mothers, for the good they may do; and to have one set of expectations for mothers and another, lesser set for fathers. Experts also tend to pathologize mothers when they fall short of idealized expectations of motherhood.

Seattle attorney Martha O. Eller notes a disturbing trend: "We are very disheartened by social workers' and psychologists' willingness to ignore issues of domestic violence, over-emphasize the value of a working father and under-value the contributions of a full-time homemaker, and [their] general tendency to despise a woman for having boyfriends without carefully inquiring of the father along the same lines. The [child] guardians *ad litem*, including psychologists, tend to evaluate the mothers harshly, even more so than the judges."

Some mental health professionals have encouraged fathers to consider co-parenting or joint custody as their *right* and encouraged mothers to consider co-parenting or joint custody as their *obligation*, both of which are "in the best interests of the child." Unbelievably, mental health professionals tend to trust what a father tells them and to distrust almost everything a mother says. They routinely minimize male violence and routinely pathologize the normal female response to violence. For example, read the following evaluation from a Michigan case:

The mother presents as a tense, suspicious person rigidly fixated on her ex-husband's so-called potential for child abuse. She and the maternal grandmother, an overly intrusive, controlling woman, have convinced this child to fear her father. While the father admits to engaging in mildly inappropriate fondling behavior with his young daughter and to an incident of "joyriding" with her, I believe these were isolated occurrences and would not occur if the father-daughter relationship was stabilized. The father's continuing inability to pay child support should not be used to deprive him or his child of their relationship. I recommend visitation to the father and therapy for the mother to help her deal with her pathological dependence on her own mother.

Here is an evaluation from a New York case:

The mother claims that her son has been terrorized by his father during so-called drunken rages. She claims that the father allegedly threatened to kill the boy's dog if his son didn't obey him. The wife claims she has been battered and that her husband tried to control her every waking hour. I don't see this. She is too self-confident, too bossy. This woman has her own business and earns more than the father does. The father has been in treatment for alcoholism and says he is now recovered. He lives with the paternal grandparents, who are prosperous. The boy needs to live with male role models, his father and grandfather, especially since his mother has a career and is obviously hostile to men.

It made no difference to either evaluator—one a man, the other a woman—that both fathers were verified as having been treated for mental illness and alcoholism, had been fired from jobs for "losing their tempers" and for repeated absences, and had often "disappeared" from home. That both mothers had been their children's sole support, psychologically and economically, and had sought help from the police, hospitals, and, in one case, a shelter for battered women. None of this impressed the evaluators. Incredibly, these reports—and they are typical—found the mothers "guilty," the fathers "innocent."

How can one fight such an incredible catch-22?

At some level, the evaluators do believe that the fathers have done something "wrong," but they don't want to penalize them for their actions. In fact, when allegations of paternal violence are believed, the father is then exonerated by virtue of having a mental illness. While male mental illness is seen as either temporary or amenable to "therapeutic" intervention, women are often seen as suffering from near-permanent mental illnesses. Judges have been reluctant to order a wife batterer or child abuser out of the house or into jail; based on such psychiatric evaluations, they have instead ordered violent fathers into therapy or mediation. Violent or mentally ill fathers rarely lose their rights to visitation or custody; mothers, however, do. The following paragraphs are from an Illinois case and a Rhode Island case, respectively:

> I guess I had a post-partum depression. I was always so tired, but I couldn't sleep. What if I fell asleep and my babies needed me? I was all they had. I might not have needed pills or a two-week stay in a hospital if my husband had helped or allowed me to hire someone for the twins. When I put myself into a mental hospital, my in-laws persuaded my husband to move in with them, start divorce proceedings, and take custody away from me. Twice, when I and my parents, who finally decided to help me, tried to see my babies, my in-laws physically threw us out. The third time they had us arrested. The police threatened us. The judge said I was too sick to be a mother.

> My ex-husband is charming, well-dressed, well-spoken, and comes from a very powerful family. He first beat me two weeks after we were married. The beatings continued. When I was pregnant, he kicked me so hard between the legs that he broke my water. I gave birth prematurely. During that beating I grazed his arm with a fork. I also pressed charges. He said I'd gone too far and I'd have to be punished. On the basis of his version of what I did with the fork, the custody psychiatrist stated that I was the abusive spouse. The psychiatrist prescribed a minimum of three years of therapy to cure my violence. He recommended that I have limited, supervised visitation and that sole custody go to my ex-husband and his live-in housekeeper. The judge agreed. I haven't seen my child in three years.

"Good enough" mothers behave (and are trained to behave) differently toward children from the way "good enough" fathers do. Most mothers give birth to children after successful pregnancies. Most "birth" and adoptive mothers do not physically abandon or physically abuse their children once they have gotten involved in caring for them.

Some mothers do physically neglect their children. A small (and unknown) percentage of mothers sexually abuse, torture, and kill their children.

All other things being equal, the majority of mothers *physically* nurture and support their children adequately, continuously, and in nonviolent ways.

All mothers are psychologically imperfect. Some are also psychologically abusive.

Most fathers are trained to neglect their children physically. Many fathers physically abandon their children. As we have seen, perhaps one in seven fathers (and stepfathers) sexually abuses his daughters; perhaps 50 percent of fathers economically abandon their children.

All fathers are psychologically imperfect. How many are also psychologically abusive? Most? Some? Few?

In a woman- and mother-hating culture, it is emotionally difficult or psychologically forbidden to acknowledge female or maternal superiority even—or especially—in the areas of female "specialization." In a man- and father-idealizing culture, it is emotionally difficult or psychologically forbidden to acknowledge male or paternal inferiority even—or especially—in the areas of male nonspecialization. These are two of the reasons we "forget" that a "good enough" mother is different from a "good enough" father.

As adults, we respond "indignantly" to news of an abused child. We experience child abuse as something extraordinary, not ordinary; as something that *other* parents, mainly *mothers*, do; not as something that our *own* parents, or *fathers*, once did to us; not as something that we as parents do to our children; and not as something that fathers allow to happen to large numbers of children in their name and without their protest.

As adults, we confuse images of maternal psychological imperfection with maternal psychological and physical unfitness. For example, the idea of a mother's locking her child into a room arouses our rage and a deep sense of heartbreak. (Why? Were we all once left in rooms alone? If so, do we think that this constitutes "child abuse"? Does it?)

The idea of a mother's verbally tormenting or refusing to speak to her child at all or the idea of a mother's neglecting or beating her child provokes the greatest fury and terror in us. (Why? Did our mothers or fathers beat us? If not, why do we so empathetically identify with the image of an abused child? Are we by nature altruists?)

As children, none of us could escape or protest whatever minor or major abuse we suffered at maternal and paternal hands. Now, in one mighty adult voice, we vent our long-suppressed fury at the *mother* in the child-abuse headlines. She is utterly evil and can never be rehabilitated. (How can she be? She is a "stand-in" for so many mothers.) She is very powerful. This time she must not escape us.

Given male violence (or indifference), how can our own *mothers* accept or defend the way things are? (And they do, they do. . . .) How can our own mothers bear to hear our cries and do nothing? How can they leave us alone in the tiny rooms of our lives?

Given male violence and our fear of it, we scapegoat mothers instead. (They are trained to "take it" without killing or abandoning us.) Given male violence and our fear of it, we ask: How dare any mother refuse to become pregnant? How dare any mother have an abortion or abandon, abuse, or kill a child—because if she can, then there is no respite on earth, no one to bear the brunt of *our* imperfections, and no one to save us. We, the innocent, are damned.

Medea—not Jason, not Creon—is still the one we blame.

In summary, an ideal mother is very different from an ideal father. A real mother is also different from a real father. Traditionally, an ideal mother is expected to choose married motherhood for her future at a very young age. She is expected to become pregnant, give birth, psychologically "bond" with her children, and assume bottom-line responsibility for her children's physical, emotional, and economic needs. She is also expected to behave in physically nonviolent and psychologically self-sacrificing ways.

Nevertheless, this female socialization into and practice of motherhood is devalued and taken for granted. We experience the same parental abuse as "worse" when a mother performs it. We condemn mothers more than fathers for failing the parental ideal, for performing parental work inadequately, for being psychologically imperfect, and for being physically abusive.

With such double standards and anti-mother biases, what kind of custodially challenged mother would automatically be viewed as a "good enough" mother? (A person might say, "There must be something wrong with her. Why else would her husband or the state challenge her?")

Do judges, priests, politicians, psychiatrists, or social workers view unwed, imprisoned, or "career" mothers as maternally fit? Would they view their custodial victimization as unjust? Do white married mothers or white social workers view nonwhite or welfare mothers as maternally fit?

Most custodially challenged mothers blame themselves for being imperfect. What kind of custodially challenged mother would view herself, or be viewed by other challenged mothers, as a truly "good enough" mother?

I decided to study sixty custodially challenged, predominantly white mothers who had internalized the Western ideals of motherhood and were demographically similar to the majority of divorced white mothers in America. These sixty mothers were custodially challenged in every geographical region of the United States and Canada between 1960 and 1981. In addition, I interviewed fifty mothers who were black, brown, yellow, and red. Some, but not all, were part of this study. They are very much a part of this book.

In general, the sixty mothers I studied married as virgins—or they married the first man they slept with. They both married and gave birth at relatively young ages. They assumed the bottom-line domestic, emotional, and primary child-care responsibilities of traditional marriages. In general, these mothers stayed at home until their youngest children were of grade-school age. Both psychologically and physically they put "work" or a "career" second to motherhood.

During our interviews together, these mothers casually and matter-of-factly described performing at least twenty-five very specific maternal domestic and child-related chores—quite separate from domestic chores that are husband related.[52]

As I noted in the introduction, I was exploring a worst-case scenario. Could a "good enough" mother ever lose custody? Could she lose custody to a relatively uninvolved or abusive father? Could this happen more than once? Could this happen often?

In my book *Women and Madness*, I allowed each of my sixty interviewees to establish what would ultimately be a collective portrait of the mental health profession. I employed this approach with custodially challenged mothers.

However, I also interviewed fifty-five fathers who battled for, won, or gave up custody. These independent interviews confirmed many of my conclusions about the range of paternal custodial motives.

The study you are about to read is a study of "good enough" mothers. Unbidden and silent, the mother Medea accompanied me to each interview.

4

Do "Good Enough" Mothers Still Lose Custody of Their Children in North America Today?

···············

The Results of an Original Study

One night in the early summer he came home with photocopies of custody judgments in which the custody of very young children was given to the father. He threw these papers at me saying, "See, this proves I'll be able to take the baby away from you." I tried to read the papers, but I couldn't understand the legal language. I tried to ignore his threats, but they were unremitting. I tried to understand what was troubling him, but it was beyond my twenty-year-old grasp. I felt overpowered, helpless, trapped. Where could I go where he couldn't follow me? What can a pregnant woman do? As he battered me with words, all I could do was cry. And as I did, he'd take my tear-contorted face and press it against the nearest mirror. "Look! See that face? It's the face of a crazy woman!"

—*Bonnie Lee Black,* Somewhere Child

Studies of American custody battles tend to confirm that fathers custodially challenged mothers and that many fathers arranged paternal custody privately or won judicial or "kidnapping" custody of their children.[1]

In a comprehensive study of divorce and child support, Drs. Lenore J. Weitzman and Ruth B. Dixon found that 63 percent of the Los Angeles fathers who fought for judicial custody were successful. The authors noted that 90 percent of divorcing mothers retained child custody, but that as the result of an increase in divorce, the actual number of fathers winning custody had increased "dramatically."[2]

They also confirmed that divorce is impoverishing mothers and children, that most fathers do not pay child support, and that most judges do not order fathers to pay adequate or enforceable amounts of child support.[3]

This study is an important one. However, it is not based on interviews with the embattled parents. As such, it is unable to tell us much about the kind of father and husband who fights for custody or about the kind of mother he challenges.

Studies of judicial trends in custody are important and rare. However, like statistical studies, they are also psychologically limited. Neither the case-law analyst nor the appellate judge personally interviews the embattled parents, their witnesses, or their lawyers, nor do they observe the behavior of the trial-court judge.

Courtroom transcripts are not usually available to case-law analysts. In any event, such transcripts do not convey the nonverbal behavior of courtroom participants, nor do they reveal what the trial-court judge refused to "hear" or admit as evidence.

In an excellent study of case law, attorney Nancy Polikoff found that judges had a strong "paternal preference" in cases of contested custody. She noted, "In interpreting the significance of [certain judicial decisions], it is necessary to bear in mind that there has not been a revolution in child rearing, and mothers still bear most of the responsibility. Therefore, data showing a success rate for fathers in courtroom battles of one-third to one-half during the 1970s, suggest the possibility that men who have not been the primary child-care providers are prevailing over women who have been."[4]

How many fathers currently have custody of their children? No one really knows. Do more fathers have custody of their children in 2011 than had it in 1911 or 1811?

In the mid-1980s researchers estimated that the number of households headed by divorced or separated fathers had increased by 71 percent, that five hundred thousand fathers had sole legal custody of their children, that between twenty-five thousand and one hundred thousand formal custody disputes were occurring annually, and that forty thousand fathers had won judicial custody *each year* since 1977.[5]

Such estimates never include the number of fathers who won "kidnapping" custody of their children. Nor do they include the number of fathers who privately coerced mothers into "agreeing" to paternal custody, nor the number of fathers who obtained custody because mothers became ill, were hospitalized for long periods, died, or were genuinely unfit.[6]

American mothers have probably lost more children to paternal kidnapping than to judicial decision. *Parental* child kidnapping is an almost all-male crime. Conservative estimates range from one hundred thousand to one hundred twenty-five thousand child snatchings a year.[7] Dr. Richard Gelles estimated that four hundred fifty-nine thousand to seven hundred fifty-one thousand parental "child snatchings" have occurred each year.[8]

I would estimate that within a single decade at least two million fathers won "kidnapping" custody and that four hundred thousand won judicial or courtroom custody. In a single decade, nearly 2.5 million fathers probably won custody of their children in *quantifiable* ways.[9]

This statistical "guesstimate" does not include the number of children separated from their mothers each year by the state because either the children or their mothers committed crimes and were institutionalized.[10]

As I noted in the introduction, such a statistical estimate not only is partial and conservative, but it also represents only the tip of the American custodial iceberg. Each *publicized* custody battle terrorizes mothers in unmeasurable and unknown ways.

·····

A number of researchers have studied the psychological and medical consequences of divorce among both men and women, and the measurable effects of a conflicted marriage or a "bad" divorce on children.[11] The most influential (or most often quoted) of these studies focus more on fathers than on mothers, more on children than on mothers, and more on paternal rather than on maternal expressions of parental longing.

Most studies about custodial fathers concentrate more on what fathers *say* about themselves as parents than on observations of what they do. Pro-paternal-custody researchers have not viewed paternal custody historically or politically, nor have they explored how custodial fathers parented during

marriage or after divorce or whether they parent differently than noncustodial fathers do. Male custodial parenting is almost never compared to female
custodial or noncustodial mothering.[12]

Dr. Deborah Luepnitz published an excellent study of joint custody.
Luepnitz interviewed sixteen custodial mothers, sixteen custodial fathers,
eleven joint custody parents, and ninety-one children. She found that sole
and joint custody fathers fought long, hard, and "bitterly" to win custody.
They had higher incomes, more support systems, and less of an "authority"
problem with children than did sole or joint custody mothers.

Luepnitz's divorced mothers and fathers all adopted some "crossgender"
skills—that is, fathers became more "domestically" competent; mothers,
more "economically" competent. Luepnitz's children were measurably similar psychologically, whether they lived with their fathers, their mothers, or
with both parents in joint custodial arrangements.[13]

As a social scientist, Luepnitz cannot and does not argue in favor of joint
custody, nor does she "confirm" that male fathering and female mothering
are alike. Ideologically, Luepnitz believes that genuine *co-parenting* would
be ideal during marriage and, if practiced, should continue as joint custody
after divorce. Luepnitz calls for "further research" to study whether joint
custody is better, per se, for children than are other "conflict-free" custodial
arrangements.

Dr. Patricia Pascowicz published a study of noncustodial motherhood.
Ideologically, Pascowicz is a champion of a woman's right to be a (good)
"absentee mother" without being treated as a social pariah. Her arguments
are eloquent and passionate. However, the majority of Pascowicz's question-
naire respondents (61 percent) lost or relinquished custody against their
wills. The remaining mothers relinquished custody as the result of serious
emotional problems (18 percent), a desire for self-realization (17 percent), or
a belief that the children's fathers were more nurturant (4 percent).[14]

The majority of Pascowicz's "absentee" mothers both felt and were horri-
bly victimized. All were treated as social pariahs. Only 14 percent ever again
gave birth to or adopted children. Some of Pascowicz's mothers, however,
did develop themselves economically, intellectually, and emotionally after
becoming "absentee mothers."

Dr. James R. Turner published the results of his interviews with twenty-
six divorced fathers who had fought for and won sole custody of their
children. Two-thirds of these fathers did not have close or nurturing relationships with their children during marriage, were "upset" by their wives'

pregnancies, and were not "involved" in the birth process. According to Turner, these fathers (who were in the majority) sought custody out of "anger" at their wives and/or because they felt their ex-wives were "poor parents." They "waited" an average of two years before moving for custody.

One-third of Turner's fathers sought custody immediately upon separating. Turner reported that these fathers were "pleased" with their wives' pregnancies, "involved" in the birthing process, and, according to them, "involved in at least half of the child care activities during marriage." These fathers sought custody in order to "maintain a close relationship with their children."[15]

What kinds of fathers custodially challenge a "good enough" mother? Are they similar to most other divorced (or married) fathers and husbands? Are they exceptionally nurturant—or exceptionally abusive—fathers and husbands? Do they pay child support? Do they see their children regularly and behave in nonviolent ways?

Why do these fathers fight for custody? How often do they win? Why do they win? Can a "good enough" mother really lose custody of her children? If so, why? How is the psychological parenting of mothers and fathers viewed in a custodial confrontation? How are "good enough" mothers psychologically affected by having to battle for custody against their will?[16]

I interviewed each one of the sixty mothers in my home or office or in hers. The interviews lasted from two to ten hours and took from one to three days to complete. Three-quarters of each interview was taped. I also read and analyzed each mother's trial transcript, legal deposition, psychiatric report, and relevant private correspondence—when it was available.[17] I transcribed and then analyzed the taped portion of these interviews, both statistically and thematically.

WHAT KINDS OF MOTHERS WERE CUSTODIALLY CHALLENGED? (TABLE 1)

As a group, these mothers were married by the time they were twenty-one and had two children by the time they were twenty-seven. Half the mothers were married between 1951 and 1964; half were married between 1965 and 1974. Their marriages lasted for an average of nine years.[18]

As a group, these mothers had completed an average of three years of college.[19] Of these mothers, 30 percent had professions in teaching, nursing, social work, psychology, science, and medicine; 10 percent were serious artists who were unpaid or poorly paid; and 60 percent had no professional-level skills when they married or when they separated. In addition, 87 percent of these mothers had never worked full-time or at "careers" once they became mothers.

Fathers who battled for custody had an average income that was five times greater than their wives had at the moment of separation. *This was true both for "poor" and for "rich" fathers.*

Sixty percent of the mothers had no professional or marketable skills. They worked immediately or within two years of their separation as non-unionized domestics, factory workers, laborers, clerks, saleswomen, and school aides. Some mothers worked as secretaries. These mothers did not have jobs that promised them a better economic future. They did not learn any on-the-job skills. Most important, their work didn't pay very much.

Of the group of mothers, 94 percent were white; 77 percent were heterosexual. Fifteen percent of the heterosexual mothers eventually remarried or had live-in boyfriends. Half the mothers were of Protestant origin; 23 percent were of Catholic origin; 27 percent were of Jewish origin.

WERE THESE MOTHERS REALLY "GOOD ENOUGH" MOTHERS?

Fifty-eight mothers (97 percent) successfully gave birth to children after pregnancy and labor. Two mothers adopted infants at birth. All mothers, whether they worked outside the home or not, psychologically bonded with their children and were their primary caregivers.

Most mothers personally attended to all their children's physical and emotional needs. A minority supervised others in assisting them with certain maternal responsibilities. Custodially challenged mothers fulfilled the following twenty-five child-related responsibilities:

1. Breast- and/or bottle-fed infants;
2. Changed six to eight diapers a day until their infants were toilet-trained;
3. Toilet-trained their infants;
4. Nursed their infants through every illness;
5. Taught each infant how to eat;
6. Taught each child how to speak;

TABLE 1: COMPARISON OF SIXTY NORTH AMERICAN MOTHERS AND SIXTY NORTH AMERICAN FATHERS WHO BATTLED FOR CUSTODY (1960–1981)

MOTHERS		FATHERS	
1. Religious origin		1. Religious origin	
Catholic	14 (23%)	Catholic	11 (18%)
Protestant	30 (50%)	Protestant	26 (43%)
Jewish	16 (27%)	Jewish	23 (38%)
2. Average number of years married	9	2. Paid alimony	6 (10%)
3. Average number of children	2	3. Paid child support	20 (33%)
4. Responsible for the primary child care of children under eight	60 (100%)	4. Involved in the primary child care of children under eight	8 (13%)
5. Mothering styles		5. Fathering styles	
Traditional	60 (100%)	Traditional Patriarch	36 (60%)
		Peer-Buddy	10 (17%)
		Smother-Father	14 (23%)
6. Physically abused their husbands	0	6. Physically abused their wives	37 (62%)
7. Estimated median annual income at time of separation	$5,000	7. Estimated median annual income at time of separation	$25,000
8. Had live-in stepfathers, maternal grandmothers, or live-in boyfriends	9 (15%)	8. Had live-in stepmothers, paternal grandmothers, or girlfriends	31 (52%)
9. Kidnapped their children	7 (12%)	9. Kidnapped their children	22 (37%)
10. Engaged in brainwashing campaigns	0	10. Engaged in brainwashing campaigns	34 (57%)

7. Taught each child how to walk;

8. Taught each child how to read;

9. Shopped for children's food;

10. Shopped for children's clothing;

11. Cooked for children;

12. Sewed for children;

13. Ironed for children;

14. Cleaned for children;

15. Called and waited for repairmen, salesmen, and others;

16. Helped children with their homework;

17. Helped children with their psychological problems;

18. Chose religious and private schools or special lessons for each child;

19. Chose and transported children to and from dentists and doctors;

20. Transported children to and from birthday parties and athletic and cultural events;

21. Planned and carried out all family holidays and birthday parties;

22. Planned and worked out the details of children's summer camps;

23. Met and maintained contact with teachers, parents' groups, and other parents;

24. Found, trained, and supervised babysitters and housekeepers;

25. Assumed responsibility for sick children, whether the mothers worked outside the home or not.[21]

WHAT KINDS OF FATHERS CUSTODIALLY CHALLENGED "GOOD ENOUGH" MOTHERS?

In this study, eight of the sixty fathers interviewed (13 percent) were involved in the primary child care of their children. Eighty-seven percent of the fathers weren't responsible for any of the previously mentioned twenty-five chores. An exceptionally good husband sometimes "helped out" with one to three of these chores; an unusually good husband felt "responsible" for one to three of these chores.

According to mothers, about 20 percent of the fathers "helped out." For example, a father might "babysit" for one child while a mother nursed another sick child, or a father might shop with a list created by his wife. Some fathers "helped" their wives put children to bed or took the children out while mothers rested or did other domestic tasks.

In general, fathers earned money and left the children and housework to their wives. Most mothers never expected or asked for their husbands' help with household tasks. Those mothers who did were met with disbelief, indifference, or hostility.

During marriage and/or the custody struggle, 62 percent of the fathers physically abused their wives. More than a third (37 percent) kidnapped their children; 57 percent engaged in serious child-brainwashing campaigns. Half the fathers remarried, had live-in girlfriends, or had help from their mothers.

As a group, fathers earned *five times* as much as mothers. Although these fathers had been domestically and reproductively serviced by their wives for an average of nine years, only 10 percent paid any alimony, and only a third paid any child support.

Ninety-four percent of these fathers were white; 87 percent were heterosexual and/or sexually active within marriage; 13 percent were homosexual, bisexual, or sexually celibate.

In terms of religion, 43 percent of the fathers were of Protestant origin; 38 percent were of Jewish origin; 18 percent were of Catholic origin. The information I have about these fathers is based on my interviews with their ex-wives.

In *Women and Madness*, sixty interviewees each contributed to a collective portrait of the mental health establishment. I employed this same approach with custodially challenged mothers.

I also interviewed fifty-five custodially embattled, custodial, and noncustodial fathers. Five of these fathers had been married to five of my maternal interviewees; thirty were fathers' rights activists. These interviewees confirmed most of my findings based on the interviews with mothers.[22]

HOW WAS THE *PSYCHOLOGICAL* PARENTING OF MOTHERS VIEWED?

Maternal styles of psychological parenting were closely scrutinized by fathers, relatives, neighbors, judges—and children. Highly controversial or popular (mis)interpretations of complex psychoanalytic *theories* were used to terrorize mothers—especially those involved in courtroom battles. As I've noted previously, idealized motherhood exposes all mothers. No mother can embody the maternal ideal perfectly enough to ensure her custody in a battle.

All sixty mothers had internalized certain standards of ideal mothering. These mothers were the first to blame themselves for minor or major psychological "failings." Mothers were often accused of psychologically abusing their children when they disciplined them—that is, when they set curfews and demanded that homework be done, rooms cleaned, and domestic chores shared. Mothers were also accused of being psychologically "abusive" or "inadequate" for refusing to give up or "let go" of their children (a real catch-22!).

Husbands, lawyers, and judges *accused* mothers of wanting their children "as meal tickets because they can't function in the real world." Mothers who worked were also viewed as psychologically abusing their children because they had to work or wanted careers.

HOW WAS THE *PSYCHOLOGICAL* PARENTING OF FATHERS VIEWED?

Paternal styles of psychological parenting remained invisible. Judges, lawyers, relatives, children—and mothers—minimized an individual father's long-term absence or abusive presence. As I've noted previously, the *ideal* of fatherhood is very sacred and essentially symbolic. As such, it protected these fathers, including those who really were psychologically unfit.

Fathers adopted three main fathering styles: the absent and authoritarian Patriarch (60 percent), the Peer-Buddy (17 percent), and the Smother-Father (23 percent). Some fathers exhibited only one fathering style; others combined two fathering styles.[23]

Patriarchal fathers ruled through "symbolic" authority rather than intimacy. Some patriarchal fathers were never home; some were passive at home; some were psychologically demanding and competitive at home. All were emotionally distant or emotionally inept.

Patriarchal fathers tended to be more interested in older than younger children, harder on sons than on daughters, and hostile to daughters who were not sufficiently "feminine." Patriarchal fathers considered themselves perfectly good fathers. None was involved in child care or domestic labor.

Peer-Buddies were also patriarchs who tended to be permissive, playful, and "boyish" with their children. Such fathers left discipline up to their wives and then opposed or mocked the need for discipline.

The Smother-Father demanded an exclusive "bond" with his children—one in which he was seen as the better "mother" or as a self-sufficient pansexual mother-father. Smother-Fathers were tenacious, seductive, and very overwhelming. They convinced everyone, including their children, that they were more generous and self-sacrificing than mothers. Their children often thought that satisfying their fathers' emotional needs, including rejecting their mothers, was a way of being paternally loved.[24]

WHERE AND FOR HOW LONG DID PARENTS BATTLE FOR CUSTODY?

Of the battles, 58 percent took place in the American Northeast. The remaining battles (42 percent) took place in the American South, Midwest, and West and in Canada.

Custody struggles lasted an average of three stressful years and involved a total of one hundred forty-one children, 56 percent of whom were boys. The average age of the youngest child was six when the battle commenced.*

Custodially challenged mothers and challenging fathers did not give up easily. Mothers endured protracted litigation, poverty, and violence; fathers fought for children who were already toilet-trained, verbal, and of school age.

The stress involved included the father's protracting or dramatizing litigation, withholding of child support, prohibiting the children to visit the mother, "seducing" and brainwashing the children against the mother, denying the mother the ability to move or forcing her to move in order to see her children, prohibiting the mother from having a lover, and "legally" kidnapping the child or receiving mandatory joint or split custody of the children.

WHY DID FATHERS CUSTODIALLY CHALLENGE "GOOD ENOUGH" MOTHERS? (TABLE 2)

In addition to loving their children, fathers battled for custody for at least eight reasons. Two-thirds of the fathers (67 percent) had some economic motive: for example, they didn't want to lose or share the marital homes or other financial assets with custodial ex-wives. Some fathers wanted to provide for their children—without depriving themselves or their second

---

* The children ranged in age from breast-feeding infants to teenagers.

wives of comfortable middle-class lives. Since such a father couldn't afford to subsidize two wives, he chose to sacrifice his first wife custodially.

Those fathers (25 percent) who were fairly prosperous refused to subsidize their ex-wives' motherhood for both economic and psychological reasons. Such fathers were addicted to "jet set" lifestyles. They couldn't psychologically afford to cut back in order to subsidize their first wives' custodial motherhood.

Most fathers believed that *wifely* disobedience was a form of maternal unfitness and that "uppity" wives deserved to be custodially punished. Nearly two-thirds (62 percent) of the fathers viewed their ex-wives as punishably "uppity."

"Uppity" behavior included nonmarital sexual activity during marriage or after divorce, returning to school or work, holding independent religious or political opinions, or initiating a divorce against a husband's wishes.

Nearly a fourth (23 percent) were Smother-Fathers. These fathers believed they were the superior parent and/or that their children needed only one parent. Smother-Fathers, Patriarchs, and Peer-Buddies all loved and needed their children—as obedient inferiors, as domestic servants, and as personal genetic allies in a hostile world.

In addition, 25 percent of the fathers fought for their children because they—or their second wives—were infertile. Perhaps such fathers needed daily, visible proof of their (former) spermatic potency; perhaps they also wanted to "award" children to their (infertile) second wives.

HOW OFTEN DID FATHERS WIN CUSTODY?

In court, 70 percent of the judges ordered children into paternal custody; 70 percent of the private arrangements also resulted in paternal custody. Within two years, 82 percent of all custody battles resulted in paternal custody.

Only five mothers—8 percent—retained custody without having to keep battling. These mothers either "gave up" their rights to alimony, child support, or other marital assets or agreed to whatever paternal visitation was demanded. In addition, two of these mothers agreed in writing never to allow lovers into their homes overnight.

Thus, when fathers *fought* for custody, they *won* custody. Challenged mothers were custodially vulnerable—no matter how maternally fit they were.

TABLE 2: THE EIGHT MAJOR REASONS SIXTY NORTH AMERICAN FATHERS BATTLED FOR CHILD CUSTODY (1960–1981)*

FATHERS' REASONS FOR ENGAGING IN CUSTODY BATTLES	NUMBER OF FATHERS (percentage of fathers)
1. Economically and psychologically refused to subsidize their ex-wives' motherhood by paying alimony or child support; didn't want to move out or sell marital home or liquidate and divide other marital assets; wanted companionship of and control over the children they had to support	40 (67%)
2. Punished "uppity" female behavior (desire to return to school, work, or career or to have an independent intellectual, religious, or social life)	37 (62%)
3. Punished maternal nonmarital sexual activity (heterosexual and lesbian) during marriage and after divorce	29 (48%)
4. Punished wives' initiation of divorce	27 (45%)
5. Had patriarchal concept of children as paternal "property" and thus punished and prevented ex-wives from moving away (the Apartheid factor)	19 (32%)
6. Had patriarchal concept of children as paternal "property" and thus initiated divorce and forcibly separated mothers from children by physically ejecting mothers	16 (27%)
7. Had patriarchal concept of the male as the "superior" parent and competed with mothers for exclusive intimacy with children (the Smother-Father factor)	14 (23%)
8. Were infertile or were remarried to infertile wives	15 (25%)

* Eight custody battles took place between 1960 and 1970. The remaining fifty-two battles took place between 1971 and 1981. An individual father can have more than one motive for fighting. The paternal population as a whole had an average of two reasons for fighting.

Paternal legal persistence and maternal poverty, plus paternal brainwashing and kidnapping, led to maternal "agreement" in court or on the eve of a trial—or, in general, to sole paternal custody.

WHAT KINDS OF FATHER WON CUSTODY JUDICIALLY VERSUS PRIVATELY? (TABLE 3)

Fifty-nine percent of the judicially successful and 50 percent of the privately successful fathers physically abused their wives or initiated a violent divorce. Such fathers believed that wives could be unilaterally discarded and that children are a form of landed personal property, not part of a movable maternal unit. Mothers are not entitled to children any more than they are entitled to the marital house or furniture. A third of these fathers (32 percent) also moved for custody when their ex-wives needed and wanted to move out of the father's immediate geographical orbit.

As for the children, 36 percent of the judicially successful and 19 percent of the privately successful fathers kidnapped their children; 45 percent of the judicially successful and 31 percent of the privately successful fathers brainwashed their children. Nearly half the judicial fathers (49 percent) and 44 percent of the privately successful fathers opposed their ex-wives with "mother competitors."

After separation or divorce and prior to obtaining custody, three quarters (77 percent) of the judicially successful and all (100 percent) of the privately successful fathers refused to pay alimony. Moreover, 42 percent of the judicially successful and 69 percent of the privately successful fathers refused to pay any child support.

Mothers were not rescued from individually violent men by police officers, social workers, lawyers, or other family members. Judges did not rescue mothers from violent men either. On the contrary, the large number of domestically violent fathers, including those who kidnapped their children, were not imprisoned, fined, or custodially punished. Of the 12 percent of the mothers who kidnapped their children (table 1), 80 percent were imprisoned, fined, or custodially punished.

HOW DID 82 PERCENT OF SUCH FATHERS WIN CUSTODY?

Fathers had many motives for fighting; they also *won* custody for more than one reason or in more than one way. At least seven reasons were involved.

Money played an important role. Judges, relatives, children—and often mothers themselves—viewed paternal economic superiority as in the child's "best interests." Money also allowed fathers to persist in their legal battles for a long time without having to suffer economically themselves. Money allowed fathers to kidnap and seduce their children economically. The paternal withholding of money gradually devastated the maternal-child unit, both economically and psychologically.

TABLE 3: SELECTED VARIABLES ASSOCIATED WITH FOUR KINDS OF CUSTODIAL ARRANGEMENTS (1960–1981)				
	PATERNAL CUSTODY		MATERNAL CUSTODY	
FATHERS (*n*=60)	judicially ordered (*n*=26)	privately arranged (*n*=16)	judicially ordered (*n*=11)	privately arranged (*n*=7)
1. Physically abusive	59%	50%	54%	29%
2. Brainwashed children	45%	31%	54%	0%
3. Opposed mother with "mother competitor"	49%	44%	81%	0%
4. Initiated the divorce violently	29%	50%	27%	0%
5. Kidnapped children	36%	19%	64%	43%
6. Saw mother as "uppity"	64%	50%	27%	0%
7. Did not pay alimony	77%	100%	82%	100%
8. Did not pay child support	42%	69%	64%	43%
9. Involved in primary child care	12%	6%	27%*	14%

* Three fathers were involved in some primary child care in 30 percent of the court cases.

Sixty-two percent of the fathers used violence to win custody. They physically battered, psychologically terrorized, and physically ejected mothers from their homes; they kidnapped and, with the help of "mother competitors," brainwashed children.[25]

Judges upheld the views of 59 percent of the fathers who viewed mothers as punishably "uppity" and 57 percent of the fathers who viewed mothers as punishably "sexual." Mothers who wanted (and needed) to move away were judicially prevented from doing so.[26]

In this study, fathers who won courtroom custody were very violent men. They were even more violent than were fathers who privately pressured mothers into giving up custody. They battered their wives; they kidnapped and sometimes brainwashed their children (see table 4).

Those mothers who were able to battle successfully for custody tended to have jobs or careers or to have married or given birth at later ages. Those mothers who gave birth at the youngest ages tended to lose custody, both judicially and in private arrangements.

How does the age at which a mother first gives birth relate to her ability to defend herself custodially? Perhaps women who are married and become

TABLE 4: SELECTED VARIABLES ASSOCIATED WITH FOUR KINDS OF CUSTODIAL ARRANGEMENTS (1960–1981)				
	MATERNAL CUSTODY		PATERNAL CUSTODY	
MOTHERS (*n*=60)	judicially ordered (*n*=11)	privately arranged (*n*=7)	judicially ordered (*n*=26)	privately arranged (*n*=16)
1. Average age at birth of first child	27	26	23	22
2. Has profession	57%	36%	40%	38%
3. Initiated the divorce	57%	64%	40%	31%
4. Committed adultery	29%	54%	47%	31%
5. Were physically abused by husbands	39%		59%	
6. Endured paternal kidnapping	59%		36%	

mothers at the youngest of ages were chosen by or "attracted" to the most violent and patriarchal husbands. Young, dependent, and isolated mothers may have been further weakened by the restrictive bonds of marriage, the burdens of motherhood, and their own traditional values.

Woman's need to be a "good girl" results in her inability to fight with her husband in public. "Good girls" are also reluctant to lie in court or adopt violent means to obtain custody of their children.

It is important to remember that "bad girls" have an even harder time in custody struggles and that mothers are custodially vulnerable whether they married at very young or at slightly older ages.

WERE CUSTODIALLY CHALLENGING FATHERS MORE INVOLVED IN HOUSEWORK OR CHILD CARE THAN OTHER FATHERS?

Most of the custodial fathers (87 percent) did no housework or primary child care, although many criticized and denigrated their wives' competence in these areas. Twelve of the custodial (20 percent) "helped out" with maternally organized child-care chores; eight (14 percent) were involved in the primary care of their children.

These eight men were all Smother-Fathers. Their child-care activities included holding their children exclusively or secretively for hours on end, keeping their children up very late, and expecting their children to listen to paternal problems and assuage paternal anxiety. In a sense, Smother-Fathers treated their children more as "wives" than as children.

As I have noted, "good enough" fathers in general do not physically or psychologically take care of a home or a child the way "good enough" mothers do. This seems to be true about custodial fathers as well.

Studies of paternal involvement in housework and child care do not exist or are too experimental in nature to permit us to compare custodial paternal behavior with that of other fathers.

DID CUSTODIALLY CHALLENGING FATHERS ENGAGE IN LESS CHILD ABUSE THAN OTHER FATHERS?

Of the custodial fathers, 67 percent impoverished their wives and children, 62 percent physically abused the mothers of their children, 57 percent engaged in anti-mother brainwashing campaigns, and 37 percent kidnapped their children. Three percent were incestuous fathers. In my opinion, these are all forms of child abuse.

As we have seen, very few studies on paternal child abuse exist. Thus we cannot compare custodial fathers with the paternal population in general.

DID CUSTODIALLY CHALLENGING FATHERS ECONOMICALLY ABANDON THEIR WIVES AND CHILDREN LESS THAN OTHER DIVORCED HUSBANDS AND FATHERS?

Over the years, 33 percent of the custodial fathers paid (some) child support; 10 percent paid (some) alimony. Fathers who fought for custody were probably no more domestically involved, in terms of housework and child care, than fathers are in general. They were as domestically violent to their wives, perhaps even more so, than husbands are in general. The fathers were physically and psychologically abusive to their children in ways for which no comparative data yet exist. They were somewhat more economically abusive to their wives and children than separated and divorced fathers are in general.

DOES THIS STUDY PROVE THAT MORE NORTH AMERICAN FATHERS FOUGHT FOR OR WON CUSTODY BETWEEN 1960 AND 1981 THAN EVER BEFORE?

We do not know if mothers were custodially challenged or victimized more frequently between 1960 and 1981 than between 1860 and 1881. It is almost impossible to confirm a statistical increase in a previously uncharted area.

This study can and does confirm the custodial vulnerability of "good enough" mothers. It also confirms the ease with which a domestically violent father or one with no previous involvement in child care can win custody.

This study can and does confirm that "good enough" mothers have no enforceable right to freedom from male domestic violence, no enforceable right to alimony or child support, and no right to initiate a divorce unilaterally, pursue a career, move away, engage in nonmarital sexual activities, or hold any opinions opposed by their husbands—without risking a custodial challenge.

WHAT TREND OR HIDDEN TRUTH DOES THIS STUDY REVEAL?

As children became more of an economic burden than an economic asset, maternal custody became more common. In the twentieth century, maternal custody also meant maternal poverty. This study reveals that once "respectable" mothers (white and formerly married) are divorced and impoverished, they are custodially vulnerable in the same way that members of a racially, ethnically, morally, or criminally despised group are.

Historically, fathers (and the state) claimed custody of children as their absolute religious and legal right and as their children's best economic provider. In this study fathers also claimed custody on the grounds of male economic and psychological superiority.

Historically, fathers claimed custody of children as their absolute economic right.*

In this study, some fathers also claimed children for paternal economic advantage; all fathers claimed children as a form of psychological "wealth."

Respectable mothers were unprepared for the consequences of divorce. They were stunned when their unchosen poverty, their career achievements, and their sexual independence were viewed as maternal crimes. Respectable mothers were also surprised when police officers, lawyers, judges, neighbors, and relatives did little to protect them from male violence—including that of a custody battle.

I would like to introduce you to these mothers in the following chapters.

---

* Children performed domestic, agricultural, and wage labor for their fathers.

5

The "Sexual" Mother

....

Anna Karenina Today

If motherhood is the highest fulfillment of women's nature, what other protection does it need save love and freedom? (Doesn't marriage) say to woman, only when you follow me shall you bring forth life? Does marriage not place a crown of thorns upon an innocent head and carve in letters of blood the hideous epithet. Bastard? Were marriage to contain all the virtues claimed for it, its crimes against motherhood would exclude it forever from the realm of love.

—*Emma Goldman,* Marriage and Love

How can a woman go into this marriage contract with a man who she thinks is so mean that, in case of a quarrel, he wouldn't even support his own children? If she thinks he is such a man, why should she marry him? I suppose truth and mutual faith are the first principles of love. At any rate, I believe as a wage-earning woman, that if I make the great sacrifice of strength and health and even risk my life, to have a child, I should certainly not do so if, on some future occasion, the man can say that the child belongs to him by law, and he will take it from me and I shall see it only three times a year! Any intelligent woman who reads the marriage contract, and then goes into it, deserves all the consequences.

—*Isadora Duncan,* My Life

WHAT DOES MY STUDY TELL US ABOUT THE CUSTODIAL VICTIMIZATION OF DIVORCED MOTHERS WHO ENGAGE IN SEXUAL ACTIVITY?

Ten mothers were custodially challenged for post-divorce sexual activity. Of these, 30 percent were married to maritally celibate, inactive, or impotent men. Seventy percent were sexually abused or neglected by their husbands. It is very dangerous for a wife to be married to a sexually inadequate husband.[1]

•••••

We are now in nineteenth-century St. Petersburg. Anna Karenina—Tolstoy's hero in the novel that bears her name—is estranged from her husband Karenin and in love with Count Vronsky. When Anna discovers she is pregnant, she desperately summons Vronsky, who literally bumps into Karenin at Anna's front door. "After meeting Vronsky, Karenin drove to the Italian opera. He sat through two acts and saw everybody it was necessary for him to see. [Karenin's] feeling of anger with his wife, who would not observe the rules of propriety, gave him no rest. She had not complied with his stipulation [not to receive her lover in his house], and he must punish her and carry out his threat to divorce her and take the boy away."

Anna's morphine addiction and her suicide start here—with her right to motherhood absolutely jettisoned by her need for love. Anna is a social pariah. Karenin refuses to divorce Anna; Vronsky cannot marry her; society cannot include her. Anna gives birth to a girl. Vronsky grows more distant every day. Vronsky says,

> "My daughter is by law not my daughter, but Karenin's. I cannot bear the falsity of it!"
>
> "Someday we may have a son," he went on, "my son, and by law he would be a Karenin. He would not be heir to my name or property. There would be no legal bond between us.
>
> "[All my children] would be Karenins. Think of the bitterness and horror of such a position. Conceive the feelings of a man who knows that his children, the children of the woman he loves, will not be his, but will belong to someone who hates them, and will have nothing to do with them! It is horrible."

Vronsky has described Anna's position exactly. However, he remains unaware that Anna's legal status is even worse than his own. Anna has lost her son, her lover, her maternal and social identities—all for the sake of passion. Anna mistrusts herself and her world. Moments before she kills herself, Anna says, "'There go some school boys, laughing. Seriozha? I thought that I loved him, and used to be moved by my own tenderness for him. Yet here I have lived without him. I exchanged him for another love. . . . Are we not all flung into the world for no other purpose than to hate each other, and so to torture ourselves and one another?'"[2]

After Anna's suicide, Karenin does claim Anna and Vronsky's love child as his legal child.

· · · · ·

I have interviewed Anna Karenina in America today. She is here, in this chapter, and she goes by many names.

Catherine greets me at her door in autumn. Her hair is as red as the falling leaves. She wears a long dress over her riding boots.

"Come in," she says. "I'm so glad you've come by." Catherine's skin is unlined; her figure girlish. She is the mother of four teenagers. I cross the threshold into another century.

A candelabra, love seats, and footstools crowd the room. The piano and chime clocks are silenced by velvet drapes. Upstairs there are four children's beds covered with dolls and animals. There are framed paintings and photographs of children in every room. No child appears to be more than ten years old.

She is waiting for her children to return.

"It was the fifties," she finally says. "I wanted six children to love. I married in order to have children. Dr. McQueen seemed very marriageable, very much a family man. He had no friends or close family.

"Dr. McQueen was always very secretive. For instance, whenever he went to the dentist, he refused to let me see the inside of his mouth. I thought that was very strange. Years later, when it was clear that our marriage was floundering, he also refused to open up to discuss anything.

"He didn't make love to me for ten years. I tried to discuss this chastity or impotence with him. He wouldn't hear of it."

I can see her smiling at parties, where she is ashamed to admit that her husband doesn't touch her—ever—and doesn't make love to her—ever. She is a slight figure on her side of the bed, still awake at two o'clock in the morning, planning to bake brownies.

Catherine is weeping now. "After seventeen married years I was starved for an affectionate relationship with a man. I found someone. We were very discreet. Somehow, Dr. McQueen found out. He pinned a scarlet letter on me, one I could never rip off. He had our town buzzing. He never spoke to me again, but he spoke against me to everyone.

"Thomas convinced my two youngest children that I didn't love them because I'd slept with another man. He also made them feel that he'd shrivel up and die without them. My boys were thrilled by his attentiveness. They perceived me as the strong one and began turning away from me. I was devastated.

"Once I was an heiress," Catherine says. "We lived in a twenty-room mansion that my mother gave us. My money paid for the children's private schools. I let Thomas handle my inheritance. He insisted on it. He also managed my mother's money. He put all her money—and mine—into a trust for the children. When the divorce came up, he threatened to have my mother declared mentally incompetent if I didn't give up my claim to the children."

Family Court

Thomas's Lawyer: We contend that Mrs. McQueen carried on an openly adulterous affair. This seriously questions her fitness as a mother. I would like to call the family priest as my first witness. Father Creeley, did Mrs. McQueen bring the two McQueen boys for their Catholic instruction?

Father Creeley: No. Their father did. I never saw Mrs. McQueen. Of course, she's not Catholic. She didn't even attend her youngest boy's confirmation.

Catherine's Lawyer: If I tell you, sir, that Mrs. McQueen brought the two older children to their Catholic instruction before you took over the parish, and that Mrs. McQueen was in the hospital during her youngest son's confirmation, would these facts influence your opinion about her involvement in the church?

Father Creeley: No, it wouldn't.

Are they trying her for not being Catholic? Or for requiring surgery?

"One night, about two months after the custody trial, our car was in the driveway piled high with suitcases. I ran into the house. 'What are you doing?' Thomas was packing another suitcase. I was absolutely frantic.

"'I'm taking the children away. The judge has given them to me.' I was horrified. My teenagers were out. My two youngest boys were already asleep. The next morning they were all gone.

"I was so lonely, so ashamed to be without my children. People avoided me. I wanted to tell my side of the story, but I was damned if I was going to explain myself to a town that thought the worst of me. I moved away. When strangers ask about my children, I either lie—or feel like a liar no matter what I say.

"I miss the children. They are my whole life."

WHAT DID BETTINA, JOSIE, AND BONNIE DO?
WHAT DID THEIR HUSBANDS DO?

These "sexual" mothers married as virgins before they were twenty-one. Catherine and Josie were forced into sexually celibate marriages by their husbands. Bettina and Bonnie were married to openly adulterous husbands.

In 1964 Bettina married John, her childhood sweetheart. She had three children by the time she was twenty-four. John traveled the corporate road "four out of every five weeks." He was open about his extramarital affairs. After five years, Bettina began an affair—and told John about it. John beat her up. He became obsessed with Bettina's infidelity. Bettina said, "John hit me each time he knew I had been with my lover. I guess he was right. He was within his rights to do that. I did commit a sin. I must have hurt him terribly."

Within three months of Bettina's first affair, John had kidnapped the children. He demanded that Bettina give up her lover. She did. John then agreed to pay her rent and minimal child support—if she never had another affair. He refused to divorce Bettina, live with her, or forgive her. He threatened to take the children "any time" he heard she was "misbehaving." John moved out—and took their eldest son with him as a hostage. Bettina said, "My eldest boy was the easiest child to live with. His father left him alone with a housekeeper for weeks at a time. He wasn't permitted to visit us. This went on for a year. Eventually my son came to visit for Easter. He refused to return to his father. He said it was too lonely. His father allowed him to stay with me. I've always blamed myself for his suffering."

Bettina's punishment for her one adulterous affair far outweighed her crime. She was economically shorn and sexually traumatized. When I interviewed her in 1981, Bettina still had never slept with or dated anyone. Perhaps Bettina was too timid. Why didn't she bring her case before a judge?

Josie did. Josie married at eighteen and was a mother at nineteen. After a year of enforced marital celibacy, Josie moved out. Within six months, she fell in love with a black man. "We live in the South," said Josie. "My husband Ron's father is a former politician. They tried to have me and my boyfriend fired from our jobs. Our offices were ransacked. My boyfriend's home was fire-bombed. His friends were leaned on. Threats were made. During the custody trial, they called me a filthy whore. I lost custody of Laura when she was only three. My mother-in-law became her mother. I was only allowed to see her every other weekend for six hours."

Josie was not permitted to enter Laura's home. Whenever Laura said she wanted to live with her mother, they weren't allowed to see each other. Within a year, Josie had fallen into a deep depression. "A friend pulled me out of it. She told me that if I tried to kill myself or got admitted to a mental hospital, my ability to fight for custody or for more liberal visitation would be compromised forever."

Josie decided to go to law school. Four years later she was admitted to the bar. Josie said, "The day I was admitted to the bar I called Ron. I threatened to ruin his business if he didn't let me have Laura for two months every summer. I told him, 'If I don't get my daughter, I'll ruin your reputation and your business.' I knew enough to implicate him in enormous corruption. I got my summer visitation."

Josie has never remarried, never lived with anyone, and never had another child. If only Ron's family hadn't been so powerful! If only Josie's husband had been more sexually active. . . .

Bonnie's husband was. Frederick believed in "smashing monogamy." While Bonnie stayed home taking care of their two children, Frederick had a series of one-night stands and affairs. He also "loved" Bonnie very much. Then Bonnie had an affair. "Fred lay on the couch for three or four days, just staring at the ceiling. He repeated over and over again, 'You have just taken away my manhood. My trust in the human race is gone.' He really pinned the scarlet letter on my breast. He kept at me day and night, accusing me of not really loving him. He acted as if I had murdered him."

A year later, when Bonnie moved out, Frederick physically prevented her from taking the children.

LUCY, LINDA, AND LORETTA: WHAT DID THEY DO?
WHAT DID THEIR EX-HUSBANDS DO?

In the mid-1950s Lucy had dared initiate a divorce from an adulterous husband. Lucy was custodially challenged because she went out on a *date* after her divorce. By that time her ex-husband, Stanley, had already remarried. Lucy had no family or economic resources. She and her three-year-old son were entirely dependent on Stanley's economic largesse. Stanley became enraged when he learned of Lucy's date. "He called the man I'd dated and threatened him," said Lucy. "He harassed this man's parents. He stopped sending rent money. I got an eviction notice. He threatened a custody battle—based on my 'sexual immorality.' I was twenty-one and terribly naive. I believed I was some kind of outlaw."

For years Stanley's maniacal possessiveness prevented Lucy from remarrying or forming a lasting, stable relationship with another man. Stanley's second marriage and second set of children didn't seem to diminish the ardor of his vendetta. Lucy said,

> He wanted to see me dead. I'd rejected him: I didn't put up with his sexual infidelity and his emotional absence at home. The minute I went out with another man that was justification for him to get back at me. This was proof that I was no good. He was used to controlling everything. When I became a moving piece, not a fixed piece in his universe, he vowed to get me, to slow me to a standstill. His means of doing that was by withholding child support. I once asked him, "How can you do this to us?" He said, "You're not going to let him starve. I know you're not going to deprive him of anything. What I'm doing is hurting you, and you're the person I want to hurt." He was very clear and exceedingly up front about it.

Lucy was awarded custody of Michael. However she privately agreed to a joint custody arrangement on paper. In return Lucy got minimal child support. Within eight years Michael had chosen to live with his father and stepbrother.

When she was twenty-one, Linda married Frank, her childhood sweetheart. Frank traveled a great deal and was openly adulterous. They battled about his constant absence from home. After twelve years, Frank moved out. Two years later Linda began dating a man. "One Sunday evening, Frank walked in unexpectedly," said Linda. "He was wearing a leather jacket. He looked just like the Gestapo. He pointed his finger at Carl (my boyfriend) and said, 'You, outside. You have no business seeing my wife.' I was mortified. We began yelling at each other. Frank punched me in the eye. I fell. He punched me in the stomach. I doubled up. Then he left. He came back a little later to say he was sorry. By that time my eye had closed and I was vomiting blood."

Linda was hospitalized for eye surgery. Frank's rage grew when Linda refused to "forgive" him. At this point, Frank began arguing about alimony and expressing a joint custodial interest in children whom he'd never parented. Linda said, "Frank was a good provider. He was never home. He was also infertile. I wasn't. He wouldn't allow me to have artificial insemination. I agreed to adopt instead. Maybe he's afraid some other man will make me pregnant and one-up him. So he wants his 'legal' kids."

Ex-husbands were enraged by their ex-wives' sexual activities outside of marriage. Ex-husbands were also enraged when their ex-wives remarried. For example, Loretta's husband, Peter, drove her away with his repeated (and irrational) accusations of infidelity. Loretta began a postseparation love affair. When Loretta remarried, Peter felt "replaced" in his children's affections by Loretta's new husband. He initiated an intense campaign for custody of his three sons. Loretta said, "He's made our life hell. He quizzes the boys constantly. He wants them to spy on us. He's competing with Vincent, my husband, something fierce. He believes Vincent will get the boys to love him more than they love their father. He doesn't want them to get used to a stable life with me and Vincent."

WHAT IF A MOTHER IS A SEXUAL OUTLAW?

With soft blue eyes and angel-blonde hair, Amber is Botticelli's Venus at my door. She is a young topless dancer with a custody problem, and she is very scared. She removes her ballet slippers, stretches out scarlet painted toes, loosens her blouse, breathes deeply, and begins.

"I got married because I was pregnant. My family never forgave me for sinning. Victoria was born when we were both eighteen. I left Dennis when Victoria was six months old. He was too violent to live with.

"I found an apartment and got on welfare. For eight months, I was cooped up breast-feeding and babysitting. Dennis wouldn't give us any money. He wouldn't 'babysit' for me. He offered to take Victoria completely. He thought it would bring me back to him.

"I took care of Victoria for two full days and nights each week. I also cleaned the house and did all the laundry for Dennis. My sister—who never helped *me*—helped Dennis during the week. She said I deserved to be horse-whipped for giving Victoria up. I enrolled in two college courses and started waitressing.

"When Dennis realized I wasn't coming back, he moved six hours away by bus. I had nightmares about Victoria. I couldn't concentrate in school. I was guilty and I missed her. That's when I decided to dance topless. As a waitress, I earned eighty or ninety dollars a week. Dancing, I earned eighty dollars a shift.

"When Victoria was two and a half, Dennis agreed to joint custody. I got to take care of her every day. Dennis was dating a lot of different women and finishing college. I was his ideal babysitter, child-care center, and cook all rolled into one. He also had me right under his thumb.

"Dennis said he'd let Victoria live with me if I stopped topless dancing. I took her. He refused to give me any money. I kept dancing. How else could I support us?"

Naked women dancing are our fertility goddesses—held in contempt. Nailed him to a cross, caged her genitals in shame. Continuous red neon breasts: obscene adoration, sacred love.

"Within two months, Dennis yanked Victoria out of school and disappeared with her. When we finally found him, Dennis wouldn't let me see Victoria alone. He wouldn't even let us go into the bathroom together.

"Dennis got into a fistfight with my roommate's boyfriend. He pushed the doorman down as he ran away. He jumped into his car and nearly ran someone down in the street outside. Finally! Dennis had gone berserk in front of other people. The police arrested him. Everybody—the doorman, my roommate's boyfriend, the pedestrian—pressed charges.

"Dennis's lawyer got him out of jail in twenty-four hours. The judge released him without bail, once he understood it was a 'domestic matter.'

"Dennis practically lived on my street corner, watching my apartment. On my lawyer's advice, I snuck away like a dog to another borough. I put Victoria in private school with strict instructions not to release her to anyone but me. We never went out. We were both Dennis's prisoners.

"My lawyer was really freaked by my dancing. It really annoyed her. 'Why'd ya have to dance?' she'd ask me over and over again while she kept demanding more money. I want to mother Victoria the best way I can. Not in terror of Dennis's kidnapping her. Not ashamed of what I do to support us."

The dazzling girl dances for men only and thinks she'll stay young forever. Do women feel betrayed by her sexual indifference to them? Or by how her dependence on men mirrors their own? Or is it the fate of the dancing girl that frightens women, reminding them of men's contempt for female flesh, the liberties they permit themselves with it, forbid to women: ma soeur, ma mort.

•••••

These "sexual" mothers all were sexually repressed. Their sexual experiences within marriage had been limited and unsatisfactory. Their undamaged longing for sexual affection was miraculous; its consummation heroic; the resulting assault on their right to motherhood cruel and unjust.

6

The "Uppity" Mother

. . . .

CREON

> You, with that angry look, so set against your husband—
> I am afraid of you—why should I dissemble it?—
> You are a clever woman, versed in evil arts

MEDEA

> Through being considered clever I have suffered much.
> If you put new ideas before the eyes of fools
> They'll think you foolish and worthless into the bargain;
> And if you are thought superior to those who have
> Some reputation for learning, you will become hated.

JASON

> How hopeless it is to deal with a stubborn temper.
> For, with reasonable submission to our ruler's will,
> You might have kept your home.
> As it is you are going to be exiled for your loose speaking.

> —*Euripides,* Medea

WHAT DOES MY STUDY TELL US ABOUT FEMALE-INITIATED DIVORCE AS A FORM OF CUSTODIAL PROVOCATION?

Nearly half the mothers (47 percent), and nearly a third of the fathers (27 percent) initiated the divorce. Some fathers behaved as if they "owned" both their wives and children and "allowed" their wives to take care of their children—as long as they took care of their husbands too. Once these husbands became convinced that their wives were about to "steal" paternal property (her domestic services, "his" children), the divorce escalated into a custody battle.

After twenty years of marriage, Nora could no longer live holding her breath in fear of her husband's violence. She envisioned living under her own roof, five or ten minutes away. She dreamt of breathing properly again. Their children ranged in age from eighteen to six.

Nora talked to her husband in soothing tones. She talked to him in firm tones. She suggested divorce counseling. His rage was hot red, volcanic. She attempted suicide, perhaps to convince him or herself that she would rather die than stay married.

For nineteen years, she had been the ground beneath his feet. What would he stand on if she left? Terrified that he'd float off into space forever, he kidnapped two of their children for six months.

Nora whispers when she speaks. Her hands are never idle. Fiercely tender, they knit a child's sweater, bake whole-grain bread, make tea.

"I am no longer an ordinary mother," Nora says, looking around her kitchen one afternoon, lowering her voice even more. "When one of the children is late coming home, I panic. Have they been kidnapped again? For years I lived with Lester in terror. I didn't know it myself. I always had to tiptoe around him. I thought we were a very successful marriage.

"When I talked to him about a divorce, he choked me until I was unconscious. Then he tried to murder my motherhood. He told people I was unfit. Neighbors stopped looking me in the eye. Some stopped speaking to me. I thought I was imagining it—or going mad.

"When I still insisted on a divorce, Lester started a custody battle that lasted two years. I was examined by three different psychiatrists. It's hard to imagine a worse punishment. Remembering it brings tears to my eyes. One psychiatrist said my self-esteem was too low for me to be a good mother. Another one said that my career was bad for the children, that my research was a cover-up for my hatred of men.

"Those were awfully long days to sit in court." Nora closes her eyes. "It was dreadful to be there alone. Some friends and colleagues came. Some volunteers from a local women's center also came. My attorney once asked the judge, 'Is there something about Nora that bothers you?' The judge said, 'I'm bothered by that coterie of women that she continually brings here.'"

"Nora, what happened to your career?" I ask.

"My career was kidnapped together with my children. I missed appointments and deadlines. For nearly three years I was more involved with detectives and lawyers than with other scientists. My company asked me to leave. I had no savings left. All I had were the clothes in my closet and five hungry mouths to feed."

How easily respectability and security are stripped from the female body. Nora's nakedness is unremarkable. She is now undistinguishable from all other women who are not and have never been successful scientists.

"I took a job at one-third my previous salary. I borrowed money to hire a lawyer to fight for money. Five years after the kidnapping, three years after the custody trial, a judge awarded me a substantial sum of money. Lester refused to pay anything. He told the judge he'd rather go to jail. Lester has never tried to see the children. He doesn't call or write or send birthday cards."

Can a woman under torture carry on as usual? Can she keep pretending she isn't being tortured?

A clock ticks; another chimes. We sip Nora's tea in silence. "I'm in hiding," she explains. "I don't want to be looked at anymore. I just want to bring home my paycheck and take care of my children. I'm not ready to do without the pleasure of their company yet."

What if a mother not only initiates a divorce but dares to become a successful artist? Ella Mae is a painter and sculptor. She married a lawyer. From the beginning, Donald resented and opposed Ella Mae's work—even though she worked at home, dinner was always ready, and the house was always clean. Ella Mae was devoted to their infant daughter, Mary. She said,

> During the day I would feel very happy, very whole, very satisfied with my work in my attic studio. Mary gurgled or slept right beside me. It was blissful. Donald was becoming more and more unhappy. He hated his job. He had no friends. Here I was, this happy person. When he'd come home, he'd just have to knock me down.
>
> After I sold my first painting, he demanded that I pay for my own oils and canvases. I did. As I became more successful, he demanded household money. As long as I could actually sell one of those damn paintings—he wanted me to pay for Mary's clothes. I was like some dog he could kick. After a year and a half I decided I deserved a better life than this.

Donald wouldn't move out. He wouldn't let Ella Mae take "anything he'd paid for": the iron, the first-aid kit, her sewing machine. He wouldn't give her any child support. Ella Mae outraged him by managing to survive that first winter without heat or hot water. By spring, she had sold a painting. She made new friends. Within a year, she was under the "protection" of another man, whom she eventually married. Ella Mae said,

> There was nothing Donald could do to hurt me. He was very frustrated by my successful escape. He couldn't forgive me for my strength. He thought I was a monster with no feelings. He thought I should be destroyed.
>
> For seven years I mothered Mary. I grew as an artist. I forgot that Donald had a score to settle with me. He sent twenty dollars a week for her. He thought this was a lordly sum. He thought he was a good father. This amount didn't increase in seven years.

Ella Mae divorced her second husband. Her reputation as an artist and her feminist awareness grew. She began living with an emotionally supportive younger man. When Mary was nine years old, three things happened: Ella Mae was asked to coordinate a national show of women's paintings, Mary developed a learning disorder that required special medical and educational attention, and Ella Mae decided to request an increase in child support. "At Donald's request," said Ella Mae, "Mary was with him for one month every summer. I was working on the art show. Donald hired a detective who posed as a magazine photographer. He took pictures of my home and interviewed me about the art show. After Donald thought he had a good-enough case, he refused to return Mary. He accused me of being a 'bohemian' and of 'having orgies.'"

Donald was a local lawyer with a substantial and respectable practice. Donald was remarried and had two other children. Despite Ella Mae's unblemished record as a full-time mother, a judge ordered Mary into her father's permanent custody. He allowed maternal visitation only at "Donald's discretion." Ella Mae said,

> Seven years after I left him, Donald began to exact his revenge. First, he got custody. He didn't let me see Mary for a year. Then he let me see her, now and then, for a day at a time—if I was very grateful, and never demanded her back.

After a year, Mary was no longer the child I knew. She wore tiny pearls and an expensive little suit. She wouldn't look me in the eye. She talked about her swimming pool and her ballet classes. My Mary! So quiet, so ladylike. What had Donald done to her? How could he punish a child in order to get at me? How could he do to her what he wanted to do to me?

You know, I've painted women as heroines and goddesses. I'm Demeter, and Mary is my Persephone. But I couldn't force Donald to return Mary to me—not for a single summer. I lived with Mary for three thousand days. Since I lost custody nine years ago, I've spent about forty days with her.

Donald is my most powerful teacher. Whenever I think my success has moved me out of the female ghetto, I remember: I am without Mary.[1]

What if a mother has no artistic "calling" and no "bohemian" sexual life-style but needs to move away in order to pursue a livelihood, a career, or a chance at a new life?

WHAT DOES MY STUDY TELL US ABOUT FATHERS WHO WANTED TO MOVE AWAY WITH THEIR CHILDREN?

Nearly a third (31 percent) of the fathers who *won* custody moved away afterward. Half these fathers obtained court approval to do so; a third moved away without entering the court system or without mentioning their intended move in court. One-fifth of the fathers moved away by permanently kidnapping their children.

WHAT DOES MY STUDY TELL US ABOUT MOTHERS WHO WANTED TO MOVE AWAY?

Nearly a third (32 percent) of the mothers wanted to move away. With one exception, they all were prevented from doing so with their children. Judges (and others) all viewed children as their fathers' "landed property," not as part of a movable maternal unit. Judges also viewed the paternal right of visitation as more important than the maternal right to survive economically and psychologically.

For example, Beth was privately forced into a joint custody arrangement. She received no alimony and no child support. Her children lived with her for half the week. When Beth found employment in a nearby city, she petitioned the court to have the children with her for fewer days—but on weekends. She said, "The judge told me to live on welfare. He said I couldn't just move these kids or change their established living pattern. I moved away. I had to in order to survive. Then I had to beg, whine, and wheedle weekend visitation on my own as a favor from my husband. I had to pay their fare down or my fare up. The court wouldn't order my ex-husband to share travel costs with me. After all, I was the one who decided to move."

The belief that working, career, or remarried mothers will neglect their children is very great. The belief that such mothers will neglect children more than their working, career, or remarried fathers will remains virtually unshakable.

Miki is tall and very elegant. She moves swiftly across the room, her eyes masked in pain. She starts speaking abruptly. "Ten years ago, I married a white student. Together, we organized radical demonstrations. Pretty soon, Alvin became cynical and contemptuous. He began to criticize the masses—and me.

"We were living in Alvin's two-bit hometown. I was a trapped animal, far from home, a full-time mother with a minimum-wage factory job. I couldn't pursue politics or music. I had no child care and no encouragement. When the kids turned five and seven, I moved out. Three weeks later, Alvin moved a girlfriend in.

"When I got a lawyer, Alvin stole my car. He refused to sell our house and divide up the proceeds. He threatened a custody battle if I demanded anything. He scared me. I gave up all my economic demands.

"Over the next year I began to yearn for San Francisco. I put out feelers. My parents said I could live with them or with my brother, who had young children. I could study the piano again. The kids could spend summers and vacations with Alvin. What difference would our moving to San Francisco make? Alvin traveled four months every year. *He* wasn't stuck in the Midwest. *I* was.

"Alvin got an order restraining me from leaving the state with the kids. By this time, my daughter Suzi was hostile to the idea of San Francisco. She screamed that she would be mugged there. She cried a lot. 'It's all your fault,' she said. 'The divorce and the custody battle. You're a bad mother.' Sam, my son, kept totally quiet.

"My lawyer told me there was no way I could lose custody. I believed him. Five days before the trial, Alvin married his live-in girlfriend. He began talking about how this white stepmother would be a very stable influence.

"Alvin's lawyer mocked the idea of my having a career as a concert pianist. He accused me of wanting to go to San Francisco to have 'boyfriends.' He accused me of feeding my kids un-American (Japanese) food.

"Didn't anyone notice that my children looked Japanese? Didn't anyone care about their mother's ethnic heritage? One of Alvin's witnesses was a neighbor who had once told me to 'go back to China.' I always wondered what they called me and my kids behind our backs.

"My lawyer called me two weeks after the trial. He said, 'I've got bad news for you. The judge gave Alvin custody of both children.' Alvin pulled the kids out of bed in the middle of the night and drove away with them.

"I fell apart. I begged a close friend to persuade him to let me see the children that evening. He refused. I drove by the house alone. I sat outside in the car, crying. His new wife finally sent Suzi out. She was like a zombie, straight-faced, arms at her side. Alvin followed her out. He sat down on my fender, watching everything. I tried to hug Suzi, but she held herself very stiffly. Sam hugged me, but very carefully. I could feel how scared he was.

"Alvin finally had ultimate control over me. It's as if he had the atom bomb.

"I immediately appealed the decision. I wrote and called organizations everywhere to join me in protesting this racist and sexist decision. No Japanese or civil rights or feminist organization wanted to get involved. My only support came from a group of black women social workers. They wrote a group letter to the judge on my behalf. It only infuriated him.

"Does the state have the right to force me to remain hobbled to my ex-husband's definitions of home? Do my determined and effective steps toward independence mean I am unstable? Does wanting to live with my Japanese-American family in San Francisco define me as 'rootless'? Are white married males the only people with 'roots'?

"I feel a little like a slave whose master owns my children. I'm not supposed to be free. But if I manage to escape, I'm supposed to leave my children behind as my master's property."

What if a mother exercises her conscience and her civil responsibilities by exposing government corruption? Can such an exercise in public virtue result in her private custodial punishment?

Jessie is such a mother. She said, "The Civil Air Patrol shaped my personality. I was trained to survive in the desert and to participate in rescue missions for downed planes. My mentors are American patriots, soldiers, idealists.

"Mark and I married when we were both eighteen. I became a mother at twenty and again at twenty-three. While Mark was in Vietnam, I took care of the kids, finished college, taught Sunday school, ran our house—and still had time for political campaign work.

"Mark came back a changed man. He drank. He beat me and the kids. He refused to look for work or to go for counseling. After two years, Mark drifted off. He rarely visited or even called the kids.

"I was offered a job in the Census Bureau based on my volunteer campaign work. I was very excited until I realized that Wade, my boss, was running his own political three-ring circus. He provided girls, booze, and pot for the party regulars. My job was recruiting the 'girls'—and manipulating the census findings.

"I went to my immediate superior in tears. He calmed me down. Then Wade called me in. 'If you persist in talking against me, I'll destroy you politically. I'll spread rumors about your sex life.' Within hours, my office was moved. I'd come into work and find my files missing, my phones dead. I'd be ordered to travel fifty miles to a meeting. When I'd arrive, there wouldn't be any meeting. People stopped talking to me.

"Then Wade fired me. Within three weeks, I found another government job in another state. I was there when the bureau scandal hit the newspaper. Apparently, another employee had called the papers. Wade thought I was behind it. He went on a drunken rampage. He found Mark and took him into court. Wade told the judge, 'This is Mark Morehouse—you know, the guy married to the one who's causing all that trouble. She's up and left the state.' That was it. The judge gave Mark custody. Mark went into hiding with the kids.

"Four months later, my appeal of the custody decision came to trial. Mark admitted he had a bad temper and an unstable work history. He admitted hitting me and the kids. He admitted not seeing the kids for more than a year. Mark's lawyers grilled me for two hours on whether I supported the Equal Rights Amendment."

Judicial Opinion

The father can provide a more stable home environment. That doesn't mean that the mother cannot in the future provide a stable home environment, but we do have a problem with her. She's moved. She has a new job. She had other problems. She is going to have to show this court that she has become stable enough to take these two children out of their home state and provide for their needs. There has been a substantial change in conditions. Based upon that finding, and in the best interests of the children, I am remanding the children to the custody of the father.

"Mark dropped out of sight again. The judge didn't order any maternal visitation. Whenever I wasn't at work, I was interviewing lawyers and meeting with the Justice Department. After eight months, my lawyer was finally able to arrange visitation for me.

"Lea had lost a lot of weight. Devon was withdrawn. He kept picking at himself. He was covered with sores. My lawyer convinced a judge to order temporary custody on medical and psychiatric grounds. He ordered a new custody trial in my new state.

"Mark flew right up with *his* custody order. He and the local police removed the kids from school. The school called me at work. I ran over, crying. The kids were crying behind a locked door. When the police took them away, they wouldn't even let me say good-bye.

"I went into the church across the street. I threw myself on the floor before the cross and cried my head out. I couldn't stop crying. That night I sat on the children's beds all night. I left their half-eaten breakfasts in the refrigerator for months. It was worse than if they were dead.

"A week later, my doorbell rang. It was the sheriffs department with a warrant for my arrest for having 'kidnapped' the children. I was arrested as a fugitive from justice.

"I hired two criminal lawyers: one in each state. I already had two custody lawyers: one in each state. There were three civil lawyers working in D.C. to build the criminal case against Wade.

"One of my lawyers finally convinced the U.S. attorney general's office to get beyond 'this is a family argument' and look at the custody case itself as an obstruction of justice. I was extradited one month later. I was terrified that I'd be killed in prison. Wade could easily make it look like suicide. 'Depressed mother kills herself.' I had visions of me swinging from my Sheer Energy panty hose in my cell.

"They allowed me one visit with my children—under armed guard. I had to pay a hundred dollars for the armed guard. Wade was indicted one day before my trial. Mark didn't press any kidnapping charges. He just turned the kids back to me.

"If you're going to take women's children away, none of the rest matters. If women fear they'll lose their children, we'll all just move one step backwards away from careers, and into deeper servitude. I would have done anything to get my kids back.

"Women: whatever you do, don't quit fighting for your kids."

The Lesbian Mother

HOW WERE BISEXUAL, LESBIAN, AND NONLESBIAN MOTHERS ALIKE?

Lesbians and nonlesbians were all "good enough" mothers. Dr. Ellen Lewin has suggested that "concern for [their] children" is the major reason lesbian mothers leave their marriages.[1] Several studies have suggested that the psychological "organizing principle" among both lesbian and nonlesbian mothers is "motherhood and a concern for children."[2]

Of the bisexual and lesbian mothers, 57 percent left husbands who were "previously absent" fathers, 43 percent left physically abusive husbands, 36 percent left husbands who subsequently embarked on brainwashing campaigns, 29 percent left husbands who kidnapped their children, and 14 percent left husbands who physically abused their children. Some mothers left husbands who neglected them—as well as their children. For example, Elizabeth said, "My husband was never home. He had no time for me or the kids. He put off having lunch alone with me for nearly two years. I couldn't stand the loneliness anymore. I thought I'd have a better chance either to meet someone else, or at least to concentrate on my kids in a happier frame of mind. I wasn't even gay when I started to talk about separating. It's the first thing my husband accused me of. He's treated me as a 'dirty dyke' ever since."

San Francisco, 1981. Alix and I recognize each other from our TV appearances, embrace, and sit down in her company cafeteria, whispering. In press conferences, before handheld cameras, Alix never used to whisper.

They won't hurt me on television, she must have thought, not in front of so many witnesses. In Dallas, they shot the president on television. All witch burnings are public events. Just didn't believe it meant us, too.

She begins. "I was a proper married lady. After ten years I moved out. My husband, Andrew, kept John, our eight-year-old. He 'allowed' me to take Luke, our four-year-old, if I was willing to accept financial responsibility for him. I moved into a household of single parents and went on welfare.

"After a year, I became emotionally involved with one of the mothers in the household. Andrew was outraged. He kidnapped John to Italy, where they lived with Andrew's parents for a year. When Andrew returned, my parents met him at the airport. They all demanded that I stop being a lesbian and return to my husband—who was still willing to take me back.

"Had I the remotest understanding of what court is like for any mother, let alone a lesbian, I would have done something—anything—to work things out privately. At the time I honestly believed that a judge would see that I was a good mother, and that Andrew had never been too involved with the boys.

"I was grilled about my lesbianism for one solid hour. I was blamed because the media attended the trial. The judge said he would not be 'dictated to' by a bunch of 'women's libbers.' My own parents took the stand against me.

"On a Saturday morning, two weeks after the trial, I received the judge's verdict. It was contained in a seven-page harangue against lesbianism. The judge wanted to 'save Luke from the stigma of being raised by a lesbian mother.' On Monday morning, while I was in court trying to get a stay of this order, the police came and took Luke away."

There is a loud silence: a house suddenly emptied, by legal violence, of a mother's child. A sneaker left behind. Crayons. A dentist appointment that won't be kept.

"I was allowed to see both boys every other weekend for one full day, but never overnight. Within a year it was clear that John had closed his heart to me. Luke was 'failing' kindergarten! After nine months of legal struggle, the same judge who'd taken Luke away from me agreed that he was doing badly, and needed some 'maternal nurturance.'

"The judge ordered Luke into my custody. Simultaneously, he granted Andrew's request to take both boys on a summer visit to their grandparents in Italy. Of course, Andrew never came back. For a year I was a shadow in slow motion: exhausted, and out of step with my life.

"When my parents finally realized they had done themselves out of their grandchildren, they helped me hire an Italian lawyer and detective who confirmed that both boys were too well guarded to 'snatch' back. After a six-month struggle, I arrived in Rome with legal custody of both boys—in America.

"Italy does not have to recognize an American order. My lawyer doubted that I could win in an Italian court. I was a radical lesbian foreigner. The case would take years. I left Rome and went to see my boys. I found them playing on the beach."

Mother-woman, stage left, watching the waves break, and the untouchable, growing sons.

"At first, Luke was afraid to come near me. Then, all at once, he came over and said, 'I'm coming back with you.' Just like that. I wanted to take him off the beach and right to the airport but I had no passport, no clothes for him. What if he changed his mind along the way? What if the police found us and arrested me?

"I decided to talk to Andrew. I asked him if he thought it was good for 'his' sons to be raised without ever seeing their mother. He said that a lesbian wasn't a mother anymore."

HOW WERE BISEXUAL, LESBIAN, AND NONLESBIAN MOTHERS DIFFERENT?

Of the custodially challenged lesbian mothers, 71 percent were "bonded" with domestically supportive female mates when they battled for custody. Only 17 percent of the nonlesbian mothers were remarried or "bonded" with (supportive) mates during their custody battles.[3]

Nonlesbian mothers were totally unprepared for what happened to them; lesbian mothers knew that their lesbianism would be custodially held against them. However, lesbian mothers were devastated when their own *mothers* actively opposed them in court.

Both lesbian and nonlesbian mothers were asked to make certain inhuman choices: between their right to mother and their right to lead self-determined lives. However, judges demanded that lesbian mothers choose not only between their children and "careers" but—paradoxically—between their children and their maternal "right" to domestic, emotional, and economic support. Heterosexual fathers are not asked to choose between their children or their supportive female partners. They are judicially rewarded for having domestic support.[4]

Lesbian mothers were warned repeatedly against exposing their children to an openly lesbian "lifestyle," lest it damage them emotionally or lead to their social ostracism. Lesbian mothers were also warned that their children would suffer emotionally if they lived with anxiously "closeted" mothers. Judges (and others) seemed convinced that lesbian mothers would "produce" lesbian children—whether they hid or exposed their lesbianism.[5]

Both lesbian and nonlesbian mothers suffered poverty, isolation, chronic fatigue, and the absence of supportive extended families. In addition, lesbian mothers were not or did not feel welcome as *lesbians* among nonlesbian mothers, who were either married or husband hunting. As *mothers*, lesbians were not or did not feel welcome among lesbian *nonmothers*, who disliked or were uninterested in children at a gathering for adults.

The lesbian mothers I interviewed felt most nourished by their partners, sometimes by their lawyers, and by other lesbian mothers who had not lost their children. Lesbian mothers were welcomed by other lesbians as long as they left both their children and their maternal concerns at home.

> **Rae:** I live in a wonderful lesbian feminist collective. No one else is a mother. No one wants to co-mother or babysit for me. They can't. All their energy goes into surviving and helping other women survive. They feel that children are a luxury. I guess they don't want to be reminded of what they can't afford. One of the women in the house lost her children in a custody battle. Maybe it's too painful for her to relate to kids yet.

> **Alix:** During my court battle, the lesbian and feminist communities supported me in every conceivable way. Afterwards, when the spotlight moved on, so did the activists. These women were not interested in babysitting for one male child as a way of defeating patriarchy. They pitied me for being stuck with the task.

UNDER WHAT CONDITIONS WERE LESBIAN MOTHERS ALLOWED TO RETAIN CUSTODY OF THEIR CHILDREN?

Two lesbian mothers were privately allowed to keep their children by agreeing not to live with their partners, not to allow them or any woman lover ever to spend the night, not to make any economic demands on their ex-husbands, and not to oppose or interfere with the visitation patterns of their husbands' choosing. In each case, the involved children were forced to give up their ongoing ties to a second female parent and to live with a mother deprived of all domestic and economic support and emotional and sexual affection.

Melanie weighs a hundred pounds in a jumpsuit and looks eighteen. She is twenty-four and the mother of two sons. A judge—and her own mother—viewed her lesbianism as more dangerous to her children than her Marine husband's alcoholism and domestic violence.

"I'm very nervous," she says. "I'd better start talking right away, OK? When I became pregnant, I refused to have an abortion. Momma wanted me to quit school, leave town, and give the baby away. I refused to do this. When I gave birth to Robert, Momma was thrilled. She took Robert over completely. I'd be warming a bottle and she'd already be feeding him.

"I met Jerry. He was willing to marry me and to adopt Robert. Momma was thrilled. Jerry started drinking as soon as I got pregnant. I thought everyone's husband did that. After Mikey was born he didn't stop. Momma threatened to take both kids away from him. It did no good. Then Jerry joined the Marines and we moved away.

"Jerry never hit the kids. He didn't see them that much. He hit me. I was bruised all the time. Sometimes he'd just slam me up against a wall or start choking me. He'd knock me down the stairs or twist my arm so badly that I'd be in pain for days. He said if I ever left him, he'd kill me."

Melanie smiles for the first time. "And then I met Molly at my factory job. We became friendly. After a few months, Jerry wanted the three of us to sleep together. I slept with Molly alone—after Jerry had shipped out. I'd never known love that was loving before. Molly started helping me with the house and with the kids.

"Somehow my momma found out about Molly and told Jerry. One day, I was walking down the street with the kids. Before I knew it, three policemen came after me. They grabbed Robert, my six-year-old, and Mikey, my two-year-old, and drove away. An hour later, a social worker arrived with some 'papers.' It seems that Jerry had temporary custody of 'his' son, Mikey. 'My' son, Robert, would be kept in a state home until our trial.

"It took me a day to locate Robert. He was hysterical. Jerry had told him that his grandmomma was coming to get him. My lawyer convinced the authorities to release Robert to me. Mikey must have thought I was dead.

"After three months, a judge ordered maternal visitation with Mikey once a week, but never overnight. When I'd go to pick him up, Jerry would stand there and say, 'You can't win in court. You're a lesbian. Didn't you see *Kramer vs. Kramer?* Fathers can win now. It's about time the men showed the women that they can take care of kids, too! He's my son. I want him. I don't want him being brought up by lesbians.'

"Jerry treated Mikey like a trophy. He'd take him to a barbecue, show him off for fifteen minutes, then get rid of him. He kept Mikey in the Marine day-care center all day. At night, he left him with different sitters. Soon, Jerry was calling me to babysit. But he still wanted custody.

"A few weeks before the trial, I happened to call a friend back home. She said she was so glad the kids were coming back. 'Your momma has fixed up a room and is buying furniture and toys.' My momma came to court, with her pink suit and her pink gloves, as Jerry's witness. She said she'd never seen him drink or beat me. 'Sad to say,' she told the judge, 'it's my daughter who's the unfit mother.' She was stabbing me with each word. 'Relax and smile,' my lawyer whispered. 'Don't break down here.' I could hardly breathe. I was dying."

The Court-Appointed Psychological Report

Mrs. Bates is a shy, demure and private person who is somewhat socially inhibited. Because of her passive personality she didn't stand up for herself in this marriage. She declares that she has been afraid of her husband since he forced himself upon her while intoxicated. Her eldest son, Robert, shows care and nurture. He was verbal, friendly and relaxed. He related on a most positive level.

Private Bates feels that he deserves custody because his wife is a lesbian. He is afraid that his son and stepson will be sexually confused. He is disturbed that they are so positively attached to Melanie's female lover. Bates's drinking difficulties are of some concern to this examiner.

The examiner wishes to emphasize that he considers both parents as fit caretakers: and recommends joint/physical custody of the youngest child.

"Momma expected to get Robert. She didn't. I did—at least temporarily. I don't think I'll ever talk to Momma again. She really likes kids until they're about ten years old. Then—well, I'm her child. Look what she did to me.

"The judge gave Mikey to Jerry. He said that two women couldn't raise a boy without a man. Jerry's real proud of himself as a father. Meanwhile, Mikey has grown very quiet. He won't play with other kids anymore. He calls me a 'bitch.' We just found out that he's begun to hit his head against the wall in day care.

"My lawyer asked Mikey's teacher whether she or another mother would testify for us. So far, no one is willing to testify against a Marine—or for a lesbian."

WHY IS MATERNAL LESBIANISM VIEWED AS A DISEASE?

Judges sometimes allow lesbians to keep their children—if they agree not to *practice* their lesbianism. Somehow, lesbianism is viewed as an infectious disease. If a mother agrees not to engage in relations with another (infectious) woman, then her disease is viewed as "arrested" or at least as noninfectious.[6]

By contrast, the child of a heterosexual mother is not necessarily seen as infected by her mother's compulsive heterosexuality. Heterosexual bonding is not viewed as an infectious disease.

Heterosexually adulterous or uppity mothers were also custodially challenged and victimized. They did not excite the same visceral disgust that lesbians did. Disgust is, in this case, a form of terror, as well as a form of revulsion against that which is forbidden—but still enchanting.

Many heterosexual men yearn for sexually active women but cannot comfortably conceive of heterosexual women (or wives) in this role. Many heterosexual men are also terrified of their own homosexual or bisexual longings and remain "unaware" of the relationship between such feelings and their sexual behavior within marriage—for example, their sexual passivity, disinterest, or selfishness.[7]

Lesbians in general arouse disgust when they look or behave like men—that is, like womanizers who (apparently) want to possess and control women. Heterosexual men—and women—cannot tolerate the *idea* of woman-hating and womanizing behavior in female form, nor can they tolerate the *idea* of man-hating, man-avoiding, or man-izing behavior in female form.

Both heterosexual men and women are also terrified of gender blur. They target and scapegoat the "mannish" in lesbians and the "girlish" in male homosexuals. Lesbians and male homosexuals may themselves either despise or cherish these (troublesome) bisexual characteristics.[8]

Lesbian *mothers* arouse disgust, terror, and envy when they act as if they, like fathers, are entitled to certain rights without reciprocal maternal obligations. For example, Cecily's husband threatened to "crucify" her as a "welfare dyke" if she didn't relinquish the children to him. She did so.

But his disgust grew as Cecily began to succeed economically. Her lesbianism was supposed to lead to downward, not upward, mobility. It was also supposed to inspire disgust, not love, in her children. Cecily said, "He can't stand to see how much I've achieved. I was supposed to die in the gutter. My kids were supposed to despise me. They don't. My ex-husband feels he got robbed. He sees me as scot-free. He's tied down. He has to pay for their college tuition. I don't. He calls me the lesbian bitch who escaped." [9]

How dare Cecily have a good relationship with her children when she has not undergone the sacrifice that patriarchy demands of mothers? How dare she assume the paternal prerogatives of giving up custody and still retain her children's love?

Women are allowed to live with each other and apart from men as long as they are heterosexual or celibate and they obey male gods—both on earth and in heaven. When a woman lives with another woman by choice, or when a lesbian has or wants to have children without being a man's wife, she is viewed as a threat to patriarchal law and order.

In creating a nonheterosexual family, the lesbian mother sets a dangerous example for all women. What if women refused to marry men who were not emotionally or sexually nurturing but who were at best only good economic providers? What if women refused to mate genetically with husbands or fathers who were not "maternal"?

Lesbian motherhood also arouses disgust in heterosexual women because it criticizes the conditions under which most women have to mother—and the consequent development of maternal "machismo." A "real" woman is someone who can mother a man's child with no domestic, emotional, or economic support from that man—without becoming a "man hater" and turning a child against his or her father or against men in general.

If a lesbian refuses to serve the needs of an adult man, how can she be trusted to serve the even more insatiable needs of his male children? For example, Harold demanded that Laura meet their son Barry's insatiable and father-created needs for a female servant. He also demanded that Laura join him and his student Margo in bed. Within a year, Laura and Margo were in love. Within two years, Laura was facing a "lesbian custody fight."

Margo: Once Harold felt he wasn't in complete control, he began calling us dirty lesbians. He called Laura a rotten mother. He tried to convince *me* that she was schizophrenic. He started to work on Barry. He'd tell him that he couldn't trust us, that we weren't real women anymore.

Laura: Once we separated, Harold would call Barry four to five times a day. He'd interrupt him during meals and bedtime preparation. Pretty soon, Barry started saying: "I have to call my father to see if it's all right to see this movie."

Margo: We were Barry's servants. We did his laundry; we cooked for him; we cleaned his room. Harold was his real parent. Barry began to reject me. "You stole my mother away from me. You stole her away from my father—you ruined our family. I hate you."

Laura: By the time Barry was seven he hated us and loved his father. He kept telling me I didn't love him. Meanwhile, his father never let him have a childhood. He had Barry wait on him hand and foot. Harold was confined to a wheelchair since his college accident.

Margo: Once, before Barry went to live with Harold, he took a picture of himself, together with me and Laura to school. His teacher refused to put it up with the other family pictures on the bulletin board. She said that we weren't a real family.

8

The Mother Married
to a Violent Man

....

Sixty-two percent of the mothers reported being the victims of domestic physical violence. Of these mothers, 30 percent were physically battered (pushed, slapped, kicked, punched, knocked unconscious, or raped) by their husbands on a regular basis during marriage. Some mothers required hospitalization. Thirty-two percent were physically attacked by their husbands after initiating separations or divorces.

Margaret is the mother of five children. She was a battered wife who, after twenty years of marriage, finally deserted her "whipping girl" post. This so outraged her husband that he moved out, withdrew all economic support, remarried, and began a campaign for custody. A large woman in bright cherry lipstick, Margaret weeps before she can speak.

"My husband, Ernie, was in charge of everything. I wasn't allowed to do anything on my own. Once I enrolled in a class at our local junior college. Ernie said, 'I don't want you going to school.' I stopped right away.

"I was an abused woman. I just didn't know it. See?" Margaret says, holding her right hand. "These fingers are broken. They can never hold change. When I went to the hospital to have them set, Ernie stayed with me to make sure I would say I caught them in the washing machine.

"I was always too afraid to report him. Finally, I told him I couldn't take it anymore. Ernie told me I'd regret the day I was born if I divorced him. He smashed a chair over my head. He broke my arm. After that, I stopped lying for him.

"I hired a lawyer. He told me to take the money out of our joint account. 'Don't bother looking for the checkbook,' I told Ernie. 'I took all five thousand dollars out.' With that, everything went—the mirror, the bed. He destroyed everything in the bedroom. And he beat me up.

"I got an order of protection. I used the five thousand dollars up. Then I went on welfare. Ernie got married a year after our divorce. That's when he started to visit the kids. He also started a custody action. I wasn't even worried. What judge in his right mind would give my six-, eight-, and eleven-year-olds to this crazy man?

"The judge gave Ernie custody of all five kids. She said Ernie had a good income, a nice large house, a new wife—and I was living on welfare. I couldn't give my kids over to that man. Not the two youngest. I went into hiding with them at my mother's house. I wore a wig when I went out to shop. We never answered the door. Two policemen and my own lawyer said I had to give my babies to Ernie or go to jail."

"The kids were supposed to spend Christmas with me. At six p.m. on Christmas Eve, Ernie drove up with them. 'They won't stay unless you drop your action for alimony. This Christmas is just a taste of what you'll get. I'll take them and you'll never see them again.' I said, 'I'm not going to drop my action. I happen to need something to live on also.' He just packed them into the car and off they went. Jingle Bells.

"A few months ago, my oldest son came to see me. He told me that he'd had a drug problem, that he had been in a mental hospital and was on probation. I was beside myself. No one had contacted me. No one thought he needed his mother. He said, 'Ma, I never meant to hurt you.' We sat and cried."

Margaret laughs for the first time. "Well, I told my divorce counselor I was married to one in a million. If you turn against him, forget it. But how could Ernie get custody legally? Because I left him? Because I had no money? How could I have money? I was a mother."

WHAT KINDS OF PSYCHOLOGICAL ABUSE DID PATRIARCHAL FATHERS ENGAGE IN?

Patriarchal fathers verbally and socially humiliated their wives, withheld verbal and emotional support, were emotionally overdependent and demanding, or sexually abusive or neglectful. A number of husbands belittled, closely "supervised," and publicly denigrated their wives' housekeeping and child care. Some husbands were particularly sadistic.

Ella Mae: When I was at the end of my first pregnancy, Donald demanded that I iron every shirt and handkerchief he owned before I left for the hospital. He demanded a week's worth of meals all cooked and frozen. He said I shouldn't think that I could stop being a wife just because I was about to give birth.

I was in bad shape after I gave birth. I was breast-feeding. My legs were still swollen. I had difficulty walking. The first night Mary cried, I asked Donald to bring her from her crib into our bed. He started yelling at me. He said he wouldn't cater to my laziness. He said I'd have to go get her myself. I crawled on my hands and knees to her crib.

Sue Ellen: I came down with pneumonia, I had a fever of one hundred and five. I called Curtis at his girlfriend's house and asked him to please drive me to the hospital. He did—with her sitting in the front seat. They took the kids back to her house.

I was in the hospital for a month. Curtis brought the kids to see me once a week for one hour. He waited outside. When I was discharged, I took the bus home. I remember it was snowing. The apartment was very cold. All the furniture was gone except for a child's bed and some cooking utensils. The telephone was turned off. There was an eviction notice under the door. I borrowed eggs and coffee from a neighbor. Curtis came over the next day to tell me we were getting divorced. He said that since the kids were already living with him, he didn't have to support me, that I should go on welfare. He'd let me see the kids every other weekend.

WHAT DID I LEARN ABOUT MALE DOMESTIC VIOLENCE FROM INTERVIEWS WITH CUSTODIALLY EMBATTLED PATRIARCHAL FATHERS?

Many of the battling fathers whom I interviewed expressed "murderous" feelings toward their ex-wives. Defiantly, bitterly, matter-of-factly, they said, "I want to kill my ex-wife," "She doesn't deserve to live," and "She should be dead."[1] These fathers acted as if disobedient wives were unworthy of mercy or compassion. They were surprised when their ex-wives displayed human emotions upon being custodially victimized.

For example, Luke believed in the sanctity of the father-controlled family. He moved out after his wife had committed adultery. He was too upset to see his children for nearly a year. When he heard that his wife was involved in yet another love affair, he moved for custody and divorce. "I don't know why she got so wild after the judge gave me custody. She physically attacked me outside the courtroom. Would a normal woman do that? How could I let her bring my kids up? She's really crazy. When I told her that she could only see the kids under my roof, under my supervision, she screamed and cried and hit me again."

WHAT KINDS OF PSYCHOLOGICAL VIOLENCE DID SMOTHER-FATHERS ENGAGE IN?

Fourteen (23 percent) of my custodially challenged mothers were married to Smother-Fathers. I interviewed nine additional Smother-Fathers who were also battling for custody. A Smother-Father believes that *he* is the mother or that he is a better mother than his wife is. Smother-Fathers experienced their intimacy with their children as primary and often mystical. They denigrated their wives' mothering abilities and lauded their own parenting skills as superior.

Shawn: From the time he was born, my son William couldn't sleep if I didn't hold him. It would take hours each night to get him to fall asleep. I'd have to have the right pitch in my voice to soothe him. I'd have to stroke his forehead just so. It took two years before he could sleep without me being in the same house. I had a harder time putting him to bed when his mother was around.

Once, when William was two and a half, I had a very loud fight with my wife. Afterward, William clung to me in a great panic. The only way I could calm him down was to take him into the bathroom, fill the bathtub with warm water, and hold him in the water. I got into the bathtub with him and turned the light out. It was dark. It was warm. It was quiet. I talked to him very softly. His mother was not part of the world for the time being. I wouldn't even let his mother into the bathroom.[2]

Linus: My daughters are the most important thing in my life. I don't think their mother appreciates or enjoys them as much as I do. From the moment they were born, just being with them gave me more pleasure than sex does. I stopped working in order to be with them. I don't want anything to get in the way of my role as a father.

Debra does not concentrate intensely every minute when the girls are with her. I do. I think they give her a headache, especially after working all day. I'm always fresh for the girls. I live each moment with them vibrantly. If I don't win sole custody of these kids, the whole purpose of my life is over.

Eric: Fran was always jealous of how easy it was for me to relate to the kids. I have more fun with them than she does. I have the nesting ability. Fran has accused me of being the mother hen. I am. That's why I work at home. I like being in touch with the flow of their lives every minute.

The idea that child care is a burden is the biggest fraud perpetrated by women on men in this country. There's nothing to it. You can do everything with kids. They don't have to disrupt your life at all.

It became clear, upon questioning, that Eric, who does work at home, does not do the cooking, the shopping, the cleaning, the laundry, the chauffeuring, or the scheduling of his children's appointments. A paid housekeeper, supervised and supplemented by his live-in girlfriend, does "all that unimportant crap."

The most extreme Smother-Fathers still exhibited an aggressively "male" strategic expertise and persistence.*

For example, some Smother-Fathers physically and psychologically battered their wives, kidnapped and brainwashed their children, refused to pay child support, and, above all, refused to give up until they had obtained exclusive possession of their children, both psychologically and legally.

Eric: I will not do things the way Fran wants them to be done. I don't think kids have to go to bed *exactly* at eight p.m.,

---

* We may remember that *all* the Smother-Fathers in my study obtained custody.

lights out, no TV, and no whispering. I'm not running a concentration camp. She is. I refuse to limit the number of calls I make to the kids when they're with their mother. That's interfering with my continuity and peace of mind. I'll call back twenty times if she won't put them right on the phone. Or I'll go over and demand to see them.[3]

Linus: I have joint custody now, but within a year I'll have sole custody of both girls. There's no way I can lose. I'm working on this full-time. Debra has a full-time job and spends her spare time trying to meet a new husband.

I'm also smarter than she is. For example, I persuaded Debra to let me enroll our eldest daughter in a private school near me. I said I'd pay the tuition instead of child support. Tuition is deductible. Child support isn't. What this means is that my youngest daughter is hearing all about a really great school from her sister. She wants to go, too. Only I have the money to send her. And I have certain conditions for doing it.

Smother-Fathers overidentified with their sons. In some cases, this meant strict supervision of a boy's achievement. In other cases, this meant spending enormous amounts of time doing things together without a mother present. Some Smother-Fathers preferred "boyish" activities; others preferred their sons to join them in adult activities.[4]

In a father-idealizing culture, absent and emotionally distant fathers already have a mesmerizing effect over their children. Present and emotionally intimate fathers probably have twice the mesmerizing effect on their children. In my opinion, this effect was more negative than positive.

Smother-Fathers seethed with unrepressed woman and mother hatred. They envied and romanticized the female condition and disliked real women. Many were loners and "paranoid" about the entire world. Lucy's ex-husband divorced both his wives and kept all his sons. Lucy said,

For years everyone, including me, believed that my ex-husband was a devoted father. At his funeral, my son Michael unexpectedly made a speech. He said, "It's all bullshit. He was never a good father. The truth is that my father was at war with the whole world. The only people he wasn't at war with were my brothers and me. We were his little soldiers. We were his eyes; we were the only human beings he would trust to help him in his war against the world. He trusted us because he thought he controlled us completely And he did."

WHAT DOES MY STUDY TELL US ABOUT INCESTUOUSLY VIOLENT FATHERS WHO BATTLED FOR CUSTODY?[5]

Two of my custodially challenged mothers were married to incestuous fathers. Emily blames herself for having demanded her husband's participation in child care. "He wasn't properly socialized. He didn't know how to put limits on his selfishness. When my daughter was two, I was bathing her one day. The moment I touched her clitoris, she said, 'Daddy.' I touched her again, and she said, 'Daddy.' Maybe the abuse began then."

Emily had access to information about incest. She routinely requested a file on incest from a colleague.

> The articles all suggested that incest tends to be protracted unless it is interrupted by an outside intervening factor. While I was reading, I would alternately tell myself that nothing was happening, that nothing had happened, and that nothing would ever happen again. The articles said it was the mother's responsibility to get the child away from the father. I called some friends who worked in this area. They said that I should either leave him or get counseling, but that I should never leave my daughter alone with him. Then I began reading about custody battles that incestuous fathers actually won.

When I interviewed Emily, she was plagued by fear and guilt. She was guilty for having married her husband in the first place, guilty for not leaving him sooner, guilty for finally leaving and placing her daughter at grave risk in terms of a custody battle, guilty for leaving and being unable to provide her daughter with a stable economic life.

WHAT DOES MY STUDY TELL US ABOUT THE INCIDENCE AND DIFFERENTIAL TREATMENT OF PATERNAL VERSUS MATERNAL CHILD KIDNAPPERS?

Twenty-two fathers (37 percent) and seven mothers (12 percent) kidnapped their children. Of the paternal kidnappers, 18 percent were never found or returned voluntarily after an average of three years. *None* of these fathers was economically, legally, or custodially punished. Of the smaller number of maternal kidnappers, *80 percent* were both found and punished. This pattern is true in general.[6]

WERE MATERNAL AND PATERNAL KIDNAPPINGS SIMILAR?

After years of being their children's primary parent, 70 percent of my custodially embattled mothers were legally, judicially, or physically prevented from seeing their children entirely or from developing a normal visitation relationship with them.

> **Norma:** When I'd arrive for visitation, I was told that all four kids were suddenly out with friends or relatives. By the time my lawyer got to a judge, the kids themselves said they didn't want to see me. I told the judge they'd been brainwashed. I told the judge that they obviously thought *I* hadn't wanted to see *them*. I told him that whether they wanted to see me or not, they needed me and I had a right to visitation. The judge told me that he couldn't force adolescents to see their mother.
>
> **Rachel:** I came to pick up the boys at the appointed time on Friday, late afternoon. Their father came out of the house barring the doorway. "They're still doing their homework, you whore," he screamed, loud enough for everyone to hear. He moved sideways toward me with a snarl on his face. Then my boys came out, very quiet and ashamed. On Sunday morning, eight hours before I had to return them, this madman was pounding on my window, "I want my boys back now." He was stopping my neighbors on their way to church, to tell them I'd lost custody because I was crazy and unfit. I couldn't afford any trouble with my landlord or the police, so I dressed my boys and let them go home early.[7]

Despite such provocation, very few mothers who had lost custody kidnapped their children.*

---

* No custodial mother kidnapped her child after the child was returned by a non-custodial paternal kidnapper.

Mothers were exhausted by the custody struggle and, unlike fathers, couldn't count on any economic, legal, or emotional assistance for a kidnapping venture. Unlike fathers, custodially embattled or victimized mothers had no organizations or networks to turn to for information, advice, or support.

Most mothers were also reluctant to subject their children to a fugitive and impoverished existence. They were afraid of breaking the (male) law and being denied access to their children on a permanent basis.

Of the maternal kidnappers, 100 percent had been their children's primary parent; 14 percent of the paternal kidnappers had been involved in primary child care. *All* the maternal kidnappers had been paternally prevented from seeing their children; *none* of the paternal kidnappers had been maternally prevented from seeing or maintaining a visitation relationship with their children.*

Nearly two-thirds (64 percent) of the paternal kidnappers went on kidnapping "sprees." No maternal kidnapper did this. A spree usually indicates that a parent does not intend to keep the child or that he is desperate and incompetent as a parent. Children described driving around a lot, moving from motel to motel, using false names, eating junk food, and not seeing anyone they knew. After retrieving such children, mothers described them as disoriented, hostile, frightened, unwashed, and sometimes ill.[8]

Some children thought that being kidnapped by a previously unavailable father was an "adventure." However, kidnapped children were often permanently angry and disappointed that their mothers hadn't rescued them. They also blamed themselves for their father's violence or thought they were responsible for provoking it and capable of appeasing it.

Twenty-five percent of the paternal kidnappers told children that their mothers "were dead," "hadn't loved them anyway," or "must never be discussed." Many of these children rejected their mothers forever or for a long time after reuniting with them. None of the maternal kidnappers told children that their fathers were "dead." They didn't have to. Maternally kidnapped children knew that their mothers had been prevented from seeing them. Children who were unhappy about this or who were paternally abused in other ways knew that their fathers were very much alive.[9]

One-third of the paternal kidnappers did not go on sprees. They planned their kidnappings very carefully. Such fathers were all assisted by mother

---

* Some mothers attempted to prevent *violent* ex-husbands from visiting. They were unsuccessful in finding legal assistance to prevent such paternal visitation.

competitors—girlfriends, second wives, paternal grandmothers—who took care of the children, maintained the home, and often joined in disparaging or lying about the absent mother.[10]

WHAT HAPPENED TO PATERNAL KIDNAPPERS?

Paternal kidnappers rarely were pursued or found. Those fathers who returned voluntarily or who were apprehended were not economically fined, jailed, or custodially victimized. This nonpunishment of male domestic violence and child abuse is also true in general. Unlike mothers, paternal kidnappers are usually pitied—or heroized.[11]

On December 29, 1981, a father named Rudy Johnson entered a class action lawsuit on behalf of men as a custodially discriminated class. Johnson had kidnapped his own children from Alaska and had taken them to Washington, D.C., and then to California and Spokane, Washington, where he was arrested and imprisoned. Johnson sought and received sympathetic and glamorizing attention from the media and financial and psychological support from other fathers' rights activists. Incredibly,

> one of the [fathers' rights] organizations held Johnson's children as hostages while Johnson negotiated with Spokane officials until certain of [*sic*] his demands were met. He was released on $1,000.00 bail and allowed back to the State of Alaska under a "good-faith" agreement. His demands being met, he received all sorts of pro-father publicity on his "imprisonment" for "loving" his children. He was arrested again in Alaska and again released. He now has many legal loopholes and technicalities to concentrate on in order to side-line the actual offense for which he was arrested.[12]

Paternal kidnappers were not apprehended or punished. Very often their maternal *victims* were the ones whom police officers, lawyers, judges, social workers, and relatives punished. In *Legal Kidnapping*, Anna Demeter describes how her small town blamed her when her husband kidnapped their two youngest children: "Is anything justified for a man who must punish an uppity woman? [Demeter is uppity only because she wants a divorce.] Do people here really feel that a man's wife has no right to reject him and should in that event be punished; and that to steal her children and run away, especially to leave her with a perplexing tangle of debts, is an appropriate and perhaps even an admirable solution? Why do these unspoken reactions still leave me breathless with protest?"[13]

Dorothy won judicial custody in her home state. Her ex-husband then kidnapped the children to another state. After a year, Dorothy found them. She appealed for custody in a second state. She said, "The new judge held my lesbianism against me. He didn't care that my ex had kidnapped the kids, disrupted their lives, and lived on public welfare. Now he was remarried and a high earner. This judge didn't put my ex in jail or fine him or take the kids away from him because he kidnapped them. He ordered *me* to repay the welfare department. He ordered *me* to pay child support in order to see the kids. My ex-husband, together with his wife, was already earning four times what I was. Where is the justice?"

Maureen describes a mother's typically incredible contact with the police and with her children's school during and after episodes of male domestic violence: "The first summer after I moved out, Kenneth disappeared with the children. I broke into our house to look for clues to where he might have gone. A police car pulled up, screeching. Two officers came out with guns drawn. I had proof I was co-owner of the house in my pocketbook. They still arrested me and charged me with breaking and entering my own home.

"After I found the children and brought them back, Kenneth barricaded himself in their classroom with a baseball bat. The school officials called me. They refused to call the police. They said he was the legal parent of his children and it would look bad for them to get involved in a private dispute. When I got the kids home, Kenneth broke my apartment door down. I called the cops. They came without their guns drawn. They sat Kenneth down, talked to him, actually shared a beer with him. They just made him promise to pay to fix the door.

"The second time Kenneth kidnapped the children, he 'hid' them at home with him. I first got a court order for their temporary custody and asked two policemen to come with me. I showed them the court order. I asked them to wait outside, and to help me only if Kenneth became violent. They weren't about to be dictated to by me. They went in and had a nice fifteen-minute man-to-man chat with Kenneth. They came out without the children.

"One policeman said that possession was nine-tenths of the law. The other said that Kenneth obviously loved them—he wanted them, didn't he? Kenneth wasn't going to hurt his own children. They suggested we both sleep on it, or have a friend sit down with us."

WHAT HAPPENED TO THE MATERNAL KIDNAPPERS?[14]

Two mothers were pursued by their ex-husbands and jailed by the authorities.

> **Rachel:** After I kidnapped my sons, we moved to another state. For nearly a year I worked as a social worker. We played music together every night. I supervised their homework. Their father wasn't there to interfere or downgrade me. A year later, the FBI and my ex-husband broke the door down. My head split open. My heart cracked. They threw me in prison for three weeks. Afterward, I was not permitted to see them at all, not even under court supervision. I was not allowed to attend their school graduations or Bar Mitzvahs.[15]
>
> **Jessie:** I obtained temporary legal custody of my kids the first time they were allowed to visit me in a year. My ex-husband, his lawyer, and the local police swooped down on me with a warrant for my extradition and arrest. The kids were moved from school without being allowed to say good-bye to me. Within a month, I was arrested, formally extradited, and jailed on kidnapping charges.

One mother was pursued by her ex-husband, who found her and beat her so badly she required hospitalization.

> **Georgia:** Without anyone's help I drove clear across the state with my son. Within a week, my ex-husband and his brother found us. He beat me up so badly I thought I'd never walk again. He threatened to kill me if I ever came near Bernard again. I still send letters, but I've never gotten an answer.

Two mothers were economically penalized by their ex-husbands and physically prevented from seeing their children, who were in turn simultaneously subjected to intense anti-mother brainwashing campaigns.

The maternal victims of paternal kidnappings are never the same again. Mothers whose children are returned to them live in fear of a second kidnapping. Those whose kidnapped children were brainwashed against them or who suffered other psychological aftereffects live with difficult or increasingly unmanageable children. Those mothers who never see their kidnapped children again live in acute mourning—forever.

Helen's son was kidnapped when he was six years old. She has not seen him since. I interviewed her after three years of mourning.

"My husband, Willie, was my childhood sweetheart. He changed as soon as I became pregnant. Anything set him off. He'd yell, throw things at me, punch me in the face, push me up against a wall. 'The baby!' I'd scream. 'If I break your finger, will that hurt the baby?' he'd sneer.

"Then our son, Justin, was born. I thought Willie would change when he saw what a beautiful child we had. He didn't. After a year of marriage, Willie moved out. He didn't see me or Justin very much. I divorced him when Justin was a year old.

"Willie began coming around when Justin was two. He'd turn up with one of his girlfriends. They'd take Justin out and 'forget' to bring him back, sometimes until the next day. Justin liked having a father. I didn't have the heart to deprive him of one just because Willie hit me and wouldn't pay any child support.

"When Justin was about four, Willie came over when my mother was visiting. He picked a fight with me. I went to call the police. Willie ripped the phone out of the wall. He slugged my mother. He grabbed Justin and ran. Willie got into an accident with another car on the corner. Justin was trying to get out of the car. Willie grabbed him by the neck and threw him into the back of the car.

"My mother took Willie to criminal court. They pooh-poohed her. They told her that grandmothers shouldn't get involved. She dropped the charges. I took Willie to court. I requested an order of protection and a psychiatric evaluation of Willie. The judge refused both my requests. He said that Willie obviously loved me and wanted me back. Why didn't I consider getting remarried—for the sake of my child?

"When Justin was five and a half, he began to refuse to see his daddy. He said, 'I love Daddy but he's fucked-up in the head.' Justin described how Willie beat up his girlfriend and sent her to the hospital. He said, 'Mommy, I was so scared.' This time Willie was indicted.

"I visited his girlfriend in the hospital and offered to be a witness for her. Willie put a thirty-eight to my head and threatened to kill me if I went through with it. Then he began threatening to kill his girlfriend if she didn't drop the charges. I decided to leave town. I went to live with a relative in another state.

"Willie went into court, claiming I was a prostitute and a dope fiend who'd kidnapped his only son. The same judge who'd refused to order a psychiatric on Willie gave him custody of Justin. Within two months, Willie found us and snatched Justin on his way to school. The police couldn't help. It seems that Willie had already shown them his custody order.

"I flew home. I went into court with my parents. This same maniac of a judge returned custody to me on paper. He didn't have the real Justin to return. I moved back in with my parents. We hired detectives. I went to meetings of other parents whose children had been snatched. I cried night and day for a year. Between the crying and the meetings, I had a hard time keeping a job.

"Then something happened to me. I don't know how to put it into words. I couldn't handle myself physically. I couldn't wash my hair. I couldn't put on any makeup. I couldn't go out of the house. I couldn't sleep. I couldn't sit still. My gynecologist checked me out and said it was mental. He put me on Valium. He gave me sleeping pills. I began to drink.

"I've been looking for Justin for three years. I fantasize a lot about how it's going to be when I find him. Will Justin run into my arms? Will he refuse to talk to me? My ex-mother-in-law told my mother that a nice girl was taking care of Justin. 'Helen isn't nice. She left my Willie, and he loved her. She made him crazy when she walked out on him. She should blame herself.'

"'You're a mother yourself,' I cried. 'How would you feel if you could never see your son?'

"'I can't,' she said. 'Because of you.'"

9

Paternal Brainwashing

· · · · · · · · · · · · ·

A year had passed since Seriozha last saw his mother. Since then her name had never been mentioned. During that year he had been sent to school and had learned to know and like his schoolmates. The dreams and memories he had cherished of his mother, and which had made him ill after he had seen her, no longer filled his mind. If they did come back now and again, he studiously drove them away, regarding them shameful and fit only for girls, not for boys who went to school. He knew that it was his lot to remain with his father, and did his best to get used to the idea.

—*Leo Tolstoy,* Anna Karenina

Brainwashing is a form of coercion used against a foreign or domestic enemy of the state and by many cults against its young or vulnerable members.

Prisoners and cultists are usually detained against their will, beaten, threatened, deprived of sleep, and exposed repeatedly to a specific set of beliefs. Despite "informational overload," the prisoner, the cultist, and the child being paternally brainwashed are all isolated. They are without access to previous or conflicting beliefs and without access to their families of origin. Powerful and charismatic father figures (or actual fathers) demand that they renounce all other family or ideological ties.

Cults have been viewed as psychologically destructive for separating people from their past relationships and beliefs.[1] If strangers can brainwash *adult* prisoners and cultists, imagine how easily a child can be brainwashed by a father whose authority has long been upheld by that child's mother and by society in general.

Preferring to live with one's father while maintaining a good relationship with one's mother is not the same as violently rejecting one's mother. The paternal brainwashing of children is a conscious and systematic attempt to force children into rejecting their mothers—that is, into committing psychological matricide.

A successfully brainwashed child doesn't want to see his or her mother at all. A successfully brainwashed child intensely mistrusts and dislikes his mother. He may believe that she is dead, has abandoned him, doesn't love him, or is too "selfish" to be a good mother.

How can a father "brainwash" a child who has been close to his mother? In view of our cultural idealization of fathers and dislike of or readiness to criticize mothers, a father need only accelerate this pre-existing dynamic. For example, in *About Men*, I described how normal boys begin to disidentify with their mothers in order to become "men."[2] In *Every Mother's Son*, Judith Arcana imagines the "mental process" of young boys in this way:

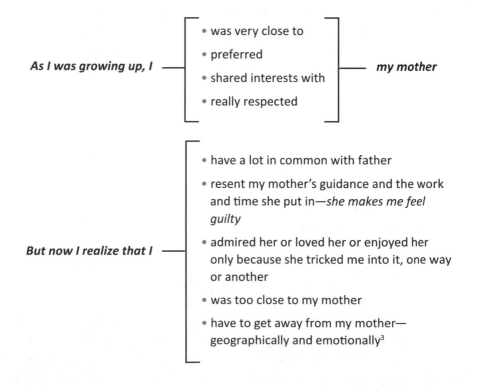

As I was growing up, I
- was very close to
- preferred
- shared interests with
- really respected

my mother

But now I realize that I
- have a lot in common with father
- resent my mother's guidance and the work and time she put in—*she makes me feel guilty*
- admired her or loved her or enjoyed her only because she tricked me into it, one way or another
- was too close to my mother
- have to get away from my mother—geographically and emotionally[3]

As we have noted, mothers are expected to do more than fathers are, and they are blamed by others, including their own children, when they fail to meet idealized standards. A father's absence, neglect, or abusive presence is, comparatively speaking, overlooked, minimized, or denied by most children.

Children are also physically, psychologically, and economically weaker than their parents. Under stress they tend to "align" themselves with the parent they're more afraid of or distant from or with the parent they newly perceive as emotionally "weak" and "needy." Children also tend to align themselves with the "winning" parent.

THE USE OF PHYSICAL FORCE IN PATERNAL BRAINWASHING

Force may be defined as applying the full weight of one's power to outrival an opponent. *Physical* force may take the form of kidnapping a child—or threatening to do so. It may involve physically preventing a child from seeing his mother totally or intermittently.

Children are easily intimidated by paternal physical violence. If a girl once observes her father hit her mother, if a boy himself once has been beaten up by his father, fathers need display little subsequent physical force to be obeyed or to be psychologically "persuasive." Physically intimidated children "know" that their fathers can use force.

Children often deal with their physical helplessness by minimizing its importance or by denying that they were physically intimidated. A brainwashed child may ultimately refuse to acknowledge to himself that he was *forced* to do anything. His terror can be measured by how intensely he rejects his mother.

Not all physically intimidated children *reject* their mothers. For example, Deena was evicted from her house and physically prevented from seeing her children. Deena "secretly" spoke to her children every day on the phone. She and her children were afraid of their father. If he could get rid of their mother, what couldn't he do to them? These children did not *reject* their mother. However, they did not resist their own physical captivity.

Many children who were physically prevented from seeing their mothers rejected their mothers for not "being there" or for not "rescuing them." Many such children became convinced that their mothers were "dead" or "bad."[4]

In *Legal Kidnapping*, Anna Demeter describes how her paternally kidnapped son dealt with his endangered situation by learning to adore his captor and mistrust and hate the mother who rescued him.[5] Bonnie Lee Black, in *Somewhere Child*, describes regaining a four-year-old paternally kidnapped child who remained angry with and mistrustful of her for six months afterward.

Rose was a battered wife. Her husband decided to have her psychiatrically imprisoned for wanting to attend a meeting against his wishes.

"Mother's Day is a very sad day for me," Rose says, smiling sweetly. "When Steven was seven, a close friend found out that Larry had obtained a psychiatric commitment against me. I ran away with the clothes on my back. I borrowed money for a lawyer and sued for custody of Steven. Larry brought his psychiatric commitment order into court and waved it around. 'Your Honor, the woman's crazy. She can't be alone with my boy.' The judge let Steven stay with his father temporarily.

"Sometimes Larry turned up at my job with Steven. 'Okay, Rose. Here's your son. Look at him. Have you seen enough? Don't say I don't let you see him.' Once, I went to the house to see Steven. Larry chased me off the property with a shotgun.

"Larry's widowed mother moved in. She had a poor relationship with Larry. I guess she wanted Steven as a way of having Larry. She didn't have anyone else. I appealed to her many times in bitter tears. I was the mother of this child. Couldn't she understand? 'I don't want to talk to you. Don't bother me,' she'd say, and hang up.

"I finally had my day in court one year later, when Steven was eight. In court, Steven ignored me. He wouldn't look me straight in the eye. He kept looking down. He lied. When they asked him where he wanted to be, he said he wanted to be with his father. He said that I beat him.

"The judge gave Larry custody but did order visitation with me immediately. Steven ran away from me on the street. The police brought him into court the next day. The judge ordered him to go with me again. An hour later, Steven started talking to me as if we'd never been separated. We went to a vacation park. He kept saying, 'This is fantastic!' He was very happy. At night he had a nightmare. He screamed, 'Mommy! Stay with me, stay with me.' This was in his sleep. He really clung to me that night. During the day he acted as if everything were okay.

"Just before our next scheduled visitation, Steven called me at work. 'I don't want to be with you. I don't want to spend any time with you.' He kept repeating it over and over again, as if he were a robot. I would call Steven on the phone. I did all the talking. He might say yes or no. Afterward I'd cry. I wrote Steven cards and letters. I sent him gifts for his birthday and for Christmas. He never wrote to me.

"Whenever I ask him, 'What's wrong?' he says, 'Mom, we have no problems. You know I love you.' He refuses to discuss his father or his grandmother with me. Last year, on his eighteenth birthday, Steven called to ask me for money for college books. I was overjoyed. I offered him my gasoline credit card.

"He's visited me once or twice since then, but the only steady communication we have is when I get his credit card slips every month."

THE USE OF ECONOMIC FORCE IN PATERNAL BRAINWASHING

Half the successful brainwashing fathers (52 percent) economically seduced and manipulated their children. These fathers did not use physical force or intimidation—they did not have to.[6] American children have been taught by television and their parents that they are entitled to the best *things* in life. Why should a child remain behind with an impoverished mother when she or he has an economic alternative?

Fathers who brainwashed economically offered their impressionable and divorce-impoverished children the following things: a room with a television set, a pony of their own, the use of a family swimming pool, new and expensive clothes, luxurious vacations, a summer home, and expensive athletic lessons. Fathers also offered their children a higher standard of living in general.[7]

These fathers went beyond material bribes. They convinced their children that their mother's poverty was her own fault; that she *had* money but was (selfishly) using it for herself, "not for her children"; that her "choice" of neighborhood was dangerous; that the "right" kind of children wouldn't like or associate with them; that their "shabby" clothes and inability to vacation properly were a detriment to their (future) social life.*

THE USE OF PSYCHOLOGICAL FORCE IN PATERNAL BRAINWASHING

Brainwashing fathers exerted psychological force in four major ways: by paying attention to (paternally) neglected children, by "smothering" them

---

* Children are conformists. Perhaps the children of divorce are even more so.

with paternal neediness, by devaluing their mothers, and by replacing their mothers with mother competitors.

A mother competitor is not a stepmother who lives with or marries a man who already has custody of his children. A mother competitor is someone who actively participates in the battle for custody and in the brainwashing campaign.

Many fathers manipulated their children in these four ways, in addition to seducing them economically or physically separating them from their mothers.

Psychological Brainwasher Number One: The Previously Absent Father

Most children have already "had" their mothers. They assume they can "have" her again whenever they want her. However, a previously absent or minimally present father has to be grabbed, on his terms, in order to have him at all. If a father (a prized commodity) demands that his children live with him, the demand is sometimes hard to resist.

> **Bonnie:** My youngest wanted to live with me. His father told him: "If you live with her I won't see you or speak to you. You'll be a stranger to me. I won't let you come back to me when and if you change your mind." Of course, he must have cried a lot when he said this.

Psychological Brainwasher Number Two: The Smother-Father

Some Smother-Fathers openly demanded that their children choose between their sad fathers and their "selfish" mothers.

> **Catherine:** My ex-husband really had no social or emotional life other than his children. He must have burdened them terribly with his fears of isolation and loneliness if they stayed with me. He complained to them about his health a lot. Maybe they were afraid he'd have a heart attack without them.
>
> **Beth:** Our kids knew that their father chose to work part time in order to spend more time with them. They knew he refused ever to hire a babysitter. He kept telling them I was selfish compared to him. He should have told them I was normal and he wasn't. They began to mistrust me. They acted as if

I were the strong and selfish one and he were the weak and giving one. They certainly didn't think there was anything unusual or abnormal about a father's making such a total commitment of time to his children.

Psychological Brainwasher Number Three: The Devaluation of the Mother

A child who is physically separated from his or her mother or psychologically and economically seduced by a previously absent father does not have to *hate* or reject his or her mother. Theoretically, such a child may still miss his or her mother—and be allowed to say so. Theoretically, such a child might insist on seeing his or her mother regularly—and be allowed to do so.

This does not occur when the mother has been systematically devalued. A child who hates and rejects his or her mother has long been encouraged to disobey her authority and suspect her maternal altruism. Such a child has long been encouraged to gather information against the mother for the father's custody case. Such a child has long been encouraged to criticize the mother in front of other adults, to lie (or to "forget" the truth) in court, to run away from the mother's home, and ultimately to refuse to see the mother at all.[8]

A mother's devaluation is in progress when children begin to speak in their father's voice. A brainwashed child also begins to imitate his father's treatment of his mother. If he is very young, he may repeat what his father says, without necessarily internalizing its meaning. For example, Melanie's two-and-a-half-year-old son "began to slap me and say 'Mommy's a bitch.' Then he'd hit my lover and say she was a 'double bitch.' Then he'd hug his big brother and say 'My brother's okay.' He would say 'Mommy's mean to me. Mommy whips me.' It was so sad. He didn't really know what he was saying but he seemed obsessed with saying it anyway."

Preadolescent children are ambivalent about having to reject their mothers.

Bonnie: From the start, my eleven-year-old refused to visit me. My eight-year-old came regularly—at first. He'd arrive and immediately unpack his clothes. Then he'd take everything out of the dresser, put it back in his suitcase, and scream, "I'm leaving. You're no good. I don't have to stay." I would go to pieces when he did this. He was showing me myself—

Loretta:
leaving him. He was also adopting a high hand with me. He wanted to punish me for his father's sake. Maybe for his own sake, too. Then he'd call his father and tell him to pick him up. His father encouraged him to do this.

Loretta: After I got married, my ex-husband began seeing the kids a lot. My eight-year-old began spying on me. He'd tell his father things about us. He'd tell *us* that his father hated me. He'd announce that he was going to live with his father, that his father was already working on it. Then he'd start crying and refuse to leave me. He began to have tantrums and nightmares.

I interviewed Loretta and her ex-husband, Lemuel, separately. During my three-hour interview with Loretta, Lemuel called to speak to their children twice. The older boy hovered at the kitchen doorway as I interviewed his mother. He told me that "he had to hear if his mother was saying anything bad about his father. If she did, he had to tell his father."

Teenagers were less ambivalent about taking sides. Some did so with a vengeance. Gail's teenage son grew cold, disobedient, and physically violent toward her. She said,

He would scream at me, "This is not your house. You don't own it. You've taken it away from my father. You've ruined my father's life. Women get everything. Men get nothing." He began to do just what his father told him to. When I said he couldn't play hockey until he did his homework, he climbed out his bedroom window, screaming that his *father* said he could play hockey. I tried to stop him. He whacked me with his hockey stick. Eventually he didn't listen to anything I said. He treated me without any respect. He treated me more and more like a servant. "Get me this, get me that."

Marta's teenage son began to treat her with contempt just as his father did. He verbally belittled her and physically avoided her. He minimized her complaints, called her crazy, and occasionally cursed her. Marta said: "My son also called his ten-year-old sister a dumb cunt. He called me a lazy cunt. My daughter giggled and flirted with him in response. When I wept about losing custody, my son told me to see a shrink."

Psychological Brainwasher Number Four: The Paternal Replacement of the Mother with a Mother Competitor

Of the successful brainwashing campaigns, 64 percent involved the active leadership or cooperation of a mother competitor, 82 percent of whom were virulently competitive. In addition, 59 percent were infertile; were married to (newly) infertile husbands; or, as the paternal grandmother, aunt, or "older" housekeeper, could no longer get pregnant themselves.[9]

No mother competitor was involved in 32 percent of the successful brainwashing campaigns. Smother-Fathers waged 88 percent of these campaigns. Also, fewer and less virulent mother competitors were involved in the nine failed brainwashing campaigns.[10]

The mother competitor maintained a battling father's home domestically and emotionally. She also assumed responsibility for child care. Some mother competitors merely assisted fathers in devaluing mothers; others far outdid men in this area. Some mother competitors also functioned as legal secretaries and legal strategists for the custody battle.

> **Lucy:** My husband's new wife Mindy came right into my office, plopped her legal papers down, smirked, and left. Another time she came to my office and started talking very loudly against me. She was completely unconcerned about whether this would get me fired or not. To shut her up, I signed whatever she wanted me to.
>
> Mindy backed my ex-husband tooth and claw. I have to conclude that their marriage was somehow based on his vendetta against me. She considered herself a good wife if she could help him get revenge against me. She was a *very* good wife.

Mother competitors verbally attacked, publicly humiliated, and physically prevented mothers from seeing or speaking to their children.

> **Norma:** Beverly, the new wife, told me she felt it was her Christian duty to protect her husband and *my* children from my bad temper and unpredictable behavior. "Why don't you go to court against us again, you greedy bitch? You're not fit to be the mother of George's children."

Beverly used to hang up on me whenever I'd call. When I'd arrive at their house, George would send her out to deal with me; she'd pretend he wasn't home. Beverly would lie outright about why the kids weren't around. She'd slam and then lock the doors. She'd pull all the shades down. Sometimes she'd say my kids weren't there when I could hear them. Sometimes she'd say that they didn't want to see me.

Adele: There was a reception line at my son's bar mitzvah. My ex-husband's live-in girlfriend was standing next to him and acting like the mother of my son. I didn't cry or run away. I tried to act very proud of my son.

PATERNAL GRANDMOTHERS AND HOUSEKEEPERS

Georgia and Ruthie both faced virulently competitive paternal grandmothers.

Georgia: She thought that my son belonged to her. She thought she was a better mother than I was. She was about forty. I was only eighteen. When her son and I separated, she wasn't about to let me steal her grandson.

Ruthie: My ex-husband was easygoing. My ex-mother-in-law talked against me to our kids. She told them I was crazy and selfish for wanting a divorce. She kept telling them that I was choosing a career over my own flesh and blood. My son got very withdrawn. My daughter began to yell at me.[11]

Adele faced three mother competitors: a live-in girlfriend, a paternal aunt, and an ex-housekeeper.

Adele: My ex-housekeeper really loved the children. She also needed her job desperately. My ex-husband offered to raise her salary if she'd testify against me. My ex-sister-in-law coached her. In court, she read aloud from a carefully constructed list that detailed all the times that I was presumably "out" or asleep over a seven-year period. The poor woman didn't look up or say hello. She couldn't face me.[12]

THE MOTHER COMPETITOR IN HER OWN VOICE

When she was twenty-one, Sheela assumed responsibility for forty-year-old Leopold's home and his two genetic children. She "managed" his custody battle against his first wife. After ten years of marriage, Leopold custodially challenged Sheela for the children she'd mothered, including their genetic child. Sheela said, "Leopold was my professor. I adored him. I thought he was a genius—and very sexy. Leopold was already involved in separating from his wife when we fell in love. At the time, Leopold's children were two and three.

"I thought their mother, Lana, was a very cold woman. She had a busy career. She traveled as much as Leopold. She must have been in her middle thirties. How could she mother properly? Leopold didn't want me to talk to Lana. He said she hated me and would only be looking for weak spots to use against *him* in court.

"I loved doing things like making birthday parties and 'special' dinners for them. I really hated certain chores—like taking them to and from places and keeping track of all their activities and whereabouts. But I knew how important it was that the day-care teachers saw how involved I was. I knew we'd need them as witnesses. I started keeping a diary and taking pictures of everything I did with the children.

"We won custody hands down. Lana didn't bother to see them very often after that. He told the children to call me the Sheela Momma.

"As I got older and Leopold did too, he became more demanding and supercritical. He began to have temper tantrums. He accused me of being fat and crazy. He openly began to have affairs with his students. When I moved out, he moved my mother-in-law in. He hired the most expensive lawyer in town to get custody of all three children.

"I did get custody of my biological child. Leopold kept 'his' two children. The oldest boy keeps running away to live with me. I have to send him back. Leopold has made visitation very difficult. Do you know who gave Leopold the money for his expensive lawyer? Lana did."

Mary Zenorini Silverzweig fell in love with Stanley Silverzweig, the much older married father of three girls. Despite—or perhaps because of—this impropriety, Mary became obsessed with proper appearances and with the Christian and patriarchal "salvation" of his daughters. Silverzweig, in her book, *The Other Mother*, writes, "I wanted to have [everyone] say some day, 'She's done wonders with those children. I don't know what they would have done without her.' . . . I clothed them, groomed them, trimmed their hair, and tied it in ribbons. I'd get up early to cook breakfast—or spend hours cooking dinner, so each meal would seem like a special occasion. We baked bread and cakes and cookies together. We went shopping and read to each other, did housework and played."[13]

According to Silverzweig, for two years Stanley called his daughters every night to discuss their "coming to live with us." During this time, Mary took them on numerous shopping expeditions for expensive and "feminine" clothing. Stanley spent one hundred thousand dollars on lawyers. Mary coordinated all the legal meetings and chauffeured the children back and forth. Mary and Stanley bought three new houses and took a Caribbean vacation, a European vacation, a trip to the Grand Canyon, and a honeymoon trip to Italy. These things, plus a "white wedding," did little to eliminate Mary's irrational desire to be the "first" and "only" woman in Stanley's life: "The overpowering urge that I felt as a second wife was to bury the first, to lose the past in the frenzy of the present, and least of all to be reminded of anything that smacked of past intimacy, sex, loving devotion, or familial bliss. I refused to acknowledge that there had been one single moment of anything resembling happiness in his first marriage."

When Mary discovered that her "enemy" had become a lesbian, her missionary zeal knew no bounds. Mary relished the victory of true womanhood over lesbianism. In her own voice she describes the following parent-school scene:

I [sat] with the teachers, dressed in a linen suit, stockings, and high heels, the way mothers used to dress when they visited the private schools that I had attended. Roberta sat on the other side of the gym, alone, in jeans, and a peasant blouse, her bare feet in sandals. Leslie [Roberta's daughter] would glance over her shoulders, first in one direction then in the other.

When it was all over, and the two hundred youngsters broke ranks wildly for summer vacation, Leslie stood and waited, not knowing what to do with the mess that confronted her. I waved; Roberta just watched. Leslie . . . came to me. . . . "Shall we go? We have an errand to do, and then we'll pick up the little ones for the weekend." My arm was around her shoulder; I was selfish enough to want to make the most of my triumph.

I separately interviewed Roberta, her female partner, her lawyer, and her two youngest daughters. Both girls hovered at the doorway suspiciously, asked me if their father knew who I was or what I wanted, and continued to eavesdrop on our conversation even after they had been ordered to their rooms.[14]

HOW MANY MOTHERS OF SUCCESSFULLY BRAINWASHED CHILDREN EVER SAW THEIR CHILDREN AGAIN? HOW DID THEIR CHILDREN RELATE TO THEM?

A third of the mothers (33 percent) have never seen one or more of their brainwashed children again. Forty percent of the mothers have seen their brainwashed children "sometimes" or after the passage of five years. A fifth of the mothers (19 percent) have seen their brainwashed children regularly. Eight percent of the mothers were still struggling against a brainwashing campaign when I interviewed them.

The effects of a successful brainwashing campaign can be deep and long-lasting. I interviewed one mother whose daughter had been kidnapped and brainwashed against her when she was six years old. Ten years later this mother managed to locate her missing sixteen-year-old daughter. She told me,

> At first she refused to see me at all. She finally agreed to one meeting. The first thing she said was "I love my father very much." The second thing she said was "Why did you try to abort me? Why did you beat me up when I was a child?" The third thing she said was "My father is both a mother and a father to me. He would never, never lie to me about anything."
>
> She told me that she "knew" I had left her, married another man, and had other kids. (All untrue.) She said she didn't want to see me again, that it would kill her father—who has a "bad heart."[15*]

The majority of rejected mothers kept trying to see their brainwashed children. They wrote, called, and sent birthday cards and presents. Rejected mothers were angry; they also forgave their children.

---

* This mother was not part of the study reported in chapter 4.

Maureen: Even as I'm battling for my kids, I'm angry at them. Why should I have to compete for my kids in order to keep being their mother? Why should I hold onto children who want the best economic "deal" more than they want a mother? Why don't they offer to get part-time jobs to help me, instead of complaining about what a drag it is to be poor?

Adele: My son refused to see me for four years. Then, *he* approached me. I try not to mention the past. It might hurt him or drive him away. That's the last thing I want to do. In my heart, I've even forgiven his father in the hope it will allow *both* my children to become friendly with me.

WHAT IS THE PSYCHOLOGICAL SIGNIFICANCE OF ANTI-MOTHER BRAINWASHING?

The forced separation from either parent, but especially from the mother who reared him, constitutes a traumatic and lasting form of child abuse. Any child who hates or rejects his mother is probably doomed to guilt forever. The need to deny such guilt may lead to the supression of *all* authentic feelings—especially those of love, anger, grief, self-confidence, and hope.

Daughters who commit psychological matricide may mistrust and dislike themselves, other women, and *their* daughters as much as paternal incest victims do. Sons who commit psychological matricide may remain emotionally armored against heterosexual intimacy. John Edward Gill, in a discussion of parental kidnapping and brainwashing, notes that

> being kidnapped is a lot harder on a child, in fact, than a real death. In an actual death, the other parent is their support and would have experienced the loss too. But in a child snatching, the child has no way of talking about it, which alienates the child even more from that absent parent.
>
> Families come together when someone dies. Relatives fly in from other states. They support each other. Children see uncles, aunts, cousins. They know they belong. Stolen children see practically no one. There are no reunions and family dinners, no offer of help. There is just hiding.[16]

I did not formally study brainwashed children for this chapter. I did observe and interview eight such children, who ranged in age from eight to sixteen. All these children were unusually pale, guarded, and suspicious. They immediately asked me who I was, what I was doing with their mothers, and whether their fathers knew about me or had sent me. All eight children held themselves rigidly. Not one child engaged in "easy," expressive, or extensive conversation.

Dr. John G. Clark Jr. has treated and studied five hundred current and former adolescent and adult cult members. He notes that "although it is possible for those who have left cults to integrate their experience into their lives in healthy ways, many are unable to [do so]. Among the common negative characteristics exhibited by the former cult members studied, are depression, guilt, fear, paranoia, slow speech, rigidity of facial expression and body posture, indifference to physical appearance, passivity and memory impairment."[17]

A REJECTED MOTHER IN HER OWN VOICE

Terry married at twenty. She had two sons by the time she was twenty-three. Her husband was a hardworking physician. She says, "I had my boys when Clark was still in medical school. I was basically a happy mother and a completely neglected wife. I went back to college when Ricky, our youngest, started kindergarten. Clark was furious. He belittled me constantly. He said I could go to school—as long as his dinner was on the table when he came home.

"We never had much sex. Now we had none. I finally began an affair. I insisted we go for marriage counseling. It was too late. Clark moved out—six blocks away.

"He started spending more time with the boys. I was delighted. I continued my secret affair with Andy, the man I've lived with ever since. Clark was busy and very lonely. I fixed him up on some dates. Within three months he was living with a woman.

"Then 'little things' started to happen. For example, Bert, my seven-year-old, told me that he wasn't dressed properly. Ricky, my six-year-old, said he was 'dirty.' His father had told him so. Bert began questioning me about what I did with the money I got from his father. He once accused me of spending 'his' money on a plant for myself.

"Clark married his live-in girlfriend. They took the boys with them to Disneyland on their honeymoon. Their honeymoon was centered on the children. The boys were made to feel that this is the way things should be.

"When they returned, Ricky asked me why I sometimes went away overnight with Andy without taking them along. Bert said it wasn't right for Andy and me to live together without being married. Both boys started criticizing everything I did. 'Daddy says if you really loved us, you'd stop school until we're all grown up,' or 'How come you hate housework so much? Daddy's wife loves it.' Clark began a compulsive letter-writing campaign to instruct me in the duties of motherhood:

An Excerpt from One of Clark's Letters

The clothes you packed for the boys were appalling. Their sneakers are worn and dirty. Bert's outfit was a ridiculous combination of a blue and white vertical striped shirt and blue checkered pants. All the buckle holes in Ricky's belt are torn together into one large useless opening (see my diagram). Also, Ricky's red striped shirt is missing several buttons. Ricky's undershorts, pajamas and red coveralls are faded and dull. Please supervise their bathing more carefully and insist it be done daily. Your own health habits are unimportant to me but those of Bert and Ricky are of great concern.[18]

"Clark suddenly stopped all his child-support payments. His lawyer told me they were prepared to move for sole custody if I didn't agree to joint custody. In court, Clark's lawyer kept referring to me as the 'liberated lady.' He kept saying I was living in sin with Andy.

"Ricky wouldn't look at his father or at me. Bert wouldn't look at me at all. Both boys seemed very pained and torn. I didn't have the heart to put them through any more. After one day in court, I agreed to joint custody. The judge told Clark that if he interfered with our arrangement, he'd flip sole custody back to me.

"My lawyer assured me that no physician with a big practice would just pick up and disappear. Friends assured me that kids eventually resent the parent who forces them to choose. The next morning, Clark, his wife, and the boys were gone. They'd moved five hundred miles away. It was legal. They hadn't moved out of the state. I was devastated. What could I do? Start another lawsuit? Uproot myself and move next door to him? Compete with Clark in tearing the boys apart?

"Clark made visitation very, very hard for me. Although I had to travel five hundred miles, Clark literally wouldn't let me through his front door. He wouldn't let me pick the boys up until late Friday afternoon. He demanded they be back precisely at six p.m. on Sundays.

"About a year after they moved, Clark allowed the boys to spend ten days with me at Easter time. On their ninth day with me, Ricky and Bert had a fight. By accident, Bert snapped Ricky's hand back. Overnight, it got very swollen. I asked Clark to look at it. A week later I received a letter telling me that the boys were forbidden to visit with Andy and me—because Andy had broken Ricky's hand!

"I tried to get through to the kids. Clark's wife refused to call them to the phone. Then Clark unlisted their number. I didn't want to put Andy through a public scandal. He was a divorced father himself. I remember telling Andy that I didn't want Clark to die before the boys came out of this on their own. I wanted them to understand what he'd done first.

"For two years and nine months Clark didn't allow me to see my sons. Then Clark wrote me, 'recommending' one two-hour visit with Ricky. 'If it goes well,' he said, we can 'discuss the possibility of another visit.' Apparently, Ricky had continued to pester him about seeing me. Now, both boys visit me regularly.

"Lately Bert has complained to me about his father. I do not encourage him. I'm afraid that Clark is capable of blaming me for Bert's normal teenage rebelliousness—and interfering with visitation again. I'm afraid of something else, too. Any man who can cut a mother out of his children's lives is capable of cutting his children out of his life.

"Clark tried to kill me. He used my flesh and blood as his weapon and his shield. He got away with torture and attempted murder."

10

The "Voluntarily" Noncustodial Mother

. . . .

MEDEA

    Since it is the King's will to banish me from here—

    I am going into exile from this land;

    But do you, so that you may have the care of them,

    Beg Creon that the children may not be banished.

JASON

    I support what you say. In the end you have come to

    The right decision, like the clever woman you are.

    Medea, why are your eyes all wet with pale tears?

    Are not these words of mine pleasing for you to hear?

MEDEA

    It is nothing. I was thinking about these children.

JASON

    You must be cheerful. I shall look after them well.

    Why then should you grieve so much for these children?

MEDEA

    I am their mother.

    O children, O my children, you have a city,

    You have a home, and you can leave me behind you,

    And without your mother you may live there forever.

But I am going in exile to another land
Before I have seen you happy and taken pleasure in you,
Before I have dressed your brides and made your marriage beds.

—*Euripides*, Medea

On March 23, 1885, "at about five minutes to nine in the morning," Charlotte Perkins Gilman, the American feminist writer, gave birth to her daughter, Katherine. Gilman was devastated by a severe postpartum depression. Despite a "loving and devoted" husband, a "German servant girl of unparalleled virtue," an "exquisite baby," and a maternal grandmother installed to "run things," Charlotte "lay all day on the lounge and cried."

Psychiatrist Dr. S. W. Mitchell warned Gilman not to engage in more than "two hours of intellectual life a day." He forbade her to "pick up a pen, brush, or pencil for as long as [she] lived." He ordered a long period of "bedrest" and a lifetime of complete "domesticity."

In 1887 after four years of marriage, Gilman and her husband agreed to divorce. "Better for that dear child to have separated parents than a lunatic mother," wrote Gilman. In 1894, exhausted by illness and by her inability to secure adequate domestic assistance, Gilman entered into a joint custody agreement with Katherine's father. "No one suffered from [my decision to share my child] but myself. Since [my ex-husband's fiancée] was a good friend to me and to my child; since the father longed for his child and had a right to some of her society; and since the child had a right to know and love her father, this seemed the right thing to do."[1]

For years, Gilman could "never see a mother and child together without crying." She would "make friends" with any child in order to "hold it in [her] arms for a little." Thirty years later, writing about this, she had to "stop typing and cry as I tell about it." Nevertheless, Gilman was furiously condemned for giving up her child. "To hear what was said and read what was printed, one would think I had handed over a baby in a basket. In the years that followed, [Katherine] divided her time fairly between us, but in companionship with her beloved father, she grew up to be the artist that she is, with advantages I could never have given her. I lived without her temporarily, but why did they think I liked it? She was all I had."[2]

Little has changed today. Few people distinguish between a mother who has lost judicial custody of her child, a mother who chooses joint custody, and a mother who is coerced into giving up custody of her child for economic, emotional, or "career" reasons.

All noncustodial mothers are viewed as "unfit" or as unnaturally "selfish" mothers.

WHAT DO MY INTERVIEWS TELL US ABOUT NONCUSTODIAL MOTHERHOOD?

In a sense, forty-nine (82 percent) of my maternal interviewees had become noncustodial mothers. However, only eight mothers (13 percent) viewed themselves as partially or fully responsible for their noncustodial status or as "benefiting" from it in terms of their subsequent emotional, financial, or philosophical development.

I interviewed twelve additional mothers, all of whom described themselves as "voluntary" noncustodial mothers. Strictly speaking, these twenty mothers gave up fighting a losing battle; they didn't give up their children. Most mothers caved in for economic reasons; many were also forced to choose between some form of self-realization and a traditional style of mothering.[3]

A number of voluntary noncustodial mothers wanted to leave very abusive marriages. Bonnie was hounded out of her home by an adulterous husband who couldn't forgive her single act of adultery. She was forced to leave her children behind as hostages. Bonnie remains guilty for escaping and blames herself for losing her children's love. She told me, "If I couldn't live with him, if I thought he was a raving maniac, how could I leave my children with him? But I did. I ran from his temper, his sulking, his threats. He convinced my children that I'd abandoned them. I would still tell another mother to save herself if she was drowning like I was. You do have to swim to shore. You can't always carry everyone else with you."

A number of noncustodial mothers wanted to leave bad, rather than abusive, marriages; did not have enough money to support a child alone; and were also interested in "self-realization."

> **Rae:** I earned thirty nine cents on my husband's dollar. How could I support my daughter and develop myself, too? I was in an economic bind. I figured that if I moved out with Joy, it would be very difficult to make her father take her on weekends, to make him support her, to make him do

anything I wanted him to do. I couldn't guarantee her a continuing father. I couldn't guarantee her a decent standard of living. His position would have been: "You wanted out. You're stuck with her."

A number of noncustodial mothers were forced by their husbands to choose between their careers and *traditional* motherhood. Alicia was in the theater long before she became a mother or decided to divorce.

Alicia: My husband couldn't stand to lose both me and our daughter. I asked him to come and live in New York. He just laughed at me. I told him I'd be willing to take her with me and move in with my mother. He fought me for custody. The first time, I won, but the judge wouldn't let me leave the state. So I gave up custody.

Things didn't work out very well for my husband that first year. I agreed to take my daughter back. I settled her in with my mother and enrolled her in a good private school. Just as things were settling down, my ex-husband wanted her back. He was newly remarried and felt he could provide a better home for our daughter. I could have fought him again. I chose not to. This is my only life. I can't live it in an unhappy marriage. I can't live it fighting a constant custody battle. I can't live it without my music.

Carla chose to give up responsibility for her preadolescent and teenage children. Such responsibilities, which she shouldered alone within marriage, made it impossible for her to seriously pursue a career. Carla felt devoured by her children's endless needs—in view of the fact that she had satisfied these needs for so long. She said,

My husband didn't understand that I wanted to concentrate totally on my work, sixteen hours a day, six days a week. After fourteen years of being a housewife and mother, I didn't want to worry about having to attend school plays or give parties and listen to everyone's troubles. My husband didn't understand why I seemed to be having so much trouble managing a career plus my grown up family.

I told him that he wasn't prepared to do for me what I'd done for him. I needed to be totally relieved of duty in order to concentrate. I couldn't manage two things at once anymore.

WHAT DO MY INTERVIEWS TELL US ABOUT NONCUSTODIAL FATHERHOOD?

I interviewed ten noncustodial fathers. In two cases I was also able to interview their children and ex-wives. These fathers hadn't *wanted* sole custodial status, just as most mothers hadn't *wanted* noncustodial status. Most noncustodial fathers also believed that their children were "better off" with their mothers or that no judge "back then would have awarded custody to a father."[4]

Fifty percent of these noncustodial fathers did not see their children at all, or very often. Sixty percent paid no child support. Eighty percent paid no alimony.

Lyndon is a successful businessman. His wife ended their ten-year marriage because of his open love affair with his secretary. Lyndon said,

> My wife Carol was a materialistic ball-buster. She looked down at me for being so successful. She thought she was really smarter than me. Cathy was my first experience of love. I had to have her. I loved my kids. I would never have pushed Carol for a divorce. She pushed me. Her pride just couldn't stand my having an open affair. She thought she'd make out better economically if we were divorced. She thought she'd get revenge on me for having something good in my life.
>
> I was a good father; I didn't want to choose between my kids and Cathy. I hate Carol for making me choose. I won't send her any alimony. I send the exact amount of child support my lawyer agreed to, no more and no less. I'll pay half their college if their mother comes up with the other half; if not, well, Carol should have thought of that sooner.

Morris has three college-age children. After eighteen years of marriage, Valerie, his wife, left him to "fulfill herself." She left her children behind. Morris said, "Let Valerie send her kids to college on her 'fulfillment.' I have to worry about myself now. I need my money to attract the kind of woman

I want. Valerie is not the only one entitled to fulfillment. The kids are closer to her than to me. Why should I keep sacrificing to send them to college?"

I interviewed Valerie, Morris's ex-wife. She described the marriage as follows:

> Morris was very wrapped up in his career. He had very little time for his family. When he spent time with us, he was demanding and difficult. He rewarded his children only when they were submissive and obedient. He never rewarded them for being independent or for questioning his rules. When they were in real trouble and needed his protection, he always disappeared.
>
> I'm very bitter that he won't pay for their college. How can a man live with his own children for twenty years and just shirk off all responsibility? Did he support them only as long as I was there, giving him wifely service?

Bruce earned ten times what his ex-wife earned. Bruce sent her and their four children about one fifth of his earnings in child support. He said, "I was wrong to sacrifice my life to my family. I was in harness when I was twenty-two. My wife had everything she wanted: me, children, a big house, no pressures. My wife wanted four kids. Not me. I'm not going to mortgage my whole life so that *her* kids can go to college. *She* needed the kids. It's a neurotic thing with her. Let them learn to fend for themselves. It will probably do them some good."

Bruce's children were reluctant to complain about their father. The older children said they "couldn't take sides." The youngest, a twelve-year-old, said, "I think Daddy loves us, but he's awfully busy. He can't see us very much. He sends Mom money every month, but it's not always the same amount. Mom says it's not enough to support four kids. My older brother has to work after school. I will, too. Last Christmas Daddy went to Florida. He sent each of us a box filled with the stones and shells he picked up on the beach as our Christmas present."

MARALEE AND ROGER: A COMPARISON

Maralee is the mother of two teenagers and a ten-year-old. She was referred to me as a "feminist" noncustodial hero. Maralee didn't work for six months after each of her children was born. She worked part-time and then full-time, but she was always available for children's illnesses, PTA meetings, and other commitments. She also chose her children's clothes, babysitters, housekeepers, schools, and camps. She did or supervised the cooking and cleaning for her entire married life.

Maralee was married to an exceptionally devoted father. Upon divorce, he wanted to assume bottom-line responsibility for their children. He supported Maralee's desire to start graduate school. He assumed the children would have unlimited access to their mother. Maralee, who had married at twenty, moved four blocks away. Her mother condemned her: "My mother had told me from the time I got married that my husband would resent me because I was a working woman. Then she said my children were going to resent me because I was a working mother. Then, when I told her I was leaving him and not taking the children, she said, 'Well, I'm not telling anyone. I refuse to acknowledge it. Get a psychiatrist. You're really sick, and you're going to feel awfully guilty.'"

Maralee's former neighbors and friends condemned and ostracized her and punished her children. "We were a close-knit group of coffee klatchers on my block. But when I left without the kids, there was suddenly this chill on the block. When I would come to pick up the kids for something, the other mothers cut me dead. I would say hello to one of my neighbors, and she would go right on walking down the street. Suddenly, the mothers didn't allow their children to sleep over. This behavior continued for years."

After interviewing Maralee in New York, I visited her at her Midwestern home. As we settled down to talk, Maralee's three children burst in. Within one hour of my arrival, I observed Maralee cook "early dinner" for her children and afterward help one son with his homework and one daughter solve a "fashion" problem.

In a Mexican or African village, Maralee could easily pass for a traditional mother, whose children were sleeping five minutes away in their father's house. In the eighteenth century in Europe or America, she might be an oddity among mothers, the only one who refused to send *any* of her surviving children to a wet nurse, a military academy, or a convent. Maralee might be an oddity among (working) poor mothers today—for having so much spontaneous time to spend with her children.

In the heartland of America, Maralee was condemned as a selfish career woman who dared move four blocks away from her children. Maralee sees herself as a besieged feminist hero. I see her as a traditional mother who, after years of married motherhood, moved four blocks away.

Roger is the twice-divorced father of two children. He was divorced from his first wife when his son, Jeff, was a year old and from his second wife when his daughter was two years old. For eight years, Roger didn't see Jeff at all. When Jeff was ten, Roger began seeing him sporadically. He also sent gifts and money "when he could." He said: "I knew Jeff wasn't starving. My first wife was remarried to a nice, respectable guy. My son had everything he needed. When I got divorced the second time, I began to think about really getting to know both my kids. I wanted to learn what it meant to be a father."

Roger did not view his late-blooming paternal desires as "too little, too late." The passing of youth and, with it, professional ambition made Roger's exploration of the father-child bond newly attractive. When Jeff's stepfather unexpectedly died, Roger offered to try living with Jeff "for a while."

Roger developed a buddylike relationship with the fourteen-year-old Jeff. To the envy of single mothers everywhere, father and son divided up the tasks of shopping, cooking, and home maintenance. When Roger worked late, he said he was not "guilty" about Jeff's fixing his own dinner, Jeff's putting himself to bed, and his not having a running ticker tape in his own head of Jeff's every need. Roger said,

> Jeff has to remind me about the eye doctor, because it's something I'm not used to. So he'll say, "Hey, Dad, it's been fifteen months since I had my eyes checked, can you call the doctor?" Then he'll put a note on the refrigerator to remind me, and I'll get the doctor. This just happened last week, so it's fresh in my mind.
>
> With Jeff coming into my life, I had a very clear sense of the genetic link between us. I heard Jeff using expressions that I use all the time. Sometimes it felt like I was having a conversation with myself when I talked to him. The things that he was interested in, the ways that he would approach things, reminded me of myself. I don't think I really felt my own identity as a father until I experienced this.

Roger was a noncustodial father for nearly fourteen years before he became a custodial father. During this time, he doesn't remember suffering any "guilt" for not building a relationship with his son, nor does Roger seem guilty about the "peer-buddy" relationship he adopted as his parenting style. On the contrary: Roger feels that Jeff had been "well taken care of without him and that, to his (everlasting) credit, he was 'there' for his son when he 'finally needed him.'"

Maralee was a custodial mother for nearly fourteen years before she became a noncustodial mother. She expressed "guilt" and described frequent bouts of depression about her noncustodial status, even though she lives four blocks away from her children and is available to cook, sew, and "babysit" for them.

Maralee is viewed as a social pariah. By comparison, Roger is viewed as something of a social hero.[5]

HOW DID NONCUSTODIAL MOTHERS DESCRIBE THEMSELVES? HOW WERE THEY TREATED?

All the voluntary noncustodial mothers experienced their status as deviant or as historically novel. No one located herself anywhere in history. These mothers had so internalized the American twentieth-century standards of ideal motherhood that at some level they judged themselves as failures. This was true even for those mothers who were proud, defiant, or even casual about their noncustodial status.[6]

The self-blame and sense of deviance displayed by voluntary noncustodial mothers was tragic because their custodial status was essentially a forced situation; because these mothers did not want to sever their psychological or physical relationships with their children; and because 80 percent of these mothers lived close by, continued to see their children regularly, and were available for emergencies and for continued sewing, ironing, and cooking for their children or their ex-husbands.*

Patricia Pascowicz published an excellent book entitled *Absentee Mothers*. All her mothers had, at one time, been their children's primary caretakers; 60 percent had become noncustodial mothers essentially against their will; 50 percent continued to live near their children. Nevertheless, Pascowicz's mothers (like my interviewees) were denounced for "abandoning" their children—both by others and by themselves.

Some of Pascowicz's mothers lost relatives, friends, and jobs as well as children. Many mothers denied that they were being ostracized or that such ostracism bothered them. One mother wrote that she "attached no importance" to various "unpleasant remarks." Pascowicz notes, "Yet [she] has

---

* Four "voluntary" noncustodial mothers (20 percent) were physically or psychologically denied access to their children.

moved far away from all her relatives; has had no contact with them at all for many years; and changed her first and last names 'because I didn't like the name I had.' Although she says that her absentee motherhood 'is pretty much accepted,' she has kept it a secret at work. [When questioned further, she said she was] immune to encounters with strangers [and didn't want] to discuss them."

Several of my maternal interviewees were ostracized or bitterly attacked by their own children.

> **Carla:** My daughter cried all the time and said I was ruining her image at school. My son withdrew into a shell. My husband walked around feeling so sorry for himself that he "couldn't" make the proper arrangements for the house and children. I got blamed for this, too.
>
> **Glenda:** Even though my ex-husband was a wonderful father, and although we presented a solid front on the custody issue, I got lots of funny looks and rude questions, even from the kids. He got lots of sympathy and praise.

Nearly a fifth (19 percent) of Pascowicz's mothers did not identify themselves with other "absentee" mothers. None of her mothers sought others "like themselves" for support. Neither sympathy nor compassion was extended to them by people "unlike" themselves.

The most apparent difference between noncustodial mothers and fathers is the overwhelming *expression* of guilt by mothers and the overwhelming *silence* of fathers on the subject of guilt. Noncustodial mothers expressed guilt for not living with their children even if they lived nearby and saw them regularly. Noncustodial fathers expressed no guilt even if they lived far away or saw their children only rarely. Why did noncustodial mothers talk so freely about their maternal guilt? Why did noncustodial fathers *not* talk about their guilt?

The similarities that exist between noncustodial parents are more superficial (or situational) than psychologically substantial. A noncustodial father is treated as "ordinary"; a noncustodial mother is treated as extraordinary. A noncustodial father may have arrived at his noncustodial status without a prolonged public or externally traumatic battle. Noncustodial mothers rarely have.

Though fathers earned more money than mothers and were psychologically used to "paying" for their children, they nevertheless described feeling "angry" about having to "buy" or "entertain" their children. ("Why can't we just behave normally, as if we lived together?") Noncustodial mothers said similar things.

However, while fathers and mothers both disliked having to "structure time artificially" with their children, some fathers were really complaining about having to structure child-oriented time. As men, they weren't used to doing this. They were more comfortable integrating their children into adult activities.[7]

Mothers may dislike structuring time with their children for other reasons. Mothers who have been their children's primary caretakers are used to an organic way of relating to children. They know that intimacy and expressions of love are achieved gradually over a long and continuous period of time. Mothers also know that children express what's on their minds only to steadily accessible parents.

Thus many noncustodial mothers were actually suffering from an absence of intimacy with their children. Some noncustodial fathers were suffering from having to do "women's work" for the first time; others were actually enjoying intimacy with their children for the first time.

A noncustodial (or custodial) father received more domestic "help" from others than his (heterosexual) maternal counterpart did.[8] The paternal grandmother, a girlfriend, a new wife, neighbors, and the wives of colleagues were willing to keep him "company" or include him in their own family activities. Neither women nor men were as willing to help or socialize with noncustodial or single custodial mothers and their children.[9]

Dr. Deborah Luepnitz noted that divorced fathers had an easier time of it "domestically" than mothers did "economically." The fathers she studied felt that "divorced parenthood elevated their status"; her mothers believed that it "lowered" theirs. Luepnitz also noted that sole or joint custodial fathers developed a "relaxed style of authority" and fully expected their children to help them with domestic chores. She writes, "It was a little surprising to find that even the father of a seven-year-old conceived of his relationship with his son as a 'partnership.' The father said: 'I'm easier than I would be with two parents in this house. It's he and I; he's my partner in our twosome—so it's important that he love me. I am more reluctant to discipline him. I'm indulgent—but at least I'm aware of it.'"[10]

WHY DO *WOMEN* CONDEMN NONCUSTODIAL MOTHERS?

Why are rather ordinary mothers condemned after they have already been custodially and violently victimized by financial, medical, or legal circumstances? Why are creative or career mothers whose husbands have forced them to choose between their maternal rights and "self-realization" condemned? Why are mothers who have done a good job of bearing or rearing their children for years condemned when they turn custodial responsibility for their children over to willing and competent fathers?

Why are noncustodial mothers condemned by women—especially by traditional custodial mothers? Perhaps such mothers believe that men, including fathers, cannot be trusted with children, that men are not capable of tender, unselfish, and nonviolent behavior toward children under daily domestic stress. Perhaps such mothers (erroneously) believe that father-child violence, including abandonment, neglect, abuse, and incest, occurs only when a mother is not a sufficiently obedient *wife*.[11]

Perhaps traditional custodial mothers condemn noncustodial mothers when they themselves have lost children to kidnapping or disease, when they or close friends have suffered infertility, repeated miscarriages, stillbirths, and adoption difficulties. How dare any woman give up what they and so many other women want so badly?

Perhaps a traditional custodial mother is also afraid of losing her husband to an independent noncustodial mother. Perhaps the rise in male-initiated divorce and the paternal flight from family responsibility is blamed on the reproductively or custodially independent woman.

A traditional mother is also deeply threatened by any mother's custodial victimization. She may find it easier to blame the victim (as too rebellious) and to disassociate herself from such a rebel than to hear what the noncustodial mother is saying.*

Thus traditional mothers may *blame* rather than sympathize with another mother for her noncustodial status. Maybe she *was* too "uppity." Maybe she chose a superficial (male) career over a deep (female) "calling." How dare she champion this misguided choice as "liberating"? How dare she expect sympathy from other mothers?

Women who condemn noncustodial motherhood are also exercising a form of maternal machismo. Woman's right to male protection has been

---

* This is a psychological defense against feeling threatened.

based on her ability to take care of others, both emotionally and economically, under the most adverse conditions. A really macho mother-woman is not supposed to complain or demand any emotional nurturing for herself. According to Pascowicz,

> In the case of single mothers, especially, there seems to be no limit to the supply of blood. The single mother is to comfort, clean, dress, feed, support, love, and entertain her children around the clock and the week and the year. She is to largely ignore her own needs; to avoid the company of men for the sake of preserving her children's morals and not having her own challenged by the court. And then, if she is lucky, if she is good enough at total self-sacrifice, she will be given the privilege of continuing to carry the entire and very real burden of raising her children.[12]

The image of a noncustodial mother is one that signals many forbidden messages: that both the price of remaining within an abusive marriage and the price of single motherhood is simply too high; that an economically overburdened, emotionally starved, and professionally undeveloped mother may be bad for her children; and so on.

It is very painful for a traditional custodial mother to seriously contemplate any of these possibilities.

The noncustodial mother who doesn't present herself as a victim may enrage custodial mothers. *She is seen as assuming a father's prerogative.* ("How dare she when I can't?") How dare any mother behave like a (male) absentee landlord who returns at harvest time to sample the fruits, to have them sent over regularly for her pleasure?[13]

· · · · ·

In the early 1970s Cecily became a noncustodial mother. When we first met, she described herself as having freely chosen her noncustodial status. As we spoke, the freedom of her choice gradually became questionable—to both of us.

"I'd been married for eight years. I had three children, a two-, a four-, and a six-year-old. After countless knock-down-and-drag-out fights, my husband, Eddie, packed his bags and moved out. I remember that he took the kids along to keep him company while he hunted for an apartment. To have five spare minutes to myself was seventh heaven.

"Eddie bought a Harley-Davidson and began careening around the countryside. I couldn't get a rational word out of him. 'What do you expect us to eat?' I said. 'That's not my problem anymore,' he said, and disappeared. Eddie comes from a wealthy family. I wrote to his parents to ask for help in feeding the children. I also wrote to my parents. Eddie's mother wrote and said, 'Sorry, he's over twenty-one, and we're no longer responsible for him.' My parents sent me two hundred and fifty dollars, told me 'there was no more where that came from,' and wished me well. I applied for welfare.

"I'd put off my own education so Eddie could start on his PhD. Now I was facing ten years of single motherhood on welfare. Eddie moved about five hundred miles away with a girlfriend. I called him and said I was on my way to move in with him. I asked him to meet us at the Greyhound bus terminal. Eddie panicked. He agreed to send me a hundred dollars every month and to pay the mortgage on the house.

"A year later Eddie turned up with Harriet. 'Why don't you let the kids live with us? You could go to school full-time.' I went to a therapist. He said I was crazy to consider giving up my children. I told him, 'I want to do something with my life. I've been changing diapers for a thousand years. I always wanted Eddie to do his share. Now he's offering to.' Friends said I'd regret it.

"I finally decided against it. Eddie could study for days without ever 'hearing' the kids. I could never leave them alone with him. If he was working on a paper, he wouldn't smell the house burning. Back then I also believed that mothers were supposed to create a perfect environment for their children. How could I trust the creation of that perfect environment to an emotional cripple and a girlfriend who might not stay?

"Two years went by. Eddie married Harriet. I began what turned out to be a six-year relationship with a woman. Violet made it possible for me to go to graduate school. Violet mothered me. She helped me take care of the kids during the week. She was available to help Eddie and Harriet out on the weekends.

"It was too good to last. Violet loved the children, but after a year she didn't want to shop, cook, clean, and chauffeur them around anymore. Eddie chose this moment to announce he was moving for custody. 'You'll never be able to keep them once a judge knows you're a dyke.'

"Harriet couldn't have any children of her own. She was willing to take care of mine. I'd been living on three hundred dollars a month with the children. Eddie offered me four hundred dollars a month to live on for three years if I let the children live with him.

"I didn't understand exactly why Eddie wanted the children. He's a scientist and a very distant, reclusive man. Maybe he needed 'background' noise to feel like a human being. He needed something to tie him to the earth. Children are perfect for that.

"I think Eddie wanted to punish me for managing to grow educationally, and for becoming a lesbian. It offended his sense of what should happen to a mother abandoned by her husband. Then there was Harriet, who had nothing to do since she finished typing Eddie's dissertation.

"I was a very ambitious mother. I was also becoming professionally ambitious. I resented bitterly not being able to manage both. I know now that if I'd had the money to hire people to clean the house, babysit, and manage the children's schedules, I would have fought to keep them. Instead, I accepted Eddie's deal.

"Eddie began to feel like the one who got robbed. He saw me as scot-free. I traveled. I did what I wanted to do. He was tied down. He had to live with the children during their teenage rebellions. He began to call me 'the bitch who escaped.' He's jealous of the warm relationship that's evolved between me and the children. He feels I've gotten away with murder.

"Eddie calls me an 'unnatural' mother. He says I'm the most despicable example of humankind. If he had his way, I'd never see any of my children again. 'You sold your children to me.' I used to cry when he said this. I was guilty that I'd given my children to such a man.

"I was convinced that I'd be punished for it by losing them. They'd reject me or hate me. For years I never kept any of their pictures around. I guess I was ashamed not to be living with them. There's a whole area of pain and longing I never talk about. I don't think I'm as close to my children as other mothers are. Sometimes I miss my children a lot.

"But I have a career I'm proud of. I've created a whole life for myself. I can go for days without thinking about my children. And they haven't died. And they love me. And I love them."

Three years after our initial interviews, Cecily called to tell me that her college-age children were living with her weekends, vacations, and summers. She said, "Harriet left Eddie. He didn't want to run a large house on his own, especially since the kids were all in college. He 'dumped' them on me. I'm really thrilled to have them. He knows I can afford only a one-bedroom apartment. It is a bit crowded. . . ."

11

The Price of Battle

· · · · · · · · · · · · ·

Mothers Encounter the Psychological and Economic Law

> This story (of my children's kidnapping), and the classic myth about Ceres, whose child Proserpina was stolen by Pluto, god of the underworld, remind me that (this is) a Common Woman theme. The kidnapping of our children is a threat that we all live with, a pain that cuts away at our very hearts, a loss that calls forth every reserve of strength and wit and courage.
>
> —*Anna Demeter,* Legal Kidnapping

Every custodially challenged mother I interviewed felt as if she were the one "on trial." Some mothers also experienced being "on trial" as a *déjà vu* experience. Why?

Are all mothers afraid of being "tried" for maternal imperfection? Do mothers recognize their custodial trials as a private nightmare come true? Or do they also feel like the everywoman "on trial"? Is some kind of collective memory at work here?

For three centuries the women of Europe and colonial America were on trial for witchcraft. On December 5, 1484, Pope Innocent VIII declared a "Holy Inquisition" against "witches"—that is, against those who had "strayed from the Catholic Faith" and through "incantations, spells, and charms" caused "horrid offenses." The European witchcraft trials were based on the

Malleus Maleficarum ("The Witches' Hammer"). The *Malleus* claimed that most witches were women because women are innately inferior and innately predisposed to "evil."

> Women are feebler in the mind and body than men, [women] are intellectually like children; have slippery tongues; are more credulous; have weak memories; it is a natural [female] vice not to be disciplined, but to follow their own impulses without any sense of what is due; [women are] inferior in understanding spiritual things; are vain, and are more subject to carnal lust, which in women, is insatiable. Three general vices appear to have special dominion over wicked women, namely, *infidelity, ambition, and lust.... When a woman thinks alone, she thinks evil.*[1]

Women accused of witchcraft and custodially challenged mothers were both accused of being sexually insatiable and adulterous and of causing male impotence. Both were accused of being too economically or psychologically independent—for women. Some accused witches and custodially victimized mothers were, in effect, accused or condemned because their *husbands* were violent and adulterous or wanted to obtain "cheap" or even "profitable" divorces—that is, they coveted their wives' wealth, property, and intimate relationship to their children.

When a husband custodially challenges a mother, the stage is psychologically set for a witchcraft trial. In a custody battle, the myth of female evil is palpable. Mothers are suspected because they are *women*. A mother's premarital, extramarital, or postmarital activities are assumed, closely examined, and used against her.

As we have seen, custodially challenged mothers are presumed guilty and must prove that they are innocent. In courtrooms, intimations of maternal unfitness assume the bizarre and surreal tones that characterize a witchcraft trial. For example, Miki was accused of "keeping her children's clothing in wicker baskets instead of in a bureau" and of "feeding them strange [health] foods." Nora was accused of "not having a basketball hoop in her driveway." Adele was accused of her children's failure to "live up to their IQ potential" in school.[2]

Judges (and other state officials) treated mothers with barely disguised contempt and suspicion. Maternal testimony rarely carried as much weight as that of the father. Catherine's judge refused to listen to witnesses describe her excellent mothering. However he listened carefully, and at great length, to the description of Catherine's adultery by her father and to all those witnesses who came to praise the "prince/father." More than a third of the mothers challenged in court cases (in my original study) reported this same courtroom experience.[3]

Judges, police officers, and social workers hesitated to offend any "prince." They found it easier to believe that a mother was lying than to believe that a father had committed incest or any other domestic crime.[4] Many mothers were cut short when they tried to introduce evidence of a husband's reign of terror or economic greed. Expert witnesses—psychiatrists, psychologists, and social workers—are our "special investigators." As we have seen, many are anti-mother and pro-father. It is easy for any custodially challenged mother to be "diagnosed" as an unfit mother.[5]

Nora, my interviewee, and Elizabeth Packard, the nineteenth-century woman whom I write about in chapter 1, were both psychiatrically diagnosed as "paranoid" because *they* mistrusted the investigating psychiatrists. According to Nora's court-appointed psychiatrist, "[Nora] maintained a controlling posture in my contacts with her, screening my questions for 'relevance,' and carefully modulating her own emotionality. She evinced an increasingly wary, guarded demeanor. Nora asserted that her position was forthright and accommodating, but that the investigator's behavior was at times biased, unprofessional and offensive."[6]

Nora's court-appointed psychiatrist recommended paternal custody. He also described Nora as "paranoid" about her husband, Lester, who had tried to strangle her and who had also kidnapped their youngest children. "Nora's paranoia about the children's father would be very detrimental to the children's mental health. My opinion is that, even if her fear were founded—which I do not consider it to be—the very fear itself represents a clear, present, active repressive force on the children's emotional development."[7]

As we have seen, many psychiatrists, psychologists, and social workers refused to believe that a father would sexually molest his own child. They felt that any mother who accused a father of incest was crazy, unfit, or herself at fault. A state social worker and court-appointed psychologist actually used the phrase "a mad witch" in referring to Brigette, who accused her ex-husband of incest. Brigette and Arlene, another mother of an incestuously abused daughter, were both described as "paranoid," "rigid," "overprotective," and "obsessed with incest" by court-appointed experts.[8]

Paternal rape and incest were medically established in both cases. Experts nevertheless persuaded the involved judges to continue paternal visitation. According to one expert, "A complete cutting of contact with the natural father could conceivably confuse the child or send a 'message' of negativity. Most importantly, it would traumatize the child. She is strongly attached to her father."[9]

A custody battle challenges a mother's psychological identity and her intimate relationship with her child. As such, it assaults both her perceived status and her deepest sense of experienced self. In addition, it weakens her self-esteem by crippling or prematurely ending her ability to fulfill her maternal obligations.

> **Terry:** A custody battle involves profound fears on a daily basis. The pain and anxiety it generates are intense and never ending. Your whole identity is on the line. Your children are on the line. Your ability ever to love and trust again is at stake.
>
> **Adele:** A custody fight is worse than a nightmare. Each detail in your life becomes distorted, magnified. It feels likely you're the criminal on trial. Even when you win, you've lost your peace of mind forever. You can never take anything for granted again.

Each mother expected to have a primary, lifelong, and uninterrupted relationship with her child, from the moment she decided to get pregnant, knew she *was* pregnant, gave birth, decided to adopt, or met her adopted child for the first time. Such mothers had no reason to anticipate custodial challenges.

All mothers were psychologically stressed by "normal" marriage and motherhood. Many mothers were also psychologically stressed (and weakened) by physically violent husbands. Divorce itself, even from an abusive husband, was psychologically stressful, quite apart from the issue of custody. The burdens of being a single mother were overwhelming, quite apart from the issue of custody.

As we have seen, custodially challenged mothers were continuously and savagely battered by physical, economic, legal, and psychological violence. For example, nearly two-thirds (62 percent) of the mothers were either legally or judicially battered. The remaining mothers were legally abandoned to their husbands' violence.

Mothers were psychologically depressed by how easily fathers could use the law against them and by how hard it was for them to use the law to protect themselves.

> **Lucy:** I kept expecting some judge to say, "Bad man, stop doing that. Don't mistreat your ex-wife and child. You've gone too far." But no judge ever said, "Enough is enough!" No one.
>
> **Winifred:** My life was put on permanent hold by the number of trial postponements. The first time it happened, I asked my lawyer if postponements were allowed. He laughed and told me to get used to it.

It is more psychologically devastating to be tormented or betrayed by an intimate than by a stranger.[10] Many mothers were paralyzed by ex-husbands who continually threatened to destroy or "murder" them psychologically. They couldn't believe that husbands could treat them as strangers or enemies and not as the mothers of their children.[11]

> **Edna:** I lived in the shadow of his rage for so many years. To feel it out in the open against me was even worse than I'd anticipated. He needed to annihilate me totally in order to accept my wanting to leave. He lashed out as if his survival demanded my death.
>
> **Angela:** Just before the first custody trial, Paul said: "Believe me, if you don't give me those kids, I am going to make it so tough for you that either you will kill yourself or you'll be ready for a mental hospital!"[12]

A number of husbands continued to punish their wives even after they had won custody. For example, whenever Norma called to speak to one of her children, her ex-husband adopted a controlled and monotonously "dead" voice. He would remind Norma to be careful, respectful, and brief and to assert, complain, and threaten nothing.

Then, and only then, would he agree to call one of their (brainwashed) children to the phone. Whenever Norma sounded too uppity or lost her emotional "cool," her ex-husband, in a voice devoid of emotion, would say, "Okay, *you* blew it. I'm starting the countdown. One, two, three. You have yourself to blame. Remember, the judge said he can't force them to visit you if they don't want to. Four, five, six. I'm hanging up now. Seven, eight. The phone will be off the hook for the next few hours. Nine. Don't call back for a month if you want my cooperation in seeing the kids. Ten."*

Mothers whose children were paternally kidnapped never stopped suffering. Gradually, with a sharp permanent intake of breath, they began to understand how much their husbands must have hated them or not perceived them as *human*.

> **Bonnie:** It is a terrible thing for a mother to lose her child to Time. Death is an end; Time is a continuum. With death you grieve for days and months. With a live loss you grieve forever. The pain never ends because you can't forget your child is alive and missing.[13]

Mothers were also psychologically tormented when their ex-husbands didn't seem to be suffering economically yet forced them into grave poverty; when ex-husbands refused to assume any of the burdens of child care while they watched mothers stagger beneath that very burden; and when ex-husbands remained sadistic even after they themselves had fallen in love, re-mated, or remarried supportive women while watching mothers go without sexual and emotional intimacy or support of any kind. Mothers were psychologically stressed when other "intimates," such as their own mothers, refused to support them or actively betrayed them.

> **Bonnie:** My mother called me Charlie Manson. She blamed me for everything.
>
> **Sharon:** It was very hard for women to stand by me. My mother was terrified. After all, why did I want out of a marriage when she hadn't left *her* marriage—and her marriage was worse than mine? I think women weren't secure enough to support me.

Friends betrayed mothers by refusing to "get involved," by being unable and unwilling to confirm that unjust victimization was occurring, and by being unable or unwilling to comfort or attend to mothers in a state of mourning.[14]

---

* I listened to three hours of tapes that Norma had made of such phone conversations over a four-year period.

Ella Mae: I experienced custody as a matter of life and death. Friends said I was overreacting, that I could never lose custody. Then, when I lost, they said I was overreacting, too, that lots of mothers lost kids. My daughter wasn't even dead. The battle ate up my core identity. It forced me to question our whole social contract. How could this be allowed to happen? How could friends not understand what was happening?

Terry: My best friend told me to "stop feeling so sorry for yourself. Your kids are better off with their father. He'll pay for their education. They'll have everything you wanted them to have."

MOTHERS' PSYCHOLOGICAL RESPONSE TO PSYCHOLOGICAL AND ECONOMIC STRESS

Approximately half the mothers became welfare recipients upon separation. This meant economic impoverishment, humiliation, and a vigorous enforcement of paternal visitation.

Janet: When I was positive that my husband was sexually molesting my two sons, I made him leave the house. He was having some kind of nervous breakdown. He went to live with his mother. I went on welfare. His union disability benefits were much higher than our welfare benefits. He wouldn't give us any money unless he saw the boys. I refused. Eventually, a judge got him to pay welfare back—but only if he got his visitation.

Emily: The welfare worker was very suspicious of me. "Why should a white educated woman need to go on welfare?" If I did, something must be seriously wrong with me. Maybe I couldn't be trusted with my daughter. Maybe I was crazy. She kept sending investigators over to look for any bank accounts or secret jobs I might have. They grilled me like I was a criminal suspect.

Ninety percent of all fathers paid no alimony; 87 percent of the fathers who battled in court paid no alimony.[15] We must remember that these mothers had been married for an average of nine years, had borne and raised an average of two children, and had performed all the traditional wifely and domestic services. For only room and board, these mothers had performed tasks far beyond the economic reach of most working men. In addition to being unpaid housekeepers and nursemaids, some mothers had earned money during their marriages; some had worked for their husbands as unpaid secretaries, bookkeepers, and accountants; some had brought financial dowries into the marriage.

Judges and husbands consistently overlooked such unpaid and economically invaluable labor. The same judge who removed children from career mothers also told noncareer mothers to get jobs and become economically independent.

Few mothers fought for alimony. Some knew that their ex-husbands couldn't afford it; some mothers felt guilty because they had initiated the divorce. Once the fathers raised custody as an issue, maternal demands for alimony usually ceased. As Lillian Kozak, former chair of the Committee on Domestic Relations for NOW–New York State, pointed out, "When you tell a woman 'You're going to lose your children,' or, 'You stand an even chance of losing your children,' every ounce of fight for her financial rights goes right out the window. Even when she knows it's probably a bluff, she doesn't want to take the chance."

The case of Myrna Labow of Connecticut provides us with a chilling example of what can (custodially) happen to a mother with young children who insists on alimony and child support. Myrna filed for divorce from her wealthy lawyer husband, Ronald, who had adulterously lived apart from her and their children for years. After a *four-year* fight, the court awarded Myrna seventy-five hundred dollars a month in child support and alimony, as well as continued custody of the children. Ronald refused to comply with what the court ordered. Instead, he used every maneuver to weaken his ex-wife economically and psychologically. Finally, when he was seventy-six thousand dollars in arrears, he moved for custody of his son.

Ronald claimed that Myrna was "mentally unfit" because of her "obsession" with money. Several psychiatrists testified for him. One psychiatrist assured the judge that, in his *psychiatric* opinion, Myrna was receiving enough money. Her demand for the court-ordered money was proof of "irrational" behavior. The New York Supreme Court "was critical of [Myrna's] behavior on the witness stand," seeing it as "an obsession with [the] enforcement of her rights." The court awarded Ronald Labow custody of his son. After two more *years* of fighting, the New York Appellate Court reversed this decision.

In my study, 67 percent of the fathers paid no child support. However, fathers at all income levels tended to pay child support more often than alimony. Some child support was paid by 56 percent of the high-income fathers, 40 percent of the middle-income fathers, and 17 percent of the low-income fathers.[16]

Many fathers economically battered the very children they wanted to reclaim. During the 1960s, Lucy received no child support. She went back to court *thirty times* in an attempt to have her court-ordered child support enforced. The fathers who did pay child support felt heroic about doing so. Many overlooked how insuffcient their payments really were. Those fathers who won custody and could economically afford to subsidize maternal visitation refused to do so. *Two* fathers (4 percent) out of all the custodially triumphant fathers helped facilitate maternal visitation.

Sixty percent of the mothers had no professional or marketable skills. They worked immediately or within two years of their separation as non-unionized domestics, factory workers, laborers, clerks, saleswomen, and school aides. Some mothers worked as secretaries. These mothers did not have jobs that promised them a better economic future. They did not enjoy the work they did. They did not learn any on-the-job skills. Most important, their work didn't pay very much.

Mothers under siege were afraid of losing custody because they were (poor) "working" mothers. They were also afraid of losing their jobs because of too many lawyer or court-related absences. Rachel said, "I missed so many teaching days that they suggested I take a leave of absence or risk losing my license. I didn't want to jeopardize my continuity in a good school. I wasn't getting any child support. I couldn't manage on my income alone. But I had to appear in court or at my lawyer's office in order to fight for child support. It was an impossible situation."

None of these mothers was able to "go home again"—at least not with their children. Maternal families of origin lived in another state or were poor, old, or deceased. Parents were also reluctant to take responsibility for daughters and grandchildren. Some maternal grandmothers blamed their daughters for their economic predicaments and counseled reconciliation.

Cecily: My husband's parents, who are very wealthy, said they weren't responsible because he was over twenty-one. My folks sent me a check for two hundred and fifty dollars and wished me luck. I went on welfare.

> **Rae:** My mother thought I was crazy for getting divorced. She wouldn't give me any money to help me keep my daughter with me. She only blamed me when I was forced to give her up for economic reasons. She had no pity for me. She didn't even grant me the right to feel bitter about anything.

Abigail was the only mother who turned to her father for help. She said, "My mother disapproved of my leaving my husband. She didn't think that his beating me up was a good-enough reason to leave. My father hit *her*, and she managed to live with him for twenty years. My mother simply didn't understand my leaving. My father, *who lived alone*, didn't think his nervous system could withstand three grandchildren in the house."

Trials by fire tend to kill, maim, or sear most people rather than to ennoble them. Amazingly, this was not true for mothers *in relation to their children*.[17] However, mothers internalized the hostility directed against them in ways that were painful and self-destructive.

Seventy percent of the mothers under siege never became apparently "dysfunctional." No one human, however, can endure such hostility and stress without becoming demoralized psychologically or medically. Thirty percent of the mothers became dysfunctional in the following ways: Four mothers developed life-threatening illnesses, including adrenal failure, a brain tumor, asthma, and an immune deficiency disease. Eight mothers attempted suicide. Three developed alcoholism, and three had "nervous breakdowns" during or after battling for custody.

Those mothers who resorted to tranquilizers, alcohol, or tears were afraid this meant they were "going crazy" or that their husbands would use it against them. Maureen said, "I began to have anxiety attacks for the first time in my life. They were horrible. But I was more worried that my kids might tell their father, or that it might happen in front of my lawyer."[18]

Custodially challenged mothers reported anxiety, depression, insomnia, and never ending "fatigue"; they spoke of becoming "irritable" or "withdrawn"; they described themselves as temporarily or permanently unable to experience sexual "desire" or orgasm.*

Mothers also reported becoming "silent" or "secretive" about their custodial status as a way to cope with being pariahs. Patricia Pascowicz noted that

---

* Overburdened mothers who are not under custodial siege often report feeling this way.

"absentee" (noncustodial) mothers tended to "disassociate" themselves from other (bad) "absentee" mothers and "denied" or minimized the importance of their social ostracism. They also became secretive."[19]

Some mothers dealt with their feelings of rage and helplessness by minimizing their loss or by "looking on the bright side."[20] However, most mothers never again felt "safe."*

Mothers also suffered a serious loss of (maternal) self-esteem and self-confidence.

Ella Mae: When I heard the judge award custody to my ex-husband, I just crumpled up, sobbing. I had to be pried out of my seat. I stood up with my head down to walk out of the courtroom. The first thing I saw when I looked up was my ex-husband. I leaped on his back like a lion and clawed him. I had my bag, and I hit him with it. I never killed him. It made me wonder what I'd ever kill for. Probably not even to save my own life.

Ellie: Once I realized how easily I could lose Daniel, something in me snapped. If I kept loving Daniel as much as I did, and I ever lost him, I wouldn't survive it. I think I began to protect myself by loving him a little less. He may not know it. But I do. If Daniel ever becomes an unhappy child, I'll always think it was my holding back that did it.

WHAT IS PSYCHOLOGICALLY SPECIFIC TO MATERNAL CUSTODY VICTIMIZATION?

Most heterosexual mothers remained "mateless"—that is, sexually and emotionally celibate or sexually nonorgasmic—during and after their custody battles.[21] They blamed themselves for their own deprivation.

Helen: I wish I could live a normal life, even marry. But who could marry someone with a hollow heart? It's hard for me to have feelings for a new man. Would he do this to me, too? Steal my children?

---

* No one is "safe" in the world. We just don't think about this until we experience a crisis or disaster personally. After being victimized, the feeling of total helplessness is very devastating. It is destructive to oneself and others to mask this feeling.

Beth: I'm a pariah. I'm spoiled human goods; I'm not light company anymore. I'm bitter. It makes people uncomfortable.

Cindy: I really need a deep love. But I cry a lot. I'm moody. I'm thirty-five. I'm not capable of putting up with too many male demands or tricks. Does this mean my love life is over forever?

Does it? Only 17 percent of the heterosexual mothers remarried (or re-mated) before, during, or within two years of battling for custody, while 47 percent of their ex-husbands re-mated or remarried during the same period.[22]

What about having other children? In my study, 29 percent of the fathers genetically reproduced other children before, during, or after the custody battle. An additional 21 percent were actively trying to do so or said they would have children in the future. Thus, 50 percent of the fathers were still engaged in the process or possibility of genetic reproduction. Of the fathers who were not, 25 percent were infertile or had infertile second wives.[23]

Winning custody didn't necessarily satisfy a father's reproductive "needs." Nearly half (47 percent) of the *fertile*, custodially "triumphant" fathers remained reproductively engaged.[24] Why wasn't custody of existing children enough to satisfy their reproductive needs? Some fathers may have had another child in order to "reward" their new wives for taking up the burden of primary child care or as a way of re-experiencing the paternal role with a more obedient wife in tow.

Did *losing* custody depress a father's desire or ability to reproduce himself genetically? To some extent it did. Only 19 percent of these fathers had other children. Nevertheless, 38 percent said they still wanted to have children. Thus 59 percent of the fathers who (initially) lost custody were still psychologically engaged in the practice or in the possibility of genetic reproduction.[25]

What about mothers? *Only 4 percent of the custodially embattled mothers still of childbearing age ever gave birth again.* Whether they won or lost, 96 percent of the mothers did not plan to give birth to or adopt any children in the future.[26] This is similar to Pascowicz's "absentee mothers," only 15 percent of whom ever had children again.[27]

Why did so few mothers ever have children again? The superficial answers are obvious. Custody battles drained mothers emotionally and economically. Also most mothers viewed themselves as psychologically too "old," too "traditional," and too poor ever to have children *with* husbands or, paradoxically, without being married.

Georgia: I never, never wanted to have another child. Losing my son thirteen years ago ruined my life. I have always used birth control or had an abortion since then. I could never face trusting another man or myself enough to risk another custody struggle.

Lucy: For years, my ex-husband kept pulling our son away from me. He ruined my whole experience of mothering. When my son actually went to live with him eight years ago, I knew I would never have a child again.

Cecily: Never again. No way. I already have three I wasn't allowed to keep.

The two mothers who did give birth after losing custody denied the biological blow to their bodies by becoming more psychologically conservative. Both remarried affluent men; both were obsessed with the importance of wifely obedience. They reacted with horror to my questions about whether they would commit adultery, move for a divorce, or seek an independent career in the future.

There are deeper explanations of why mothers did not engage in the reproductive process again. Mothers still felt they *were* the mothers of their (irreplaceable) children. They were unwilling to admit that an irreplaceable child was lost forever and unwilling to risk "failing" another child.

We are so used to maternal victimization that even psychological castration or sterilization remains invisible to us—because *mothers are women.*

Imagine that a *man,* whose psychological identity is based on his ability to earn a living, is accused and convicted of a crime he hasn't committed. Imagine that his wife, children, and parents testify against him, never appear at all, or desert him after his conviction. Imagine that he is forbidden ever to earn a living again—that is, he must develop an entirely new psychological identity. Imagine that he is blamed for being victimized and not permitted to complain of his fate. Imagine that he becomes a social pariah to *women,* the only beings he has ever trusted. Imagine that he "trusts" women less. Imagine that he can therefore never have children again.

It is easy to imagine such a man as one of Stalin's or Hitler's victims, easy to summon up sorrow and pity for what has been done to him. What we cannot do is see this man's imaginary fate as analogous to that of all mothers under custodial siege.

Strictly speaking, no such analogy would be necessary if men and women were exactly alike. They are not. A custody battle would equally threaten and devastate those fathers who have been reared all their lives to be "mothers"; those fathers who became pregnant, gave birth, and were the sole primary caretakers of their children from birth; those fathers already socialized from childhood to blame themselves for any problems their children develop; those fathers who are without familial and financial support during custody battles and without the kind of public fighting spirit and support networks a legal or public battle requires; and those fathers who are then ostracized for being forced into a noncustodial parental role.

In rage, grief, wisdom, and protest, mothers "closed up their wombs." Mothers didn't have any more children because the experience of having to battle for custody was psychologically castrating. Many mothers described feelings of bodily mutilation.

> **Melanie:** It's like taking part of your body away from you. No matter how happy you are, there's a part of you that's missing. You may have to live with a longing and an emptiness, as if your arm has been ripped off. Always you'll feel your missing arm: your phantom child.
>
> **Ellie:** If you miss a year of your child's childhood, it's gone forever. Being separated from my son felt like a limb was amputated. I had terrible nightmares about bodily mutilation and family massacres.
>
> **Nora:** When my children were kidnapped, it felt like a vulture had ripped out two still-lactating breasts, leaving two huge, gaping holes.
>
> **Dorothy:** It's just the worst thing you could ever imagine. To me it was like my entire family was wiped out in a wreck. Everybody I ever cared about was gone all at once. But they were alive. I just couldn't see them. And I was alive, too, but somehow I was dead. I was missing some vital parts.[28]

12

The Mother-Lawyer Relationship

. . . .

"You won't lose them," [the lawyer] said. "Don't worry."

"I daresay I won't, but I don't like the thought that I might. It's bad enough having to worry about them dying without this as well."

—*Margaret Drabble,* The Needle's Eye

I warn women constantly not to hire an attorney if he's divorced or if he's in the middle of a divorce. I've heard too many stories of how female clients were screwed royally by lawyers who were acting out against their own wives.

—*Lillian Kozak, former chair, NOW–New York State,*
Domestic Relations Task Force

ACCORDING TO MOTHERS, WHAT DID A "GOOD" LAWYER DO?[1]

In general, mothers described 45 percent of their lawyers as "good." This means that almost 50 percent of lawyers were positively rated according to their harshest critics—but that almost 50 percent were negatively rated. Seventy-four percent of these lawyers were men; 26 percent were women. According to my mother interviewees, a "good" lawyer was

1. Emotionally supportive, consistently patient, and never verbally humiliating;

2. Accessible during office hours and nonoffice hours, especially for emergencies;

3. Able to distinguish between stress-induced "nervousness" and chronic "mental illness";

4. Hard-working, knowledgeable, willing to explain what was happening, and able to "hear" maternal requests;

5. Economically reasonable or willing to wait to be paid; and

6. Dedicated to mothers on principle or to the particular mother.

Adele, Tracey, and Leslie all lost one or more children to paternal kidnapping or brainwashing. Here is how they described their "good" lawyers:

> **Adele:** My lawyer was an angel. He was my father's friend. He knew me since I was a child. He was also part of my ex-husband's professional circle. He broke with that circle for my sake. He took a very minimal retainer. My lawyer didn't just fight for custody. He got me decent child support, alimony, and a cash settlement. He convinced the judge to let me move away. There was nothing he could do when the children decided to live with their father anyway.

> **Tracey:** My lawyer was my friend before she became my lawyer. I felt guilty for leaving my husband. I was willing to give up everything but my children. She kept reminding me of how abusive he'd really been and how he'd turned my eldest child against me. She refused to take my case unless I'd let her fight for child support, alimony, and half the cash value of the house.

> **Leslie:** I hired my lawyer right after the kidnapping. For years, she stayed a hundred percent behind me. I paid her very well, but she did things that money can't buy. She let me call her at home. When she saw me get psychologically shaky, when I couldn't get out of bed mornings, she just waited for me to recover my strength. She always treated me like I was a good mother.

"Good" lawyers were limited by their clients' poverty, by the domestic *law* in America, by the individual judges before whom they argued their cases, and by a husband's capacity for physical, psychological, and economic violence.

ACCORDING TO MOTHERS, WHAT DID A "BAD" LAWYER DO?

A "bad" lawyer was

1. Overbearing, impatient, self-important, and verbally humiliating;

2. Inaccessible in general and inaccessible for emergencies during or after office hours;

3. Incompetent without knowing it or being able to admit it;

4. Lazy, overcommitted elsewhere, and/or cowardly;

5. Unwilling or unable to explain the limitations of the law or to use the law creatively in order to deal with such maternal concerns as disruptive or abusive paternal visitation, nonpayment of child support, brainwashing, and kidnapping;

6. Money-hungry or contemptuous of maternal "demands" in view of maternal poverty; and

7. Sexist, sadistic, and/or against alimony or sole maternal custody on principle.[2]

Mothers were initially comfortable with their self-important male lawyers. This changed as each lawyer became inaccessible—without producing any results. Many lawyers (wrongfully) assumed that mothers always win sole custody and that fathers aren't serious about custody, but they only used it as leverage to obtain economic or visitation gains.

Catherine and Rose both had nice lawyers who were custodially inexperienced, underestimated what was needed in order to win, and, for different reasons, were consistently underprepared.

Catherine: My lawyer was sympathetic and supportive. A friend recommended him. He turned out to be a tax lawyer, not a divorce lawyer. He handled my case very badly. He thought I was obviously such a supermother that we didn't have to line up too many witnesses. He encouraged me to get a job and move out of our bedroom. He said no judge would use this against me in a modern courtroom. He was wrong. In court they said I had completely washed my hands of the house and the children.

Rose: My lawyer didn't have the right papers prepared for our first day in court. He was also late for our first court hearing. Actually, he wasn't around very much. Years later I discovered that his wife had been dying at that time. Why didn't he tell me he couldn't handle my case? Why didn't he recommend someone else?

Once a lawyer had determined that a mother wanted her children *more* than she wanted an equitable (or equal) distribution of marital assets, he often appeared puzzled or *annoyed* by her urgent and continuing requests for child support and alimony.

Cheryl: My first lawyer kept pleading with me not to expect any child support. He said my husband didn't earn enough money. But I had no job. I was supporting my daughter. I was facing welfare. My lawyer didn't seem to understand that my husband's earnings were a fantastic sum compared to my zero earnings. Did I have to be married to a millionaire in order for my lawyer to feel justified in going after what I really needed?

Sally's ex-husband kept spontaneously dropping in on his children and then not showing up for regularly scheduled visitation. Sally's professional and social schedule was constantly invaded, which further weakened her in terms of the custody struggle. "My lawyer pooh-poohed what my husband was doing. He said there was nothing that could be done *legally* about it anyway. I said, 'What about charging him money for lateness or depriving him of the next visit?' My lawyer got very angry. He asked if I thought my private life was more important to my kids than seeing their father was. He said he wanted no part of driving a father away from his kids."

Maureen hired a "bomber." This is the name for a very expensive lawyer with a reputation for taking rich husbands (or wives) "to the cleaners." Maureen gladly suffered his supercilious and authoritarian style. She was more troubled by his fee schedule. "He knows what he's doing, but he's a real bastard. He has me adhere to a very strict fee schedule. When I can't meet a payment deadline, he does exactly what he told me he'd do: he'll stop submitting papers and he wont take my phone calls until I'm paid up."*

Sixteen percent of the mothers challenged in courtrooms were challenged by ex-husbands who were *themselves* lawyers or who were politically, professionally, or personally well connected to their lawyers or the presiding judge. In these cases, no mothers' lawyers had any incentive to risk offending a male power network. Mothers were powerless and relatively poor. Lawyers are not trained (or rewarded) for risking their careers for the sake of abstract justice on behalf of strangers.[3]

> **Ella Mae:** My lawyer was enthusiastic until he took a good look at the lineup in the courtroom. He told me not to get my hopes up too high. He said that the judge had once been a partner in my ex-husband's current law firm. He said that any judge, but especially this one, would view my ex-husband as the more desirable parent. My husband was local. He was a lawyer. I was living in another state. I was a nobody. My lawyer really threw the fight. He had to stay in that town after I left.

Fathers' lawyers routinely and falsely accused mothers of "sexual promiscuity" or "mental illness." *Mothers'* lawyers believed or became "worried" about such accusations. For example, Carrie's husband had her psychiatrically imprisoned and then used her hospitalization as proof of her mental illness. Carrie said, "My husband's lawyer kept yelling that I was a hospitalized schizophrenic who was dangerous to my children. He said I hated my husband and punished him by having so many children, that my fertility was part of my being out of touch with reality. I could understand it if my lawyer needed the facts to refute my husband's accusation. But my own lawyer began to believe the accusation was true. He treated me as if I were a little bit crazy."

Lucy was accused by her ex-husband's lawyer of being an "illegitimate" child. He kept threatening to confront her with (nonexistent) "pictures." Lucy said, "Suddenly my lawyer yelled at me for wearing sheer stockings to court. That's just about the only kind of stockings I had. They're comfortable and they look nice, but he told me I was presenting myself as a whore.

---

* If a mother isn't rich herself or doesn't have a rich husband, she will never meet a "bomber."

He also kept asking me about the pictures as if they really existed and I was lying to him."

Several mothers described lawyers who tried to talk them out of alimony "for their own good" and who urged them to consider joint custody "for their own good." Linda's lawyer kept pointing out all the advantages of joint custody: "My lawyer was a noncustodial mother herself. That may be fine for her. It's not what I wanted. She kept at me. She told me I wasn't doing my kids a favor by keeping them from their father or by staying at home full time myself. I can't help but think that another lawyer would have fought harder for what I wanted and deserved."

ARE THESE "BAD" LAWYERS REPRESENTATIVE OF MOST LAWYERS?

In her study of joint custody, Dr. Deborah Luepnitz found that half her maternal interviewees thought their lawyers had served them incompetently. Luepnitz's maternal interviewees, like my own, reported being treated with contempt and derided for asking too many questions. They had a hard time finding lawyers who would return their urgent phone calls, let alone give them moral support.

> My first lawyer was just horrible. I was getting absolutely nothing [economic]. The day I was supposed to close on the house, I decided to call another lawyer. He read through the papers and asked me if I had been caught in adultery because he had never seen such a terrible settlement. I was getting $750.00 out of a property worth $14,000.00. [My husband] had forged my name on a mortgage, and the first lawyer refused to fight for me.
>
> My lawyer in January had done nothing about the fact that my ex has never made a single child support payment. He assured me that [my husband] does have to pay, but nothing gets done. [He] doesn't return phone calls or even answer my letters. It makes you feel like you're invisible—that there is nothing you can do to make the law work for you.[4]

DOES EVERYONE HAVE TROUBLE WITH DOMESTIC LITIGATION?

It is important to note that most poor people can't afford lawyers. Legal self-defense costs a lot of money in America. On June 1, 1981, the U.S. Supreme

Court ruled that indigent parents (mothers) were no longer entitled to "free" legal aid in cases of wife battering, marital rape, incest, child abuse, and nonpayment of child support—nor were they entitled to this aid in custody battles.[5]

Divorce lawyers in general are ambivalent about practicing domestic law. Unless a millionaire husband (or wife) is involved, domestic litigation is poorly and slowly paid, never ending, frustrating, and without status.

Some divorce lawyers therefore "take on" a spouse as if he or she were IBM or General Motors. Such a fighting spirit is often effective in terms of protecting economic and property interests (a house or stocks and bonds, for example). However, both husbands and wives report that such an approach often escalates rather than de-escalates a divorce and custody battle and that it is ineffective in achieving custodial, economic, and visitation arrangements that either last or work.

Nevertheless, despite a unique set of biases against fathers who want custody, fathers still have less trouble with their lawyers than mothers do. Fathers have more money to hire lawyers than mothers do. They also have something "in common" with their lawyers—even if it is just being male and married, male and divorced, or male and fathers. Both male and (especially) female lawyers are more "sympathetic" to fathers than to mothers.[6]

In Luepnitz's study, her paternal interviewees all reported "positive" experiences with their lawyers. Several of her fathers cited their lawyers as important members of their support networks. One father, the owner of a company, spoke to his lawyer every morning for fifteen minutes "just for moral support" for the first three weeks of his custody battle. Many of Luepnitz's fathers found lawyers among their colleagues, peers, or relatives. "Even the father with the ninth grade education who worked as a fork lift operator had a lawyer who was a friend. They belonged to the same rifle club."[7]

Unlike fathers, most housewives and traditional mothers have no previous experience with lawyers or are used to dealing with their *husbands'* lawyers, accountants, and insurance brokers. Most housewives and mothers do not have independent professional or personal friendships with people who happen to be lawyers, nor are they trained to choose such experts carefully, to deal with them effectively, to stand up to them assertively, or to leave them when it seems appropriate. Most housewives and mothers have no old-girl-network power chips to ensure consumer-controlled legal representation. In fact, women are sometimes at risk when they behave like informed legal consumers—that is, "too pushy."

But miscommunication is a two-way street. Most lawyers have as much trouble understanding their maternal clients as mothers have in making themselves understood. There are structural and psychological reasons for this.

WHAT KINDS OF TROUBLE DO MOTHERS AND CUSTODY LAWYERS HAVE WITH EACH OTHER?

Traditional lawyers are often sexist—that is, they view women as inferior, dependent, naive, and in need of male "protection." This chivalry applies to a lawyer's mother, sister, daughter, and wife, as long as his wife isn't suing him for divorce, alimony, or custody.*

If a woman is not a lawyer's blood relative (or someone whom a lawyer's blood relative cares about), he is under no *familial* obligation to "protect" her from the consequences of her vulnerability. On the contrary: if she is a stranger, a member of a despised class or race, or sexually or economically too uppity for a woman, the lawyer himself may wonder about her right to custody.

In addition to—or precisely because of—such unspoken structural and ideological biases, the most serious miscommunication exists between the nicest of male lawyers and their nicest women clients. The feminist philosopher Eleanor Kuykendall describes one of the major double binds that *all* women face:

> Women, like schizophrenics, receive contradictory messages about the kinds of sentences they may speak or write in order to be taken seriously. Women are caught in a linguistic dilemma requiring them to speak and write nonassertively in order to be perceived as women, but requiring them to speak and write assertively to be taken seriously as persons. [Women] identify themselves as women when they utter such sentences as "I think that perhaps what we want is to be strong women," or else they cannot be taken seriously as women, because if they utter directly assertive sentences like "We want to be strong women," it is inappropriate for their gender.[8]

---

*Antitraditional or antifamily lawyers are often sexist, too.

Imagine how double binds and "contradictory messages" operate between a mother under custodial siege and her lawyer. First, it is important to understand that mothers suffer their catch-22s without awareness and without being able to articulate them.

For example, a traditional mother is not socialized to fight *against* her husband and/or in a *public* arena. When a mother does this, she experiences herself as out of context. Her lawyer may experience her as too nervous, too indecisive, and too ambivalent.[9]

Many traditional mothers say one thing when they mean the very opposite.*

For example, a mother may actually smile because she is angry. She may issue orders as self-denigrating suggestions or complaints. ("I know I don't know anything about this, and I'm probably being silly, but don't you think you might do it this way and not that way—for my sake?")

Such double-message emotional behavior is unprofessional. It may indeed remind a lawyer of his wife or mother. He may respond accordingly. ("Since you don't know what you're talking about—you even admit it yourself—why don't you just leave everything to me and not bother me about it anymore?") His response is also unprofessional.

As a traditional mother grows uneasy or outraged by her lawyer's inaccessibility, neglect, or incompetence, she may complain about him privately to her women friends. She will complain to her lawyer very slowly and indirectly.

A traditional mother acts as if her lawyer is her husband. She doesn't want to go through a double divorce, one from her husband or children and simultaneously one from her first lawyer. She acts as if her sexual or maternal reputation will be ruined if she behaves "polygamously" with lawyers.

Beyond the economic realities involved, mothers find it psychologically hard to move on to a second lawyer. Amber, a nontraditional woman but a traditional mother, described her fears about leaving her first lawyer: "What if he won't give me my money back? What if he won't transfer my papers if I don't pay him in full first? What if he delays my case because he's angry I've left him? What if he convinces my new lawyer that I'm nuts? What if I leave

---

* They are supposed to behave this way in a family setting. When they do so with strangers in public, it is not equivalent to a male or female professional's choosing to behave this way for some public gain.

him and no one else will take my case in the middle? What if the second lawyer doesn't trust me because I've already left one lawyer?"

Mothers under custodial siege are emotionally very needy. Some male lawyers refer their women clients to psychotherapists; some routinely allot a certain quota of time for "hand-holding." Some lawyers have affairs with their female clients.

Most male lawyers deal with their overly needy women clients by finding ways of keeping them at bay. They adopt brusque, authoritarian, and supercilious styles. Some lawyers terrorize women clients into soft-spoken submissiveness as the price they must pay for even limited access to their own lawyers.

A traditional male lawyer is unhappy—that is, he feels impotent—when he fails to protect a helpless woman client from male violence. He may therefore minimize the violence or blame it on her.

When a father kidnapped a child, lawyers *never* blamed themselves, the law, the judge, or even the father-kidnapper. If pressed, they blamed the mother for something she did or failed to do, or they essentially told her to "relax and enjoy it."

Nora's husband kidnapped their two youngest sons; Helen's ex-husband kidnapped their only child.

> **Nora:** My lawyer told me not to worry. He said: "We know he really loves the boys. So your sons must be all right." But I (the mother) thought: Doesn't my lawyer understand that kidnapping is a violent crime, undertaken only by a very angry and distraught father? What if my husband is so distraught he just fails to take ordinary precautions against all the dangers that this world offers to little children? His state of fury and disorganization must be frightening, if not actually abusive to our sons.

> **Helen:** I had two legal aid attorneys, a woman and a man. They both were blind to my ex-husband's psychotic behavior. They were overworked, but they also had experience with what a violent man can do. They didn't really take it into account. They didn't fight hard enough to have his visitation supervised or ended. When I yelled at them, they said that even the judge's order of protection hadn't prevented it from happening. They told me to be grateful for what they had done. And that I didn't even have to pay them.

When a traditional mother lurches unsteadily into her version of "male" assertiveness or persistence, her lawyer experiences her as unpleasant, unrealistic, or even crazy. ("I've submitted all the papers. I told her we have to wait for the judge to act. What does she expect me to do? Come over in the middle of the night and shoot her husband?")

Traditional lawyers, like everybody else, expect an ideal mother to be assertive only to help her husband or to save her children's lives. Otherwise, she is not expected to "fight like a man"—that is, to win by any means.

What if a mother and her lawyer both think her child's life is genuinely endangered by paternal custody but she decides that fighting too hard will only hurt her child more? What if her lawyer therefore decides that she doesn't really want custody or isn't a "good enough" mother and therefore stops working on her case—and blames her for losing custody?

What if a mother believes that her child's life is endangered by paternal custody but her lawyer disagrees with her assessment? What if he thinks she's fighting for her own selfish reasons and therefore isn't a "good enough" mother and he stops working on her case—and blames her for losing custody?

What if a custodially challenged mother decides to fight like a man—that is, to win? What if she actually tells her lawyer that she wants her husband out of her life for good?

One thing that may happen is that her own lawyer will view her as a potential Medea.

Ida's husband paid no child support, exercised visitation only when it was "convenient" for him, and alternately threatened to kidnap or abandon his child completely. Ida said, "My lawyer kept checking me out to see if I was against my daughter's having a relationship with her father. I once said I thought it would be a lot easier on me and probably better for my daughter not to see her father. My lawyer bawled me out and warned me that such an attitude was legally inappropriate and made him personally uncomfortable besides. He could understand my wanting to fight for child support but he couldn't go along with my desire to avenge myself against my husband by interfering with visitation."

When a father talks about getting a mother out of the picture, his lawyer may think he must be referring to an unfit mother. Why else would a father go so far as to fight for custody or deprive his children of their mother?

Most lawyers warned mothers not to belittle their children's fathers at home, no matter what they did or failed to do. Lawyers warned them not to manipulate their children into taking sides and not to use nonpayment of child support—or even male domestic violence—as an excuse to prevent paternal visitation from taking place.

This is very different from what male lawyers tell fathers to do. Lawyers expect men to "fight like men"—that is, to win by any means possible. Lawyers advise fathers to take full advantage of their superior economic status to exert psychological and judicial leverage. Lawyers do not forbid fathers to turn children against mothers.*

Male lawyers are not *surprised* or psychologically threatened by their male clients' physical or psychological terrorization of their ex-wives. This is because they identify with or understand what another man (or father) may be feeling. Sharon described a three-year legal ordeal. Her male lawyer, not her husband, delivered the emotional *coup de grâce*:

> My husband swore to destroy me. He nearly did. When the jury finally announced that I had the right to be divorced, I didn't even know who was the plaintiff and who was the defendant. All along I felt that I was the one on trial, that I was the one defending myself. My ex-husband broke down in tears when this verdict was rendered.
>
> My lawyer said to me: "You bitch, if you rub his nose in it right now, I'll kill you." I didn't do anything. I couldn't even breathe at that moment. I just wanted to hold myself together and not cry in front of my lawyer and those other men.[10]

Most male lawyers don't identify with their female clients' *husbands* as shockingly as this lawyer did. However, most lawyers—male and female—are not often traditional parents. They do not identify or empathize with traditional mothers. A lawyer may feel "protective" toward a properly "feminine" mother, but lawyers do not see themselves in her.

---

* Such lawyers do not tell mothers to take full advantage of their preexisting psychological intimacy with their children. They unconsciously expect mothers to bypass exercising any (unfair) advantage.

HOW DO LAWYERS EXPECT MOTHERS UNDER CUSTODIAL SIEGE TO BEHAVE?

Many lawyers expect mothers to be ideal, not merely good or "good enough." They expect an ideal mother to provide a good father for her children—whether one exists or not. (Hence, don't tell your kids their father won't pay child support.)

If a custodially challenged mother displays genuine regret about the divorce, blames herself as well as her husband for it, feels strongly that her husband has an inviolate right to his children no matter what, refuses to destroy his paternal reputation, refuses to fight for economic rights harder (or as hard as) she does for custody, refrains from annoying her lawyer—and even manages to express her gratefulness to him—no matter what he has or hasn't been able to do, then and only then will she be seen as worthy of her male legal protector.[11]

Marta hired four successive lawyers within a six-year period. Unlike most of my maternal interviewees, she was able to borrow money to hire some really well-recommended and expensive lawyers. Otherwise, her story is typical.

"After ten years of marriage and three children, my husband suddenly excluded me from his life. He said he'd grown beyond me. He began to exclude me from his vacations with the children. He closed our joint bank accounts, canceled my credit cards, and ordered me to leave our home. I had done nothing wrong. Why was this happening?

"I borrowed money from my brother-in-law and hired the most expensive lawyer I could find. This lawyer cautioned me not to move out of the house no matter what happened. If I did, I could be accused of abandoning my children. My husband started bringing women home. He began to curse me in front of the children. He also threatened me and hit me.

"My lawyer said I had to 'sit tight' until our first hearing. Why couldn't he get me a household allowance? Why couldn't he get my husband to stop mistreating me? Why couldn't he get my husband to leave the house? Why couldn't he arrange for me to move out with my children and then pay child support until our first hearing?

"Two years went by without a hearing. In the beginning, my lawyer saw me once a week. The first six months he always returned my calls. After that I could never get him on the phone. Whenever I did, he sounded angry and said he had no time for small talk with me.

"Three years later, my husband served *me* with divorce papers. I borrowed more money from my brother-in-law. I hired another lawyer. He took my money and also never returned my phone calls. He finally called me with an offer. I could have the house if I gave up custody of the children. 'You could sell that house and live off the proceeds for ten years—if you're careful.'

"What kind of mother sells her children for a piece of real estate? What kind of lawyer repeats such an offer so matter-of-factly?

"My lawyer knew I was economically desperate. He told me that most fathers don't end up keeping their children. 'You're always complaining about money,' he yelled. 'Well, here it is. If I were you, I'd take it.'

"I was losing weight. I wasn't sleeping. I looked ten years older than my husband. I borrowed money again, this time from one of my husband's relatives, to hire my third lawyer. I wanted to live with my children, and I wanted the money to support them. My husband admitted earning two hundred and fifty thousand dollars on his last income tax return. He owned four houses and had many investments.

"My third lawyer's 'strategy' consisted of letting the judge see how motherly and ladylike I was. I wanted a more aggressive strategy. I wanted my lawyer to subpoena my husband's accountant, stockbroker, fund raiser, and executive secretary. How else could the judge appraise my husband's income and assets? How else could I prove that this man couldn't be home with the children, as he claimed, if he was out at meetings every night?

"My lawyer didn't do any of this. He thought I'd appear too conniving if I concentrated on my husband's money rather than on just getting the children. In fact, he did a turnaround. He warned me to be careful of what I said about my husband. He said it might hurt his career or turn the judge against me.

"This trial is about giving him the legal right to take away my career or identity as a mother. But I'm not supposed to defend myself by telling the truth because it might hurt my husband's career!

"The judge granted my husband sole custody of all our children as 'the more economically stable parent.' I was ordered to move out of the house. I was awarded enough money to live on for three years. 'Be grateful,' my lawyer said. 'Other women don't get anything.' After years of marriage, it turns out I wasn't the 'better half' after all. I was only the family servant who could be pensioned off.

"I tried to hire my fourth lawyer. He said I couldn't win an appeal unless my husband's economic circumstances had worsened. 'Get on with your own life,' he advised me. 'You have a golden opportunity to start over.' I'm forty-eight years old. I work in a boutique. I do needlepoint. I get up every morning. But my heart isn't in it.

"In four years my children have never once stayed overnight with me. 'Oh, Ma,' they say, 'you don't have enough room for us.'

"I told them that the American Constitution has no room for mothers in it."

13

The Mother-Judge and
Father-Judge Relationships

....

Every judicial decision wielded a terrifying amount of power over each mother. Every mother was judged not by a jury of her peers, but ultimately by one judge. (Of course, the same is true for each father, too).

Were my maternal interviewees judged in representative ways? To answer this question, I first surveyed judicial trends in contested custody throughout the nineteenth and twentieth centuries (see chapters 1 and 2).

In this chapter, I focus on judicial decisions in three major areas. I do not discuss every judicial decision on record, nor do I cite all the exceptions to the major trends. I concentrate on decisions that are representative of most custody contests or that reveal the values of patriarchal law quite clearly.

Most trial court decisions are not easily available. Cases that are *appealed* are reported in legal journals. Appeals court judges never meet the interested parties. Therefore, trial court judges have an enormous amount of unmonitored power and information. They are the only judges who observe, question, and draw conclusions about plaintifs, defendants, and witnesses.[1]

Judicial decisions vary from judge to judge, state to state, and year to year. Judicial decisions also vary for the *same* judge over time. Judicial language is sometimes illiterate, sometimes literary. Judicial thinking ranges from dull to learned to brilliant. Judicial decisions can be morally insane, radically compassionate, and sometimes practical. They are rarely just.

Nonverbal judicial behavior—the thunderously raised voice and eyebrow, the disbelieving smirk, the bored or angry face—is never conveyed in the written judicial order. Neither are the full or true stories of the embattled parents.

Most mothers under custodial siege are rarely "heard" by judges. This is the importance of my in-depth interviews. The fact that my interviewees were "good enough" mothers and still lost 70 percent of the time allows us to imagine all that is missing or overlooked in other judicial orders.

Judicial decisions are shaped by many factors—for example, by the judicial mediocrity encouraged by political patronage, by the low prestige and financial remuneration of domestic law, or by overcrowded court calendars. Decisions are also shaped by the most blatant and unchecked sex, race, and class biases.

Most judges have mainly been white men who have never taken care of a child. The token number of women and black judges have probably not been full-time practicing mothers either. If they were, they were not trained to value motherhood over a career.*

Most judges undervalue women, devalue mothers (doing mothers' work), and overvalue men, especially as (symbolic) fathers. The National Judicial Education Program published the results of a study which confirmed that, in the past, judges were biased against female *lawyers*, as well as against female plaintiffs and defendants. Eighty-six percent of the women lawyers in the study reported that their peers made hostile remarks or degrading jokes against women; 66 percent said that judges did the same thing.[2]

Many judges did not identify with women in the courtroom. Judges also have different standards of behavior for men and women in general and for their courtroom behavior in particular. For example, judges are not comfortable when mothers under custodial siege are surrounded by supporters—especially by other women. Real "ladies" are supposed to arrive in court alone, sustained by their own ideal motherhood.

During a trial a mother must be moderate in her display of emotions; she must also, on patriarchal cue, display the right emotions. "Hysteria" must be avoided, as must coldness, anger, and verbal or nonverbal expressions of hostility toward anyone. Women must not curse or lose their tempers.

---

* *Sometimes* women and blacks are "harder" on women and blacks than men and whites are—when they have the token opportunity and unspoken mandate to behave like white men.

For example, Tennessee Judge Steve Daniel jailed Sheila Porter, a pregnant mother, for twenty-two hours after she had uttered the word *hell* during her custody hearing. Judge Daniel criticized Porter for her "construction site language" and awarded her ex-husband custody of their four children.[3]

As we saw in chapter 2, judges were custodially prejudiced against career mothers and against sexually or politically active mothers. They were also custodially prejudiced against working or impoverished mothers.[4]

IN MY STUDY, HOW MANY JUDGES ORDERED CHILDREN INTO PATERNAL CUSTODY? WHAT KINDS OF FATHER WON CUSTODY?

In my study, 70 percent of the thirty-seven judges ordered children into paternal custody.*

As we have seen, 59 percent of the judicially successful fathers physically abused their wives; 45 percent embarked on brainwashing campaigns; 36 percent kidnapped their children. No child support was paid by 42 percent of the judicially successful fathers; 77 percent paid no alimony. Of the judicially successful fathers, only 12 percent were previously involved in primary child care.

Wife abuse, nonpayment of child support, brainwashing, and kidnapping were not necessarily considered proof of paternal unfitness. Judges upheld the views of 59 percent of the fathers who viewed mothers as uppity and 57 percent of those who viewed mothers as punishably "sexual." Attorney Laurie Woods, formerly the director of the National Center for Women and Family Law, noted that "the same judges who overlook or refuse to see any connection between a man hitting his wife and his fitness as a father have no trouble seeing a connection between a woman smoking marijuana or living out of wedlock or pursuing a career and her maternal fitness."

THE JUDICIAL AND LEGISLATIVE DEVALUATION OF MOTHERS AND MOTHERHOOD

In chapters 1 and 2, we saw that, in a contest, either mothers had no right to custody or visitation or they could lose whatever right they had if the judges viewed them as immoral. The maternal presumption (or the "tender years"

---

* Of the judicial decisions, 62 percent took place in the Northeast; 38 percent in the Midwest, West, South, and Canada. See chapter 4.

doctrine, which holds that children need their mothers or mother-figures when they are very young) was always interpreted as one of several judicial options to be exercised in the child's "best interests." The maternal presumption was never interpreted as a maternal right. In fact, the child's "best interests" were usually seen as synonymous with *paternal* rights.[5]

From 1900 to 1950, presumably the height of the maternal presumption, *moral* mothers routinely lost custody of their older children in contests. Judges seemed to think that a male child over five years of age no longer required his mother's tenderness. Girls tended to require their moral mother's or a moral mother surrogate's tenderness somewhat longer.[6]

Until the 1920s, the most moral of mothers and the most tender of children were not entitled to any child support. Since the 1950s, the maternal presumption has not only been viewed as secondary to the child's "best interests" but also viewed as "sexist." By the late 1970s, two-thirds of American states rejected it as a customary presumption.

Between 1950 and 1986, judges continued to view white married mothers as custodially worthy—until they committed an immoral act or became dependent upon welfare. The mother on welfare is married to the entire state legislature, each member of which views her as a lazy, promiscuous cheat. The sum allotted to her for mothering is an exact measure of the state's devaluation of mothers, mothering, and children.

Judges usually ordered child-support payments that matched the state's economic valuation of motherhood. Judges and legislators did not worry about child-support *enforcement*. (If necessary, a mother could always turn to welfare.) Judges were reluctant to award any alimony, let alone support that was adequate or long-term. "Let mothers work—it's what the feminists want."

Joint distribution of property didn't mean that wives got 50 percent of everything. On the contrary. Where large amounts of money were involved, wealthy men hired expensive lawyers to delay judicial action and expensive accountants to hide their assets. Above all, they purchased time with which to terrorize and humble their wives and to persuade judges that their wives had grossly overestimated how much they were really worth.

Some lawyers argued that a wealthy father, by definition, would be the better custodial parent. Lawyers had no trouble persuading most judges that a wealthy man's wife had *already* been well subsidized up to the time of divorce, that she was lazy, parasitic, and financially greedy. A wife (of any age) was viewed as perfectly capable of working—especially if she was not going to be the custodial parent, or her children were already grown, or her grown children were already amply provided for by their wealthy father.[7]

Judges and legislators were more willing to divide *children* "jointly" than to divide a man's business "jointly." Judges, lawyers, and legislators had no trouble with devising tortuous "comparable worth" formulas—in the service of the *male* acquisition and retention of income, assets, and property. They had, and still have, a great deal of trouble dividing a "man's" money in half and with any "comparable worth" formulas in the service of the *female* acquisition or retention of income, assets, or property.

Despite sentimental lip service given to the sacredness of the mother-child bond, most judges take female mothering for granted and view it as an easy job. Judges express their devaluation of *mothers'* doing mothers' work whenever they decide that past maternal performance can be canceled by later "uppity" behavior.[8] Maternal labor is devalued whenever judges award children to stepmothers or paternal grandmothers, as if any female surrogate is the same as the mother. It is devalued whenever judges decide that fathers who have done no primary parenting in the past are now equally fit parents.

As I have noted, in 1975 New York Judge Guy Ribaudo awarded sole custody of two children to their father, Dr. Lee Salk. It was clear that Kersten Salk, not Dr. Salk, had reared the children from birth "without the aid of a governess" and that Dr. Salk would undoubtedly require the aid of a "third party" housekeeper-governess were he to gain sole custody. Kersten was not accused of being an "unfit" mother. The court used "an affirmative standard" to decide which parent was "better fit" to guide the "development of the children and their future."

> It is the judgment of this court that permanent custody of both infant issue is awarded to the father Dr. Lee Salk. . . . Since the birth of the children, Dr. Salk has exhibited a vast interest in the various stages of the children's development, his interaction with the children is not due solely to the fact that the father is a child psychologist. Dr. Salk is indeed a very bright, essentially stable person whose ability to conceptualize accurately and appropriately is quite superior—a fact which is reflected in turn in a high degree of competency to render proper and realistic judgments and skill in mastering effectively problems within himself and his environment, including those related to his children.[9]

Kersten Salk's full-time housekeeping and mothering was discounted in favor of Dr. Salk's professional psychological expertise and intellectually exciting lifestyle. In an unpublished paper, Kersten Salk wrote: "This decision was part of the backlash against the feminist movement. I was a victim of circumstance. Judge Ribaudo filmed an interview with NBC before he released the text of his decision to counsel. . . . The basis of Judge Ribaudo's decision seems to have been Lee's professional and material attainments."[10]

The feminist demand for equal pay for women who wished to work in formerly "male" spheres was used against women in the *female* sphere of mothering. Mothering became a gender-neutral activity, something that either gender could perform regardless of different socialization or different track records. For example, as we have seen, a Kansas court awarded one-year-old twins to a working father rather than to a mother who could stay at home with them. Even though it considered the "tender years" presumption as one factor, the father was found to be able to provide the better home environment. The higher court, in upholding the decision, made it clear that the mother could lose, even if she was fit, under the "best interests of the child" standard.[11]

In a similar attempt to be sex neutral, a judge awarded a two-year-old son to his father. Since both parents were fit, "an award to the mother *because* she was the mother, and as such the primary caretaker, would violate the requirement of sex-neutrality. The appellate court noted the faulty logic and reversed."[12]

Attorney Nancy Polikoff analyzed another case in which the North Dakota appellate court upheld the father's custody of three children: "The mother argued that it was unfair for her to lose her children because she chose to stay at home with them, foregoing career opportunities. But the court, in a cruel twist of the customary logic, stated that it would not be more fair to deprive the father of custody because he did not stay home during the day."[13]

Not all judges discriminate against stay-at-home or "good enough" mothers, nor do all judges do so in the spirit of affirmative action or sex neutrality. The West Virginia Supreme Court, in a landmark decision, enunciated a "primary caretaker" presumption—that is, whichever parent actually did the child care should be the preferred or presumed custodian in any contest. The court spelled out the chores of a primary caretaker:

1) preparing and planning of meals; 2) bathing, grooming and dressing; 3) purchasing, cleaning, and care of clothes; 4) medical care, including nursing and trips to physicians; 5) arranging for social interaction among peers after school, i.e. transporting to friends' houses or, for example, to girl or boy scout meetings; 6) arranging alternative care, i.e. babysitting, daycare, etc.; 7) putting child to bed at night, attending to child in the middle of the night, waking child in the morning; 8) disciplining, i.e. teaching general manners and toilet training; 9) educating, i.e. religious, cultural, social, etc.; and 10) teaching elementary skills, i.e. reading, writing, and arithmetic.[14]

THE JUDICIAL OVERVALUATION OF GENETIC, LEGAL, ECONOMIC, AND SYMBOLIC FATHERHOOD

Considering the epidemic nature of males' abandonment of their families, judges are impressed by fathers who fight for paternal recognition, visitation, and custodial rights. A father need only satisfy minimal criteria in order to be seen as a father and as a good-enough father. Judges view a father as fit if he bears a genetic relationship to a child, was once married to the child's mother, or now *promises* to support the child at least at state welfare levels. If a mother has once been legally married to the genetic father of her child, she risks losing custody and child support and being fined and even imprisoned if she is seen as interfering with a father's right of paternal recognition, physical access, psychological relationship, and control over his children.

Attorney Joanne Schulman describes a case in which she represented a custodial mother who wanted her alcoholic ex-husband's *visitation* structured so that he would not drive his child anywhere. The father never responded to complaints or appeared in court. Nevertheless,

> The judge literally threw a fit. He threw files at me in the courtroom. He said, "I will not slander that man. I will not give you that kind of visitation. You are putting on public record that this man has a drinking problem. That man is not even here to defend himself." The judge was that man's attorney. The judge cared more about the man's reputation than about the kid who might be killed driving around with an alcoholic. Even when I produced evidence that this man had been

convicted of drunken driving, the judge threw a fit again. He had a tantrum. He threw files all over the bench again.*

Attorney Martha O. Eller of Washington State notes that in real life, unlike in the film *Kramer vs. Kramer*, mothers who have physically abandoned their children can rarely regain custody. However, fathers who have abandoned children completely can, at any time, reopen their claim to custody. Eller has said, "I am defending several child custody modification actions right now where the fathers' connections with the children are astonishingly minimal since the parties' separation, and yet they are being given careful consideration for custody modification."[15]

A New York father sued his ex-wife for allegedly refusing him visitation. This father apparently saw his daughter quite "irregularly." According to Judge Getzels, the father

did not live up to his assurances that he would arrange his business schedule to come in from Hong Kong every three months. By visiting less frequently, he failed to exercise his right. When he came, he put business before his daughter and was really available only one day out of ten he would be in New York. When he did get to visit with the child, she was afraid to be left alone with him. After this visit [the three-year-old girl] became incontinent and her behavior regressed. She was afraid to be left alone with him. It was the opinion of a child psychologist that the regression resulted from the trauma of [the girl's] seeing her father. The child feels abandoned by her father. She has been observed walking up to strange men, tugging at their trousers and saying, "Daddy, Daddy." She tells neighbors that she has no father. Two therapists are willing to testify that unsupervised, irregular visitation is detrimental.[16]

Judge Getzels did not find the mother in "malicious" or "willful" contempt of court. Nevertheless, he ordered that visitation (with prior notice) be continued. He reminded the mother that it was her duty to "encourage visitation and to foster the child's loving relationship with her father. No evidence was adduced that irregular visitation is harmful or that supervision

---

* Schulman notes that laypeople usually deal with this anecdote by assuming it's an isolated example. The only people who don't see it as isolated are other lawyers.

is necessary. . . . So vital is the relationship between the noncustodial parent and child that *interference* with that relationship may be found to be inconsistent with the child's best interests as to raise *a question as to the fitness of the offender to retain custody* [author's italics]."[17]*

A judge in West Virginia ruled the following: "Unless a divorced father's failure to support was contumacious, wilful or intentional, or visitation would be detrimental to the children, visitation should not be denied on grounds of non-support."[18]

New York Judge Ralph Diamond delayed a mother's petition for child support because she had allegedly violated the *unwed* father's *visitation* privileges. The mother claimed she "did nothing to prevent the child from visiting with her father." The judge noted that the child "hated" her father and refused to see him. Judge Diamond ordered a new visitation schedule away from the mother's residence and held her petition for support "in abeyance, pending the outcome of the new arrangement." Judge Diamond wrote, "It is clear that the law at a minimum requires a custodian to do something to encourage and to foster the relationship between the child and the noncustodial parent to aid in gaining visitation. A custodian may not simply remain mute and passive and in so doing impede the visitation order of the court."[19]

Five years after her divorce, Frances Daghir Coughlin lost custody of her children because her new *husband's* temporary move to France was seen as interfering with paternal visitation. Khalil Daghir had abandoned the home. Frances was a stay-at-home mother who had since "provided a good home for the three children." Khalil had, in fact, been judicially viewed as incapable of "adequately caring for the children while working full time" and as someone who "might remove the children to Lebanon on a permanent basis, if he had custody."

Frances offered to subsidize Khalil's travel expenses and to "balance out" his visitation by allowing him two continuous months each summer with the children. Nevertheless, the judge granted Khalil custody. "So zealously do the courts guard the relationship between a non-custodial parent and his child, that any interference with it by the custodial parent has been said to be an act so inconsistent with the best interests of the child as to, per se, raise

---

* Note that the judge considers the father's visitation rights more important than the child's distress and more important than the extra work (and pain) this distress causes her mother.

a strong possibility that the offending party is unfit to act as custodial parent."[20] Thus, the *right* of paternal *visitation*, which few judges ever monitor in terms of its frequency or quality and which cannot be mandated, is often considered more important to children than their ongoing relationship to their "good enough" biological and full-time mother.[21]

Perhaps Mrs. Daghir's remarriage was judicially perceived as "selfish" or as unfair to her ex-husband's paternal territoriality. By contrast, judges *like* stepmothers and do not view their taking over a mother's children as unnaturally proprietary.

It is important to stress that such paternal rights exist without reciprocal obligations. For example, Kimberly Anne Louden asked the California courts to compel her natural, unwed father, Owen C. Olpin, to visit her. The court decided that paternal visitation is a "right and a privilege" and that such a "right is not reciprocal, and hence, the plaintiff ha[s] no right to compel her adjudicated father to visit her."[22] The courts claim they cannot force a father to visit his child or to behave nonviolently and responsibly when he does visit. However, the courts can and do order paternal child-support payments withheld or custody removed from the mother who is perceived as interfering with the paternal "right" of visitation.

Virginia Judge Joseph Peters Jr. awarded *custody* to an unwed father after he had kidnapped his two-and-a-half-year-old daughter. The father claimed maternal "interference" with visitation. The judge also acquitted the father of the assault, battery, and kidnapping charges.[23] Attorney Doris Jonas Freed commented: "[This decision] is the logical extension of the rights of fathers. They [unwed fathers] now stand substantially in the shoes of wedded fathers."[24]

THE JUDICIAL NONPUNISHMENT OF MALE DOMESTIC VIOLENCE: DO JUDGES IN GENERAL BEHAVE IN THE SAME WAY THAT JUDGES IN MY STUDY BEHAVED?

In my study, none of the fathers who physically abused their wives or ejected them from their homes was fined, jailed, or deprived of visitation or custody. This was true for mothers who never saw judges and for those who did. In general, relatively few batterers and their female victims are seen by judges. Those who are tend to be (1) discharged without penalty, (2) ordered into (anti-mother) counseling, (3) ineffectively ordered to "stay away," or (4) allowed (improperly) supervised visitation.[25]

Attorneys Joanne Schulman and Laurie Woods observed an increase in the number of battered wives being threatened with custody battles. Louise Armstrong noted the following:

> Where a woman is battered and threatens to leave, the batterer may counterthreaten that he will sue for custody. "Go on, leave. You'll never get the kids." At the least, he can use the threat to trade her financial demands down. Where the battered wife or mother of the sexually abused child seeks the seemingly simpler "no fault" divorce, she forgoes establishing the [claim of] battering or molestation. This makes any later claims seem no more than vindictive. With "no fault," the father will normally be awarded weekend custody, and will therefore retain constant access to her and the children.[26]

Judges did not relate wife battering to child abuse or to parental custodial unfitness. Judges rarely offered effective redress to a battered mother who was *also* fighting for her children's physical and psychological safety. Judges sometimes harassed and intimidated the female *victim* of male battering. A New York woman pressed criminal charges against her husband: "The judge asked her if this was the first time she had been beaten up. After observing court proceedings that morning, she knew that if she answered 'yes,' like all the other women had, her husband would be released with virtually no penalty. So wisely, she answered 'No, this is not the first time.' The judge dismissed the case, responding, 'Well, it sounds like you must enjoy getting beaten up if it has happened before. There's nothing I can do.'"[27]

Battering husbands learned that judges wouldn't treat their violence seriously. Battered wives learned not to expect any judicial help. Even when a judge hears a wife's request for an order of protection, "most [such] hearings, especially those without attorneys, last no more than minutes. Few women ever have the chance to explain to judges their unique fears about further violence or their concerns about child snatching."[28]

Child snatching is an almost all-male crime. Since the early 1980s, the FBI has had jurisdiction to pursue and arrest parental child snatchers. The FBI "snatched" two of my maternal interviewees. Perhaps the first parent seized by the FBI was a *mother*.[29] Nancy Lemon, staff attorney for the Mid-Peninsula Support Network for Battered Women in California, described how one mother was punished in 1983 for kidnapping her child. "The mother was denied her court-ordered visitation totally by her ex-husband. She finally kidnapped her thirteen-year-old son and drove to another state with him. She was picked up within weeks and put in jail for five months. In April 1983 she was convicted of kidnapping as a felony. That means she can't ever vote, she can't have any friends who are felons. Her visitation is supervised by the court. I have never heard of a father-kidnapper being treated this way."

Granted, domestically violent husbands may retain visitation or even win custody, but can sexually abusive and incestuous fathers retain visitation or win custody of their child victims? As we shall see, the answer is a resounding yes.

Some judges and legislators believe that a father has the right to discipline his child physically. This way of thinking may also be used to justify a father's sexual use of his child.

Most judges would not claim that incest constitutes "fit" paternal behavior. On the contrary. Judges do not often jail fathers for incest. Judges are reluctant to believe that a particular father is actually guilty of incest or, if he is, that he should be deprived of visitation or custody. Judges find it easier to assume the mother is lying or to order (anti-mother) family counseling. Judges are sometimes more concerned with the paternal right to counseling than the right of his victims to safety.

In 1980 a Kentucky mother, Mimi J., discovered that her daughter was being sexually abused. At five her daughter said that "Daddy was putting something he called his 'penis' in her front and back. 'It hurt,' she said, 'and there was this sticky stuff.'" Mimi consulted a psychiatrist and a pediatrician, both of whom confirmed the girl's story and hospitalized her. Mimi then tried to prevent her ex-husband, a fifth-grade schoolteacher, from having any access to his daughter. Mimi's ex-husband admitted in court that he had engaged in "sex education" with his daughter since she was two and a half.[30] Judge Richard Revell said that *he* didn't believe a father would sexually abuse his own child. Judge Revell ordered the girl into her father's custody. He denied Mimi any maternal visitation. In fact, he ordered her to jail for lying on the stand and for trying to ruin a man's reputation.

Mimi J. never served this one day sentence. My information about this case was first obtained through media coverage and then through the National Center for Women and Family Law. Dr. Paul L. Adams, a friend and colleague, told me that he was the expert witness for both mother and child in this case. He wrote a book about his experience—one that no publisher was interested in publishing. Dr. Adams told me that Mimi J. has not been allowed to see her daughter at all.

In 1982 I received two unsolicited dossiers in the mail. Both contained information about two different incestuous fathers who had battled for custody in Wisconsin in the late 1970s and early 1980s. Legal depositions, trial transcripts, judicial decisions, psychiatric evaluations, and accompanying event chronologies were included in both dossiers.

The first mother, Brigette O., married Anthony O. in September 1978. Anthony battered Brigette before and during her pregnancy. Their daughter, Nicole, was born in November 1979. When Nicole was five months old, Brigette left Anthony. She reported that

> he only visited when he felt like it. Sometimes he left us alone for months. Sometimes he begged me to return or threatened and harassed me when I wouldn't. His child support was irregular at best. I applied for and received welfare. When Nicole was less than two, she began to come home very upset after each visit with her father. She cried a lot, couldn't sleep, and didn't eat right. After one visit, when she was two years old, she screamed with pain when she urinated. I saw that her vagina was red and sore. I took her to the Sexual Assault Treatment Center. They reported "suspected sexual abuse."

From this moment on Brigette tried to suspend, restrict, or have paternal visitation properly supervised. The first welfare caseworker who investigated the situation described Brigette as a "horrifying mother with sharp teeth," a "mad witch." On March 29, 1982, Judge Patricia Curley removed Nicole from her stay-at-home and remarried mother. She ordered Nicole into her working, unremarried, and incestuous father's custody. Judge Curley was heavily influenced by the court-ordered psychiatric report which described Brigette as "paranoid about child abuse."*

Judge Curley did not view Brigette as an unfit mother. Her "unfitness" consisted of continuously attempting to separate her daughter from her "loving" father. The judge ordered maternal visitation "every other week."

Within four months, Nicole, who was by now three and a half years old, had perennially reddened genitalia. Nicole also tried to kiss and tickle adult men on the lips and on the penis. "On September 11, 1982, Nurse Cathy

---

* Another psychiatrist, whom Brigette had been seeing for a year and a half, strongly disagreed with this court-ordered assessment of Brigette's "paranoia." His opinion did not carry the judicial day.

Mallory examined the child and found the hymen was broken and the skin around the vagina stretched to the point of being thin and raw. The vagina was open .75 cm, where it had been a pinpoint less than one year before, as noted in the medical records."[31]

A psychiatrist, a psychologist, and a child abuse counselor all confirmed Nicole's sexual abuse. A court-appointed psychologist described Nicole's behavior in this way: "Suddenly she stopped in midstream, grabbed herself in the crotch and stated, 'He touched me down here! With his peanut!' She then began to jump around once again, became quite agitated and kept repeating this. The process of verbal expression was now more intense than it had been throughout the evaluative procedure. She then began to grab outward from her crotch as if holding an imaginary object and began to move her pelvic area up and down, and then made motions as if she was shaking the imaginary object and stated, 'Get it all off!'"

This particular psychologist still believed that Brigette "focused" on the sexual abuse to Nicole's detriment. He described Brigette as a good mother but one he personally didn't "like." In his report he focused more on Brigette's "paranoia" about incest than on the *fact* of paternal incest: "This mother is a decidedly unfriendly person. Although she is nervous about our interview, she exhibited bizarre laughter at inappropriate moments. This mother admits to being beaten by her own father. I believe she is paranoid and oversensitive on this very subject and capable of ruining the relationship between a loving father and his daughter. This mother is rigid, overprotective and obsessed with incest. This obsession is unhealthy for her daughter."*

This expert persuaded the court that *both* parents should enter treatment.†

He argued against separating Nicole from her father: "A complete cutting of contact with the natural father could conceivably confuse the child or send a 'message' of negativity that the child has not assimilated as of yet, and most importantly, it would traumatize the child—she is strongly attached to her father."

On October 5, 1982, after an emergency hearing, Judge Curley reversed her previous ruling and returned Nicole to her mother's custody. She said,

---

* As I read this report, I momentarily forgot that the *father*, not the mother, was committing a crime. I began to think: Aha! So *she's* not mentally healthy either!
† Throughout the court proceedings, Anthony maintained his innocence. The court-appointed psychologist said he had "amnesia" about the abuse—probably caused by Anthony's own *mother's* having abused him in the past!

"This court is satisfied that something is happening to this child. I do not know what that is. I am going to allow, obviously, for visitation between Anthony O. and his daughter. . . . Even if [the experts] were convinced that there was some sexual abuse going on they would encourage and require [Mr. O.] to remain a vital figure to this child. He's not going to go away. He's going to be this child's father."

Judge Curley allowed Anthony O. to resume his weekly visitation. (Note that when Brigette lost custody, she was allowed visitation every other weekend.)

In July 1983, *eighteen months* after Brigette first discovered that her daughter was being incestuously abused, she was still trying to find a neutral person, trained in child sexual abuse, to supervise paternal visitation.[32]

What if a mother flees the state to protect her daughter from being sexually molested by her father? As we will see, she may be arrested and extradited; her daughter may be returned to her incestuous father—unless the governor can be persuaded to intervene.

In April 1982 Arlene W., my second Wisconsin mother, did run away. Here is an edited chronology of the events that led to her flight.[33]

In the summer of 1977, Arlene W. met Red E. Early. In 1978 Arlene became pregnant. She moved in with Red for three months. He began drinking heavily and was physically abusive. Arlene moved out. Andrea W. was born in the fall of 1978. Red visited Arlene in the hospital but was barred by the hospital staff for his "abusive" behavior. Arlene went on welfare. When Andrea was 3 months old Red forced his way into Arlene's apartment, and beat her so badly she was hospitalized. Early in 1979, Red's paternity was established by the Welfare Department. Visitation was allowed with 24 hour notice. Red was physically abusive to both Arlene and Andrea during several visits, Arlene decided to refuse further visitation.

In the fall of 1980, Red legally demanded overnight visitation twice monthly. Judge John E. McCormick told Arlene to "give a man a second chance." He ordered visitation for one weekend day and one half weekday. Visitation began. At this point, Andrea started "acting out" behavior: aggressive hitting, crying, clinging, not sleeping, wetting herself, vomiting. Andrea complained of being hit by her father—and marks were detectable. Arlene complained to Family Reconciliation Worker Carolyn L., who said that a father had the right to hit a child.

By early 1981, Andrea started saying that her father "hurt" her. She also cried when she urinated. She had a rash on her buttocks. Arlene noticed that Andrea's vaginal area was reddened. She took her to the hospital's Sexual Assault Treatment Center. The hospital report concluded that Andrea had been sexually abused, that her bad vaginal abrasions were caused by penile rubbing. The rash on her buttocks had been caused by ejaculation. The Sexual Assault Treatment Center ruled that there were to be no further visitations. Arlene was told that the police would be calling her for a statement.

In the spring of 1981, the Sensitive Crimes Unit of the District Attorney's Office became involved in the case. D. A. Jeffrey Kremers said he believed that Andrea had been sexually abused, but that because of her age (2½) she would not be able to testify in court. Consequently, charges could not be filed against Red. The D.A. recommended no visitation. However, this recommendation of the criminal court had no effect on the visitation order by the Civil Court.

In the spring of 1981, Red appeared in Judge John E. McCormick's courtroom. Arlene W. was charged with contempt, due to the denial of visitation. A psychological evaluation was ordered for all parties. The D.A.'s office supported Arlene in the hearing. The psychologist confirmed that Andrea had been sexually abused. Judge McCormick ordered visitation. Having six children of his own, he said he could not believe that a father would sexually abuse his own child. Arlene would be held in contempt of court if she prevented visitation. Visitation was to take place under supervision in the courtroom.

In the fall of 1981, Red demanded a new court hearing on visitation. Afterwards, he was also allowed to have Andrea on visits outside the courthouse. Judge McCormick told Arlene that if she intervened with visitation it would be cause for reversal of custody. Arlene's attorney refused to represent her if she didn't comply with the visitation order. She retained a new attorney—the former D. A. of Sensitive Crimes Unit, Jeff Kremers. Supervised paternal visitation outside the courthouse was upheld.

Andrea often returned home after visitation with her vagina quite red and severely irritated. Sometimes she was not abused. When she was, her mother, feeling desperate, called all the agencies again, but no action was taken. By late fall of 1981, Arlene W. refused to allow any further visitation.

Early in 1982, Arlene appeared again before Judge McCormick. Red demanded a *male* psychologist. He claimed that the previous psychologist was a woman and biased against him. The judge ordered a new psychological evaluation done by a man. The court-ordered male psychologist presented a classic profile of an incest abuser. Supervised paternal visitation was still upheld. Judge McCormick informed both parents that the matter was closed, that he did not want to see either parent back in court again. He told Arlene that interference with visitation would lead to the harsh penalty of loss of custody.

After exhausting every legal means available to separate Andrea from her sexually abusive father, Arlene fled Wisconsin to her brother's home in the state of Washington. She went on welfare and enrolled Andrea in a Montessori school and an incest treatment program. Wisconsin Judge McCormick now demanded Andrea's extradition. In January 1983, the Tacoma welfare department sent Arlene a notice to come in for a review. It was a ruse. Police arrived with a warrant for Arlene's arrest. They separated her from her daughter, denied her bail and the use of the telephone, and jailed her for four days.

Feminists, ministers, psychiatrists, incest victims, experts, academics, jurists, the department of social services—all launched a campaign against Arlene's extradition. Washington Governor John Spellman was persuaded to hold a fair hearing on the matter. On March 31, 1983, Governor John Spellman decided not to extradite Arlene for the "crime" of protecting her daughter from incest.

Arlene W.'s unedited "Chronology of Events" documents the profound isolation and vulnerability of a battered, unwed, and welfare-dependent mother who has discovered paternal incest. It also documents the state's absolute refusal to believe or assist her. "Sympathetic" bureaucrats continually urged Arlene to expose her daughter to more sexual abuse in order to get "better documentation." Arlene was forced to watch her daughter being destroyed—not just by her unwed biological father but also by her state "father."

Arlene and Brigette's ordeals involved facing a cabal of judicial, penal, welfare, and mental health experts who were all committed to assisting incestuous fathers and failing to protect mothers and children from male physical, sexual, and psychological violence. The judges in both cases refused to punish the male criminal and punished their female victims instead.[34]

Judges have not been educated about incest. No one has. Our educators and mental health experts have often denied its existence and its importance. They have also blamed the victim's mother and assured everyone that counseling will help. As we shall see, custodially challenged mothers of incest victims continued—and continue—to lose custody. Some custodially challenged mothers of incest victims vowed to go to jail rather than comply with court-ordered visitation.[35]

Question: *What is going on?*
Answer: *Patriarchal law is going on.*

In the twentieth century, under patriarchal law, male contractual property rights supersede female natural property rights. Mothers have obligations without reciprocal legal rights. Fathers have rights without reciprocal obligations. Under patriarchal law, men carry more custodial weight than women do; fathers carry more custodial weight than mothers do. This is true for fathers who do not support or visit their children.

SUMMARY AND JUDGMENT

Simply put, contemporary judges are biased against mothers in custody disputes.

In a contest, judges always favor paternal custody when the challenged mother is allegedly mentally ill, accused of a crime, or maternally inadequate or unfit. Judges also favor paternal custody when the challenged mother accuses her *husband* of mental illness or of paternal unfitness, including incest.

In a contest, judges favor paternal custody when the challenged mother has less money than her ex-husband, less money than the unwed father of her child, or, in certain cases, less money than the child's sperm donor. Judges *also* favor paternal custody when the challenged mother works, has a "career," or has to move in order to work.

In a contest, judges favor paternal custody when the challenged mother commits adultery, lives with a man out of wedlock, or has an illegitimate child. Judges favor paternal custody when the challenged mother is a lesbian, holds minority political and religious opinions, or leads an "alternate" lifestyle.

In a contest, judges favor paternal custody when the father has remarried and the mother remains single. If, however, a mother remarries or if she needs to move in order to remarry, judges favor paternal custody to protect paternal "private property" from a stepfather's encroachments and to guarantee paternal visitation.

Judges favor paternal custody when the challenged mother is against joint custody, when the challenged mother is seen as interfering with paternal visitation (without necessarily moving away), or when the children are over a certain age or are boys.

Judges *do* favor maternal custody—when the challenged mother is the Virgin Mary, one who is white, wealthy, and backed by her father, God.

Are judges morally insane? To what extent are judges merely being "practical" when they award children to their economically superior fathers? Is there some other explanation even for the most outrageous custodial decision?

There may be. Traditional judges share an unstated and perhaps unconscious belief that men are more violent than women and that male-dominated families contain or minimize male violence. According to Louise Armstrong, male domestic violence is judicially unpunished because judges perceive "household violence . . . as *domesticated* violence, with the violence potential of less powerful males perceived as a fixed quantitative phenomenon which has to go *somewhere*. It would not hurt as a hedge to leave each individual male an 'appropriate' victim or two. This is the woman and child as lightning rod theory."[36]

Most judges are apparently convinced that the law cannot prevent or punish the male abandonment of women and children. However, perhaps they unconsciously believe that the law can be used to stem the tide of *female*-initiated divorce. Judges view mothers who abandon their husbands as genuine threats to public law and order. When judges custodially punish mothers for adultery, they specifically write about patriarchal marriage as the "bedrock" of social order.

Each mother who displeases or leaves her husband is refusing to absorb one man's potential for public violence. Such mothers are also setting a bad example for other women. Most important, since the state doesn't guarantee or enforce equal or comparable wages in the marketplace for women, most (single) mothers are fated to swell the state welfare rolls.

Patriarchal law is a system of maintaining public law and order among *men*. It has traditionally been based on the legal sacrifice of women and children in the private realm. Judges are, perhaps unconsciously, attempting to uphold *public* law and order when they render morally insane decisions in the *private* realm.

14

Court-Enabled Incest in the 1980s and 1990s

. . . .

Many custodially embattled mothers who have been battered and whose children are being raped do not usually impress professionals as credible or even as sane. Some have suffered abusive childhoods and married abusive husbands who, in turn, are now abusing their children sexually; thus, these women are already "on the ropes." And that's before they get trapped in the court system. Once there, unless they are very wealthy and have very solid family support, their fragile coping mechanisms are no match for what happens next. Thus, by the time the system has had its way with them, they are sometimes their own worst advocates.

What this means is that custodially embattled "protective" mothers—understandably—often behave in extremely "emotional" ways. They are long-winded, need to describe each detail, and cannot follow instructions when asked to get to the bottom line; they are also hostile, suspicious, and "paranoid." Some such mothers may also be incredibly demanding, manipulative, needy, and without boundaries. They have been tortured. They have not gotten over it. These mothers are not capable of behaving in a businesslike or professional way. From their point of view, how can they? Why should they? Their children's fate and their lives are on the line. However, such behavior may impress others as "wild" or "primitive."

Thus, many custodially embattled mothers are not "likable." Unlike their male abusers, they may lack the same kind of easy (sociopathic) charm and affability; their foot is still caught in the trap, so to speak. This makes it easy for lawyers, forensic evaluators, and judges to dismiss them as mentally ill and/or as completely untrustworthy. As I've previously noted, such mothers have sometimes been severely abused in childhood and/or have chosen a series of violent men. Why this happens is an important question that I will answer with another question: Why are so many men violent?

Although these mothers may be difficult to represent, they may still be telling the truth—and may still be trying to protect their children. They may also be very good mothers. But, like the survivors of a nasty war, they have been rendered permanently "different," perhaps unpleasant, certainly overwhelming, and, as such, a real challenge for their advocates.

Let me introduce you to Linda, a California-based mother who responded to my call for stories by first calling my office about seven times. I spoke to Linda once. I told her that my office was not equipped for frequent conversations but I nevertheless encouraged her to send me her "story" and to supply documentation. In this case, I'm very glad I did. She was a custodially challenged, battered mother whose young and precious daughter had been both sexually and physically abused both by her own father and by his family. Linda, to her credit, kept careful documentation of her entire case. She sent it to me together with letters written by two physicians and a fairly prominent law professor who was involved in her case. I will draw upon both this mother's story and upon the documentation.

In the mid-1980s, after a whirlwind courtship, Linda married Rocco, a man in Los Angeles. She became pregnant almost immediately. She left a good job in the area and moved to another county in California so her husband could be near his family. (Her family was far away and highly dangerous to her). Almost immediately, Rocco began to beat her, severely and continuously, and to verbally and psychologically torment her. She called the police many times but was too afraid to press charges. The police sometimes filed reports. And yes, when she panicked and actually called home, her family told her that she should "stick with her man," that it was her job "to make it work," and that she should "never turn to the police."

When Linda became pregnant a second time, her husband beat her up and forced her to have an abortion. Linda did not leave him until he beat her while she was holding her one-year-old daughter in her arms. Then she left immediately. From that moment on, she was an excellent and resourceful mother.

The courts ordered Linda and Rocco into joint legal custody, with physical custody going to Linda but with her husband allowed unsupervised, liberal visitation. However, the court ordered a psychiatric evaluation which forever damaged Linda's standing. I reviewed the court-ordered psychiatric report, which is dated March 14, 1988. It made my blood boil.

Dr. Marc Lawrence began this way: "The emotional and psychological relationship between Linda and her daughter Sue has been loving, supportive and healthy enough to have brought 20-month-old Sue to a thriving and developmentally appropriate state. Linda has done most of the child care. . . . The pair is deeply attached and well bonded." Thus, Dr. Lawrence admitted that Linda was a good and loving mother, that the child was obviously close to her and in very good developmental shape. However, the psychiatrist was uncomfortable with how *emotional* Linda was about the possible loss of her daughter.

Even more important, he is concerned with what she *might* possibly do in the future, although no harm had been done and the "father does not have the same depth of involvement as seen with the primary caretaker." Nevertheless, he fears that the mother's *emotionality* "threatens to" harm her daughter *in the future*. He wonders whether Linda will be able to "give her daughter the psychological and physical space she needs, especially in the direction of her father."

Yes, the psychiatrist admits that her husband constantly "provokes" Linda but still feels that the mother's "out of control emotional expressiveness" might *in the future* "harm" her daughter and that—ideally—the "father *should* learn how to express emotional warmth and nurturing, and the mother *should* learn to take control and become more rational."

What world is he living in? Does he believe that by rewarding the nonprimary caretaker, ostensibly a violent and incestuous man, with joint or sole custody, it will teach him how to become more "warm and nurturing"? Apparently he does. Thus, he recommends that "legal custody should be joint. . . . The parents should meet together weekly in therapy to resolve their differences." He does not believe that the child should be "given over completely to either parent." But he does envision the child spending more and more time with her father. One must ask why.

This psychiatrist lives in a dream world—one that is quite dangerous to vulnerable children and women. Clearly he does not believe that men are violent or incestuous. But, even if they are, Dr. Lawrence believes that female "emotionality" might be even more dangerous. Above all, the misguided doctor actually believes that therapy can resolve evil.

In my opinion, this psychiatrist is some kind of domestic war criminal. But his thinking and his report are not at all unusual.

For three and a half years, Linda raised her daughter on her own with no financial assistance. But she lived in perpetual fear. She had to endure verbal and physical violence at the beginning and end of each paternal visitation. Linda's ex-husband would not give up—nor would he come on time to pick his daughter up. He would not return her on time either, nor did he turn up, as expected, on her third birthday for a family party.

Rocco, with the help of his mother and sisters (all of whom denied that he was a violent and dangerous man), then fought a vicious and prolonged custody battle. One sister-in-law or another would refuse to return Linda's child to her; she would curse Linda and lock the door.

Then, when Linda's daughter was nearly four years old, a disturbing pattern emerged. Suddenly, her little girl would return from a weekend with her father bruised, exhausted, distressed, sorrowful, and sometimes with swollen eyes. She would be dropped off at her day-care center. The workers would invariably call Linda at work and suggest that she immediately take her daughter to see her pediatrician. She did so. The pediatrician began to document what "appeared to be signs of potential sexual molestation." According to Linda, her four-year-old began "acting out sex acts and stating that she was afraid of the penis."

Two independent pediatricians went much further. On June 10, 1989, in a letter to Linda's private lawyer, Dr. Cyril M. Ramer, the first pediatrician, noted that this "brilliant, charming, captivating, courteous," verbally sophisticated, and happy-go-lucky child had begun to "stutter." She seemed "traumatized," almost "catatonic," and she had a "significant black and blue mark on her inside thigh which was still there a week later. . . . It was after this first incident that Sue started not wanting to go visit her father. Sue would plead with me, 'Don't want to see daddy, please.' This child has now begun to curse her mother, calling her foul four letter words which Linda has never spoken."

In this first pediatrician's view, the visitation periods away from her mother are "much too long. . . . She is being taught to hate Linda or at least to 'act' like she hates Linda when she is with her father. She has begun to use the word 'hate' and to say, 'Ma Ma Ca Ca, flush down the toilet.' She is also back to 'thumb sucking.' This child has regressed to about an ordinary 18 month old, insisting on being held her entire visit." In addition, the pediatrician writes, "She may be in danger spiritually. The child and her mother are Jewish, the father is not. He broke all Sue's Jewish memorabilia and said they were bad things. Her father said she definitely was not Jewish and he didn't like Jews. My greatest concern is not her spirituality. My greatest concern is her spirit. How much can this incredibly gifted young child take without her spirit broken?"

On June 6, 1990, after the first pediatrician had written to her lawyer, Linda filed an application and declaration to the court. Linda wrote the following:

Two months ago I had a very disturbing conversation with my daughter when she was at her father's house (over the weekend). She was very agitated and kept repeating that she was cold. When I picked her up from school that Monday, she seemed very sad. She said that "Daddy sweat on her and that is why she is cold." She then climbed onto my back, lay down, and made grunting sounds and thrust her lower body onto mine. She said "This is how Daddy sweats and he is too heavy on her." I was shocked. She also complained loudly about pain in her rectum and had difficulty urinating. Her rectal area was inflamed and red.

Last weekend my daughter phoned me on the Sunday from her father's house and begged me to bring her home. She was crying and her father wouldn't let her talk to me. I was very worried and called the police. A few days later, she told me unsolicited that "the little spoons with grease on them hurt me." When I asked her what she meant, she described how her father put the spoons with grease on them inside her "behind and doo-doo." She also said: "I don't like the taste of the snakes in my mouth on the foot up and down—and it's not really a penis you know. I spit it out afterwards." She said her father told her I would be angry if she told me about this and "Daddy would put doo-doo on me and will kill us."

She also said, "Let me show you why it hurts," and she had me go on all fours and thrust her finger into my rectum in an angry fashion. I stopped her and held her because she was crying.

On June 27, 1990, a second physician, J. William Evans (probably court ordered), wrote to the court case worker, copied the police department, and reported the matter to Child Protective Services "with regard to possible sexual abuse." I want to quote from his letter extensively.

I am writing with regard to Sue, a child I recently reported to Child Protective Services, with regard to possible sexual abuse. At this point in time, I have seen Sue on three separate occasions, and the concern I have is that this child appears to have significant conflict in talking about her father and talking about the problems in her relationship with her father. As we discussed on the telephone, what is difficult to determine is precisely what has happened with regard to potential abuse. Her story tends to change; and, she also becomes quite reluctant to talk about charged issues.

In my first encounter with Sue, she spoke to me in a very warm, engaging manner. She talked to me about how her father put grease on her eyes: "Dad puts grease on my eyes, but stopped now." She also stated that "Dad has lots of secrets." Later in the interview, she became very quiet when asked about her father, and what was notable in that first session was how non-verbal she became when asked questions about her father, as opposed to her almost precocious language capability in talking about other areas of her life. Her play productions with me involve primarily mothering characters and female children, and there was no overt evidence in her play of any sexual abuse.

Her second session with me involved, again, very little disclosure of information, except she stated that her father had threatened to kill her. As she put it, "He said he would kill me and kill my mother." Again, she was quite reticent to talk when asked specific questions about her father, and what was notable was her silence in contrast to other productions during that interview.

In her third meeting with me, she talked about an Uncle Marco, who she said had stabbed her in the hand. She frequently, during that session, would seem to interchange Uncle Marco and her father, but again was generally quite reluctant to talk about any charged issues. During my time with Sue, I did attempt to use the anatomically correct dolls to elicit information from her. She was curious about the dolls, and was curious about anatomical parts. The only potentially specific comment she made was that she had seen her father's penis, but would not go into any detail regarding specific events or abuse.

As I stated in my report, I think the presentation of this child is quite suspicious and bears careful investigation. It seems reasonable to me at this point in time that contact with the father be suspended or carefully supervised, at least until the outcome of the investigation is clear. Complicating this picture is the severe anxiety that the mother is experiencing, with regard to the child's allegations; and, it makes it very difficult to sort out the details when Sue's anxiety is so great.

Linda's allegation, coupled with these two medical letters and, as we shall soon see, the utter incompetence of at least two of the mother's lawyers, spelled doom for both mother and child.

First, the county immediately and inappropriately removed Linda's daughter from her care and keeping—presumably because they feared the mother "might" kidnap her child to protect her from "suspected" child sexual molestation.

Linda was grilled on the stand about whether she had "concocted these false charges or not." Linda's own lawyer did not stop this line of questioning, nor did she point out that Linda had been a very good mother for the last four years. She also did not call Dr. Ramer or Dr. Evans. Indeed, although (or perhaps because) she had no case prepared, Linda's own lawyer persuaded her client to drop all charges and agree to never raise them again.

Good, competent lawyers have been advising their female clients for a long time not to allege sexual abuse, especially when physicians have documented it as such. I am not talking about physicians who say that there are "possible," "probable," or "suspicious" signs of sexual molestation. I am talking about physicians who find clearly and without a doubt that a child has been sexually molested. Lawyers have learned to advise clients not to mention either "probable" or "definite" sexual abuse for one simple reason: They now know that the mother will invariably lose custody and may lose unsupervised visitation as well.

And, as I've previously pointed out, many of the mothers whose children are being sexually abused are themselves battered wives who may have also been incest victims. They do not always "present" well, and they may not do well on the stand. However, I am not saying that this was true in this case.

Tragically, Linda's first lawyer was totally incompetent. The same lawyer who failed to represent Linda competently was eventually disbarred in 1997 for a variety of reasons. The details are too baroque and too bizarre, but suffice to say that this thoroughly incompetent lawyer—who was well paid—did absolutely nothing and did nothing right, including refusing to turn the file over to her client. This soon led to the abusive father's getting custody and moving far away from where the mother lived and worked. Linda was only granted expensive, supervised visitation at a distant location. The supervisors were women who were incredibly "hostile" to her. Thereafter, Linda was represented by a series of tragically incompetent lawyers, another one of whom was also subsequently disbarred for incompetence.[1]

In 1990 Linda wisely contacted Dr. Judith Wallerstein and Janet Johnston for help; they connected her with the prominent family law professor Carol S. Bruch. Here is just a small part of the amicus curiae brief that Professor Bruch wrote to the court. It mainly concerns jurisdictional issues and the incompetence of Linda's current court-appointed lawyer. The brief is long, but I have shortened it for you.

> I am Professor of Law at the University of California, Davis, where my teaching, research and public service responsibilities include the field of family law, in which I have taught since 1973. . . . My professional interests include child custody law, both in domestic relations court and in the juvenile court. Under the juvenile court law, the country has an obligation to promote reunification of the family for all but the most extreme cases, as defined by statute. The brief argues that this is a case requiring reunification efforts in which the country's obligation has not and is not being met. Rather, unreasonable obstacles to contact between the child and her mother have been imposed by country officials.
>
> The mother is entitled to competent legal representation under the Welfare and Institutions Code. The brief argues that she is currently not receiving such counsel. Her rights are being prejudiced as a result, as are the rights of the child, who has had no visit with her mother since current counsel's appointment in May. In the brief, I ask the court to dismiss the juvenile court proceedings, returning the case to the competent domestic relations court.
>
> On the basis of expert professionals whose testimony was never presented to the court, I consulted two professional colleagues. . . . Each is experienced as a clinician and has served as an expert witness in molestation cases. If, as I am told, none of the expert witnesses on Ms. XX's behalf whose materials were in the files I read were called to testify as the time of the County court's initial jurisdictional hearing, my own professional assessment is that Ms. XX was not competently represented at that time.
>
> Because of continuing difficulties with her representation, I have found myself rather deeply involved in this case, although I have met none of the parties or involved professionals personally. It is my

fear that things have gone seriously awry in a way that endangers the court's ability to carry out its functions that has sustained my (quite extraordinary from my standpoint) involvement in this case and prompts this brief.

Whatever the conditions at the time of the court's assumption of jurisdiction, there appears to be no current basis to argue that the mother endangers her child and requires the court's continuing jurisdiction. The mother's distress at her ever-more-constricted access to her child in no way suggests danger to her daughter. The child's welfare, in fact, seems to be jeopardized by her ever-decreasing access to her mother.

The primary goal of the juvenile court law, once dependency has been assumed and the child's protection assured, is the speedy reunification of the family. Since April, I have seen no initiative taken by the country to reach this goal. I understand from multiple sources that the visits the supervisor witnessed between mother and child were successful and completely without untoward incidents of the type that presumably were the court's concern when it subjected Ms. XX to supervised visitation. Absent difficulties in the mother's interactions with her child, there is no basis for the court's continuing jurisdiction. . . . Absent abuse or neglect, the family court is the proper forum to decide all custody and visitation matters, including questions of supervised visitation by either parent.

Ms. XX's lawyer at no time discussed his preparation for his court appearance with Ms. XX or myself. We did not even know before the hearing whether he would appear, and Ms. XX, who felt she could not attend in person without prejudicing her employment, sent a letter to the court in some desperation so that there would be no danger that the court would think she was uninterested in the proceedings. Not only was her lawyer irrelevant to this process, he was unavailable throughout, and the person answering his office phone told me again that he has not picked up messages or contacted them for several days or more at a time. Once again, Ms. XX has had to do virtually everything herself as a layperson operating under serious stress, assisted somewhat by me. As I am now abroad, I can no longer actively assist her, and I think it imperative that the court appoint diligent, competent counsel for her should it not choose to dismiss the juvenile court proceedings at once.

Imagine being the mother who is going through this hell. Imagine having to live without your child—knowing that she is being sexually molested, physically abused, and brainwashed.

Finally, as Linda was fighting for her right to maintain visitation or a semblance of joint custody with her daughter, violence continued to haunt her during drop-offs and pickups. Here, in Linda's own words, is what happened to her in 1990 on a street in California.

During a visit exchange, Sue's father became enraged for some reason when I tried to say hello to her before the supervisor, who was late, arrived. Rocco attacked me and Sue, who had run into my arms for a hug, and whom I was holding. He grabbed us brutally and fiercely in a powerful grip with his large forearms from behind. Sue, four years old at the time, was caught in his grasp as well. Rocco exhibited superhuman strength in his violent rage and lifted both of us off the ground and started shaking us both violently. Sue's head started knocking back and forth, and I became terrified for her safety and need for protection from Rocco's violence. Although people witnessed this scene, no one chose to get involved and stop the violence in broad daylight on the street. I eventually became so afraid that Sue, caught in Rocco's powerful and violent shaking grasp, would be physically harmed, that I bit Rocco's large forearm in self-defense, screaming for Sue to run away when his arm was forced to release us. He held on violently, and I bit harder and harder, in an effort to save my daughter from irreparable physical harm or worse.

Finally, after a deep bite into his arm, in self-defense, Sue was freed. I screamed for her to run away, and she did, crying and hysterical, standing, shaking by herself on the street. A crowd of onlookers did nothing to stop or intervene with the violence, as Rocco kept yelling that this was a family matter and I was crazy. He then turned, faced me head on, and took his open hand, and thrust it full-force (he was an ex-football player in high-school) and hit me open-handed directly on my full face. My nose broke and, although it did not show up until at least a day later, he also gave me two black eyes. I fell hard onto the cement and lay there hysterically crying for someone to call a child advocate and care for my terrified and battered daughter.

When the police finally arrived, Rocco stood calmly and talked to them at length. I was so distressed and hysterical not only because

I'd been injured, but because my daughter had also been physically brutally assaulted as well, that all I could say in response to the cops' repeated queries to me was that they should call a child advocate to ensure my daughter's well-being. I was picked up, along with my car keys, which were still clutched in my hand. The cops put me in handcuffs, inserted me into a police car, and insisted that I had scratched Rocco's car with them, which had never occurred. I was so terrorized and in complete shock, and battered, that I was unable to respond to the two arresting officers. I was handcuffed and taken for the first time in my life to a jail. As the police car pulled away with me handcuffed in the back seat, my eyes caught Sue's, standing alone and sobbing on the street, and I knew then that I was losing her forever.

That night I was placed in solitary confinement, shackled from head to toe, and told that multiple felony charges had been filed against me. I did not understand what was going on and lay on a cot, never taken out once, for three days. I phoned my mother, desperately and pointlessly reaching out to a mentally ill, unloving, selfish narcissist, as did three friends of mine, asking her and my lawyer father, who had molested me while I was growing up, to contribute bail money. My mother said they were on their way to a party and hung up on me. On the way to the criminal trial, two prostitutes asked me if I was aware that I had a broken nose and two black eyes. I wasn't, nor was I given any medical treatment while in jail.

She dismissed her public defender when she was taken into the criminal court and tearfully told the judge the truth—that she had bitten her ex-husband while he was beating her, in a desperate effort to try to protect her young child. The judge agreed that she was a battered woman and released her on her own recognizance. She pled nolo contendere because she did not have money to pay for a competent attorney. She was charged with a misdemeanor, sentenced to probation for three years, and ordered to undergo counseling. She had never been in trouble with the law before in her life, she told me, nor has she since. At this point, she gave up all hope of ever seeing her daughter again. "I was traumatized, terrorized, and had serious PTSD."

She left the state to escape the violence, vowing to one day return to see her daughter. She moved back to her home state and began studying journalism at a university, while holding two part-time jobs as well. She lived in a convent in a small room near the journalism school. All this time she would send gifts and cards to her daughter with the help of an older woman who was a child advocate. She had no phone contact with her daughter. She writes,

> I received an urgent letter while going to class one day stating that my pro-bono lawyer had been alerted that Rocco had gone to the police, fictitiously claimed that I was involved with a militant women's group (although I hadn't been in been in California for two years at that time, and was on heavy sedation due to the fact that I had lost all contact with my daughter), and that I was a danger in terms of potentially kidnapping Sue. The attorney said that Rocco had had the police terrorize the older woman who was facilitating contact via mail from Sue to me and vice versa, and that she thereafter did not want to continue dealing with me at all.

Linda returned to California in 1995 and, shortly after returning, asked for Family Court Services to provide mandated mediation services so that she could resume visits with her daughter. She has no understanding of why supervised visitation between her and Sue was not instituted ever again. She says,

> I never had a visit with Sue, who was nine at the time the mediation occurred, and have never seen her since, except for one time in 2000, when I found the school she was attending, walked into the open hallways and through the long corridors, asked everyone if they were Sue and finally found her. I had big sunglasses on, and high-heeled flip flops. I said, "It's your mother." I have always regretted not just saying "I love you, my daughter." She freaked out completely—she was obviously brainwashed by her father—and I fled with my head hung low as fast as possible, losing my shoes as I ran to my car across the street and away from my daughter for the next ten years, fearing untold violence and retaliation by her violent father.

Yes, a mother can be beaten up in broad daylight on an American street and the police may arrest the victim and jail *her*, not her attacker. If the attacker had been a stranger things would have ended up differently. One can only hope that the police have been educated and have radically changed since 1990.

A mother never gets over this, but neither does the child. No sane father or extended paternal family would purposely allow a girl to grow up believing that her mother was dangerous to her or that she'd abandoned her. Even assuming that a mother is mentally ill or that mental illness has specifically incapacitated her (which is not the case here), for the child's sake, contact with the mother is still crucial. It should have been facilitated, not prevented. This child was not only deprived of the only mother she will ever have—she was forced to live with and had to learn to "love" her captor and rapist and his criminally colluding family.

Linda, like so many mothers, is still grieving. Her daughter is now in her midtwenties. She will not talk to the mother who tried—and failed—to protect her from having to live with a violent father. Like many kidnap victims, brainwashed children display symptoms of Stockholm syndrome. They bond with their abductors as a way of surviving. If they are not actively and skillfully deprogrammed, they will continue to believe whatever their abductors have told them.

And so, despite the serious efforts of two physicians and a family law professor and Linda's own extraordinary perseverance, this mother and daughter were unjustly separated forever by paternal violence. Linda writes, "I wish I could talk to, see, or hold my now grown daughter in my arms, even once—just once would change my life for the better and help heal the unyielding pain in my heart, where she always will be." Linda found strength in *Mothers on Trial* when it first came out, and she took the time to find a great deal of documentation for me about her case. I am very grateful to her for doing so.

Linda is certainly not the only battered, "protective" mother to whom this has happened. I have interviewed, spoken to, reviewed documents from, and heard from hundreds more.

Linda is our first custodially challenged, battered, "protective" mother. Her husband, Rocco, could never have gotten away with this without the active collaboration of his female relatives and the American court system. This next story is similar in this regard.

Like Linda, Cathy was also a custodially challenged mother of two daughters who were being sexually abused by their father. Unlike Linda, Cathy had not been physically, psychologically, or sexually abused when she had been a child; thus, she had strong family support throughout her ordeal. Initially, her parents mortgaged their home and business to make sure that she had enough money to hire lawyers. However the family never recovered financially. Cathy was also resourceful enough to find therapists for both herself and her daughters.

Unlike Linda, Cathy was one of the lucky ones. While the system did not exactly punish her battering and child-molesting husband, it did not reward him. After a five-year, hard-fought battle, Cathy won sole custody. Then, within two years, she won the right to relocate to another state so that she could live with her parents who had, by that time, retired to Florida.

Here is her story.

In the mid-1990s, I myself received a frantic phone call from Dr. Ann, a Minneapolis-based psychotherapist. She knew of my work in this area and wanted my advice. As a mandated reporter, after interviewing two sisters, one five and one seven years old, she had reported the father for the child sexual abuse of his daughters. She told me that after numerous sessions, she had no doubt that they'd been fondled, digitally penetrated, and involved in masturbatory activities. Cathy, the mother, had known nothing. One day, both girls had casually and cheerfully disclosed to a teacher "that they played with Daddy's penis." The teacher then spoke to Cathy, the mother, who took the girls to Dr. Ann, who confirmed that, in her professional opinion, the sexual abuse had occurred.

Soon after she reported the father, Bruce, he began stalking Dr. Ann's office. Dr. Ann reported him to the police, but he was never caught and charged. Years later, for other reasons, Dr. Ann moved to another state. That's when she called me again.

"That same father is outside right now. How did he find me? What does he really want? What should I do?"

We spoke at length. This man was definitely scary. Imagine being a small child—or a wife—at his mercy. Clearly he was persistent, clever, and in thrall to the Dark Side. Perhaps all he meant to do—if we give him the benefit of the doubt—was to terrify Dr. Ann, to punish her and retaliate against her for her having reported him to the authorities. Perhaps he had femicidal intentions.

Dr. Ann again reported him to the police in another state. Again he evaded their grasp. This time I asked Ann to tell me about the case and to obtain permission from the mother to share documentation with me, which she did. People who have not experienced domestic terror and all its lifelong repercussions do not understand what it can do, how it can twist lives forever after. Here is this mother's story.

Washington, D.C.–based Cathy had married in 1978. She believes that her husband, Bruce, married her because "He thought I was rich and he wanted entrée into a better social stratum. He though I was his ticket in." Like so many women are trained to do, Cathy, an interior decorator, wanted to make the marriage work. Hence, she put up with "extreme emotional abuse, which began on our honeymoon. I thought I could change him, help him."

Cathy had married someone who had a bad temper and who could not keep a job as a biomedical researcher. But when he lost his third job in less than two years, he never told her. "He got up, got dressed, packed his briefcase and left the house every single day. I never knew if he went to the library or had come home after I'd left for work." When Bruce lost his fourth job, Cathy refused to follow him to yet another city. She moved back home with her parents and sister. Bruce moved back home with his divorced mother.

In Cathy's case, her physical battering began in 1980 after she gave birth. The emotional battering worsened. Cathy told Ann, the therapist, that "he was mean, emotionally withdrawn. But he only hit me—hard—for the first time when Debbie was six weeks old. Bruce did not believe that Debbie was his daughter. How crazy is that? His mother hated me. She was not friendly towards her own granddaughter. She seemed jealous. She treated me like the 'other' woman in her son's life."

One must ask: Why do battered women remain with their batterers? Some say that they are afraid they will be killed if they leave—it is a realistic fear. Others say in retrospect that they had believed they could change their husbands and that without a husband they would have had to take low-paying jobs, which would have condemned their children to lives of poverty. Some women admit that they stayed because they no longer viewed themselves as "marriage marketable," either because they were no longer attractive or because they no longer trusted men. Domestic battering takes a severe toll on one's self-esteem.

Cathy still gave Bruce another chance and moved with him to a fifth job located in another state. In Minnesota, Cathy kept trying to make the marriage work and gave birth to a second daughter in 1982. When Bruce wasn't demeaning and frightening her, he was apologizing. He begged Cathy to stay with him.

When things got "way out of hand," Cathy began staying with friends. But, because she still lived in the same neighborhood as Bruce, he would continue to stalk her at their daughters' school and at the community center. "I would go into the center and suddenly he'd be behind me, yelling and screaming like a lunatic. Eventually, I was asked to take the girls out of the program." Bruce consistently alienated her friends and supporters by putting them at risk. He would somehow find which family she was staying with, and then call the police. "He would accuse my friend's husband of kidnapping or abusing my daughters. He would also call their workplace and report alleged crimes and improprieties. I never exactly knew what he said but always, always, I had to move on."

By 1989 Cathy had filed for divorce. Her husband managed to find her at each and every shelter for battered women to which she fled. He would bully and threaten the shelter director, who would invariably call the police. He was never arrested for doing this. She tells me, "Once, he found us in a motel which had designated certain rooms for shelter residents. He threatened the receptionist who called the police. Anytime he was actually arrested he always seemed to get out by that night."

Dr. Ann, my therapist-informant, described a series of hair-raising acts of sadism both toward Cathy and toward the daughters. Bruce would break Cathy's bones and then run away to another city so that he might claim that a stranger must have been the bone breaker. When he finally obtained unsupervised visitation, he engaged in fairly rough activities with his daughters. According to Dr. Ann, "Bruce insisted that his seven- and nine-year-old daughters kayak with him, and when they cried, he yelled at them. Bruce's version of this is that he wanted to 'toughen' his girls up and did not want to treat them differently than he would boys."

Bruce also came to the counseling center to demand his children's psychological records. He frightened the other clients, but Dr. Ann stood up to him. "He was ranting and raving. He probably views himself as the victim. Bruce focused on the loss of his rights as a father. He blamed this on Cathy, not on his own actions."

As I suspected and feared, this father became very active in a fathers' rights group. In public, he began to give speeches about how he had been falsely accused of being a batterer. Sometimes he joked that he had only hit his wife once, and lightly: "Was it his fault that she bruised so easily?"

In 1998, with Dr. Ann's permission, I once spoke to Cathy on the phone. Here's what she said.

My ex-husband bonded with a series of lawyers who became very devoted to him. I was never sure if he met them in a fathers' rights group or through business associations. His mother funded his battle against me and against her own grandchildren. At one point, my former mother-in-law was designated as the visitation supervisor. That was a nightmare for me because she kept insisting that her son would never, ever molest his girls, that I was a vicious liar. She also refused to believe that he was a batterer. Even when she saw how bruised I was or once, that I was in a cast, she always said that I could have fallen down or had an accident due to being a secret alcoholic.

Shortly after receiving sole custody and permission to relocate, the paternal grandmother sued for—and won—visitation. Cathy told me that

these visits were fraught with anxiety and fear. My former mother-in-law would secretly spring their father on them. He would jump out of the bedroom, frighten them—then get angry if they weren't delighted to see him. My daughters were not allowed to call me, and if I called, whoever picked up the phone would hang up on me.

I consider myself very lucky. I won custody, and, after many years, won the right to relocate. But Bruce never stopped haunting me. He would turn up unexpectedly at my office. He would sit in his car outside the girls' school. He would call and make threats, or call and say nothing but then hang up. It was meant to rattle me, and it did.

For a while, my poor daughters were out of control. They had tantrums. They smoked. They drank. They stole money from me. Thank God they never got into hard drugs. But they had been forced to remain connected to a father who terrified them. He would do something terrible—and then, in a very quiet voice, insist on getting them to admit that it had never happened. His mantra: "It's not nice to tell lies about Daddy."

I was naive, crazy, desperate, foolish to believe that he would ever change or that I could change him. I should have left town when the therapist, Dr. Ann, told me she believed the girls. Instead, I think I was too scared, afraid of what he might do to us if I took off, but still hoping that none of this was true, that it would all get better. Maybe I was brainwashed.

You know, it's a shame that I still can't name our real names. The retaliation could be very dangerous. This kind of man will sue me, you, your publisher, and he will take years going pro se in order to get it done. He doesn't care if he wins. He wants to torment and weaken you. This kind of man might also show up unexpectedly and ram a car through your front door when you're not home, talk against you to your neighbors and to your children's teachers, stage a ranting session in your therapist's office, threaten your employer so you'll lose your job, stalk your home. My ex-husband has done all this.

The court system did not prevent or punish Bruce for doing these things. But it did not reward him either. That means that he did not get sole custody and was restricted to supervised visitation, although only for awhile. The most significant and positive thing the court did was to grant Cathy sole custody and the right to leave the state. This is no small thing, but it took nearly seven years to do so.

The first case in this chapter has been vetted by a reliable and reputable law professor and two physicians. The second case has been vetted by a clinical psychologist. I hope that my readers now believe that such things do happen, that the mothers of raped children are not necessarily crazy, and that the court system may further punish the victims or, at best, merely not reward the battering pedophiles.

Linda and Cathy are not exceptions. They both represent what was happening in our court system during the 1980s and 1990s when battered and nonbattered mothers tried to "protect" their children from paternal abuse—including sexual assault—as well as from anti-mother brainwashing. Linda and Cathy represent thousands of mothers. I have personal knowledge of hundreds of such mothers, including "protective" mothers who chose to run and who were, invariably, caught, jailed, and deprived of even supervised visitation for a very long time, sometimes forever.

We have just viewed two cases in which mothers tried to protect themselves and their daughters from psychopathic men. They did not run away. They stayed and fought. Most mothers do. This is, at best, a fifty-fifty proposition. For example, Linda lost her daughter forever; Cathy was lucky and, after suffering for many years, won sole custody and the right to relocate. However, the lives of both mothers (and their children) were shadowed and scarred forever. Both were damaged psychologically and financially. Neither ever remarried or had more children. Both mothers had to live with the fact that their daughters had been seriously harmed because "the law" could not or would not stop violent, psychopathic fathers from having their way.

For such reasons, some mothers run away. They are invariably captured and punished. Yes, gender-driven double standards apply in kidnapping too. Thus, although mothers usually only kidnap for the most altruistic of reasons, they are punished more severely than are fathers, who tend to kidnap for reasons that are completely selfish.

Allow me to introduce you to two high profile mother-kidnappers who made headlines in the 1980s. Again, a mother's chance of success seems to be a fifty-fifty proposition.

The so-called underground railroad for runaway mothers and children did exist. I had firsthand knowledge of it. However, most of the mothers who ran away to protect their children were ill suited for outlaw lives or even for lives on the margin. Most were traditional, even deeply religious women. Many had been battered and beaten down during the course of their marriages. Most did not have powerful (or any) families backing them. These mothers did not know how to keep secrets or how to train their children to behave deceptively. Few were "political" or feminist in philosophy. And, sad to say, at the very time that such mothers needed the support of a large, national feminist political and legal organization, the majority of feminists did not want to get involved in illegal activities and were not that interested in motherhood-related issues. To be fair, most feminist resources were consumed by the fight to keep abortion legal, the fight for employment justice, the fight to end sexual and physical violence against women, and the fight for lesbian rights.

In 1985 a mother whose pedophile husband was a police officer turned to me for help. I first tried to find her a lawyer. No one was willing to risk losing her license or jeopardizing her ability to represent other clients by representing the mother, since she had already broken the law by running away. I then turned to a feminist therapist to see her young girls, who were not only on the run with their mother but were also severely traumatized. She too did not want to get involved if there were issues of nonpayment or illegal and criminal activities. Finally, I turned to a feminist who owned property and lots of acreage and asked whether a mother and her children could quietly live there for awhile. She turned me down. She said she was not running a shelter for runaways.

With the help of the director of a shelter for battered women and a convent, I sent this woman on her way—but in so doing, I got myself into trouble with the FBI, which convened a grand jury to question me as to her whereabouts. However, several days before I was supposed to be questioned, I received a call. "We have captured the felon." My criminal lawyers told me never to write to this mother, who was subsequently imprisoned for two years because she had run away. Of course, I wrote to her and met with her after she was released. When she apologized for "getting me into trouble," I told her that she "had gotten me into the history books," and I had to thank her for that.

Also, many of these early "protective" mothers naively believed that if they could only get on *The Oprah Winfrey Show* or if their stories would be cinematically documented, even fictionalized, that they would "win" both their children and the world's support and understanding. This was not true then, and it is not true today. Thus, in the past, "protective" mothers were unable to create a political organization.

However, by 1986, mother-kidnappers had begun to speak out, both publicly and, to me, privately. I found those whom I've interviewed all to be caring and responsible mothers. Their questions were always sane and heartbreaking: Do you think that my child is being sexually abused? Could I be imagining it? Do you think she'll develop a multiple personality? How long should I wait for the system to protect her? Should I kidnap her? Would you—if she were your child? Even if she's being sexually molested by her father, won't being a fugitive hurt her just as much—even more? And finally: What will happen to her if I'm arrested?

Our government should probably have placed such mothers in a federal witness protection program long ago. What they are doing is no less dangerous than what an undercover agent does when she testifies against a drug dealer or a pimp. A "protective" mother not only risks being jailed for accusing the criminal of committing a crime; she risks losing her children to that very criminal as well. In addition, such mothers also risk losing their jobs, homes, families, and health.

Many people find it easier to condemn the "protective" mother as the bearer of bad news rather than consider that what she's saying might be true. Thus people ask: Aren't these mother-kidnappers lying or crazy?

We do not have to personally like each victim of violence in order to believe her. As I've previously noted, like veterans or prisoners of war, many mother-kidnappers seem quite understandably to be suffering from post-traumatic stress syndrome. Many are economically marginal; some are themselves incest victims. This does not mean that they or their children have not been battered or sexually abused. We do know that sexual molestation exists in epidemic proportions within the family. An increasing number of people believe this, but people also seem to forget this when faced with a case of incest.

In the 1980s I was involved with two high-profile mother-kidnappers. One mother was Mary Beth Whitehead, who kidnapped her newborn daughter, "Baby M," after giving birth to her. Although she had signed a surrogate-mother contract, Whitehead did not want to surrender her child. I organized a campaign on behalf of her custodial rights. In 1987, I published *Sacred Bond: The Legacy of Baby M*, a book about this new kind of custody battle.

As I saw it, this was a battle in which a wealthy and educated couple felt utterly entitled to "buy," for ten thousand dollars, another woman's egg, womb, and nine months of gestational service. This child was created to be adopted even before she was conceived. Based on my research, it was clear that adopted children are at special risk and that American couples and individuals increasingly want designer-gene babies who do not have African features. Thus they do not adopt already existing children who desperately need a family.

I am not anti-adoption. Although my interest was primarily in the custody battle aspect of this case, I found myself having to debate the heads of adoption agencies and happy adoptive parents. They felt that what I was saying about this particular adoption and about surrogacy might cast all adoptive parents in a negative light. I also debated liberal feminists who were concerned about their own and their daughters' possible infertility. They all wanted the option of surrogacy to remain legal, inexpensive, and easily available.

In 1988 surrogacy was deemed a criminal enterprise and against public policy in New Jersey. The New Jersey Supreme Court also factored in the "best interests of the child" in their decision. I was proud to assist lawyer Harold Cassidy on this case and quite amused when, at the time, certain feminists accused me of "being in bed with the Pope" because the Vatican had also condemned surrogacy. Ultimately, Baby M had three parents and knew them all. I was recently told that, when she turned eighteen, she chose not to see her birth mother anymore.

That same year another high-profile mother-kidnapper made headlines. Unlike Mary Beth Whitehead, Dr. Elizabeth Morgan was a "protective" mother. She was also a D.C.-area plastic surgeon whose own father happened to be a former CIA operative. Thus, when Dr. Morgan observed, and experts had documented to her satisfaction, that her young daughter, Hilary, was being sexually abused by her father, the maternal grandparents fled with Hilary to New Zealand. Judge Herbert Dixon jailed Dr. Morgan for nearly two years because she would not tell the court where her daughter might be.

The therapist who evaluated Hilary called and spoke to me off the record. There was no doubt in my mind that this was a seriously endangered child. I again organized a demonstration on Dr. Morgan's behalf. Hilary's father, Dr. Eric Foretich, vehemently denied that he was guilty, and he was never found guilty in any court of law. However, a previous wife also accused Dr. Foretich of sexually abusing their daughter, Heather, and a Virginia judge did prevent visitation between Dr. Foretich and Heather.

Judge Dixon refused to relent. Dr. Morgan remained silent. Finally, in 1989, a special act of Congress freed Dr. Morgan. The act stated that in the future no judge could imprison a resident of Washington, D.C., for more than twelve months without a trial by jury for specific, stated crimes.

Freed, Dr. Morgan joined her parents and daughter in New Zealand. (At the time, there was no reciprocity between the United States and New Zealand, and thus the Morgans could not be extradited.) A movie was made about this mother, *A Mother's Right: The Elizabeth Morgan Story*, which starred Bonnie Bedelia. The bill that freed her was eventually deemed unconstitutional. Dr. Morgan remained in New Zealand for many years. When she did visit the United States, her daughter Hilary chose not to see her father.

Dr. Morgan's lengthy imprisonment haunted me. Judge Herbert Dixon had made Dr. Morgan an example of what can happen to any mother who defies the law to save her own child from paternal sexual abuse—or, if you will, who dares accuse a father of such a heinous crime.

Imagine if Elizabeth Morgan had not been a white, God-fearing, Christian, heterosexual mother. Imagine that she had not been a physician whose brother was a Justice Department lawyer, whose fiancé (later husband) was a judge, whose father was a retired CIA operative, and whose lawyer was an ex–State Attorney General. Look what can happen to an extremely privileged "insider" who is also a "protective" mother.

Interestingly enough, many of the media and psychiatric reports on Dr. Elizabeth Morgan bore an uncanny resemblance to those of mother-kidnapper Mary Beth Whitehead. I read the forensics in both cases. These two very different mothers were both described as "narcissistic," "stubborn," "manipulative," and "borderline personalities." Those who interviewed them did not "like" them and certainly did not see them as heroic. This is not surprising. Despite their vast differences in terms of class and education, both were viewed by the same kind of biased mental health experts.

How have mothers similar to Linda and Cathy, whose stories began this chapter, fared in the Custody Wars of the twenty-first century?

15

Court-Enabled Incest in the Twenty-First Century

. . . .

By the turn of the twenty-first century, things had definitely changed. Custodially challenged battered and "protective" mothers had become connected through the Internet. They could now exchange advice and information and strategize solutions. Wisely or unwisely, many began to appear pro se; they also consulted and became professional "divorce coaches." Such coaches are women who themselves have gone through acrimonious divorces and who now assist other women. Finally, mothers now hold annual conferences. For example, the seventh Battered Mothers Custody Conference, which was attended by many mothers who are also "protective," took place in January 2010 in Albany, New York. Their press release read, in part, as follows:

> Thousands of children [are] being sent to live with abusers while safe, protective parents, primarily mothers, are denied any meaningful relationship with their children. The court system has failed to respond appropriately to domestic violence and child abuse cases involving custody. There are common errors made by the courts and the professionals they rely upon which contribute to these tragedies. These same mistakes have negatively impacted battered women and children. . . . Advocates know that a variety of factors contribute to the problem—everything from gender bias to over-crowded courts, to poorly trained personnel to outright corruption.

As I did with Linda and Cathy in the previous chapter, let me introduce you to some similarly "protective" mothers whose battles began in the twenty-first century. These stories or cases all began after the turn of the twenty-first century, and many are still underway. I will focus on cases that took place in New York, Maryland, Pennsylvania, Florida, and Massachusetts.

NEW YORK

Dr. Jane Samuels's credibility is above reproach, as is her professional and expert knowledge of domestic violence, child sexual abuse, and the court system. Here is her story.

Jane is now an advocate for battered women and abused children. She is also a clinical psychologist and the mother of four children, two of whom have been sexually abused by their father. Although she has "on occasion spoken publicly about her case," she has not done so too often "because my outcome was so much better than the horrors that so many mothers endure." Technically, a gag order is still in place, she says. It is "written in the court decision, and forbids me to discuss the sexual abuse with anyone except a shrink or a lawyer. I consider it an unlawful order that I have chosen to respond to with my own version of civil disobedience."

Jane married another graduate student when she was in her midtwenties. When "the troubles" were upon her, Jane's own family supported her former husband against her and against their own grandchildren. She says,

> My brother and (former) friends testified against me on his behalf. The rest of his family, as well as four of my eight siblings, stopped acknowledging my existence once we separated.
>
> In 1998, six months after my ex-husband moved out, leaving me and our four children (then ages four through twelve), his attorney filed a motion in the county supreme court requesting regular visitation between my ex and our children. The motion included wholly fabricated allegations that I had been refusing to allow the children to visit their father; in fact, I had been asking him to take the children regularly for visits, which he rarely did. At the time, I did not realize that the filing of this motion—an "order to show cause"—was a regular feature of battered mothers' custody cases.
>
> After the court-ordered visitations commenced, my then-six-year-old daughter alleged that her father had sexually fondled her during

the middle of the night. I notified Child Protective Services. They directed me to go immediately to the county family court to file a family offense petition and to request an order of protection, so that visitation between my four children and their father could be stopped by the court.

The court issued a temporary order of protection and ordered CPS to conduct an investigation of the sexual abuse allegations. I had already fired one very green attorney, who was foisted on me by his partner, a female family lawyer whom I'd originally hired merely because, in my naïveté, I thought a woman lawyer would understand and respond to my case appropriately. The second attorney then asked the court to order supervised visitation between my two sons and their father at Family Services. This was before the CPS investigation was completed. I later learned that this lawyer was on the board of directors of Family Services, to which, apparently, he regularly refers his clients and those of opposing attorneys.

In a private meeting, this attorney—whose name I found on a list of family lawyers recommended by our local domestic violence agency—urged me to "treat this sexual abuse differently" from the way sexual abuse typically is handled, stating that my ex-husband's fondling of our six-year-old daughter was, as he strangely put it, a "mistake," as per my ex-husband's defense that he had "been sleeping" at the time he abused our daughter. CPS didn't agree; they "indicated" the children's father for "sexual abuse" and "inadequate guardianship," adding that they had "serious concerns" about the safety of the children should the father have unsupervised access.

However, during the court appearance when the judge read the CPS report, the court-appointed guardian ad litem, who had not once spoken with me and had met just once with my four children for a total of fifteen minutes, accused me of "parental alienation"—this despite the fact that CPS believed the allegations were true. As it turned out, this man had himself gone through a bitter, contested divorce and custody battle with his wife a few years prior. Because he had, upon taking on the position of law guardian for my children, immediately begun to advocate for the children's father while accusing me of parental alienation, I kept asking my attorney to have him dismissed as law guardian. Instead, the attorney defended the law guardian's behavior, refusing to comply with my request, claiming that it's "almost impossible" to get rid of a law guardian after he's been assigned to a case. Flabbergasted, I asked my attorney if he had a personal friendship with the law guardian, which he denied. However, in a written statement he later submitted to the court, he stated, to the contrary, that "Mr. X is a personal friend of mine." But when the family court judge "dropped" the sexual abuse case due to "lack of jurisdiction," merging it with the divorce case being handled (as per NYS law) by the Supreme Court, this law guardian finally resigned, citing "pressing responsibilities" at Family Court.

After the sexual abuse allegations were *founded*, my ex-husband filed for sole custody of our four children. The court recommended that a local psychologist perform the custody evaluation, to which the opposing attorney agreed. I later learned that my ex-husband had joined the Fathers' Rights Association.

As the psychologist, a woman, was conducting the custody evaluation, she had access to all of the CPS investigatory reports, including the verbatim statements made by my six-year-old and her older sister. She told us that she did not believe my daughter's reports of sexual abuse (saying to my older daughter, "Well, he didn't have intercourse with her"). She arranged for my children to meet with their father in her office for a sort of "reunion party."

In her custody evaluation report to the court, she dismissed the sexual abuse findings as, in her words, "tenuous at best," despite the fact that she had not performed a sexual abuse evaluation of my daughter and was fully aware of the CPS findings. In the written report, she recommended that I have primary physical custody, but "with great reservation." She also recommended that custody should be switched to the father if I were to engage in "further alienation" of my children from their father.

At the custody trial, she testified on behalf of my ex-husband. Her testimony included statements that she was not an expert on child sexual abuse and that she had "no opinion" regarding the sexual abuse findings. She also named the children's father the "friendly parent" while at the same time admitting that my daughter, the sexual abuse victim, did display significant signs of sexual abuse, as did my older daughter.

The final supreme court decision handed down essentially mirrored what the psychologist had recommended. I was given "modified joint custody," requiring me to keep the father informed of all of the children's activities. By the time the judgment was made, my ex had been indicated by CPS yet again, for "emotional abuse," due to his attempts to coerce his victim to recant her report of his abuse.

I was one of the lucky ones; I did not lose physical custody of my children. I raised them, to greater or lesser degrees, under the implied threat that the custody case could be legally reopened any time until my youngest turned eighteen. And my ex continued to make that threat over the years—until the children themselves warned him against ever doing so.

Today, my youngest child is almost sixteen; he sees his father occasionally. My younger daughter, the sexual abuse victim, is almost eighteen and is doing well. She has a friendly but distant relationship with her father; so does my nineteen-year-old son.

My oldest daughter, who I believe was the most traumatized by my ex's behavior, took her own life three years ago, at the age of twenty, after suffering from severe depression for several months. After she died, my ex—in true form—refused to even consider my wishes regarding her wake and burial. I do not know, to this day, whether she would be still alive if the court had protected my children from their abusive father, as I asked them to do many times.

MARYLAND

In 2002 a father punched his eight-year-old daughter in the mouth—yet he ended up with custody. According to a forensic report, this physical violence was an "indicated finding." The mother, Rita—who in no way had physically, psychologically, or sexually abused either of her two daughters—ended up losing all but minimal supervised visitation. In fact, Rita, not the father, spent three months in jail because she kept calling her children.

Why did this mother lose custody? In my view, she did mainly because she displayed "extreme emotionality," both about the paternal physical and sexual abuse of her children and about the court system that protected him and endangered both her and her children.

Just like Linda in California in the late 1980s and early 1990s, Rita was forever punished for her extreme "emotionality," which she did not suppress when dealing with social service and courtroom professionals who had tremendous power over her fate. Sadly, her "emotionality" (tears, anxiety, anger) over the well-being of her children and over her potentially losing them was seen as more dangerous to her children than their being punched in the mouth by their father, being sexually abused by him, and being brainwashed against their mother as well.

According to Rita, her husband had a bad temper, tried to increasingly isolate her, and was constantly getting into fights with his construction company clients. Rita had a college degree but chose to be a stay-at-home mother. However, she also worked as a party planner for children—a successful business that her husband forced her to give up.

Due to "cruelty, infidelity, domestic violence, and child abuse," Rita initiated a divorce. However, in 2002, as the divorce heated up, Rita's husband alleged that she had posted flyers in the neighborhood accusing him of child abuse and of being a "registered sex offender." She denied having done so and claims she told the police that he was not a "registered sex offender." Still, because she *denied* doing so, Rita was considered at risk psychiatrically. The court-appointed mental health professionals decided that Rita had "disassociated" from having done so. No one suspected that the father himself might have done so as a ruse—or that perhaps a concerned relative or friend might have done so. No one hypothesized that indeed, Rita might have done so in order to protect her children—and then was too afraid to admit it. Damned if she did, damned if she didn't. From that moment on, Rita was lost.

In 2002, just before Christmas, Rita's children were taken away from her, and sole custody was given to her ex-husband. Unbelievably, in 2003 Rita was actually arrested and spent three months in jail for calling her children too often. She says she was unaware that she was not allowed to do so. Further, she could not afford and was not given a lawyer. During this time, she was ordered to pay fifteen thousand dollars of her upper-middle-class ex-husband's legal fees. With an arrest on her record, her opportunities for certain kinds of work also became more limited.

Thereafter, Rita's ex-husband kept calling the police, falsely alleging that Rita was either violently abusing the children or breaking the law by calling or seeing them at the wrong time or for too long. As a consequence, Rita developed serious post-traumatic symptoms "when she sees police cars or hears sirens. When someone knocks on the door, she becomes very fearful, thinking that someone may be coming to falsely arrest her. . . . She has no intention of violating any court order but her past experience has left her frightened."

According to a 2008 court-ordered forensic report, the record shows that Rita had indeed been seen as "loving, devoted, and affectionate" toward her children—but that she had also approached professionals "unprofessionally"; she dared criticize them for separating her from her children and for endangering them instead. But, as the forensic report said, "Ms. X is an emotional and outspoken woman, who writes to people directly (about) how she feels without mincing words and often with little tact. This way of approaching professionals has severely backfired against her, as many professionals have reacted defensively."

However, this is not the way Rita acts toward her children—a point lost on the "defensive" professionals. In fact, there is a record of the children telling one professional after another that they really missed their mother but then pleading with that professional not to tell their father that they had said so. Apparently, they were not being allowed to say anything positive about their mother at home, including that they wanted to see her or live with her.

Incredibly, after punching his daughter in the mouth, the father recovered his visitation rights as well as sole custody more quickly than Rita, the children's primary caretaker, was ever allowed to recover custody or even liberal, unsupervised visitation. The system chose to punish this good mother and her children for nearly six years. Social service and courtroom professionals retaliated against her because she criticized them, not because she was a danger to her children. And they genuinely viewed her refusal to behave humbly toward them—or inability to do so—as proof that she was mentally ill.

According to the forensic report, Rita views her "extreme emotionality" as a consequence of "losing her parental time." The 2008 report was careful to collate all previous reports and to interview Rita as well. Everyone agrees that Rita was and is an exceptionally good mother. The psychologist listened to the tape that originally got Rita in trouble and found that the child who reported the sexual abuse sounded entirely credible and not like she had been coached. "It is unfortunate that Ms. XX's own defensive and emotional behavior has caused social services to misinterpret this event." This psychologist also found Rita's account of not having posted the flyers as logical and believable. She does not believe that Rita "disassociated."

"No one in the state of Maryland," Rita told me, "endured supervised visitation as long as I did, despite reports that my interactions with my children were quite positive, certainly more so than their interactions with their abusive father. My case involved extreme courtroom manipulation from the start. I lost custody of my children when my daughter called me crying that her father was abusing her. 'Daddy rubbed my pee pee,' she said. I recorded part of the conversation—it is hard to listen to. My ex claims I put my daughter up to it and he took my children from me." According to the 2008 psychologist, Rita showed clear signs of what she calls "legal abuse syndrome," which can afflict "people who have been engaged in ongoing litigation that has worn them down, eroded their financial well-being and led them to be perceived in ways that are unfamiliar to them."

In 2009 Rita obtained unsupervised visitation with her daughters, but she chose "not to visit with [her] children [then] because of their father's interference with [her] life."

This is a terrible tragedy. The court system enabled a vindictive, violent, and possibly sexually abusive father to destroy a good and essential relationship between two daughters and their mother. Clearly Rita is genuinely afraid that her own natural emotional expressiveness might get her jailed; she is not totally wrong. But, she is also defeated, beaten down. Her self-esteem suffered a series of tremendous blows from which she has not recovered.

PENNSYLVANIA

This case involves the kinds of byzantine details, conspiracies, and biased agendas that we are used to seeing in huge political scandals. One simply does not expect to see this kind of diabolical behavior when the welfare of children is involved. But, as this mother keenly points out, no one wants to believe that a father can be so evil to his own children and to the mother of his children; everyone wants to believe that even the greatest of male sinners can and should be redeemed. And everyone needs to keep getting paid. It does not matter if the mother and children pay a huge price in order to appease these lawyers, judges, and court-appointed therapists.

Over a nine-year period, Roberta's case has been heard in family, criminal, and civil court. The various court cases are not yet over.

This case involves serious domestic violence and even more serious child sexual abuse. For years Roberta was battered and beaten on a daily basis; her surgeon husband Max threatened her with "dismemberment" and would hold a "butcher knife to her throat." He would threaten to commit suicide in front of all the children—but he also threatened to "cut her head off" and told the children to say "good-bye" to her. She writes, "He punched and kicked all of us, threw furniture, broke appliances and often choked me. I got between him and the children and most often, he would come after our autistic son, Jonathan. He hated me for having a 'defective son' as he and my father-in-law put it and he hated Jonathan for being 'defective.' It made him feel as if he was not perfect to have such an imperfect child. All of the years of trying to live up to my promises and my religion by getting him help did not seem worth it anymore."

Thus Roberta told her husband that she would be asking for child support for their four children. True to form, he told her that "he would smash her skull into a thousand pieces and then run over it on the pavement."

In 2001 Roberta asked for an order of protection against her husband. In 2006 she divorced. Her ex-husband was only ordered to pay for five years of child support, which was officially labeled "alimony" so that it would be taxable to her and not to him. At one point he stopped paying for his children's health insurance, even though their autistic son had substantial medical needs. It took Roberta, a part-time musician, two years to finally get him on Medicaid. Now, she and her family are threatened with homelessness. On the advice of his lawyer, Max completely cleaned out his bank account at the beginning of the legal proceedings. Roberta was broke before she knew what hit her.

In 2006 Max was convicted on various counts of child abuse. Among other outrages, he had raped one of his sons and later sodomized both of his sons with a broomstick. Roberta told me that she once witnessed her husband on the verge of sodomizing their eldest son in this way. Her three other children were watching the attempted violation and screaming, begging for him to stop, but he told Roberta that it was just a joke and he would never have gone through with it. He acquiesced to therapy, but unbeknownst to Roberta, he had already sodomized and would continue to sodomize his sons after this incident. Ultimately, the fact that she witnessed the near sodomy but reacted mildly was used against her in court.

However, the corruption, inefficiency, and bias in the court system was such that the family court judge in her case mandated unsupervised visitation for the father even after the rape case had gone to trial. At one point, one of the sons ran away from his middle school, refusing to submit to visitation because he was too terrified of his father. In court, the judge ignored the children's pleas that they not be forced to endure unsupervised visitation with their father.

According to Roberta, one of the custody evaluators in her case, refused to report the abuse he had documented, lying that Roberta had never told him about the abuse. Another evaluator prepared an outrageous report accusing Roberta of being a "manipulative liar" and also claiming that she was "severely delusional and schizophrenic."

At one point, Roberta was issued a gag order, presumably to spare the children the pain and humiliation of public exposure. However, the abuser was not silenced. He went public and claimed that a "bitter wife" was making false accusations against him, a respected physician. Incredibly, the family court judge also threatened her fourteen-year-old son with foster care if he refused visits with his father. After criminal charges had been filed, the criminal court judge ordered the fourteen-year-old to visit with the very man, his father, who was being accused of raping him. Further, this judge forced the teenager to participate in "reunification therapy" with the proviso that the children could not "discuss the sexual abuse allegations with their father" in the therapy session. (Both judges happened to be women).

In Roberta's view, her ex-husband hoped that by dragging the case out, he would impoverish her and eventually obtain unsupervised visitation so that he could continue his reign of terror over his children. The fact that he had a series of girlfriends did not in any way limit or change his need to terrify, abuse, and dominate his children. When the court-ordered therapist who had originally documented the sexual abuse tried to be helpful (he opposed the "family reunification" therapy for example), he saw that the deck was stacked against protecting the children. He backed out and said "there was nothing more he could do." Only the children themselves were able to save themselves by refusing unsupervised visitation with their father. However, their mother risked being held in contempt of court and jailed because she failed to facilitate or perhaps had even encouraged her children to refuse seeing their father.

She told me that "at the suggestion of the judge, we were left with no share of the marital assets outside of one account to insure payment to the lawyers and experts, no family home, no healthcare for our adult disabled son whom my ex husband was convicted of criminally abusing . . . an amount of child support that is less than 3 percent of their father's income each year and no educational funds for the children. Please recall that their father is a surgeon who makes over one million a year." She got "no alimony after taxes and legal fees."

"Psychologically," she added, "my children have suffered through numerous problems, including depression, anxiety, post-traumatic stress disorder, and eating disorders, to name a few. They have needed therapy and medical treatment, none of which their father has paid for. Even after the state had secured a conviction in the criminal case, the family court went on to ignore the conviction, continuing to obstruct justice by its refusal to enforce health insurance for our adult disabled son."

It comes as no surprise, therefore, that one lawyer, whom Roberta consulted before this legal fiasco began, advised her to "stay within the marriage and try to get my husband more psychological help, or I would be on the street with a new baby and three small children forced to pay half of his medical school debt off with no marital assets to divide."

Sad to say, but this lawyer's advice was realistic. On the other hand, how can any mother worth her salt allow her children to be sexually, physically, and psychologically abused without fighting to free her children from such abuse? It is tragic that the American court system punishes mothers and children for exposing paternal crimes; it is reprehensible that fathers are actually rewarded when such crimes are brought to the attention of court personnel, including judges and custody evaluators.

FLORIDA

In 2004 in north-central Florida, Colette filed for divorce after eleven years of a rocky marriage in which she was persistently abused, both physically and emotionally, but in which she also gave birth to two daughters. Colette was a stay-at-home traditional mother. She did not obtain a divorce until 2007. However in 2002 Colette received a shocking call from her eight-year-old daughter's school administrator, who said that Colette's daughter had "sexual knowledge way beyond her years, that she was found 'putting dolls in sexual positions' and masturbating at school."

At that time, Colette also discovered that her husband was rather too keen on washing his daughters' vaginas. He lingered over this task when they were five and seven years old. When their mother told him to stay out of the children's bathroom, he simply refused. According to Colette, at age seven one of her daughters spontaneously said at Sunday school "I suck my Daddy's penis." She also told a therapist, "I have a secret with my Daddy and he said if I ever told I will become an orphan and he'll take me away from you." When she drew a picture of her daddy for the therapist, she drew an erect penis on legs. This information was clearly and carefully "documented by licensed professionals."

In 2006 a licensed psychologist called a child abuse hotline. She was the only one in a long line of professionals to have done so. Colette said, "She took a courageous stand to protect my children. I am still in contact with her and she is alarmed by what has happened in my case."

When Colette petitioned for custody of the children, she assumed that she was on solid footing. She had been their sole primary caretaker for all their lives. Her husband did not oppose her on custody. She said, "Never did I ever imagine in my wildest dreams that me—'squeaky clean' class Mom, soccer Mom, community volunteer, no drugs, no alcohol, no abuse, nothing—could ever lose custody and be placed on supervised visitation with only fifty-seven hours of contact in two and half years."

But that's precisely what happened. She explained, "The mandatory reporters in my case knew of the abuse and—other than that one psychologist—ignored the mandatory reporting laws and failed to protect my daughters. The custody evaluator in my case is known for what she can do for ignoring abuse in custody cases and goes after the money."

Incredibly, she accused the disclosing daughter of having "pediatric bipolar" and therefore of being an "unreliable witness." Although the evaluator initially reported that Colette had a better "psychological bond with the children than their father did," she reversed her assessment two days before trial. Colette believes some "foul play" was involved. In 2007 the judge refused to hear the testimony of the psychologist who had reported the sexual abuse and—without prior warning—orally ordered the children into their father's custody. He also limited the mother to highly restricted supervised visitation.

Colette spent one hundred forty thousand dollars on legal fees before her money ran out. She is currently representing herself in an appellate court case. She describes her struggle as one in which she is trying to "undo the judges' errors" and to reverse the "legal kidnapping" of her daughters.

You might think that Colette sounds a bit "paranoid" or naive about her ideas of "foul play" and "legal kidnapping." However, what if you knew that her husband's family was the single most powerful family in their city? Then you might better understand the kind of walls Colette encountered. Judges, lawyers, politicians, physicians, counselors, and the heads of private schools and country clubs were all either longtime friends or beholden to her husband and his family in one way or another. Or they wished to curry favor and gain some advantage.

Thus Colette, a high-school graduate, was ordered to pay child support to her husband, who, according to Colette, earned between fifty and sixty thousand dollars *every month.*

In 2007 the judge gave Colette two weeks to vacate her home. She would be allowed to see her daughters in two weeks but only at a supervised visitation center. She said,

> That day, after carpool, soccer, dinner, homework, I packed my daughters' school lunches, washed out their soccer uniforms, set their backpacks out, and went upstairs to hug and kiss them goodbye, and as they cried, I cried, telling them that I love them very much. My daughters cried, "Mommy fight for us, do something every day to try to get us back and don't ever stop." I promised them I would but never did I imagine that it would be thirty-two months without them and only fifty-seven hours of actual contact at the SV center. Now [2009], I talk to them most every day after school and before bedtime. He tried to stop my phone contact but, in 2007, my appeals attorney just said to call them. I also get to go to school events, band concerts, awards ceremonies. The judge ordered me to provide supervisors so that I could see the girls outside of the SV center. We provided fifteen people such as PTA presidents, soccer moms, business and community leaders. My ex-husband refused all fifteen, and the judge agreed with him.

To add insult to injury, her husband began an affair with a neighbor, a married woman, before the divorce was finalized. Colette told me, "He was having an affair with my married neighbor for two years during the three-and-a-half-year divorce right in front of the children—dating with them, [going to] hotels with her and the children—and he married her after the divorce and now she is their primary caregiver."

Despite these injustices, or because of them, Colette told me, "I am finding out that I have incredible strength and am very empowered to speak up about the injustice done to all of our children. I have faith in God, an attitude of gratitude, and I pray that one day justice will prevail." She wrote, "America better wake up, because if I can lose custody, anyone can."

MASSACHUSETTS

Sharon is a technical sergeant in the U.S. Air Force. She married and gave birth to a son in 2001. Sharon first noticed signs of abuse when her son was only one and a half years old. He had been staying with her husband's family while she attended a program at her air force base. The boy came home in severe pain because his genitals had been rubbed raw. She called her husband's mother and asked what had happened. "Nothing," she said. At first, she bought into the excuse because she "didn't even want to conceive" of sexual abuse. But when her son was old enough to talk, he told her what had really happened.

When Sharon found out that her son was being sexually abused, she reported the abuse to the Department of Social Services (DSS). She and her son found safety in a domestic violence shelter. The child revealed to a forensic sexual evaluator that he had been abused by his father's family. DSS documented that a paternal aunt had "bit her nephew hard on the butt, leaving teeth marks." The toddler also told DSS that his half sister "stuck Lego blocks up my butt and it's not funny!" Both a pediatrician and the child's therapist filed multiple abuse and neglect reports. According to her lawyer, the pediatrician documented injuries to the boy's genitals.

One day in 2004 as she was reading a book to her son, he climbed onto her head, pressed his diaper into her face, and said, "Mommy, suck my cock. Suck my cock, Mommy. Mommy, suck my cock." "Trying to hide my shock," she told me, "I picked him up and set him on the bed and asked, 'Who said this to you? Who told you these words?' He began to cry and said, 'I want Daddy.'"

Even then she "remained in disbelief" about what her husband had been doing to her son. "I was very slow to realize Daddy was one of the perps. I was in love; I thought I was married for life; I had a beautiful baby boy whom I love more than I ever thought it was possible to love anyone." But when her son began fingering his own anus and saying, "Daddy tickle me there for go," and then pantomiming his father's orgasm, "complete with heavy breathing," she finally accepted the truth.

In 2005 her husband sued for divorce because she had insisted that he get therapy. Incredibly, the judge in the divorce trial barred the boy's therapist from testifying on behalf of the child. The judge ignored videotaped evidence of the child "humping" both the floor and his teddy bear for up to five minutes at a time. She also ignored videotape of the son saying, "Daddy licks my pee pee," an audiotape of him pleading not to go his father for visitation, and a log of eyewitness accounts of the son using inappropriate language and sexually acting out. While the judge's concerns about the reliability of the evidence were not unreasonable, she could have at least spoken to the child herself. She never did. On the contrary: she openly laughed when the testimony was presented.

According to Sharon, her husband's lawyer accused her of being a "coacher," an "alienator," and "every other abuse excuse they typically employ." The judge agreed that she was "making up the abuse." Her husband used her own honorable military service against her by stating that since she could be "sent to the sand" at any moment, she was incapable of adequately caring for her child.

The outcome of the custody battle was, as she put it, "The complete destruction of our lives with court enforced sexual torture of my precious baby boy, sole legal and physical custody to the perpetrator." The allegedly pedophilic father was awarded full custody of the four-year-old child. Sharon was reduced to supervised visitation, for four hours per week, at three hundred dollars per week. The judge ordered her to undergo a psychological evaluation with a "court-preferred" psychologist.

Sharon wrote, "At first I was shocked that the judge 'fell for it.' Now I know that it was a setup from the git-go, and there was nothing I could do once the truth of the father-on-son rape was out." Quoting pro-mother attorney Michael Lesher, she told me, "The truth about the family courts gives the lie to some cherished American assumptions. Americans believe they are safe from arbitrary abuse of governmental power—yet child protective services, 'law guardians,' and family court judges can cast aside the norms of due process."

According to Sharon, the judge in her case, a woman, was eventually forced to retire early after Sharon lobbied the Massachusetts Commission on Judicial Conduct. Letters of complaint may have been effective. The judge was not censured—she was merely "retired," probably with her pension intact. Of the lawyers who handled her case, she writes, "five out of the six I hired were corrupt, collusive, cowering, and incompetent. I was simply fleeced, a mother with two government jobs, a juicy target sucked in by dangling my helpless child."

The advice she gives to other women is stern. "Organize the underground railway because you have an obligation to the child you bore, and the American court considers you and your baby to be a man's property to dispose of as he wishes. Wake up. . . . Change the law, and until you can accomplish that, take your child and flee. If you expect even a chance of raising your child, I would not recommend impregnation by a man. I recommend a sperm bank; they are affordable."

Incredibly, this battle is far from over. In Sharon's view, a new judge "retaliated" against her and stood by the previous "retired" judge's ruling.

Sharon still has to pay in order to see her son and then only for limited, supervised visitation. Worse: She still cannot protect him from whatever abuse he is being forced to endure.

Why would the courts enforce such a savage mother-child separation? Why would the courts, the police, the Department of Social Services, and the state attorney general refuse to believe the sworn testimony of a high-ranking U.S. Air Force veteran?

Homosexually abused children grow up to become pedophiles. There is no cure for this. And, of course, incest runs in families. It is an ongoing, intergenerational problem, a tribal or cultlike phenomenon. No one turns another member in, few escape, and anyone who tries to "tell" is denounced and shunned.

Ask most lawyers, judges, and mental health professionals whether they are in favor of raping children; all will say "absolutely not." However, like others, they resist believing that incest really exists. It is easier, even safer, to believe that the mothers involved are "lying" and "crazy" and have made it all up.

Thus, those mothers who are trying to free themselves and their children from lives of living horror, often find themselves trapped in the court system for anywhere from five to fifteen years. Some mothers may be trying to get child and/or spousal support enforced. Other mothers may be trying to end unsupervised visitation with an abusive father or to overturn an existing order of sole paternal custody or joint custody. Some mothers are fighting against orders which have cruelly forced them into expensive, supervised, and limited visitation, usually because they've alleged paternal child sexual abuse. Some mothers have faced battles over allegations of paternal or maternal brainwashing and kidnapping.

All such cases become torturous. Mothers are being condemned to spend their time and (nonexistent) money on defending themselves in court. In my opinion, they are being tortured by the legal system. I am not using this word lightly.

However herein lies a dilemma. If we want the court system to rule justly, that process takes time and costs a great deal of money. Although everything is relative, the truth is that most judges are underpaid and have far too many cases at any given moment. Most lawyers cannot afford to work forever for a wage below the poverty level, nor can they pay for all the costs that a "high-conflict," acrimonious, complex divorce might incur. Why should they? Such realities, combined with an anti-woman bias, leads to years of court-enabled torture for "good enough" mothers. Many lose both their physical and mental health under the pressure. Often, when this happens, "the system" believes that the mother was crazy to begin with. This is rarely true.

Allow me to introduce you to some twenty-first-century cases of prolonged legal torture.

16

Legal Torture from 1986 to 2010

·············

There are a number of cases that may be described as full-scale, court-assisted, perfectly legal assaults upon motherhood and mothers. The issues vary and do not involve incest allegations. However, the nature of such all-out courtroom assaults is in a category of its own. Some mental health professionals have begun to describe this phenomenon as "legal abuse syndrome." Over the years, I have heard many such stories. Here are but a mere handful of such tales.

I have chosen to share only a few details of each story, because even these small parts are overwhelming. One feels bogged down, hopeless; the cases all seem to merge together; the stories are painful to read. But imagine having to live through each and every detail when your child's safety is at stake, when you can't pay the rent or the mortgage, when you can't afford a good-enough lawyer, and when you are afraid that you will lose your mind as well as your children. Then multiply whatever you're feeling with the experience of having to endure the actual litigation, which may last anywhere from four to twenty very intense years and which will take over your waking and sleeping life. Mothers and their supportive families have routinely been impoverished by such lawsuits. Some mothers have also lost their jobs, friends, family, and their physical and mental health. Yes, the stress is that intense.

Someone who merely works in the court system as a lawyer, judge, guardian ad litem, social worker, or mental health professional goes home at night. What they do does not affect them personally; rather, they may "take their work home with them," but it is not personal to their lives. It is not *about* their lives. Like physicians or soldiers, courtroom and legal personnel often "harden" themselves in order to do the work. If not, they too will become overwhelmed by the unending misery and chicanery that passes before them.

TEXAS: TWENTY YEARS AND COUNTING

In 1986 a father won custody of his two-year-old son away from his perfectly good mother. Let us assume that the father was also a good father. Why then would a good father need to obliterate his son's good mother from his life totally and forever? Why would a good father legally kidnap his son and demand that the mother give up her parental rights if she ever wanted to see her son again? Here is what Sarah, the mother and formerly a legal secretary, said:

> When you ask your newly estranged husband where your two-year-old son is and he hisses the word "safe" at you, you have stepped into a nightmare. In 1986, my husband George "seized and secreted"—the nonlibelous term for technically legal kidnapping—our son David. Four months later, after one incompetent lawyer intent on protecting his win-loss record and one lawyer who held my case for a four thousand dollar ransom two days before trial, I listened to well-paid expert witnesses misdiagnose me based on teenage rebelliousness, heard my own mother testify for George (she later killed herself), and heard two people I thought were good friends testify against me. The divorce was granted and George was awarded custody.

This took place in a district court before a probate judge who "probably handled overflow cases."

For nearly two years, Sarah's ex-husband proceeded to use "every means at his disposal" to deny her visitation. After each of her son's visits, he would show up at her doorstep with an armed escort in order to intimidate her. Although she tried to pay child support as ordered by the court, her ex-husband's lawyer refused to take the money so that he could then sue her for nonpayment of the child support. Unbelievably, according to Sarah, this judge later killed himself after being prosecuted for corruption. At one point, he put Sarah in jail for contempt.

Sarah's ex-husband then legally kidnapped their son. "When he called me and asked me if I would sign an affidavit of relinquishment of my parental rights 'so we can get this case out of the courtroom' but promised me I could still see David—at his discretion, of course—because, after all, I would 'always be David's mother,' I asked for a few moments to think about it. I knew exactly what he was doing but I was also bankrupt." A month later, the judge terminated Sarah's parental rights; shortly thereafter, her ex took her son to another city in Texas, far away from their home.

After hearing her story, Southwest Airlines gave Sarah a free ticket to visit her son; she flew there and snuck into David's classroom to give him some Christmas presents. Her former father-in-law found her there and demanded that she leave the building, which she did quietly in order to avoid making a scene in front of her son. Her former father-in-law told her, "We've spent over a quarter of a million dollars putting you in your place, little lady, and there's plenty more where that came from so don't you go getting any ideas." They then got a restraining order on the grounds of "invasion of privacy, harassment, and intentional infliction of emotional distress." Sarah did not see her son again for another thirteen years.

Some families function as if they were cults. In a sense, they *are* cults and they view all outsiders and non–blood relations as dangerous intruders.

Sarah was determined to avoid becoming "psychologically sterilized." If her ex-husband was a bad man, that was not going to mean that all men are bad. Thus, Sarah remarried—and gave birth to two more children. She also became a stepmother to her new husband's son. "I was determined not to let 'the bad guys' defeat my spirit," she told me. Like so many of these mothers, Sarah also wrote a book about her experience to "purge [herself] of all the mental poison but I set the book aside because I was adamant that the ending hadn't happened yet. . . . Through all of this, we kept vigil for David. When we built a house in 1994, it had a room for David. Sarah kept a stocking on her mantle every year at Christmas." Every April 2, on National Reconciliation Day, she sent a letter to her ex-husband asking for permission to visit David. One year, in 2001, he accepted, and she and her new family flew to Texas to see him. "It was wonderful," she said. Then she didn't see him for another five years.

Finally, when David was in college, he got back in touch with his mother himself. Sarah wrote, "He is a forgiving person and he now has a loving relationship with both of his parents. A happy ending at last."

Sarah thanked me for *Mothers on Trial*, which was a "lifeline" for her. It helped her adopt a philosophical and long-range view, which I find simply remarkable.

It is impossible for one to know the father's motives in this case. Did he hate women so much that he did not want to "pollute" his son by having a woman in his life, especially his own mother? Did George believe that he himself could be a better mother or a mother-father to his son? Or did he have another woman whom he wanted to mother his son: his own mother perhaps, or a new wife?

In any event, in this case, a son was forced to grow up without his mother, and a mother was forced to lead her life entirely apart from her son. When they finally connected, her son was a grown man in his twenties. There is no way they can ever "make up for lost time." The court system enabled a father to get away with matricide, quite legally, in an American courtroom.

HAWAII: TEN YEARS AND COUNTING

Another father used the court and legal system in Hawaii to attack and legally batter a perfectly good mother for a full decade. Sexual abuse was possibly going on, but the case did not turn on this issue so much as on general paternal physical and psychological abuse.

In 2000 Elizabeth divorced her husband for many reasons, including "cruelty, domestic violence, and child abuse." Nevertheless, although she managed to win full physical and legal custody of their two children in 2003, she still found herself mired in litigation, which spanned ten years and involved eight different judges. Her husband was, eventually, not allowed visitation. Elizabeth calls herself a "unicorn" because she understands that her situation, however, grievous, eventually had a "rare and delightful outcome."

Elizabeth came from a "violent" home herself, which may help to explain why she put up with so much abuse for so long (the two married in 1991). She told me, "I didn't recognize it as domestic violence until I was way out of the marriage and getting help for the aftereffects of it, and even then I couldn't really believe that it really happened to me/us—it was just so surreal."

What kind of man was her husband? She explained that "my cooking was always an issue—he referred to it as 'abuse' in the divorce. Everything was always my fault, I couldn't do anything right, I was a bad mother and an even worse wife. 'Cruel' is a good word to describe it—lots of humiliating and embarrassing moments, too many tears for so many reasons."

She said, "When I needed to go to the hospital because I was in labor, he decided teaching a weekend class was more important. . . . Because I'd 'whined' that I didn't want to be alone my first day home, he sent a coworker from his office—a woman whom I'd never met or heard of before—over to 'babysit' me. He did this even though he had two weeks of paternity leave."

It gets worse. "My ex is a very scary person when he gets angry; he has a quick, volatile, and explosive temper and has scared two attorneys off our case due to his behavior. He only hit me once when I was pregnant. But, when he killed my beloved cat because 'she was getting in the way of our marriage,' I came to realize what he is capable of, and that he had no remorse for any of it."

What made her finally leave her husband? She said that "the final straw was the day he killed my five-year-old daughter's spirit; I watched him systematically strip her of her beautiful little spirit over a course of hours and was absolutely powerless to stop it. Everyday she used to ask, 'Mommy, why does Daddy hate you so much?' But after that day, she asked, 'Mommy, why does Daddy hate *us* so much?' That was it—the next day we were gone."

Throughout all of this, her family was extremely unsupportive. "My family took his side," she told me. Their attitude was, "He's a good husband and father; you must be crazy just like he said you are. Otherwise why would you be getting rid of him?"

Initially her ex-husband received unsupervised visitation. After a year, this was revoked because, she told me, "he treated my daughter horrendously: hit, shoved, slapped her, denied her food, water, and sleep, put her and my son in dangerous situations, exposed them to inappropriate adult situations and content, prevented her from doing homework and participating in social events, wouldn't let her speak to me, made her cook for him and serve him (she was only ten) and was becoming increasingly sexually inappropriate with her."

This was extremely hard on her daughter. Elizabeth told me, "After visitation had been stopped, she held me accountable for what he did to her because she was telling me what he was doing, yet I kept on surrendering her for visitation regardless. As far as she was concerned, I was allowing him to hurt her. So for three years, she relentlessly let me know how much she resented me for giving her to someone I knew was hurting and violating her. It was awful." It took her daughter three years before she was willing to touch her mother again. "Her innocence is gone," she says of her daughter, "but she was able to retain just a smidgen of tenderness."

The experience has been extremely traumatic for Elizabeth too. "Physically, I've aged more in the last ten years than I did in the first thirty. Since he stalks me unabated, monitors me, maliciously interferes in my life and relationships with others, and appears to continue in his mental decline, I'm in an almost constant state of fear and mild anxiety."

As for the court system she spent ten years in, she has only contempt for it, calling it a "devil's playground," "an infestation of corrupt, unethical, incompetent, ignorant, and arrogant individuals comingling in an incestuous pool where good and innocent souls are tormented for profit or pleasure."

Fortunately, for now, the nightmare seems to be over. While her ex-husband tried to win custody by accusing her of parental alienation syndrome, that tack has not worked so far. As she said, the system "worked" in her case for three main reasons: she obtained a temporary restraining order for incidents of abuse and escalating threats; she "followed the court orders, the directives, and even the intent of them to a T; and "I did as I was told and reported every incident and transgression my ex made to the proper authorities."

But her case will never really be closed until her youngest child turns eighteen in 2015. Until then, she's holding her breath and hoping for the best.

ILLINOIS: NINE YEARS AND COUNTING

In 2004 Florence, an Illinois mother of two who is now a forensic psychologist, finally divorced her businessman husband after years of marriage and her discovering that he had raped her much younger sister, who was nine years old at the time. After nine years of stressful litigation, she lost her home, her assets, and sole custody. She has been financially devastated. She despairs of ever being able to pay back her enormous debt. She said, "The court bankrupted me when all I did was leave a very abusive man." What kind of abuse did the court overlook where the children were concerned? This is a father who "threw his son's ten-pound book bag across the street into our yard screaming 'I'm not doing the fucking homework'"; a father who removed the furnace from the family home and replaced it with a faulty furnace that he found in an abandoned building, exposing them to frigid temperatures and the possibility of carbon monoxide poisoning; and a father who "neglected to seek medical attention for his son who had broken his hand in a bike accident while he was visiting his father."

What kind of abuse did the court overlook where Florence was concerned? Her husband threatened to have her killed if she left him; he would not allow her to work; he "would tell the kids that if I wanted money I had to give him 'nooky-nooky.' In order to feed the children I had to give him sex—painful, unpleasant sex. He would throw things at me, threaten to hit me, listen in on all my phone calls, physically kick me out of bed, threaten to have me killed by a hitman who could make it look like an accident."

What the court did was to force Florence into a joint custody arrangement. This happened in 2002. She told me, "My lawyer told me that the judge wanted me to do this, that if I didn't, he was prepared to give sole custody to my husband who had alleged that I'd been alienating the children. I knew that this would mean I would never see my kids again, the court system would do nothing to enforce my visitation. Also, I had to stay in the marital home for five years without income or child support." However in 2005 when she represented herself, she actually won sole custody. And her husband was held in contempt.

"I left an abusive marriage," she told me, "and entered a legal system that was more abusive than the marriage. My children and I have been exploited and all for the financial gain of the agents of the courts."

Florence endured four years of intense litigation. She says that she "was in court every month, sometimes twice a month with no trial/hearing. If I raised an issue I would soon regret it, as the judge would then use it as an opportunity to appoint more private professionals to our case. Finally after an expected trial date, the judge went home *sick* and no trial took place or was rescheduled. I 'crashed' and could not get out of bed for three months. I was thinking, 'How did this happen?' All I did was leave an abusive marriage."

Her children were psychologically and medically affected. One son began to suffer migraine headaches when he was seven years old; they have persisted. Another son, then nine years old, suffered from bedwetting and severe depression. He became suicidal and was also diagnosed with "emotional disturbance."

Why did everything take so long—in her case, nine years? As she sees it, "Lawyers are whores of the court. They are soulless bottom feeders who prey on victims of domestic violence. I have learned that there are a number of attorneys who are very successful and charge up to four hundred fifty dollars per hour because of their connections. We call them the 'good ole boys network' so you pay an obscene amount of money to try and get justice only to learn that these attorneys will keep the litigation going on for as many years as they can—steady income for them."

Once she went pro se, she was able to ask the judge, "What had she done for the last five years in which she'd presided over my case when visitation, life insurance, child support, medical and educational expenses were never adjudicated? The judge threatened me that she would be very creative in sanctioning me." Florence now says, "I did not understand the magnitude of being faced with a corrupt, possibly mentally ill, possibly alcoholic judge and the power they have over your life. Once you appear before one of these judges you can't get out." Florence has seen how other judges make rulings in order to "protect one of their own even if the judge has made a non-lawful decision. Judges have too much power and discretion. They make decisions for families without any accountability."

In the beginning, Florence wondered if she was the only woman in the country to lose custody after being falsely accused of parental alienation syndrome. But one day she "got an e-mail from an organization that hooked me up with other moms in Illinois who were going through exactly the same thing. I felt as if a huge boulder had been lifted from me and I didn't feel so alone. I felt vindicated. I hooked up with these moms and our group got larger. We became advocates. In 2005, I formed my own organization. I have worked on three bills with legislators and been on the radio."

Florence supports the idea of jury trials, but barring that, she advises mothers to represent themselves in court. That, she says, will "put a wrench in the racket."

When I asked her what she'd learned from her ordeal, she said, "I have learned that justice only comes to those who can afford it. A mother cannot count on our legal system for justice. Judges have their own agenda and for some it is to keep their cronies financially secure by keeping certain cases with assets trapped in ongoing litigation. I also learned that other judges will protect their cronies even when they know they have committed illegal actions."

Florence believes that if a mother goes pro se, she can demand a jury trial rather than "be coerced into psych evaluations, therapy, parent coordination, and a relationship with the numerous other court-appointed professionals."

ALASKA: SEVEN YEARS AND COUNTING

Christina, a successful businesswoman, entered the court system in 1998. She remained trapped there for seven years and endured three separate trials. At the time, Christina was in her late thirties and the mother of an infant and a seven-year-old. Despite extensive evidence of domestic violence, Christina was pressured to settle for joint custody. The various court-ordered psychologists and parenting counselors completely underplayed the issue of domestic violence and focused on the mother's allegedly "stubborn," even "unbalanced" refusal to share parenting with her husband. They had all been trained by followers of junk scientist Dr. Richard Gardner, who named and popularized the false concept of parental alienation syndrome. Thus they believed that most mothers falsely report battering and routinely and successfully brainwash or "alienate" children from their fathers. Christina was described—or rather, castigated—as "hysterical," "alienating," "over-protective," and "overly enmeshed."

Christina believes that "few attorneys will advocate aggressively for any one client. They can't afford to burn their bridges with evaluators, guardians ad litem (GALs), psychologists, lawyers, and judges with whom they will have to work on future cases. The smaller the community, the less likely they'll do so because either it won't make the judge or other professionals in the community happy, and/or it will take them too much time and work and they know the client can't afford it." Christina understands the system and what she says about it is also true for other places in the United States. She says,

> Judges have very high case loads and the fifty-fifty model is very attractive because they don't have to analyze parenting history and skills and can clear their calendars easier. When one or both parents refuse to settle for that, it seems to anger them. Most typically, the one refusing is going to be the primary caretaker—generally Mom—as she doesn't believe that arrangement is best for her kids. Then, if you add poor or abusive parenting on the part of the father, she is even less likely to accept fifty-fifty. So the judge has a predisposition to be resentful and angry at the parent—Mom—who refuses to "share." They punt their decision making to "evaluators," who already know the judge prefers fifty-fifty, and in order to keep getting assignments, have that preconceived outcome already in mind. The judges can then delay decision making until the evaluators' report comes in and often end up defaulting to the evaluators' recommendations, even though much of the report is hearsay and should not be legally admissible.

According to Christina, in her case, as expected, the co-parenting was a "disaster." The court finally ordered her husband to work on his "anger issues" but did not penalize him in any way for failing to do so. Eventually,

Christina hired a new lawyer who was able to get the GAL to recuse herself. The new lawyer argued for modified paternal visitation, given that the father lived in a one-room four-hundred-square-foot cabin that did not have a bathtub, did not have privacy, was located too far away, and did not allow the children to see their usual friends and engage in their usual activities. In Christina's view (a view shared by the court-appointed psychologist), the children were being "emotionally, physically, verbally, and mentally abused." The judge still refused to admit that the children were being "abused" but did restrict, in a minimal way, their visitation with their father.

This father constantly threatened further court actions. He remained angry and controlling toward his children. When his daughter asked to see a therapist, he refused to grant his permission; no therapist would agree to see her without it—unless he was allowed to sit in on the sessions. When their teenage daughter became fifteen, she began running away from her father's home. They had a prolonged verbal, psychological, and physical power struggle, after which her father finally "gave up."

Christina told me that "both of the kids are A students and thriving. The custody evaluator predicted that my daughter would be a promiscuous, substance-abusing dropout if she didn't have shared custody with her father. I am proud to report she is none of those things. She is taking multiple advanced placement classes, has a current GPA of 3.8, does volunteer work in her community and is a varsity and competitive cheerleader. She will attend college this coming fall, and hopes to pursue a career in law or psychology."

Christina joined and subsequently founded a number of organizations that offer assistance to custodially challenged battered mothers. She has also initiated legislation for both mothers and children.

FLORIDA: FIVE YEARS AND COUNTING

In the early 1990s Alexis, a flight attendant, started dating Patrick, a pilot. Alexis grew up in the Midwest and still lived near her family. When she became pregnant in 1993, she and Patrick got married. After their daughter was born, Alexis's husband insisted that they move to Florida, where his family and friends were located. He then began to isolate her. They had a second child, and her husband "changed"; he became "more controlling and "disrespectful." As she later learned, this was when he began an affair. Eleven years after they first met, Alexis now understood that her husband was an "abuser." He began to rape her and when she protested, he insisted that "You're my wife, I can do whatever I want with you." He broke windows, pulled down shelves, started huge arguments. He began to take a knife to her, push her against the wall with it—and then turn the knife on himself, threatening suicide.

In 2006, fourteen years after they first met, Alexis called the police for the first of forty-five subsequent calls for police intervention. They entered marriage counseling. Ultimately they would be involved with six different court-ordered psychologists. Alexis decided that her husband was having a "nervous breakdown." (Yes, he was still the captain of a plane.) He now accused her of "brainwashing" the children against him. Alexis fled to a shelter for battered women. Her husband started a phone-call campaign: He told her he still loved her, and he also told her how much he hated her. When she and the children moved back home, they found it in shambles. "It reeked of liquor, there were chicken bones all over the kitchen, the pets had been neglected."

The psychologist they had all been ordered to see viewed her husband as a "narcissist." Patrick began stalking Alexis; he also called his children and cursed them, his daughter in particular, whom he called "a bitch, just like her mother." He attempted to rape Alexis as well, and he choked her when she said she'd call the police. He then threatened to impoverish her and the children. "I'm giving it all to the attorneys; they'll be nothing left for you and those brats." She called the police, and he said, "Baby, it's a free for all now. All they'll do is slap my hand."

So far, between the two of them, "more than four hundred thousand dollars has been spent on lawyers." Both children were ordered to see their father, pretty much against their will. The daughter is afraid of her father, and does not like how he "stares at her with sexual intent." Although Patrick preferred his son to his daughter, he fought bitterly with and physically and verbally abused both children. Eventually, neither wanted to see him. The court-appointed parent coordinator told Alexis to force the children to see their father. Alexis refused. The parent coordinator resigned from the case.

Now, a pediatrician, a psychologist, and a teacher turned Patrick into Child Protective Services for "throwing his son around one weekend." The CPS investigator lied about the event and threatened Alexis with foster care for the children if she pressed charges. (No, she does not understand this either.) At this point, Patrick insisted on taking both children on a road trip, even though his son had "walking pneumonia" and subsequently had to miss one month of school. He also left both children by the side of the road—after trying to run them down with his car. Hysterical, they called Alexis; she called the police and drove to rescue them. At the time, the children were nine and fourteen years old.

This is when Patrick moved for full custody and charged Alexis with having alienated the children from him. Alexis was not allowed to stop his visitation or to gain supervised visitation. When his fifteen-year-old daughter wrote to CPS about her fears, her father physically attacked her in his car—and he told the police that his daughter was a "violent, aggressive, and out-of-control teenager." The police arrested the *child*. Finally, based on this incident, the judge stopped visitation for her daughter—but not for her son.

At trial, the judge finally saw Patrick have a full rage attack. "The veins were bulging in his neck and he was grabbing the arms of the chair very aggressively. The judge looked at him in disbelief" and finally ordered supervised visitation only. But this was two full years after Alexis had first called the police.

The litigation did not stop there. Although Patrick did have supervised visitation, he continued bringing motions asking that Alexis be held in contempt "for not allowing him to see the children." And he found a way to impoverish both his former wife and children. This meant that Alexis had to start bringing motions to have child support enforced—a tedious and expensive proposition. Patrick began bringing a series of actions aimed to overturn some of the economic features of the divorce agreement.

At this point, Alexis's health failed. "My doctor said that the divorce was literally killing me." Luckily, it was not her mental health, as that would have quickly been used against her. By December 2009, the father's motion to have Alexis and the children thrown out of the marital home was denied. His motion to have unsupervised visitation with the children was also denied.

These were great victories, but it took nearly four years of intense litigation from the time Alexis first called the police for such victories to come about. Here is what Alexis has to say now:

> This man has traumatized the children and me. I live in fear daily of what he will attempt if he sees me in public or what he will do to me in the courtroom. I know he stalks me by driving by my home and he has his parents and alcoholic friends doing drive-bys as well. That way

he can claim it is not "him" doing the stalking. Our sixteen-year-old daughter will not speak with him on the phone. I forced her to take his call in December and she had a migraine for two days. She has begged me to not force her again to speak with him. The conversation is so manipulating and coercive that she cannot do it anymore.

The psychologists who have worked with me told me that 97 percent of the men in his situation stop after they have lost in court, but he won't stop. It is very difficult to get a psychologist to stick with our case. One psychologist assigned to me by the court propositioned me—and then turned on me when I turned him down. He did not understand the danger that we faced. He did not think it was unusual for my ex-husband to demand that his twelve-year-old daughter get undressed in front of him. The judge refuses to put an end to this insanity.

Perhaps the family and civil court system is simply not set up to stop crazy, cruel, violent husbands who are also highly litigious. Perhaps, as I've previously suggested, the system would stop a man who is going after a strange woman far more quickly than a husband who is going after what he still views as his property: his family. How many times is a former husband allowed to stalk his former wife's home before he is jailed? So far, in this case, the answer is as many times as he wants.

And Alexis's is a success story. She has not lost her children physically, psychologically, or legally. She is not the one with supervised visitation—her ex-husband is. However, the same ex-husband who has been allowed to continue to sue and stalk her has also not been stopped from impoverishing his family. She told me that "currently there has been roughly three hundred fifty thousand dollars spent on attorneys, psychologists, and a custody evaluation. I have been financially drained. He could legally do this! Even after we were divorced, I was still contractually tied to him, 'married.'"

Alexis has borrowed from her parents and other relatives. She has amassed one hundred thousand dollars in credit card debt in order to pay for lawyers and medical care and maintain the family home. She still owes her lawyer seventy thousand dollars. She has lost some good, old friends who are afraid that her ex-husband will go after them if they help her. She would like to move back to the Midwest and live near her parents, but the thought of the litigation that would entail is sobering to her.

LONG ISLAND, NEW YORK: FIVE YEARS AND COUNTING

Nicole is a forty-five-year-old divorced mother who lives on Long Island. She is an academic. After a prolonged custody battle, she was awarded custody based on the report of the court-appointed psychologist. However, the divorce has utterly impoverished her and her two children. Nicole's husband does not pay child support and has applied for a reduction in support. The court has not forced him to honor his obligation. Nicole works nearby as an adjunct professor, which means she earns far less than minimum wage and has no security and no benefits.

In 2007 Nicole was offered a position at a university in another state that would amount to twenty times the money she is now earning, plus it would give her job security and benefits. She offered to renegotiate visitation and pay for her children's airfare to visit their father. Her husband rejected this— so did the judge. She said, "The judge completely didn't care that we live here in virtual poverty. Long Island is not nice when you have no money."

> Most lawyers and judges are anti-mother. It was a huge and scary wake-up call. My own lawyer treated me abusively, disliked me, lied to me, and spoke disparagingly about me. The social worker and the law guardian treated me like an "uppity" woman. My lawyer recommended that I see a therapist, who treated me with disdain. My ex told my children that "your mother is going to therapy because she is crazy." He planned to use this against me in court. I was attacked from all sides. My judge never looked at me or spoke to me. He spoke only to my ex, even though I was the primary caregiver. He laughed and joked with my ex while we were in court.

I asked Nicole what she had learned or what she would tell other mothers. She said, "I learned that my children could have been taken from me just because the law guardian was spiteful or the judge wanted to punish me for speaking out. They have way too much power. Don't trust the social workers. They have the power to take your children, and they are not qualified to make judgments. If you are poor be very careful, because they will take your children away for any little reason at all."

TENNESEE AND NEW YORK: FOUR YEARS AND COUNTING

Yolanda is the forty-one-year-old mother of a six-year-old daughter. She married her husband, a chiropractor, in 2005, right after she discovered she was pregnant. Unfortunately Yolanda gave no serious thought to the fact that her husband had abandoned a previous wife and a set of children, nor did she gauge how lazy, erratic, unstable, and even dangerous her husband really was. Yolanda is an executive administrator, and her husband demanded that she work for him in his New York office. For reasons unclear to her, her husband suddenly shut down this office and moved them all lock, stock, and barrel to Tennessee, where he opened up another office. He forced Yolanda to work until she went into labor, and he demanded that she return to work with the infant "in a car seat." Then, after spending the holidays with Yolanda's family back in New York, her husband left, phoned, and told her not to return—then he told her to return only to "pick up her possessions." He had moved out the valuable pieces of furniture and left her the "junk."

Yolanda's husband filed for divorce and demanded custody, alimony, and child support. The law guardian sided with Yolanda's husband. Yolanda told me,

> My mother has shelled out thousands of dollars for my lawyer. I have been working around the clock. He is trying to have custody tried in both states, whichever one might be more favorable to him. I am nervous all the time, even about visitation. My husband drinks. Daily. He feels that children need to fear their parents and he spanks, restrains, and cusses at our daughter. He owns a shotgun. His ex-mother-in-law wrote to me and said that she tried to have his cult-like behavior deprogrammed. The law guardian knows all this but she's kicked it to the curb. My husband says he has no money. But he has a new car, an iPhone. He was dressed to the nines in court. My mother and I are exhausted. The law guardian recommended that my husband have his daughter for Christmas. She would not allow us to share him or to split his day in half. I am scared to my stomach over what will happen.

In this case, the court stands helpless before a father's cruelty and madness.

17

The International Custody Situation

. . . .

I am worried that men are said to be the children's owner, yet I spend nine months carrying the baby in my stomach, and then the next twenty to thirty years looking after her or him. A woman has no property at home and she has no children. When she gets divorced, she goes away naked.

—Anonymous, Zimbabwe[1]

There was no court of appeal. Mother was sent away for labor reform. My father disassociated himself from Mother and eventually "denounced" her. When she came to visit us he would scream: "The children in this house need a Revolutionary mother, not a Rightist mother." The court awarded custody of the children to father. So perhaps inevitably, over the years, I came to resent my mother for making life so miserable. I began to believe that she really had done something wrong. My father and teachers said so, and my classmates hated me for her supposed crimes. At last I no longer wished to visit her despite my loneliness, and when I saw her at a distance I didn't even call out to her. I cut her out of my life just as I had been told to do, and became solitary and self-reliant.

—Liang Heng, China[2]

Early in 1980 the wife of a UN diplomat requested an emergency appointment with me. "My freedom and possibly my life are being threatened."

272 • *Mothers on Trial*

"Have you contacted the police or told your husband?" I asked.

"My husband is the one who is threatening me," she said.

May arrived at my office that evening. She told me the following:

I was born into a well-known Caribbean family. My husband and I met in Europe when we both were in school. We married upon graduation and moved to my mother-in-law's home in Africa. I rarely saw my husband after that except at large family and public events. My mother-in-law was very domineering. She did not permit me to work. I gave birth to three children in six years.

When my husband's government appointed him to the United Nations, I was overjoyed. My husband had a good salary and an expense account. He provided for his family well. He employed many servants. He also bought many homes and, with the help of friends, had a substantial investment portfolio. He kept everything in his name only. Whenever I tried to talk to him about this, he would stare at me and ask whether I or my children were hungry or without clothing. Then he would leave the room.

My husband traveled all the time. Over the years he began to drink and became something of a womanizer. He had two children with two different women. He could have married either of them but didn't—because he was a "modern" man. But he did expect me to accept these children into my home without rancor and graciously. Whenever I suggested a separation or a divorce, he would stare at me and say, "I can't allow you to desert my household. If you force the issue, I will have you declared mentally incompetent and put away. You will never see your children again."

Who would help me if I forced the issue? My husband is a tribal chief. Would his tribe or its laws find me entitled to custody and a decent settlement if I were the one who wanted the divorce? Would the laws of my own country have any power in this situation? Could I turn to the International Court in The Hague or to the United Nations itself? My own father said he couldn't help me. He said I could always return to him—but only as I'd left him, *without my children*.

If I fled my marriage anyway, what would happen to my children? My husband might punish them for my desertion. He'd treat them as the offspring of an immoral mother. He'd send them back to his family in Africa. He might never allow me to see them.

Therefore I never left. However, a year ago, when our youngest turned fifteen, I obtained my first real job since completing graduate school. My husband has been threatening to disinherit our eldest son and to have me declared mentally incompetent if I don't quit and return to running his household. What should I do? Can my husband really have me declared mentally incompetent when it's not true? Should I hire a lawyer or simply stop working? Does anyone specialize in persuading a husband to allow his wife to work?

This chapter is not based on studies and statistics, since they do not exist. It is a passionate survey of the custodial status of women from twenty-nine countries around the globe, countries in Europe, the Middle East, Asia, Africa, and South America. It is based on formal and informal interviews. It is also shaped by my reading, my travels, my work at the United Nations, and conferences that I've attended, coordinated, or about which I've read. It now also contains some recent cases.

My questions in this chapter are, quite simply, the following: Is there any place on earth in which mothers have as many rights as they have obligations, in which mothers are automatically entitled to child custody or tend to obtain it even when a father or the state contests it? Is there any place on earth in which the work of motherhood is adequately subsidized or custodially rewarded? Is there any place on earth in which a father is not entitled to custody or simply cannot obtain it if a mother contests it? Is there any place on earth in which fathers do not abandon their families or in which fathers are forced to support their children, even against their will?

EUROPE

United Kingdom

According to barrister Alec Samuels, the majority of British fathers traditionally did not want (or did not think they could obtain) custody of children.

The mother usually wins because the father does not contest the application, contests only halfheartedly, or is unable to provide for the care and attention of the child, especially during the day when he is at work. In other words, the mother wins on merit and not by reason of prejudice or presumption. Even where the mother does gain custody, she only gains day-to-day looking after. Unresolved disputes over major matters, such as religion or education, may still be taken by a father to the court for decision.[3]

When fathers *do* contest custody, they do so by accusing mothers either of sexual or "uppity" behavior[4] or by kidnapping the children. Dr. Martin Richards has noted that

> what seems to be a growing problem [in the United Kingdom] is the kidnapping of children and the taking of them overseas. Usually, but not always, the kidnapper is, of course, the father. The major problem is that very few, if any, countries will recognize the orders made in British courts so that the mother has to start afresh in the new country—assuming, of course, that she is able to trace the children. Also, British embassies have been very reluctant to provide help for parents trying to retrieve their children. . . . The major significant change in recent years [in British custody] is a growing belief that joint [not to be confused with split] custody should be the normative arrangement.[5]

In the past, the British state systematically challenged the custodial rights of poor, single, dark-skinned, immigrant, and lesbian mothers. According to Norma Steele, many such mothers traditionally faced state-imposed poverty and separation from their children. She said, "Every day we have to fight the [British] State for the custody of our children. When we come to this country, because we have the least money internationally, we are forced to leave our children behind. Then after years of hard saving and long separation, we are told they are too old to come to Britain without a work permit, which is almost impossible to get."[6]

What's changed? In January 2010 a British appeals court ordered an eleven-year-old boy to leave his mother and move more than one hundred miles to live with a father he hated and hadn't seen for more than four years. Although the judges acknowledged that the boy was doing very well with his mother, they objected to the mother's attempts to prevent her son from having contact with his father. The mother claimed that she wouldn't mind the father having a role in her child's life but that this should wait until the child was ready for it. The judges, however, argued that she was stalling and really had no intention of ever allowing contact. According to a British newspaper article,

> The appeal judges called the boy's feelings of hate for his father "irrational" and said he would suffer long-term emotional and behavioural problems if they were not reunited . . . [and] that the animosity felt

by the boy would quickly disappear once he was living under his father's roof. At the appeal, Lord Justice Thorpe said it was the third time recently that the court had upheld properly reasoned decisions in favour of fathers. Miranda Fisher, of London solicitors Charles Russell, said later that the activities of groups such as Fathers 4 Justice had tipped the balance—and courts were taking a tougher line on parents who denied contact between their children and their ex-partners. She explained: "Twenty or 30 years ago it was not the normal expectation that fathers should be involved in looking after the children. Now more mothers have full-time careers and fathers are increasingly wanting to share in caring."[7]

France

Puissance paternelle (fathers' rights) has dominated the legal codes of northwestern Europe. Mothers could retain child custody under paternal guidance; and only if husbands and the state judged them to be "moral." According to law professor Christopher L. Blakesley, French law has never expressly articulated a "maternal preference."[8] "In both France and Holland, domestic legislation emphasizes paternal rights and maternal responsibilities. Legal formulations are ambiguous, but clearly designed to favor a patriarchal system in terms of inheritance, ownership of names, etc. European divorce procedures are terrible. In many cases, the children are assigned to the 'care' of the mother, but it is the father who is invested with the authority and power to decide matters pertaining to the children's education and future."[9]

Aziza is an Afghan-French woman. Here is what she told me about her experience in France: "I was born in Kabul but educated in Europe. My marriage was arranged, but by Afghan standards, we were a modern couple. We were living part-time in Paris when the Russians invaded. We stayed on. My husband had many financial and psychological difficulties. He took a lot out on me. I opened a boutique with another woman. Compared to him, I was a great success. My husband demanded that I stop working. I refused. He accused me of being an unfit mother. He said our children needed extra supervision because we were refugees and I was never home."

According to Jamila, an Algerian-French mother,

My husband Achmed is a cruel and violent man. When I got a temporary job offer as a governess in France, I accepted it with Achmed's permission, and then stayed on illegally. For a year I worked eighteen hours a day, seven days a week, as a cashier, waitress, and domestic. I sent money home and also saved enough money to send two of my children tickets to visit me for the summer. Then I refused to send them back. Achmed actually came and found us. He beat me in the street. The police came. They understood that I was illegal. They only locked Achmed up overnight.

And then the French courts did the unthinkable. They yielded to Algerian law. Jamila said,

> The lawyer said that in Algeria, Achmed—not I—would be entitled to custody. How could I expect French custody when I wasn't even a French citizen and was, in fact, already breaking the French laws? Legally I had abandoned my husband and kidnapped his children. The lawyer advised me to go back to Algeria and live with Achmed if he would still have me.
>
> The French court gave him custody and a divorce. For two years now he has refused to allow me to see or write to my children. I am a double refugee, not only from my birthplace but from my own children.

In 1999 Frederic Dallemagne, a French citizen, and Cory Dallemagne, an American citizen, met and married in the United States. They then moved to France with their newborn daughter to live with Frederic's parents. After two months, Cory became depressed because her husband had been verbally abusing her and accusing her of not trying to adjust to French life. In 2001 Cory and Frederic moved to an apartment of their own. Frederic began beating her. Cory consulted attorneys who advised her that her chances of winning custody were very small because she was not a French resident or citizen.

Frederic drank, took drugs, and kept trying to barge into or break into Cory's home. She said that calling the police was "a joke" because they refused to write reports or arrest him, as Frederic was her husband and she was not French. Cory allowed Frederic to see the children, but his behavior was wild and frightening. The children did not want to see him. At one point, he tried to run Cory over with his car with the children inside. In 2005, Frederic kicked in the door and tried to beat her. She called the police. When the police saw the damaged door and the red marks on Cory's body, they asked her to forgive her husband and let him cool down. They told him to leave. She asked the police to file a report; they refused to do so.

At this point, she felt that she had no choice but to kidnap her daughter and flee to the United States. In 2005 Frederic filed a petition with French authorities to have his daughter returned in accordance with the 1980 Hague Convention on the Civil Aspects of International Child Abduction, to which both the United States and France are signatories. A U.S. district court in Florida sided with Frederic, citing a lack of evidence to verify Cory's account. While the Convention does make exceptions for situations in which there is a "grave risk that the child's return would 'expose the child to physical or psychological harm or otherwise place the child in an intolerable situation,' the court concluded that it could not leave the daughter with Cory on that basis because she brought insufficient proof that her husband was seriously abusing the child.[10]

Greece

According to Margaret Papandreou, former president of the Greek Women's Union,

> Until 1982, all authority and decisions involving the family resided in the husband; he could decide where the family would live, how the children would be brought up, and whether his wife would work or even take the children out of the country. Strictly speaking, a man could file for divorce on grounds that his wife was a poor house-keeper.[11] Wives were responsible for the physical care of the house, and the physical care of the children. In the case of divorce, a boy child of ten could be taken by the father, and often, he could have the girl children too, if he desired. Naturally, the attitudes that have to do with the man's position and role in the family do not automatically change when written into law.[12]

Italy

According to my Milanese informant, Virginia Visani,

> Italy is a country with strong patriarchal attitudes about the family. Maternity is still considered a woman's unique destiny and her most important function. It is understood that children under seven need to be cared for by their mother or by another female relative, such as the

grandmother. Children are assigned to the father only in exceptional cases—that is, in case of the mother's illness, or immoral behavior. A mother might also be deemed "unfit" by a judge if she works or does not want to take traditional care of her children. Children over fourteen are often allowed to decide whom they want to live with. From time to time a father claims custody or visitation as his legal or natural "right" or kidnaps his child."[13]

A remarried father kidnapped his ten-year-old son twice. The father claimed he had married a "housewife" who could stay at home with the boy. He deemed her a better mother than his ex-wife because the latter had worked outside the home for three years since their divorce.

Alma is a sophisticated career woman. She is also a traditional Italian Catholic mother. After fifteen years of marriage Alma's husband left her for a woman half his age. Alma immediately agreed to joint custody as the "progressive" thing to do.

I thought joint custody was the right thing. He was their father. He helped quite a lot with their upbringing. He had a right to remain close to them. I also thought I could rebuild my life if I had some time alone. I had the children during the week. He had them from Thursday to Sunday night. His girlfriend was only ten years older than our eldest child. They went to pop concerts and took skiing vacations together.

My children didn't lose "family life." Only I did. I grew more and more depressed. My ex-husband condemned me as too old-fashioned. My children all agreed with him. So did our friends. I became more isolated than ever. I had to watch what I said. If I was too angry or too depressed my children would yell at me. Even though I'm educated and have a profession, at heart I'm a good Catholic girl still in love with my husband. We were both forty when we separated. At forty, my mother was already a grandmother. I tried to date, but I only felt ridiculous.

I have lost everything. I am too shy and too sad to start over again. Nature is cruel to women. I can't have any more children. I always thought that when our children left home, I'd still have my husband—and then grandchildren. A career, even a lover can't replace family life for me.

Sweden

According to Cecilia Onfelt, an advocate for battered women,

> Custody battles are in the air in Sweden. Men almost always get normal visiting rights even if they are convicted wife beaters or child abusers. One particularly horrible case involved a "feminist" father who was sexually molesting his five-year-old daughter. Another case involved a father who had been threatening to murder the baby. The mother fought like a tiger and refused him access to the baby. For this she was fined $300. The court decided that the man could see the baby but not alone. A young social assistant took the baby to the man's flat, went into the kitchen and left the man with the two-year-old in the bedroom. He stabbed the baby about twenty times, swiftly and quietly, without the social assistant noticing. When she came into the room the baby was already dead. The bailiffs still went to collect the mother's fine even after the murder. I think people felt that was really a bit too much and the government stopped it all.
>
> I discussed custody with a male colleague. Should fathers have access to children regardless of their behavior? His answer was: "If I put a quarter into a candy machine and get out a candy bar, is the candy bar mine, or is it the machine's?" His metaphor told me he thought women are machines for male use.[14]

Denmark

The incidence of child abduction by unwed fathers in Denmark is so severe that a special legislative commission has been established to cope with the problem. Danish laws tend to favor mothers over unwed fathers. One out of every four children is born out of wedlock.[15]

THE ARAB AND MUSLIM WORLDS

Bahrain

Fifty-four Muslim countries have not signed the Hague Convention, which requires the return of parentally kidnapped children when the other parent has been granted custody in their home country. In these countries, the custody of children is viewed as a male religious, tribal, and legal right.

Women who grow up in these countries know this, which is why many of them do not seek divorce and "accept" second and third wives into their homes. But Western women are different.

Many traditional Arab men tend to marry those Western women who have been raised on romantic fairy tales, women who are vulnerable and trusting. The men routinely wine and dine them, treat them with great charm and every courtesy, and make outsize promises which the women unwisely believe. After they begin an affair or marry—usually after the men get their green cards—everything changes, often overnight.

For example, in 2004 Mexican-born naturalized American citizen Maria married Mohammed, a college student and Bahraini national. Later that year, their daughter, Leyla, was born in Arizona. Mohammed paid no child support and spent little time with his new family. He spent most of his time back in Bahrain. In four years, he visited only three times. In January 2009 Maria finally divorced him and received custody in Arizona.

However in 2010, after suffering some major economic setbacks that included losing her job, Maria visited Mohammed in Bahrain. Apparently he had promised her that he would get her a good job, an apartment of her own, a car, and a cell phone and that both she and Leyla would be part of a loving extended family.

He lied. He and his family, which now included a new and pregnant wife, were nice only that one time. When Maria returned, they were hostile and threatening. And Mohammed promptly filed for custody of Leyla in a Bahraini court and easily won visitation and a series of hearings.

But Maria already had custody of her daughter in an American court. Thus she tried to flee with her daughter. The two even managed to clear customs at the airport when an American embassy official told her to cross back to the other side, saying it was just a formality and they would soon be free to return to America. The American official was wrong. As soon as Maria re-entered Bahraini jurisdiction, Bahraini police seized her daughter.

"The judge told me Leyla could not leave Bahrain because her father did not want her to leave," Maria said. "They told me, 'If you want to leave, you can leave. But the girl stays.' Obviously, I wasn't going to leave my baby."

With help from a tireless advocate, Maria's case caught the eye of one of her senators. In January 2010 he sent a letter to Bahraini ambassador Houde Erza Ebrahim Nonoo, urging her to "expeditiously resolve" the custody dispute and allow Maria and Leyla to return home.

The custody dispute has not been expeditiously resolved. Mohammed won visitation-custody of Leyla for three days a week. At first, Leyla resisted. Maria told me that Leyla is terrified of her father's family and even once hid under a café table when she saw some of her Bahraini relatives approaching. She said, "I don't want to see my father. He will take me so that I will never see you [Maria] again."

Thus Maria went into hiding in Bahrain. When the police finally found her, they stormed into the house and dragged Leyla away.

Maria, shaken, told me, "When the police came, Leyla was afraid. I told her to be strong. She's only five and she's going through a very traumatic time. She was crying, saying, 'Mama, I can't sleep without you.' She didn't put on her sandals because she thought that if she wasn't wearing her sandals they couldn't take her. She hid in the bathroom so that no one would get her."

Maria's situation is grim. She also does not know whether it is safe for her to remain in the country. She has no money, no job, no financial resources, and no powerful relatives who can help her fight for her daughter. Her rights as an American citizen do not matter in Bahrain, nor does the fact that an American court has granted her custody of Leyla. Maria is traumatized, ashamed that her own naive, "trusting nature" has potentially deprived her daughter of an American future.

"Leyla is not the same little girl she was when she arrived in Bahrain," Maria told a reporter. "She has crying spells. She misses home, she misses her (older) brother. That's where our home is—our home is in Arizona."[16]

When last I spoke with Maria, she described a process of paternal brainwashing that was already fully under way after only three days. Although it took nearly three days to undo the hostility that Leyla expressed toward her mother for the first time ever, Maria remains optimistic that she can still retain her daughter's affection.

Sadly, she may not be thinking that she will have to face an "undoing" process each and every week, which will get harder and harder to do over time. Absent a miracle, Leyla's fate will be that of a servant to her father's family and a source of income when they arrange a marriage for her, possibly when she is as young as twelve.

The odd thing is that at some point, Maria converted to Islam. She told me so in a whisper. One might think that as an American Muslim she might find support from American Muslim organizations. That has not happened as yet, nor has Maria received support from the American government. Only her Bahraini lawyer, who has represented her pro bono, rose to the level of a hero. He managed to get himself arrested, briefly, when he tried to stop the police from taking Leyla.

Egypt

My respondent, Dr. Nawal El Saadawi, the prominent Arab feminist, author, and physician, researched the question of Egyptian custody for me. She wrote,

> According to Egyptian law, it is the *father* only (and not the mother) who has the *authority* over his children, males and females, until they reach the age of twenty-one. For instance, a boy or girl cannot travel outside the country without the permission of the father. If the father is away, or dead, then the authority goes to another male member of the family (and not to the mother) such as the uncle or the grandfather. Usually Egyptian mothers try to keep their children with them whether the fathers pay support or not. Fathers try to pay the least support, or avoid paying support altogether, unless forced to by the law. After divorce, the man usually remarries. The mother usually supports the children and avoids remarriage.
>
> The government modified some crucial items in the Egyptian Marriage and Divorce Law. One item is related to the right of [fit] mothers to keep custody of their children after divorce. Now, she can keep a boy until he is ten and a girl until she is twelve. The father is supposed to pay their maintenance until then. A judge can decide to prolong this period. He or she can allow the mother to keep her boy until he is fifteen and the girl until she marries. In such cases, the father has to pay the mother only for the personal expenses of the children such as food, clothes and education, and then, only according to his income.

Has this changed? Do mothers now have custodial equity in an increasingly fundamentalist Egypt? Apparently not.

During the early 1990s, the marriage of Mona and Ahmed Amer, native Egyptians who had moved to New York in the 1980s, began to deteriorate. The two quarreled frequently over Ahmed's bigamous marriage to another woman, over Mona's decision to work outside the home, and over her decision to apply for welfare. Ahmed regularly abused Mona both verbally and physically. They had three children together; two were born in America, and one was born in Egypt. Ahmed also began to try to persuade her to move back to Egypt with him, suggesting that the children would receive a better education there and that the family would benefit from living among close relatives. But Mona told Ahmed that neither she nor the children would return to Egypt. Ahmed threatened to kill Mona for her refusal. She refused to change her mind.

In 1995 Ahmed came to the family apartment to have dinner with Mona and the children. After dinner, Mona left the apartment to do some shopping. When she returned two hours later, Ahmed and the children were gone. The next morning Mona learned that Ahmed had taken the children to Egypt. Mona promptly filed a complaint in Queens Family Court seeking custody of the children. The court awarded her full legal custody of the three children and issued a warrant for Ahmed's arrest. Meanwhile, Ahmed obtained an order from an Egyptian court compelling Mona to return to the "conjugal home" in Egypt. After Mona failed to return to Egypt within three months, the Egyptian court awarded Ahmed custody of the three children. Additionally, under Egyptian law, Mona no longer had custody rights to her twelve-year-old son, since a mother loses all rights to her male child when he reaches the age of ten. The last word on the children was that they were still with Ahmed's family in Egypt.

When Ahmed returned to the United States, a U.S. district court imprisoned him for two years for violating the International Parental Kidnapping Act; however the court had no power to return the children to Mona. Only the Egyptian government had that power, and Egypt was not—and still is not—a signatory to the Hague Convention on the Civil Aspects of International Child Abduction, which mandates the return of children kidnapped across international boundaries. The children remained in Egypt.[17]

While Turkey is a signatory to the Hague Convention and is therefore inhospitable to paternal kidnappers, no other Muslim country has signed on.

Iran

According to Iranian dissident Dr. Reza Baraheni, domestic life in pre-Khomeini Iran was based on "absolute male dominance": "The children absolutely belonged to the father. He had the final say over what children can and can't do. Fathers were dictators over their children. Very traditional wives from good families could subtly influence their husbands. They could never oppose them."

Marva is a professor who has been in exile from Iran since 1981. I asked her about women's custodial status in post-Khomeini Iran. She said that "everyone is afraid. Everyone knows that they are only safe if they obey the Qur'an and public opinion. Iranian children have always belonged to the fathers and to their father's family. The husband of my close girlfriend died. They were both middle-class professionals. The paternal grandparents sued for custody of the two children. They charged my friend with being unfit because she wasn't a devout Moslem. She had many Western ideas. The grandparents won custody. Miraculously, my girlfriend still managed to escape with her life, her sanity, and her children."

With the further Islamification of Iran, it is doubtful that women's custodial rights have improved.

American-born Betty Mahmoody married an Iranian man, Sayyed Bozorg Mahmoody, in America. She gave birth to a daughter in America. Her husband invited Betty to visit his family in Tehran for a two-week visit. Once there, he installed Betty in his mothers' home, beat her, locked her up, and forced his young daughter, Mahtob, to attend an Islamic school. He also demanded that Betty convert to Islam. Although they had married in America where Mahtob had been born, both mother and daughter were viewed as the chattel property of an Iranian husband and father. After suffering terribly for a number of years, Betty hired mercenaries to help her and her daughter escape. Miraculously, they succeeded. She wrote a successful book, *Not Without My Daughter*, which was also made into a popular film. For awhile, both mother and daughter lived in hiding, in fear of being kidnapped again.[18]

Algeria

According to Algerian feminist Nadine Claire, a divorced Algerian mother is "given" responsibility for boys until they are "nine or ten" and girls "until marriage."

> But she is only working as a maid in caretaking the children—the husband can take them back whenever he feels that she is not raising the children properly. She has got to stay close to him geographically, so that he can check on her every day. Which means that she cannot build a new life, she has to be under his eye all the time. [Parents cannot adopt children.] This means . . . that at any point, the state can

take the children back. So if you don't "behave properly," if you are not a "good citizen," if you have any kind of political activity this is a continual threat. And I know some trade unionists who have just emigrated, because they couldn't stand the fear. And this of course was stealing a child, because it's not their child, right? On the other hand I also know of cases in which the family was just upset after two years, or five years, and just dropped the children back into the orphanages. So this is not adoption, not at all, and women are fighting for the rights of these children.[19]

Turkey

Naila Minai is the Turkish-born author of *Women in Islam*. She responded to my questions about custodial matters in this way:

The sexual double standard in Turkey has always influenced the court's interpretation of immorality in custody litigation. Ex-wives have been dragged back into court by vindictive ex-husbands who happened to see them sitting with male friends in public restaurants. Under the secular government, courts are more consciously pro-feminist. I could not dig up one case where the courts decided to take the child away from the mother just because she dined in public with a male friend. But the point is that no man has ever been dragged to court for dining out with a woman friend. He is not considered immoral or unfit as a parent even if he lives with a woman friend.

ASIA

China

Margery is a mother and engineer. She escaped from communist China in the 1970s.

I was born in 1935. My father was a bourgeois capitalist. After the Revolution, I was sent to a special school. I married another engineer in good party standing. In 1963, I became the mother of twins. I began to quarrel with my husband and with his family. They all felt I wasn't obedient enough to them. My husband began to spread rumors about me, implying I wasn't obedient to the Revolution. I became very afraid. I could be relocated to another province. Maybe my capitalist origins could still be used against me. I fled the country. I have not seen my children since. I have no way of knowing whether they've ever received my letters.

What could Margery have done to retain custody of or access to her children if she had been declared an enemy of the state? Could she have taken her children with her into a labor camp or into foreign exile? Margery had no claim to her children as their *mother*. Like all resources, they belonged to the Chinese state.[20]

Chinese mothers (or fathers) did and can lose custody and access to their children if the state views them as "unfit."*

Liang Heng has described how he was separated from and brainwashed against a presumably "unfit" mother. When Liang was four, his mother was routinely asked to "criticize" her work situation. After hesitating a long time, she finally criticized her section head. "It was disastrous. [Twenty years later] when she was allowed to see her file, she found out that she had been given a Rightists' 'cap' solely because of three [minor] criticisms [that she was pressured into expressing]. There was no court of appeal. Mother was sent away to the suburb of Yuan Jia Ling for labor reform."[21]

Liang's father disassociated himself from his wife. Eventually, as both a party and a family man, he denounced Liang's mother. When she came to visit their three children, he would scream, "The children in this house need a Revolutionary mother, not a Rightist mother." Eventually, after a bitter marital dispute, the court awarded custody of the children to Liang's father. "So perhaps inevitably, over the years, I came to resent my mother for making life so miserable. I began to believe that she really had done something wrong. My father and teachers said so, and my classmates hated me for her supposed crimes. At last I no longer wished to visit her despite my loneliness, and when I saw her at a distance I didn't even call out to her. I cut her out of my life just as I had been told to do, and became solitary and self-reliant."[22]

Japan

According to feminist psychologist Dr. Kiyomi Kawano (who translated my first book, *Women and Madness*, into Japanese),

---

* This is also true in the United States and in all the countries discussed so far.

Few Japanese men want custody. Therefore, most divorces result in maternal custody. Men cannot raise children. They can't even take care of themselves. Japanese men tend to be "workaholic." They live in a culture where to be "hung up" on children is considered "sissy." A Japanese man doesn't want to be "Mr. Kramer" [of the film *Kramer vs. Kramer*]. He is supposed to "die out on the economic battlefield."

One of my good friends got divorced about three years ago. She had a hard time winning custody of her children. She was lucky. She had the financial resources to keep fighting her husband for two years. There was no mother-in-law ready to take over. Most divorced mothers face severe psychological and economic problems unless they come from very wealthy and modern families. This is the reason that so many women choose to suffer in abusive marriages rather than to leave them. Needless to say, this allows men to remain arrogant.[23]

Keiko, a twenty-five-year-old kindergarten teacher, was raped by the father of one of her pupils. He threatened to expose their sexual "relationship" if she didn't become his "mistress." Keiko became pregnant. The man tried to force her to abort. A week after giving birth, Keiko asked this man to acknowledge paternity legally. His response was to have the infant kidnapped.

Eventually Keiko found her kidnapped son. He had already been adopted with Keiko's forged consent. Keiko sued for legal custody. She lost her suit in 1971. The court noted that "Keiko was unmarried," that she "kept company with the father of a pupil," and that she had had the child "without any solid plan" and therefore probably did not have "true love for the child." In 1975 Keiko kidnapped her then five-year-old son. She also obtained legal custody, but only after she paid "consolation money" to her rapist's legal wife.[24]

Korea

According to my respondent Grace Liu-Volckhausen,

All countries with a Confucian tradition have a strong tradition of paternal rights and authority. Children carry their fathers' names and belong to them. In 1960, my mother fought for women's inheritance rights in Korea. The Chief Justice met with a women's delegation. He said: "How can a field have any rights? Only the farmer, only the seed has rights." Korean women often have no [first] names. They are known as the "number-one daughter of Mr. So-and-So." Many Asian women will describe themselves as "the lady who lives next to the post office," or "the lady who is the mother of Mr. Ahn's number-one son."

Nepal

According to Nepal's national code, "A mother has no right upon the issue she has given birth to. The law is based on the Hindu concept of women as *jaya*, or one who bears children for her husband. The mother simply gives birth to children for her husband."[25]

AFRICA

Ethiopia

According to Daniel Haile, parental rights in Ethiopia are customarily exercised by the father, by his appointed guardian, or by the other men in his family. Unless the mother is considered "unfit," she customarily retains custody of children under five.

Although the code says that this is in the best interests of the children, there is reason to believe that this practice is really based upon the proposition that it is the mother's duty to raise young children who, when they grow up, become productive members of their father's homestead or business, as the case may be.

Haile also notes that in Ethiopia

in any marriage, parental rights are exercised by the father. Next, the person appointed guardian by the father, next the eldest brother, then the grandfather, the paternal uncle and then the paternal nephew. Similarly, pursuant to the Sharia rules, the father is the guardian, [and in] order of priority: the father's executor, the father's father or the paternal grandfather's executor. However, it must be emphasized that even though both the Fetha Negast (the Ethiopian civil codes) and the Sharia do not recognize the mother as legal guardian, they do not prohibit her being a guardian by appointment.

Normally, unless there are serious grounds for deciding otherwise, the children are entrusted to their mother up to the age of five years and to the father over the age of five. The father is obliged to assist the mother by providing assistance to the children under her custody, since raising children is more or less a full-time job. The end result of divorce is the transformation of the woman from a relatively unequal partner in the marriage to having full responsibility for caring for the children and no assistance from the children's father.[26]

Nigeria

According to Dr. J. O. Debo Akande, "customary" Nigerian law grants custody to the father or, upon his death, to his family. Nursing mothers are entitled to temporary custody, and in some areas children are entitled to a *woman's* care until they are seven. However "a woman's care is not necessarily the mother's care and if the father is able to make provision to have a woman look after the child he may take the child. . . . A father could defeat the mother's right to appoint a guardian for an infant child on his death. The guardian so appointed has a better right to custody than the mother. . . . The court [can] award the custody of an infant under seven to the mother, provided that she has not committed adultery [or is] considered absolutely unfit."[27]

According to Nancy Greene, formerly of the American branch of International Social Services,

> In the late 1970s an American woman lived with a Nigerian man in the United States. The father died before they could marry. She gave birth to a son. The mother took her infant son on a visit to his grandparents in Nigeria. The paternal grandmother offered to take care of the boy for a year while the mother returned to finish school in the United States. The Nigerian family then refused to give up the child. Since the boy is the only son of their only [deceased] son, they feel—and in Nigeria . . . they *have* the legitimate claim to custody. The only thing this mother can do is to go to Nigeria and physically take her child. If she makes it back to the U.S., she's home free. But how many single women have the money to do that?[28]

Southern Africa

In many parts of Southern Africa, including Lesotho, Mozambique, Tanzania, Zambia, and Zimbabwe, once a husband has paid *lobolo* (bride price), he owns all the children his wife produces and is entitled to keep them after divorce. In Mozambique, "child custody is determined not by what is best for the child, but according to which lineage he is considered to belong. Muslim children always belong to the father; in matrilineal societies their guardian is the mother's brother, and in patrilineal groups, once the *lobolo* has been paid, they belong to the father's lineage. Moreover, if the children go with their mother, for whatever reason, the father feels no responsibility to help support them."[29]

In 1975 women were allowed to initiate divorce for the first time in Mozambique's history. "People's tribunals" were established to arbitrate issues of divorce, marital property, and custody. Women's families still discouraged divorce, as the *lobolo* would have to be returned. Courts tried to convince fathers that children should be allowed to remain with their mothers and that fathers should become responsible for providing food for their children.

Fathers do not accept their responsibility to provide food for their families; they expect this to come from the plots on which their wives grow cereals and vegetables. Many men in southern Mozambique who migrate either to the South African mines or to urban or rural employment centers in Mozambique in search of paid employment use their wages to pay taxes and buy consumer goods, but they never send their wives money for food. If these husbands don't comprehend their responsibility to feed their families, serious problems can arise, especially in urban areas, where many women no longer have plots of land to cultivate.[30]

SOUTH AMERICA

Argentina

According to Argentinian novelist Luisa Valenzuela,

> *Patria potestad*—or fathers' rights, embodied by individual men or by the state—completely governs family life in Argentina. A mother I know was accused of being against the government—by her husband. She had to leave the country immediately. Her husband wouldn't let the children go. He didn't let the children see their mother's relatives either. For about ten years he kept moving them from school to school. Luckily, his attempts to turn them against my friend were unsuccessful. She was finally able to smuggle them out of the country. I have another close friend who couldn't get her children out of Argentina

for ten years, even for a visit, because her husband wouldn't allow it. She saw her children only after they turned eighteen.[31]

Brazil

According to sociologist Dr. Heleith I. B. Saffieti, Brazilian mothers are considered very "important" for children only if they are "moral" or if the father doesn't want the children.

> Most men don't fight for custody. If the mother behaved badly, custody might go to the grandparents. Generally, women keep children. This is more often a burden than a right since fathers seldom pay child support. More and more, men are abandoning their families. Fathers also are away all day working, or they're drunk, or they don't want to take on family responsibilities. Many women tolerate violence from men because it is very hard for a mother to feed her children alone. The situation in the Northeast is dramatic. For example, an abandoned mother of five children gets up at 5 a.m., prepares a small quantity of food for her children, locks them in the house, walks 5–6 miles to work, works for 4 hours carrying stones, and walks back by evening— for $12.00 a month. With this money, a family of six cannot afford to eat more than manioc flour with water.[32]

Peru

According to Nancy Greene,

> An American mother divorced her Peruvian husband and attempted to take her nine-year-old daughter back to the United States with her. The father refused to allow it. He sent the girl to live with his mother. The American mother returned to the States and attempted to get ISS [International Social Services] to help her. She obtained a custody order in the United States and returned to Peru to reclaim her child. The father had remarried, obtained his own Peruvian custody order, and sent his daughter away to boarding school.
>
> The American mother returned to Peru, found her daughter and physically took her away. The father managed to pay off some Peruvian border officials, who restrained the mother and put her in jail for several days. The mother is desperate to have her daughter. The father

won't allow it. In Peru, that is his right. It's not as though the father even sees his child. He just wants to make sure that the mother doesn't have her. The Peruvian courts will back him all the way.[33]

OCEANIA

Australia

According to Maureen, an Australian businesswoman now living in Europe,

> In the mid-1970s, my children were brainwashed against me because I had a career. My working was held up to them as proof that I didn't love them. My refusal to be tied down in a traditional way to mother-hood or marriage caused me endless suffering. My own family turned against me, once it was clear that I was not willing to fight for custody if it meant losing my job, or if it meant winning and having to be a traditional mother. No one allowed me to mother in my way. No one encouraged or supported me in my fight for liberal visitation. No one believed that I really loved my kids.

New Zealand

Lawyer Catherine Mallon traced the history of custody in New Zealand. She wrote,

> The courts have made it clear that the presumption [of the child's best interests being served by the mother] is not in any sense a rule of law and is liable to be displaced by other considerations in the child's best interests. The law has never recognized the mother principle as having the status of a rule of law. It is a factor of importance which varies from case to case. The courts over the years have consistently taken the view that where all other considerations are equal, it is in the best interests of growing boys that they should be in the care of their father.[34]

Mallon also notes that the courts do not consider it "in the child's best interest for custody to be given to the mother where her relationship with the child is destructive, where she is significantly mentally ill, or where someone else has replaced her in the child's life as the established mother-figure."

CONCLUSION

As we have just seen, once a mother has been custodially challenged, she is immediately at risk—anywhere in the world. In most non-Western countries, a challenged mother expects to lose custody *automatically*. The laws of her land, tribe, or church unambiguously proclaim her husband's primary right to child custody. The non-Western mother may be terrified that such laws may be exercised against her motherhood. However, when and if they are, neither she nor her children necessarily consider her to blame.

In the West, children are presumably never removed from "fit" mothers—or never *automatically* removed. First, there is a trial, in which every mother is presumed guilty until proven innocent. In the West, when a mother does lose custody, she is allowed to blame herself. The governments of Western developed countries do economically subsidize married, abandoned, divorced, widowed, and unwed mothers and their children—but very inadequately.

This chapter surveyed the paternal right to child custody on every continent in twenty-nine countries. In the countries surveyed, most fathers were legally, religiously, and customarily entitled to custody and to other paternal rights without having to fulfill reciprocal paternal obligations.

Just as fathers were entitled to rights without reciprocal obligations, mothers were obligated to care for and support their children without any reciprocal rights. Mothers around the globe were not automatically entitled to custody of their children by law or custom or when it was contested by individual fathers or the state. No mother could count on obtaining physical or legal custody, even of a paternally kidnapped child, in her country of origin or in her husband's country of origin.

In these countries, women had few rights as *individuals* and no rights as *mothers* to protect them from the rights that men have over women, that husbands have over wives, that fathers have over mothers, and that states have over citizens. In general, mothers everywhere are at the mercy of legalized father right—whether that right is embodied by a legal or genetic father or by the state, tribe, clan, or paternal family acting as a surrogate father.[35]

18

The Fathers' Supremacist Movement
from the 1980s to 2010

....

As we saw in chapters 1 and 2, fathers, not mothers, have had an automatic right to custody throughout history. Even after the "tender years" doctrine gained influence in the early part of the twentieth century, a father could still easily win custody if he wanted it and if he alleged that a mother was an adulteress, mentally ill, or held ideas which he (and the judge) opposed.

Thus, the idea that men began to see themselves as "persecuted" meant that they could not abide women having an advantage, even in the area of motherhood. They felt that feminism (and demands for female independence) challenged the traditional role of men as "paterfamilias," that this was bad for children, and that attacking women as mothers might bring feminism to heel. Some felt that men could be primary caretakers and should not be denied this new style of fathering. Understandably, in individual cases, where a father was actually a better parent, denying him custodial rights because he was a man was viewed as discriminatory. A number of good fathers, just like good mothers, had lost custodial and sometimes even visitation rights in vicious custody battles, often when they faced wives who were independently wealthy or judges who were biased in a variety of ways (for example, they believed that fathers should be high earners and not stay-at-home caretakers).

Initially the fathers' rights movement in America grew out of both the male feminist movement and the anti-feminist right. "Left-wing" (or feminist) fathers' rights activists claimed that fathers have an equal right to children because men can also mother. They said that "mother is a verb, not a noun" and "a man can be a better mother than a woman can."

"Right-wing" (or patriarchal) fathers' rights activists claim that children need a father-dominated family. They also claim that God is the "father" of all children and that He appointed earthly fathers as "His" children's custodians.

Both kinds of fathers' rights activists insist that they have been savagely "discriminated" against by lawyers, judges, and ex-wives in custody matters—because they are men. They also insist that, as men, they have been economically enslaved and controlled by greedy and parasitic ex-wives who have prevented them from seeing their children.

In 1968 Charles Metz asserted that "even absent from the home, the father can supply love and guidance through a good housekeeper. When he doesn't come home, his competent presence is all the more valuable. No child needs to be in contact with a parent twenty-four hours a day."[1]

In 1973 George Gilder advocated deliberately lower salaries for women and the payment of a family allowance only to "intact" two-parent families as a way of "solving" the problems of divorce, unwed motherhood, and female competition with men for "male" jobs.[2] In 1979 Daniel Amneus declared the following: "Fathers should get custody of their children; all alimony should be eliminated; women who want to compete in the work world should do so unencumbered by children, and should leave those children to fathers who will remarry women who want to stay home and take proper care of them."[3]

In June 1981 representatives from twenty-one states met in Houston, Texas, to announce the formation of the National Congress of Men (NCM). Approximately one hundred men claimed that the "greatest inequality suffered by men involved the loss of child custody, loss of home, and loss of assets upon divorce." Frederick Hayward, in his keynote address, used feminist rhetoric against women. He said, "I do not want to stop women from going out and getting high-paying jobs. I want to demand that women go out and find high-paying jobs. I am tired of being their wallet. We must give full credence to the seriousness of women's problems [but] when I look at feminists today, I don't want to call them names—I only want to call their bluff."[4]

In October 1981 John Rossler and Dr. Robert Fay, both of New York Equal Rights for Fathers, proposed that mothers or "homemakers" be ordered to provide their ex-husbands with domestic services as *their* form of alimony. "It is demeaning [to a homemaker] to imply that the only contribution valuable and essential enough to be deserving of post-marriage compensation is the financial one made by the employed spouse. We therefore resolve and suggest that 'alimony' or 'maintenance' be broadened to include . . . such spousal contributions as housekeeping, cooking, secretarial or bookkeeping work. . . . Such services to each other [should] be assigned for a specific period of time."[5]

Fathers' rights activists began to sue for custody individually and as members of an oppressed and judicially persecuted "class." On December 29, 1981, Equal Rights for Fathers of Alaska brought a class-action lawsuit against nine judges and two state experts, charging them with discriminating against fathers in custody cases. The suit alleged that judges have a "maternal preference" or follow a "tender years doctrine." The suit also called for an affirmative action program on behalf of fathers.[6]

In 1981 Gerald A. Silver, president of Fathers' Rights of America, and the second Mrs. Silver wrote that "women find sympathy wherever they turn. Men are treated as if they have no feelings, almost as if they are invisible. . . . Men who fail to pay child support are ruthlessly tracked down by federal computer bloodhounds. Women who withhold visitation are not pursued at all. A woman who is beaten by her husband will receive aid and support, and then be directed to a federally funded center for victims of physical abuse. A man who is battered by his wife is laughed out of the police station."[7]

In 1983 Maurice K. Franks, a fathers' rights advocate and lawyer, offered his (nineteenth-century) solution to the (twentieth-century) problem of the paternal nonpayment of child support:

Custody of the daughter had been given to the mother many years before, and the father (my client) had neglected to pay his full child support. The mother got a judgment against my client for back child support. There wasn't much we could do about that now. But we learned that the daughter, a teenager by now, had been working for a few years as a part-time waitress. We sued the mother, and the restaurant where the girl worked, for all wages ever paid to the girl.

We argued that where the duty of support remained with the father, the right to sue on behalf of the child also remained with the father. We then argued that wages received by the child were the property of the father, and it was the father who was entitled to the earnings of the daughter even though she may have been in the legal custody of the mother. We asked that the restaurant owner be ordered to pay a second time, since he never should have paid wages to a minor child without the father's permission. We won. A jury ordered the restaurant owner to pay my client, the father, wages that the restaurant had previously paid to the daughter.[8]

The National Congress of Men also met in Los Angeles in 1983. It "resolved" to "focus primarily on fathers' rights and divorce reform." The NCM strongly favored "joint physical and legal custody" and was concerned with ending the (unfair) economic burdens faced by divorced fathers and with assuring the paternal rights of unwed fathers.[9]

Has anything changed since then?

More fathers have taken up some tasks of primary childcare—and more fathers have benefitted from the judicial preference for automatic joint custody whether or not they have been their children's caretakers. I believe that more fathers have sued for custody, not as a bargaining chip to obtain favorable economic results but because they want their children to live with them. Fathers' rights lawyers and mental health professionals have confirmed that fathers are being "persecuted," which can mean anything. It can mean that they are not being shown the proper respect, that their wives dared to leave them, or that they are being asked to support children whose mothers are not performing wifely services.

Over the years, fathers' rights groups have become routinely quoted and consulted by the world media. They have also successfully swayed legislatures and courts to their point of view. In 2005 the *New York Times Magazine* published a cover story on fathers' rights groups titled "The Fathers' Crusade." According to this article, a new brand of fathers' rights activism has led to outsized headlines.

A British group, Fathers 4 Justice (F4J), has chapters in several countries, including the United States. F4J is famous—or infamous—in Britain for staging high-profile stunts to raise awareness about the custody rights of divorced and separated fathers. In one memorable incident, a member of F4J pelted Prime Minister Tony Blair with a condom filled with purple flour. In 2004 an F4J member climbed on top of Buckingham Palace dressed as Batman, unfurled a pro–fathers' rights banner, and spent five hours perched on a balcony ledge while security officials tried to persuade him to come down. His audacious tactic worked brilliantly; coverage of the event flooded British airwaves for nearly two days. Two weeks later, the same man, along with three other fathers, stood atop a two-hundred-fifty-foot-high suspension bridge in Bristol, dressed again like superheroes and hanging an F4J banner.[10]

Stunts like this, pulled off with superhero costumes, have become the calling card of F4J. The main public relations goal of F4J and like-minded groups is nothing short of recasting "divorced dads, en masse, as needy and lovable rather than as distant and neglectful." These mainstream groups also use humorous tactics to distance themselves from overtly misogynist groups like the Blackshirts in Australia, who are masked men in paramilitary uniforms who stalk the homes of women they feel have taken unfair advantage of the custody system.[11] Although the basics of their platform have not changed fundamentally since the 1980s, they are also distancing themselves from the more (overtly) misogynistic tone that fathers' rights groups took in previous decades.

According to Ben Atherton-Zeman, author of *Voices of Men*, in their early days of lobbying, men in fathers' rights groups "would show up and have this looming body language that was very off-putting. But that's all changed. A lot of the leaders are still convicted batterers, but they're well-organized, they speak in complete sentences, they sound much more reasonable: All we want is equal custody, for fathers not to be ignored."[12]

According to a 2009 article in *Slate*, "One of the respectable new faces of the movement is Glenn Sacks, a fathers' rights columnist and radio host with 50,000 e-mail followers, and a pragmatist in a world of angry dreamers. Sacks is a former feminist and abortion-clinic defender who disavows what he calls 'the not-insubstantial lunatic fringe of the fathers' rights movement.' He recently merged his successful media group with the shared-parenting organization Fathers and Families in a bid to build a mainstream fathers' rights organ on par with the National Organization for Women."[13]

Why has the fathers' rights movement continued to gain momentum? "One explanation that has proved attractive to some parts of the media is the idea of 'backlash,' most famously discussed by the U.S. author Susan Faludi, who describes a powerful counter-assault against the achievements of feminism. As women gain more influence outside the household, she suggests, men lose their traditional role and authority both at home and in the workplace. Inevitably, men fight back and 'gender wars' result." Another explanation is that "long-term upward trends in divorce rates and numbers of single parent families mean that fathers increasingly find themselves living apart from their children, and their relationships with them may thus be more fragile."[14]

On one level, law professors Richard Collier and Sally Sheldon write,

it may be that the Fathers' Rights movement's demand for equality should not be heard primarily as a call for practical change but rather as a demand for symbolic recognition. The failure to accord fathers equal contact time with their children may cause psychological harm to men's sense of their worth as fathers, being perceived as, according to them, of secondary importance to their children's mothers. Fathers' Rights movement websites are full of powerful and moving accounts of fathers' pain at being allowed to see their children only at formally sanctioned, narrowly prescribed times, while mothers as resident parents retain seemingly unlimited access to them.[15]

But fathers' rights groups in the twenty-first century do have concrete legislative and social goals. "Although some of the issues raised by Fathers 4 Justice concern quirks of the British custody system, most of them overlap with demands of divorced-fathers' groups in other countries: stronger enforcement of visitation rights, more shared-custody arrangements, a better public and legal acknowledgment of a father's importance in his child's life. In the United States, the influence and visibility of those groups have waxed and waned since the mid-70s, but they appear to be agitating now as never before. In [2004–2005], class-action suits were filed in more than 40 states, claiming that a father's constitutional right to be a parent guarantees him nothing less than 50 percent of the time with his children."[16] The American Coalition for Fathers and Children, a major American fathers' rights group, defines its mission as follows:

We, the members of the American Coalition for Fathers and Children, hereby dedicate ourselves and our efforts to the creation of a family law system, legislative system, and public awareness which promotes equal rights for ALL parties affected by divorce, and the breakup of a family or establishment of paternity. It is our belief through our involvement and dedication, we can have a positive effect on the emotional and psychological well-being of children.

We believe equal, shared parenting time or joint custody is the optimal custody situation.

We believe grandparents should have rights and access to their grandchildren.

We believe gender bias should be eliminated from family law and from future legislation.

We believe child support orders should be reasonable, realistically reflect the cost of the children's basic needs, and reflect the relative parenting contribution of both parents in a shared parenting plan.

We believe when parents are given equal rights, equal responsibility follows; when parents have equal access to their children and support levels are reasonable and reflect the true cost of raising a child, parents will comply with court orders.

We believe when equity is created in our laws, the conflicts inherent in divorce situations dissolve and that, in the end, this is the greatest gift which we, as parents, could possibly bestow on our children.[17]

Sounds good, yes? However, winning joint custody does not always mean that the parenting is joint or shared. One scenario: A mother "wins" the school week and responsibility for child-related chores; the dad "wins" the weekend, circus time, holidays, and vacation time. Or Dad gets his mother, girlfriend, or nanny to take care of the children three to four days a week, and the children must wearily troop from one home to another twice a week while the mother gets little or no support for maintaining the home seven days a week (whether or not the children are there). Worse: A violent husband and an abusive father can—and frequently does—win joint custody, which then becomes the way to continue his reign of terror.

As the respectability and savvy of many fathers' rights groups has grown, they have become increasingly successful. According to the 2005 article in the *New York Times Magazine*,

On the legislative front, last spring Iowa passed some of the strongest legislation to date in favor of joint physical custody—the division of the child's time between the two parents as close to equal as possible. The policy, which resembles some legislation that Maine passed in 2001, encourages judges to grant joint physical custody if one parent requests it, unless the judge can give specifics to justify why that arrangement is not in the best interest of the child.

There are dozens of Fathers' Rights groups in the [United] States, including the American Coalition for Fathers and Children, Dads Against Discrimination and the Alliance for Noncustodial Parents Rights. They may not have the name recognition that Fathers 4 Justice has on its own turf, but they work quietly behind the scenes, pushing for custody laws like the ones Iowa and Maine have passed, lobbying Congress and generally doing what they can to improve not just the rights but also the image of divorced fathers.[18]

On the other hand, some high-profile fathers' rights groups are still clearly extreme and misogynist. One such group is Respecting Accuracy in Domestic Abuse Reporting (RADAR). Kathryn Joyce reports that

> in October of 2009, National Domestic Violence Awareness Month, members of the men's movement group RADAR gathered on the steps of Congress to lobby against what they say are the suppressed truths about domestic violence: that false allegations are rampant, that a feminist-run court system fraudulently separates innocent fathers from children, that battered women's shelters are running a racket that funnels federal dollars to feminists, that domestic-violence laws give cover to cagey mail-order brides seeking Green Cards, and finally, that men are victims of an unrecognized epidemic of violence at the hands of abusive wives. "It's now reached the point," reads a statement from RADAR, "that domestic violence laws represent the largest roll-back in Americans' civil rights since the Jim Crow era!"

And RADAR has also won legislative victories. Joyce wrote, "In 2008, the organization claimed to have blocked passage of four federal domestic-violence bills, among them an expansion of the Violence Against Women Act (VAWA) to international scope and a grant to support lawyers in pro bono domestic-violence work. Members of this coalition have gotten themselves onto drafting committees for VAWA's 2011 reauthorization. Local groups in West Virginia and California have also had important successes, criminalizing false claims of domestic violence in custody cases, and winning rulings that women-only shelters are discriminatory."

Thus, explains Michael Flood, an Austrian sociologist, feminist, and ardent opponent of fathers' rights groups, such groups often "reflect the tactics of domestic abusers themselves, minimizing existing violence, calling it mutual, and discrediting victims."[19]

"Above all," Flood writes, "fathers' *contact with* children has been privileged, over children's *safety* from violence. In large part due to publicity efforts by Fathers' Rights groups, an uncritical assumption that children's contact with both parents is necessary now pervades the courts and the media. In Australia, the Family Court's new principle of the 'right to contact' is overriding its principle of the right to 'safety from violence.' In short, family law increasingly is being guided by two mistaken beliefs: that contact with both parents is in children's best interests in every case, and that a violent father is better than no father at all."

Flood continues:

> There is no doubt that many of the individual men in Fathers' Rights groups want a greater involvement in their children's lives, but these groups have done little to foster fathers' positive involvement in children's lives, whether before or after separation and divorce. The Fathers' Rights movement focuses on fathers' 'rights' rather than the actual care of children. . . . It conflates children's welfare with parental equality, ignores actual caregiving divisions of labor. . . . Many fathers' rights groups seem more concerned with re-establishing fathers' authority and control over their children's and ex-partners' lives than with actual involvement with children. They neglect the real challenges of maintaining or setting up shared parenting after divorce, arguing for one-size-fits-all approaches based on joint custody, which won't work for most families.

Flood also argues that fathers' rights groups are bad for men, not just women:

> Men who are going through a separation or divorce certainly deserve services and support. But they're not well served by fathers' rights groups. Fathers' rights groups stifle men's healing processes, constrain and harm their relations with their children, and directly compromise the wellbeing of children themselves. First, many groups offer their members identities based only in victimhood, centered on hostility toward and blame of the legal system and their ex-partners, and colored by misogynist norms. Such approaches fix men in positions of anger and hostility, rather than helping them to heal. Some groups encourage their members to engage in malicious, destructive, and unproductive legal strategies.[20]

According to writer Kathryn Joyce, "Some advocates call the men's rights groups 'the abuser's lobby' because of members like Jason Hutch," the "Batman" mentioned earlier who climbed on top of Buckingham Palace and the bridge in Bristol wearing a superhero costume. He has, apparently, "been estranged from three mothers of his children and was taken to court for threatening one of his ex-wives."[21]

In the original edition of *Mothers on Trial*, I interviewed thirty fathers' rights activists and advocates. In addition, a mother whose two sons had been physically, sexually, and psychologically abused by their father contacted me in 2010. This father was a charter member of a major fathers' rights organization in his state. She talked to me at length about her ex-husband and his organization.

THE FATHERS' RIGHTS ADVOCATE

Advocates were not obsessed with paternal custody as part of some ideological program or unspoken emotional agenda. For example, they sympathized with mothers as well as with fathers.

> **Flora:** What if a divorced mother needs to get "out from under"? Why can't we let her go, and respect her, and trust that the children's father can do just as good a job? Why not give fathers a chance? Why not give mothers the same chance?

Many fathers' rights advocates favored "decriminalizing" custody disputes and having them "mediated" out of court. They were very bitter about divorce economics—but didn't always blame their ex-wives:

> **Lemuel:** When you're dealing with average incomes of fifteen to twenty-five thousand dollars before taxes, what can you get when you chop it up? You can't divide a whole into parts and get two wholes. How can we deal with a broken family without everyone getting hurt?

Fathers' rights advocates wanted to spend "spontaneous" and relaxed time with their children. They also wanted to spend the "same" amount of time with them as before and/ or the "same" amount of time that their ex-wives did.

David: There are many fathers who won't spend time with their children. Children need both parents' love. We can't do anything about the uncommitted fathers. Why should we punish those fathers who are committed by depriving them of liberal access—even if they can't pay any child support? I refuse to see any less of my kids than my ex-wife can.

THE FATHERS' RIGHTS ACTIVIST

Most activists were trained as lawyers, psychologists, psychiatrists, and detectives. Many were also trained in assertiveness training or in techniques of emotional manipulation. Some activists used feminist rhetoric; others used patriarchal rhetoric.

Seth is a lawyer and a fathers' rights activist. For three hours he held forth on male suffering at the hands of female stupidity and cruelty. He said he "knew I'd understand and agree with him because we were both feminists." As if on cue, Seth paused, made eye contact with me, called me familiarly by my first name, and smiled. He was very self-assured and apparently used to "winning" arguments on this subject.

Seth saw no difference between his "helping out" and his ex-wife's full-time, stay-at-home motherhood. Nor did he think of *maternal* child care as "work" or as entitling a mother to custody. He said that

> if a woman changes the diapers and feeds the children, and a man doesn't, because he's working outside the home, you don't really know what special relationship the children have evolved with him. You don't know what would have happened if this man had tried or been allowed, in a sense, to *replace* his wife.
>
> Had I known how to have children without marrying or living with a woman, I would have done it. I think I'm the better parent. Why doesn't my ex-wife become liberated?

This confusion of female liberation with whatever it is a particular man happens to want and the denigration of maternal child care were shared by many fathers' rights activists.

When I could no longer bear Seth's contempt for women as mothers and because I was curious to see how verbally agile his paternal hubris really was, I shared Ella Mae's story (contained in chapter 6) with him.

"Seth," I said familiarly, "what are your thoughts about a father who doesn't see his daughter for nearly eight years except for one month each summer; who refuses to support her decently, despite his ability to do so; and who then, without warning, suddenly refuses to return her, obtains sole paternal custody on false grounds and then refuses to let her see her mother for the next eight years? Is sole paternal custody good for the child or fair to the mother—*in this particular case*?"

Without hesitating, Seth said, "Phyllis, even if the father hadn't seen his child for eight years, I'd conclude that they were having a relationship without seeing each other. Maybe he felt it more at that point. Maybe he needed the child more. Maybe he was better able to take care of the child. Maybe he had his act together more. Maybe he felt that the child was now grown and he was in a sense willing to put the child under the stress of changing their relationship."

"But, Seth, why remove the child from the only mother she has ever had for nine years? Why restrict that mother to seeing her child once a year or for a day at a time for the next eight years?" I asked.

Seth's immediate and unequivocal response was the following: "Why *not* remove the child from the mother and let her have the only father that she's ever had?"*

Martin is a psychologist-consultant. He runs groups for divorced fathers, testifies as an expert witness for fathers in custody battles, and organizes seminars for judges, lawyers, and parents on the importance of the father-child bond.

Like Seth, Martin doesn't respect his ex-wife as a mother. His sense of outrage and victimization is very real to him—and really dangerous to the wives of his male clients. Martin can exorcise and capitalize on his "divorce demon" by winning battles against other men's wives over and over again.†

Some fathers' rights activists sounded like football coaches, mercenary soldiers, or Marine sergeants. They handled every question as an opportunity to display their blood-and-guts "manhood":

Men! Make no mistake about it. There's a war on! We have an aggressor army attacking us! Men, you must put together a very tough team.

---

* Seth had sole paternal custody of his children.
† Martin has liberal visitation but was planning his own battle for sole custody in the "near future."

You need a private investigator. [As a group] you must turn over all your cases to him and to one lawyer. Then you get to control what they do. Get a local psychiatrist, throw him all your business and wow! For thousands of dollars a week is he going to say what you want? You better believe it! He'll go with you to the state legislature. Why shouldn't he? With the business you throw him, he'll be building a new wing on the hospital in your name.[22]

AN ACTIVIST AND HIS EX-WIFE

John was lionized by the press as a heroic father battling for child custody. When I called, he immediately agreed to an interview. John was relaxed and very personable.

However, either he waited for me to "agree" with him after each point or he tried to "agree" with whatever I said—even if it meant contradicting himself. John also smiled a lot during our four-hour interview—especially when he distorted the facts or contradicted himself. For example, he smiled when he said that "men are hunted down like criminals if we miss a single child-support payment and jailed if we don't pay outrageous sums of child support. These are facts. This is not just my personal impression. Since the feminist movement, most fathers have been nurturing children just as mothers do. Fathers now have a diaper relationship with their kids."

When John discussed his divorce, he began to pace. In a voice strangled with pain, he repeatedly asked me, "Can a woman who has sex with every Tom, Dick, and Harry really care about her children? Marriage is forever in my book. What kind of woman leaves with young children just because she wants to? Now that she's remarried, she thinks she's a lady. But the damage has been done."

At first, John's ex-wife, Priscilla, refused to see me. She said she didn't "trust" psychologists. Unsmilingly, Priscilla described John as a very traditional father who "lost his temper a lot." She said, "Once I left the sink full of dishes to take a fast shower. John came home, pulled me out of the shower to yell about the house being a pigsty. Then he tried to strangle me. I moved out with only the clothes on my back. Even though we both worked, he felt everything we bought belonged to him. More so since I belonged to him, too, but I was leaving."

Once Priscilla remarried, John joined a fathers' rights group, sued for sole paternal custody, and attempted to brainwash the children against her.

He claimed in courtrooms and in press conferences that Priscilla was "interfering" with his visitation. "Were you?" I asked. She answered,

> No matter what kind of visitation he has, he feels inconvenienced and deprived. Once John's visitation coincided with our daughter's hospitalization. He was very angry that he had to share his child in her hospital room with me. My husband had to leave the hospital when John arrived. Even so, John made a scene, left the hospital early, and wouldn't return.
>
> Once our son's birthday fell on one of John's visitation days. I had planned a huge party. I asked John to join us as a member of the family. He refused. He told me to cancel the party. I suggested he take our son the day before or the day after the party. He refused. I proposed extra visitation the following weekend. He refused. Instead, he had his lawyer charge me with visitation interference.*

Why are some fathers' rights activists demanding to be recognized as "mothers"? Are they romanticizing unpaid private labor now that they themselves have paid public positions? Or is it because they aren't and thus feel as economically devalued as women—but without a maternal "cover" or "fallback" position?

Why are some fathers' rights activists so angry about "uppity" wives or divorced mothers? Are they afraid of losing their strangleholds over unpaid, obedient wives? Or do they perceive "reverse discrimination" in any pro-mother decision?[23] Letty Cottin Pogrebin has theorized that "now that men have no animals to tame and no frontiers to conquer; now that women are rebellious and machines are out-thinking and displacing men, children are the last remaining subjects of domination. Rulers need subjects. . . . Men, especially, need children to anchor the bottom of the chain of command. When gender, race, and class comforts fail, children are the last order of necessary inferiors."[24]

---

* Two months after our interview, John won joint custody of his son and more liberal visitation with his daughter.

19

Contemporary Legal Trends, Part I

....

Joint Custody, Mediation, Incest, and Parental Alienation

Does the legal record support what custodially embattled mothers have said about what happened to them in American courtrooms during the last few decades of the twentieth century and throughout the first decade of the twenty-first century? What are the major changes in courtroom decision making? To try and answer this question, a team of lawyers and researchers and I reviewed hundreds of cases obtained on LexisNexis. I also talked to lawyers and judges who confirmed that the most important changes have been as follows.

MANDATORY JOINT CUSTODY: POST-DIVORCE PATRIARCHY

In 1980 a New Jersey judge was hearing a routine divorce case. At issue were alimony and child support, not custody. The mother, Susan Beck, was a traditional stay-at-home mother. Richard Beck was a high earner who provided well for his family. He was also, admittedly, an absent father. Over the weekend of the hearing, the judge happened to attend a nearby conference on joint custody. A succession of fathers' rights activists and joint-custody researchers spoke convincingly about custodial discrimination against fathers and about the "joy" of joint custody. The judge returned to his courtroom and *mandated* joint custody. He wrote,

> Even though the father did not request it, and even assuming he
> doesn't want it, I'm going to order this as something that I feel would

be in the best interests of these children, particularly because they're adopted, and I feel that adopted children need . . . the love and security of both parents. I order that these children live for four months at a time with each parent, and while one parent has the children, the other parent will visit every other weekend. Even though there have been instances of violence on the part of the husband against the wife, and while there does seem to be some strife between them, the strife seems to be about money issues and both of them evidence caring for the children and concern for their welfare; and even though there's been no probation in court, even though there's been no psychiatric testimony, and even though I haven't interviewed the children, I feel that this case would be an appropriate case for joint custody.[1]

This precedent decision was hailed as an important victory by fathers' rights activists. Richard Beck gave paternally "heroic" interviews to the press. Mrs. Beck appealed the decision and won a reversal. Mr. Beck appealed to the Supreme Court of New Jersey. The court upheld mandated joint custody. Mrs. Beck, in private interviews with me, said, "That was the worst moment of my life. Why did that judge order four months? Where did he get that magic number from? My girls were hysterical. But they had to go to their father. Luckily it didn't work out. They're back with me. Richard can see them as often as he wants. It's no more often than before. I just feel sorry for any other mother who'll suffer because of my judge's ruling."[2]

In the 1980s both fathers' rights and fathers' supremacist activists and feminist theorists posited the "withering away" of the patriarchal state once men become involved in child care. According to Dr. Deborah Luepnitz, many feminists supported the idea of joint custody as a way of "encoding" the fact that both men and women "should remain responsible for the act of spawning mortal flesh."[3] However, this was liberal theoretics, not scientific fact. Joint custody of children already mothered by women cannot bring about any hoped-for feminist revolution in human psychology. Awarding mother-reared children to previously absent, non-nurturant, or violent fathers cannot change a child's earliest gender-typed emotions, nor does it turn fathers into nurturant mothers.[4]

Jointly awarding mother-reared children to previously uninvolved fathers will certainly not upgrade children's opinions of the importance of *female* mothering, nor will it force fathers to get involved in child care before they're divorced. On the contrary. Attorney Nancy Polikoff has noted that "presumptions favoring joint custody upon divorce, regardless of who has provided care and nurturance during the marriage, actually discourage co-parenting during marriage by sending a clear message to fathers that they have a right to intimate involvement with their children upon divorce—if they choose to exercise it—no matter how detached they are from the ongoing care of their children during the marriage. . . . Although joint child rearing by mothers and fathers should be encouraged, joint custody presumptions are not carefully tailored to this."[5]

There are many reasons a father may want joint custody. He may want to make "amends" to his children for his past unavailability or for the divorce itself. He may want to deny that his marriage is over or to protest his ejection from his castle. (This is true even if he has initiated the divorce). A father may also want joint custody as a way of having his children without having to subsidize them or their mother economically and without having to contend with repeated demands for child support. According to attorney Joanne Schulman, "Joint custody is being used as a bargaining tool by men to extract more favorable property and support terms in divorce. . . . Joint custody is being used by men to avoid or reduce outstanding support orders."

A father may also want joint custody as a way of retaining the marital home and other assets and as a way of monitoring, controlling, and harassing his ex-wife. According to attorney Laurie Woods, "Joint custody would allow a father to exercise maximum control over his former wife while having minimum responsibility. Joint custody is also a good threat for fathers to use to get mothers to back down from economic demands. . . . A more serious problem involves the increasing demand for joint custody on the part of wife batterers and incestuous fathers. Battered women who fear for their safety and oppose joint custody are being punished—the courts are finding them 'uncooperative parents' and awarding custody to the batterer."[6]

Dr. Paul L. Adams and his co-researchers give an example of how both a mother and a child advocate were unable to prevent a joint-custody father from sexually molesting his daughter:

Under the guise of sharing custody and outmothering the mother, the father began performing vaginal examinations on his little girl; he cloaked his sexual abuse under the guise of "cleaning her vagina" when the little girl reported his actions to her mother. He ranted against the mother's "neglect of the girl's vaginal cleanliness" and discounted the mother's objections as emanating from her "puritanism about everything sexual." The therapist reported the case to protective services and made every effort to help the child but the protection agency found that what the father did—although admitted to be a bit bizarre—was not harmful to the girl. The court said there was no reason to change the child's life from its former status of shared custody by her parents. The therapist realized that child therapy and child advocacy [was] hampered in the 1980s and had to yield, contenting herself with being available to the mother if needed.[7]

Not all judges, lawyers, or mental health experts were initially in favor of mandatory joint custody. Many opposed it. For example, Judge Vincent R. Balletta Jr. noted that "those who strongly advocate joint custody as the 'way to go' point to . . . studies, but rarely do they fully consider the cooperation required between parents to make such a situation viable. . . . It seems almost naive to believe that parents resorting to the courts to settle their differences would suddenly interact in an imposed joint custody arrangement in a way calculated to be in the child's best interests. . . . Joint custody as a favored solution is a flawed concept."[8]

Dr. Deborah Luepnitz published the best early study of joint custody. Her study was frequently cited as proof that joint custody "works" and is "better" than sole maternal custody. According to Luepnitz, her study was "a) based on only 11 families with joint custody b) in all but one case, both parents had *agreed* to joint custody c) the sample was self-selected, meaning that the parents had agreed for their own reasons to be interviewed, and d) Finally, the study included no follow-up of the 11 families."

In addition, Dr. Luepnitz stated,

Much more research is needed before we could conclude with confidence what the best custodial arrangements for children of different ages would be. As long as joint custody is voluntary, it can work, even though neither parent initially wants it. If the fathers are not abusive or vindictive, then joint custody is clearly better for everyone involved. Making joint custody mandatory is full of painful contradictions. On the one hand, we must recognize that judges, legislators, and lawyers are mostly men and that the law is always man's law. To propose statutory change which presents a chance of eroding women's relationships to children is extremely dangerous.[9]

Early on, there was only one study about the effects of joint custody on *children*. In that study, there were no instances of court-mandated or court-coerced joint custody; the joint custody was a choice made by both parents. The study concluded that the effects of joint custody on children needed to be studied more before this arrangement could be presumed to apply in most or all cases. The Roman[10] and Greif[11] studies, which were used in support of joint custody legislation and forced joint custody awards, only studied *fathers*. The children (and the mothers) were never interviewed or studied.[12]

In the 1980s a number of studies were cited as proof that joint custody decreases the need to return to court or leads to adequate and continuous child support payments. These studies have all been concerned with *voluntary*, as opposed to mandatory (court-imposed or mediation-coerced) joint custody.

Drs. Susan Steinman, Steven F. Zemmelman, and Thomas M. Knoblauch completed the first study,[13] which compared forty-eight voluntary and mandated joint custody families. Of these forty-eight families, 32 percent "failed," 42 percent were severely "stressed," and 27 percent were "successful." They note that "the characteristics that seem to be associated with a negative outcome for the joint custody arrangement included: 1) intense, continuing hostility and conflict that cannot be diverted from the child; 2) overwhelming anger and the continuing need to punish the spouse; 3) history of physical abuse; 4) history of substance abuse; 5) fixed belief that the other is a bad parent; 6) inability to separate their own feelings and needs from those of the child."

Thirteen of Steinman's families were "successful." One hundred percent of these families were voluntary. Still, 15 percent engaged in re-litigation. Male domestic violence occurred in 23 percent of these families. Twenty families were "stressed" by their joint custody arrangement. Ninety percent of these families were voluntary. Nevertheless, 65 percent engaged in re-litigation. Male domestic violence occurred in 50 percent of these families. Fifteen families "failed" at their joint-custody arrangement. Of these cases, 47 percent had joint custody mandated. *Eighty-seven percent* of these families engaged in re-litigation. Male domestic violence occurred in 57 percent of these families.

Nevertheless, many judges and state legislators were immediately—and remain—more willing to award fathers sole or joint custody on the basis of work they *didn't* do than they are to award mothers sole custody, alimony, or marital assets on the basis of work they *did* do. Despite what such studies are really telling us, judges have chosen to pursue joint custody as the preferred solution.

The organized *movement* for joint custody (as opposed to the theory of joint custody) is not organized on behalf of mothers and children. It is organized to obtain more rights for fathers.

As we have seen, fathers' rights groups are well organized and have promoted biased, shoddy work, which judges and other courtroom personnel are predisposed to believe, partly because they themselves are biased against mothers and because they are truly trying to be "fair" to both parties so that the case will resolve.

Let's look at some of the most recent studies about joint custody. For example, in 2002 Dr. Robert Bauserman, published a review of thirty-three joint custody studies in the *Journal of Family Psychology*. He claimed that the majority of these studies documented that joint custody (both voluntary and mandated, and whether or not domestic violence and "high conflict" exists) is demonstrably good for children. Dr. Bauserman's study was quickly challenged on methodological grounds for omitting very important qualitative and national sample work, including the work done by Dr. Judith Wallerstein. In fact, he simply omitted the major studies that disagreed with what he wanted to prove. Instead, he included twenty-two (out of thirty-three) studies that were small, unpublished, and conducted by doctoral students— and he used many of the earliest, flawed studies that have been circulating for years on fathers' rights Internet sites.[14]

In addition, according to Florida attorney Elizabeth J. Kates, in 1998 Bauserman coauthored an infamous study, known as the Rind Study, in which he and two other academics supported adult-child sex as long as it was not "coerced." The authors claimed that sometimes children even initiate the sexual contact. The Rind Study suggested moving away from terms such as "pedophilia" and substituting more neutral words such as "intergenerational sex" or "adult-child sex."[15]

The lesson? This is a war, and one must know who the researchers are and what their views on certain subjects are, as well as what is right or wrong about their methodology and conclusions. In any event, in 2006 reliable researchers concluded that "the causal relationship between certain custody arrangements and child outcomes is far from clear and the empirical evidence is mostly inconclusive."[16]

Thus, there is no evidence that joint custody is any better for children than sole custody to one parent. There is evidence that joint custody is definitely worse for children when violent men—men who have battered their wives, both physically and psychologically, and abused and brainwashed their children—are involved.

Lynne Gold-Bikin, past chairman of the American Bar Association's Family Law Section, said, "Children will do well if their parents both continue to parent well after divorce. However, we are talking about parents who, when married, couldn't decide on the toothpaste. Why will they get along now?"[17]

Ideally, joint custody should begin as joint parenting during marriage. Upon divorce, it should not be judicially mandated, nor should divorce mediators or lawyers coerce mothers into it. Joint custody may work when divorced parents live within five or ten minutes of each other and have or earn the same amount of money. If fathers earn more money than mothers (or vice versa), some arrangement must be made to equalize both parents' standard of living.

Joint custody parents do not have to agree on values. They must respect their ex-spouses' right to opposing values. Joint custody is a rigorous test of parental maturity and flexibility. Few parents are capable of such maturity; fewer still are capable of such maturity after a failed marriage and a bitter divorce.

MEDIATION AND PARENT COORDINATORS

Since I first published *Mothers on Trial*, divorcing couples have chosen or been ordered into mediation or told to work with parent coordinators. According to Laurie Woods, the mediation process can only hurt women and children, upon divorce.

Mediation is a (1) private, (2) non-appealable, (3) non-enforceable approach to resolving differences (4) which is not required to be and (5) does not attempt to be consistent with any set of laws and (6) is not required to have consistent outcomes. . . . Mediation trivializes family law issues by relegating them to a lesser forum. It diminishes the public perception of the relative importance of laws addressing women's and children's rights in the family, by placing them outside society's key institutional system—while continuing to allow corporate and other "important" matters to have unfettered access to that system. Loss of one's children and protection of one's physical safety should be considered too important to entrust to any other legal system.[18]

In 1992[19] and again in 2006, University of Denver family law professor Penelope E. Bryan reviewed mediation. In her opinion, mediators are often bad news for mothers. Many are biased outright in favor of fathers, and many more take positions that subtly work against mothers' interests. For instance, "Mediators often enhance the threat women's care orientation poses to financial negotiations by appealing to emotional and relational interests and by denigrating the importance of monetary interests. This emphasis reinforces the traditional woman's socialization and obscures that obtaining an equitable financial agreement from a reluctant husband might require the wife to sacrifice relatedness and good feeling. In such an atmosphere, the wife likely will refrain from the needed sacrifice."

Moreover, Professor Bryan points out that "divorce mediators have a strong bias in favor of joint custody and coerce divorcing mothers into this arrangement." Studies show that mediation "produces a significantly greater percentage of joint custody arrangements than any other process of custody dispute resolution." On the surface, joint custody might seem like a "fair" solution. But as Bryan eloquently argues, there's a difference between what's formally fair and what's genuinely fair. "Fair" in divorce mediation isn't always fair.

Joint custody is actually bad for mothers, she explains, "because this form of custody superficially seems less threatening to mothers, its subtle political implications frequently go unnoticed. Joint legal custody often perpetuates the preexisting patriarchal family structure by allocating the day-to-day care of the children to the mother, while solidifying the ex-husband's power over important child-related decisions." Joint custody gives the father veto power over the mother's decisions. "This veto power, or the threat of its use, invades the ex-wife's consciousness and makes her ex-husband, and the male control he represents, an ever-present with which to contend. The message is clear: she may escape the marriage but will remain subject to male domination." Another problem with the ubiquity of joint-custody settlements is that women will often settle for outrageously lopsided financial deals in order to get joint custody off the negotiating table.

The problem with mediation is not just the mediators but with the mediation itself; the system has built-in imbalances that favor men over women. While mediation proponents argue that it promotes autonomy, reconciliation, dignity, and respect, mediation outcomes inevitably reflect the preexisting power differences between men and women.

How so? Bryan gives many reasons. First there's income:

> The spouse with greater income has several advantages in negotiation. He more easily can hire experts to advise him on how to negotiate or how to structure an agreement to maximize his, and minimize the other party's, interests. Moreover, due to greater self-sufficiency, he more credibly can threaten to terminate or extend the length of negotiations if the other party fails to meet his demands. . . . A wife . . . has some power over her husband during marriage because of his dependence on her for emotional and psychological support, as well as for sexual gratification. At divorce these sources of power evaporate. Thus, tangible resources probably have even more influence in divorce than in marital negotiations.

Bryan also fears that battered women will be most poorly served by mediation. She is already "damaged" in terms of her ability to fight for herself. Mediators, who have insufficient training with respect to power imbalances, will usually fail to pick up on these dynamics. And even if they did, they're bound to be "neutral" in a way that often guarantees an unfair outcome for the party who is more willing to appease and please.

This is why Bryan advocates abandoning the neutral mediator model as the best way to protect the weaker spouse. A woman with a lawyer at her side will be much better insulated from her husband's emotional sway over her. And lawyers can sometimes be counted on to be tough negotiators for women.

With the contemporary rise of joint custody and mediation, a new cottage industry has also arisen: that of the parent coordinator. Many states have defined the coordinator's role as helping the parties implement their custody plans. In some states, courts have mandated parent coordinators. Some lawyers, as well as divorcing parties believe that such coordinators, who are either mental health professionals or lawyers, can be enormously helpful—as long as they are the "right" person. If not, according to many mother-interviewees, a mother who is already impoverished by the custody battle simply ends up having to pay for one more professional "state parent," who may not have the necessary skills and who may be biased against mothers.

The courts increasingly favor "parent coordinators" who are expected to facilitate a parenting plan for still-warring post-divorce families. Often they are very helpful. In a sense, they are the "babysitters" both for the parents and for judges who cannot spend anymore valuable time on this matter. If appointed by the court, they may be perceived as the judge's point man (or woman) and, as such, may both be respected and feared. Whether a lawyer or a mental health professional brings the necessary skills to this task remains an open question.

INCEST ALLEGATIONS

As we have seen, what I've termed "court-enabled incest" has gone on in the United States since the 1980s.

On the one hand, we have studies that document that about 20–25 percent of American girls (an epidemic number) are sexually abused in childhood and that 30–50 percent of their abusers are male members of their own family.[20] Yet when mothers accuse fathers of sexually abusing children in their families, judges and others in the court system don't believe they are telling the truth.

We don't *want* to believe it, but studies document that at least 49 percent[21] of the recent maternal allegations about incest are true, not false, and that neither mothers nor child advocates allege paternal incest more often during a custody battle than at other times. Some fathers' rights activists, including lawyers and mental health experts, keep insisting that the *mothers* or children are lying or misguided. And the media continue to cite an increase in "false" maternal allegations.

I have documented cases of court-enabled incest from the late 1980s through 2010. These cases were all reported by mothers and by their supporters. Therefore I asked a lawyer to review some legal cases involving allegations of paternal incest that took place between 1991 and 2006. She randomly chose eight appellate cases from four different states. Her summary and analysis of these cases tends to support what the mothers are saying. Judges ruled against the mothers in five of the eight cases, or 63 percent of the time.

For example, in *People v. Amine Baba-Ali* (New York, 1992), the court vacated the conviction of a father for raping and otherwise sexually abusing his four-year-old daughter. The court was highly skeptical of the mother's claims because she made them in the course of "an extremely unpleasant and highly bitter divorce and custody battle." The court did not consider the possibility that the mother was unpleasant and bitter precisely because her husband had been sexually abusing their young daughter.[22]

Likewise, in the case *In re Nassau County Department of Social Services* (New York, 1991), the court argued that "the veracity of the [incest] allegations must be tempered by a consideration of the context in which they arose. Neither party disputes that when the accusations of abuse were first made by the children's mother, she and the appellant were embroiled in a bitterly contested proceeding arising out of the [father's] marital infidelity." The court assumed that the mother was engaged in retaliation but did not seriously consider the possibility that the allegations might be true. It therefore opened the door to the possibility of paternal visitation upon remand.[23]

In 1992 in Illinois (*McClelland v. McClelland*), a mother lost custody to a father alleged to have sexually abused their child. Despite the fact that the father subsequently agreed to psychological treatment and supervised visitations in the wake of those allegations, the court nevertheless awarded him custody and limited the mother to visitation. According to the court, the mother had developed severe mental illness and now believed in the ritualistic satanic abuse of her son by his father, a notion that the court determined was baseless. The mother had also been hospitalized for her apparent mental illness. According to the court, there was insufficient evidence of sex abuse by the father and expert testimony attributed the abuse allegations to the mother's mental illness. Ultimately, it is impossible to tell whether the mother was truly mentally ill, whether she was in any way a danger to her child, or whether her allegations were or were not true or were part of a psychiatric problem. However the father did agree to psychological treatment, which suggests that a court found sufficient reason to so order.[24]

In this small review of incest-allegation cases, mothers did manage to win in three of the eight cases.

In a 1993 Texas case (*In re A.V.*), the victory seems related to the fact that the mother was considered a reliable witness because she herself was a therapist; however, as it happens, the father was a therapist too.[25]

In a 1995 Illinois ruling (*People v. Yolande*), a guardian ad litem challenged the gradual return of a child from foster care to the mother on the grounds that the mother had denied the paternal sexual abuse that had landed the child in foster care in the first place. The court ruled in favor of the mother and returned the child to her, and it furthermore eliminated the expiration date for the court order protecting the child from incest. The judges wrote, "Incest is a crime that is plainly so odious and appalling to the mores of our society and absolutely contrary to the interests and well-being of any child, that an order protecting a child from the risk of incest should not be self-terminating in that regard during the minority of the child. . . . Moreover, the child's judicial protection from incest must be unyielding and may not be compromised for the purpose of family unification."[26]

In a 2006 case, *In re P.A.*, a California court ruled in favor of the mother. The father in that case claimed that he shouldn't be denied custody of his two sons just because he had sexually abused their sister (perhaps because he was only interested in heterosexual incest). Fortunately, the judges seemed to have exactly the "I see your point, but for heaven's sake" reaction one would expect of a good judge. They wrote in their opinion: "[W]e are convinced that where, as here, a child has been sexually abused, any younger sibling who is approaching the age at which the child was abused, may be found to be at risk of sexual abuse. [A]berrant sexual behavior by a parent places the victim's siblings who remain in the home at risk of aberrant sexual behavior."[27]

Incestuous fathers may win visitation. For example, in the case of *In re Brynn* (New York, 1995), a father who had previously lost custody due to his history of incest perpetration won expanded visitation. A therapist testified on the father's behalf that he was not likely to turn to his children for sexual gratification in the future—and the court accepted this testimony over the objections of the mother's expert witnesses. One reason was that the father's new girlfriend, who would accompany him during the visits, was a teacher and therefore a mandated reporter of abuse.[28] She would be reliable, yes?

Interestingly, in a confirmed case of paternal incestuous rape, the court envisioned some visitation—for the rapist. In 2006 in the Texas case *Hale v. Hale*, a father challenged a trial court order prohibiting him from visiting his daughter until a therapist's evaluation confirmed that he posed no further threat to the daughter. Prior to the divorce, the Texas Department of Family and Protective Services investigated allegations that he had sexually abused his two stepdaughters—and he admitted in court that he had done so. However, he told the court, he would never abuse his own flesh and blood. Therapists disagreed with him, and they testified that the father's conduct with the flesh-and-blood daughter was inappropriate. The appeals court nevertheless remanded the case to the lower court, insisting that more specific provisions be made for the possibility of the father resuming visitation with his daughter. The court stated, "We agree that a complete denial of access should be rare. A parent appointed possessory conservator should at least have rare periodic visiting privileges with their child and should not be denied such except in extreme circumstances."[29] One might think that the sexual abuse of two young stepdaughters would constitute "extreme circumstances." The father's argument in this case—that his abuse of one child does not prove that he is a danger to another child—is usually dismissed by the courts, as it was in *In re P.A.*

BRAINWASHING AND PARENTAL ALIENATION: A PERFECT STORM

As we have seen, while some battered mothers and the mothers of sexually abused children were protected by the legal system, many were not. Such mothers and children were not believed. Many were treated with disdain and contempt by the entire court system, which caved in to the demands and ideas of father supremacist organizations and which chose to believe the misogynist rantings of one Dr. Richard Gardner.

As the default presumption became that of joint custody and fathers were seen as equally entitled to custody—and as somehow "discriminated" against—just then, allegations of incest were increasingly viewed as "proof" that the mother had "alienated" the child from the father for which she lost custody and visitation. The allegedly pedophilic father gained sole custody. This was justified as the necessary corrective, just as Dr. Gardner had suggested.

In 2001[30] and 2002,[31] California law professor Carol Bruch summarized this history and confirmed that Gardner's work had no scientific basis, that it was mere "junk science." She wrote,

> PAS shifts attention away from the perhaps dangerous behaviour of the parent seeking custody to that of the custodial parent. This person, who may be attempting to protect the child, is instead presumed to be lying and poisoning the child. Indeed, for Gardner, the concerned custodial parent's steps to obtain professional assistance in diagnosing, treating, and protecting the child constitute evidence of false allegations. Worse yet, if therapists agree that danger exists, Gardner asserts that they are almost always man-hating women who have entered into a folie à trois with the complaining child and concerned parent. Indeed, he warns judges not to take abuse allegations seriously in the divorce court setting. . . . Gardner asserts that abuse allegations

which are believed by therapists constitute evidence of alienation by the protective parent.

This is not what true alienation is about, as we shall see.

Bruch also points out that if and when the child is placed with the "abusing parent," the "youngsters will be bereft of contact with the parent who might help them. Parent groups and investigative reporting describe, for example, numerous cases in which trial courts have transferred children's custody to known or likely abusers and custodial parents have been denied contact with the children they have been trying to protect. In less extreme cases, too, children are likely to suffer from such a sudden dislocation in their home life and relationship with the parent they trust."

In Bruch's opinion, Gardner succeeded first because he misrepresented himself as on the faculty of a distinguished university—he successfully "conned" the courts. Second, he also "conned" the media, which kept quoting him. Third, he was strongly supported by father supremacist groups, whose lawyers and members kept hiring him and others who believed as he did to testify in court cases. No one noted that Gardner was mainly self-published, that his so-called research made no sense and was not logical. The court system did not probe into what Gardner's real views were about adult-child sexual relationships or about women. Whenever the scientific basis of his views about child sexual abuse was challenged, he simply revised his tests, renamed them, and republished them. According to Bruch,

> In practice, PAS has provided litigational advantages to noncustodial parents with sufficient resources to hire attorneys and experts. It is possible that many attorneys and mental health professionals have simply seized on a new revenue source—a way to "do something for the father when he hires me," as one practitioner puts it. For those who focus on children's wellbeing, it hardly matters whether PAS is one more example of a "street myth" that has been too willingly embraced by the media and those involved in child custody litigation, or whether attorneys and mental health professionals truly do not know how to evaluate new psychological theories.

Bruch notes that the role of the forensic evaluator has expanded enormously, often in a way that is detrimental to the litigants. Also, in her view, divorcing families are now subjected to court-ordered "monitoring" and "overzealous intervention"; families that do not divorce do not face these things.

More recently, in the 2009 *Journal of Child Custody*, Joan S. Meier of the George Washington University Law School published an article titled "An Historical Perspective on Parental Alienation Syndrome (PAS) and Parental Alienation." Meier argued convincingly that PAS theory is as dangerous as it is scientifically worthless and provided a trenchant analysis of how it nevertheless managed to become so popular. As she admitted from the outset, that children of divorce are often alienated from one of their parents is a given. What is intolerable is that observations of parental alienation are "crudely used in courts to defeat abuse allegations." Tragically, she wrote, "Parental alienation . . . has come to dominate the discourse in many family courts."

Meier wrote that Richard Gardner, the psychiatrist who launched the idea of PAS, described parental alienation "as a 'syndrome' whereby vengeful mothers employ child abuse allegations as a 'powerful weapon' to punish the ex and ensure custody to themselves." According to Meier, based solely on his personal observations from his own clinical practice, he estimated that children in 90 percent of custody cases suffer from PAS and that the majority of child sexual-abuse claims in custody litigation are false. However, he did suggest that some mothers' vendettas are the product of mental illness rather than malice.

His figure of 90 percent is untrue and absurd.

The obvious problem with Gardner's ideas, as Meier pointed out, is that it completely sidesteps the question of how to objectively verify whether sexual abuse has actually taken place.

Academic studies put the lie to Gardner's arbitrary belief that mothers frequently allege child sexual abuse where there has been none just to gain an advantage in court. In 1990 Thoennes and Tjaden conducted a major study of nine thousand cases in twelve jurisdictions, which documented that child sexual abuse came up in only *2 percent* of cases. In *50 percent* of these cases, courts and government evaluators agreed that sexual abuse had indeed taken place. Despite this study and others like it, it is "virtually an article of faith" in custody courts and among forensic evaluators that there is a flood of false sexual-abuse allegations, even though that's simply not true.

If judges, lawyers, guardians ad litem, and mental health professionals had only known how extreme Gardner's views about sexuality really were, they might have reconsidered their blind loyalty to PAS theory. Meier noted that, according to Gardner, "women's physiology and conditioning makes them potentially masochistic rape victims who may 'gain pleasure from being beaten, bound, and otherwise made to suffer,' as 'the price they are willing to pay for gaining the gratification of receiving the sperm.'" As for pedophilia itself, she added, "Gardner argued expressly that adult-child sex need not be intrinsically harmful to children. He claimed that adult-child sex is beneficial to the species, insofar as it increases a child's sexualization and increases the likelihood that his or her genes will be transmitted at an early age."

Gardner blamed Western society's "overreaction" to pedophilia on the Jews, and he opposed mandated reporting of child sexual abuse, relating proudly how he once successfully persuaded a mother not to report a bus driver who had molested her daughter. To explain why mothers would fabricate incidents of paternal incest, he argued that some women are titillated by the thought of their child having sex with the father.[32]

As a remedy for PAS, Gardner advocated an absolute cessation of contact between mother and child. Not surprisingly, in cases where families have been subjected to this draconian punishment, children cut off from their mothers and forced to live with sexually abusive fathers have sometimes become suicidal, and some have died as a result. Incredibly, some judges who have bought into PAS theory have decided to put children who run away from visitation with abusive fathers into juvenile detention as "treatment" for the syndrome. When these re-educated youths then realize that they have jumped from the frying pan into the fire, they are magically "cured" of their PAS and submit to further abuse by their fathers.

Yet, as Meier wrote, "The dominant consensus in the scientific community is that there is *no scientific evidence of PAS.*" In 1996 a presidential task force of the American Psychological Association reached the same conclusion. The three courts[33] that have taken up the question of whether PAS theory is admissible in court have all decided that it is not because it lacks scientific weight, so it is puzzling why so many other courts simply take for granted that it does belong in courtrooms.

Why is this? Meier believed that "to a great extent, the influence of PAS thinking on custody courts has been driven by the 'allied' professionals who serve such courts, including custody evaluators, other forensic evaluators, and guardians ad litem (GALs)." In some states, a "handful of bad-apple psychologists" can "single-handedly create 'law' for the state." But these explanations aren't really enough, given that courts have often accepted PAS logic even in cases where there have been actual *findings* or *admissions* of child sexual abuse. As Meier wrote, "it's hard to avoid the conclusion that outright gender bias also comes into play."

Several studies have suggested that abusive fathers get custody at rates of anywhere from 46 to 70 percent.[34] And the reason for this? "The ordinary response to atrocities is to banish them from consciousness." Child sexual abuse is too horrible to contemplate, so judges and court-sponsored officials have preferred to deny that it exists. "Finally," Meier wrote,

> the receptivity to alienation theories reflects the degree to which an overriding belief in the importance of fathers—and shared parenting—shapes and dominates the psychological professions, courts, and even to some degree, the public. . . . It is an article of faith of most family courts and evaluators—despite continued debate about the empirical support—that children need "frequent and regular" contact with both parents for optimal psychological health. In this respect, the fathers' rights movement has been remarkably successful. Even a glance at leading newspapers demonstrates a fascination with fathers and fathering, and a comparative lack of interest in, or respect for, mothers and mothering.

Another contributing factor is the widespread belief that fathers are "underdogs" and that mothers have an unfair advantage in custody litigation. According to Meier, "Perhaps courts are operating from the (unfounded) assumption that men who fight for custody are particularly dedicated fathers."

Where do matters really stand today? Courts and mental health professionals do not have an easy way of acknowledging that they were misled and that they may have caused great harm to both mothers and children. Should they, can they retry all the old cases? But, quietly, pervasively, court personnel no longer refer to "parental alienation syndrome." Now they talk about "parental alienation." Even so, the American Psychiatric Association is currently trying to inaugurate a new mental disorder, parental alienation *disorder*. The matter is being hotly contested.

Now, alienation does exist. I was the first one to write about it in the first edition of *Mothers on Trial* (see chapter 9). Actual alienation is a very extreme phenomenon and one that is devastating to the alienated parent. In 2010 Dr. Bernice Shaul, a New York psychologist, delivered a lecture on this subject at the City Bar of New York. This is how she characterized it: "Alienation exists when a child who has previously had a good relationship with a parent now, after only a brief period of time, despises that parent. The hatred and contempt for one parent is not normal and is pretty psychopathic. Alienation is not badmouthing. It is not about parent's having different points of view. It is about having a child totally rejecting a parent whom they once loved."

An alienated child will curse the rejected parent and treat them with enormous cruelty. The child's extreme reaction does not match the reality of the child's relationship with the now-hated parent. The children's current statements are not factual. The child's view is "split," "polarized." Such a child will repeat the same things over and over again. A formerly beloved mother is suddenly "a slut, a psycho freak." She is All Bad. The father is All Good.

One girl would not let her mother touch her and gagged when she did. She called her "shitty lady," "monkey," and "animal" and began lining the toilet seat at home so that nothing the mother touched could touch the daughter. In this case, the father had a system of "points" for being mean to Mommy.

Dr. Shaul gave an example in which a son called his mother "a filthy bitch" and a "retard." That was on a good day. Mainly, this son and his younger sister stopped talking to their mother for *two* years. When the mother entered a room, her children would walk out. When she had surgery, no one asked how she was or offered to help her. In this case, the father also organized a "sting" operation, which involved the son spying on his mother through her computer and confronting her about an alleged affair.

Dr. Shaul described an alienating parent as someone who may "have no resources to deal with stress. The children become allies and they bolster his self-esteem." This sounds very similar to what I first wrote about in terms of Smother-Fathers and Smother-Fathers who brainwash. Although virtually all the examples Dr. Shaul chose to share were about anti-mother campaigns launched by fathers, she does not believe that alienation is a gender issue. She said that both women and men are offenders. However, the one example of an alienating mother was a very wealthy woman who was also mentally ill.

Perhaps the fact that there were judges and lawyers in the audience with whom she works required that Dr. Shaul appear "even-handed" and "fair"— even when her own expert clinical experience had yielded a fact pattern that suggested that fathers, more than mothers, were the "alienators." (Of course,

Dr. Shaul might have many other examples that she did not share in this one lecture.)

Refreshingly, Dr. Shaul proposed remedies. "A quick response is required by the court. The alienated child must be mandated to see the parent. Perhaps at first with the help of a skilled therapist. There must be vigilant case management. The more time that elapses, the more the alienation will set, like cement. If the court does not act, spontaneous re-unifications are the exception not the rule—unless the alienating parent changes their mind or dies."

Dr. Shaul did not deal with batterers or with allegations of paternal sexual abuse, but her advice is certainly appropriate when that is not going on.

20

Contemporary Legal Trends, Part II

....

Mental Illness, Gay and Lesbian Custody,
Surrogacy, and the Primary Caretaker

Mother-interviewees, as well as the forensic reports I've reviewed, provide a damning picture of anti-mother and anti-woman bias among mental health professionals. In part, mothers are not at their best under custodial siege and are often wrongfully or falsely accused of being mentally ill when that is not the case. However, some mothers (and fathers) truly are mentally ill. Courts still hesitate to view batterers as mentally ill. If the battering is documented, they are seen as criminals—and even criminals have parental rights. The same is true for male alcoholics and drugs addicts. Women who are mentally ill are in another category.

MENTAL ILLNESS

I reviewed forty-nine custody decisions that involved allegedly mentally ill mothers. These cases took place in twenty-one states between 1981 and 2009.[1] In 76 percent of these cases, mothers lost all their parental rights. In eight of the cases, both the mother and father had been determined to be "mentally ill"; both lost custody. The remaining forty-one cases all involved a single mother losing custody. Most, if not all of these forty-one mothers, were probably poor women who had neither family nor community support. This does not necessarily mean that they had not bonded with their children or were not "good enough" mothers. What it probably means is that they had no safety net when things fell apart, and they paid an ultimate price for this state of affairs. These mothers are primarily described as "mentally retarded," less often as "schizophrenics," occasionally as suffering from an "emotional" or a "personality disorder," and only sometimes as addicted to drugs and alcohol.

Nevertheless, all these mothers fought—and fought hard—to keep custody of their children.

In almost all of the cases, the judges ruled based on what they thought were the "best interests" of the child. On the whole, judges seemed to recognize that the absolute termination of a mother's parental rights is a drastic measure. They looked for reasonable, less extreme alternatives to termination—but most of the time they could see none. They took many factors into consideration, among them the love between the mother and her children, the adoptability of the children, the possibility that the mother might be rehabilitated and the amount of time that would require, the quality of foster care, any special medical care that a child might need and that a mentally ill parent might not be able to provide, and what they saw as the overriding need for stability in the children's lives.

A typical case involving a mentally ill mother took place in 1989 in Iowa (*In re Interest of K.F.*). The mother's schizophrenia followed a repetitious cycle that left her child's life in turmoil. First she would deny that she had an illness; then she would lose touch with reality, become delusional, go to the hospital, become stabilized on medication, leave, and return to a somewhat normal life. Then the dreadful cycle would begin all over again. As a result, her nine-year-old daughter was in and out of foster care for more than half her life. The judicial rulings on this case were overturned twice—first by an appellate court and then by the Supreme Court of Iowa—which shows how agonizing these cases can be. While the trial court terminated the mother's parental rights, the appeals court overturned that ruling 5 to 1. The appellate judges did this because a psychiatrist's testimony convinced them that the mother's steady improvement on a new medical regime meant that there was insufficient proof that she would be unable to care for her daughter in the future. But the Supreme Court overruled that decision, arguing that despite the child's remarkable resilience, she had clearly suffered from the strain of both her mother's unpredictable behavior and multiple foster placements, and therefore it would be in her best interest to be placed permanently in a home that could guarantee stability. This best interest, they decided, outweighed the strong bond between mother and child.[2]

In the 1986 Texas case of *Wetzel v. Wetzel*, a father accused a mother of being mentally ill when she demanded that her visitation rights be enforced. The judge terminated her parental rights. In fact, the mother had suffered from an emotional disorder at the time the marriage was breaking down, and she even abused the children at that time. But a judge subsequently restored some of her parental rights, arguing that evidence showed that she was cured and was now a stable, loving, and caring mother and was no longer a danger to her child. A mother's actions or mental condition, the judge argued, cannot be used against her later if such actions don't persist.[3]

Other mothers have had their parental rights terminated because of substance abuse. This happened in Arizona in 2009 in the case *Denise R. v. Arizona Department of Economic Security*. Here the court relied on the Arizona statute that allowed the termination of parental rights in the event "that the parent is unable to discharge parental responsibilities because of mental illness, mental deficiency or a history of chronic abuse of dangerous drugs, controlled substances or alcohol and there are reasonable grounds to believe that the condition will continue for a prolonged indeterminate period." According to the court's opinion, "a case manager and a counselor conducted a home visit; they heard appellant screaming at the children. She was intoxicated. Her children were removed from the home. Appellant participated only minimally in the services CPS offered her; she tested positive for alcohol, discontinued counseling services, stopped taking prescribed antidepressants, and was charged with DUI." The court found sufficient evidence that she was unable to be an adequate parent as a result of her alcohol abuse.[4]

Mothers also lose their parental rights due to mental retardation. One such case had a uniquely happy ending. In the 2009 Alabama case of *C.S.B. v. State Department of Human Resources*, the trial court ruled that the mother's mild mental retardation left her unable to adequately care for her daughter, who had cerebral palsy. However the mother fought back. While court records left no doubt that she had serious intelligence problems, the appeals court overturned the ruling, in effect arguing that even a very dumb mother can still be a legally adequate one. The court explained that "the mother visited the child every other week, completed parenting classes, went to counseling, submitted to requested psychological evaluations, and the results of a home study were favorable to her. There was no indication of any abuse. The evidence did not support a finding that the circumstances in the case were so egregious as to warrant the irrevocable termination of the mother's parental rights as to the child."[5]

These cases do not give us the real story or convey the human suffering involved. Therefore, allow me to introduce you to Jenny.

When she was in her midtwenties, Jenny experienced her first psychiatric "breakdown." Nevertheless, she went on to become a successful artist and teacher. In the early 1980s Jenny married, and she gave birth to two children. After six years, her marriage "fell apart." When she decided to get divorced, her husband beat her up and locked her out of their home. At the time she was still breast-feeding their youngest child. Jenny got an order of protection. Her husband responded by alleging (true) mental illness and (false) maternal incompetence.

Yes, a mentally ill woman can also be a good mother. But, as a woman, she will be shown no mercy.

In fact, Jenny's husband's continued harassment and threats led to another psychiatric episode. While she was in a hospital to adjust her medication, her husband won custody of their two young children, who were both under five at the time. Once Jenny was released, her husband refused to allow her to see the children. Her therapist testified that "supervision was unnecessary"—yet the court still ordered minimal supervised visitation. Her husband continued to harass her and created a situation in which, she says, "there was no continuity of bedtimes, meals, or discipline." In the early 1990s the couple was pressured into agreeing to a joint-custody arrangement. Jenny told me, "This was a total disaster since we were not able to cooperate at all."

Custody litigation continued for a total of eleven years; during that time her husband kept alleging that she was "abusing the children." He also began to brainwash the children against their mother. Jenny believed that a competent judge would view any father who did this—and who also demanded that his young children testify against their own mother—in a negative light. She was wrong. The children testified that they were "afraid" of their mother. They began to refuse to "come for visitation." Finally, Jenny said, "My son ran away from my home, physically assaulted me when I tried to pick him up after school, broke lamps and furniture in his room. My daughter threatened suicide and locked herself in the bathroom. Finally, after a therapist failed to turn this around, we completely gave up. My children were eleven and nine at that time."

This mother had never done anything to harm her children. However, she had been psychiatrically hospitalized at least twice and took psychiatric medication. The fact that a father had alienated his children from their mother and manipulated them to achieve his desire of sole custody with no mother in the picture did not count as much as the mother's psychiatric illness.

For six long years, Jenny did not see her children. "They did not return phone calls, they did not acknowledge cards and letters. When they would see me in town, they would literally cross the street or turn their faces away. Honestly, I don't know how I kept my chin up during that time."

And then she heard that her son had made a serious suicide attempt and had been hospitalized. Her daughter had also "made a serious suicide attempt and had been hospitalized against her will."

In 2008, six years after her children made their final break from her, Jenny's son asked to see her. She began forging a relationship with both children. She said, "Everyone told me that the children would come back to me in time, but I doubted that they would live to see that day. I love them both very dearly and feel very lucky to have them in my life." However Jenny experienced yet another psychiatric breakdown, and her precious but fragile relationship with her adult children was seriously challenged—if not temporarily shattered.

GAY AND LESBIAN CUSTODY

Compared to what existed when I first published *Mothers on Trial*, there is definitely less prejudice toward gay and lesbian parents (when faced with heterosexual challenges) and less prejudice toward gay and lesbian third-party partners. However, homophobic laws and prejudices still exist, and decisions are diverse. Whether this is due to regional differences or the discretion of individual courts is unclear.

I reviewed twenty-eight legal decisions that took place between 1988 and 2009 in nineteen states in every geographical region of the United States. These cases were all obtained through a LexisNexis search. These custodial disputes involved gay or lesbian litigants, and they fell into two main categories: (1) one parent was heterosexual and argued that the homosexual parent should not have custody or visitation because that parent's sexual orientation would be detrimental to the child, or (2) the lesbian partner of an adoptive or biological mother argued that even though she wouldn't be considered a parent by traditional legal standards, based on her past relationship to the child she is nevertheless entitled to certain parental rights. Steady progress in favor of gay rights can be seen in both of these areas over the last twenty-one years.

The first kinds of cases were all appellate decisions that took place between 1988 and 1996. In every instance, an appellate court emphatically struck down a lower court's ruling denying custody or visitation rights to the homosexual parent because of his or her sexual preference. The appellate courts agreed that there was no solid evidence that a parent's homosexuality would be detrimental to the child.

For example, in the 1988 case of *In re the Marriage of Birdsall*, a California court argued that "an affirmative showing of harm or likely harm to the child is necessary in order to restrict paternal custody or visitation" and that "evidence of one parent's homosexuality, without a link to detriment of the child, is insufficient to constitute harm."[6] In the 1992 Pennsylvania case of *Blew v. Verta*, a court determined that "there is simply no evidence in the record of a causal link between the mother's homosexuality and [the child's] acting-out behavior."[7] And in the 1994 Indiana case of *Teegarden v. Teegarden*, the court said, "Homosexuality standing alone without evidence of any adverse effect upon the welfare of the child does not render the homosexual parent unfit as a matter of law to have custody of the child."[8]

Some of the appeals courts went further in denouncing the misguided moralism of the courts they overruled. In the Washington State case of *In re the Marriage of Wicklund*, a court ruled that "the children will have to come to terms with the fact that their father is homosexual," that "hard facts must be faced. . . . There is little to gain by creating an artificial world where the children may dream that life is different than it is."[9] The Pennsylvania court went even further in *Blew v. Verta*: "Courts ought not to impose restrictions which unnecessarily shield children from the true nature of their parents unless it can be shown that some detrimental impact will flow from the specific behavior of the parent. The process of children's maturation requires that they view and evaluate their parents in the bright light of reality. . . . [The child's] best interest is served by exposing him to reality and not fostering in him shame or abhorrence for his mother's nontraditional commitment."

In the second kind of case, progress over time in favor of gay rights was also visible. I reviewed twenty-two such cases that took place between 1990 and 2009. Most were appellate cases; some were decided in supreme or family courts.

In the earliest cases, the lesbian partner of the biological or adoptive mother was treated as merely a third party with respect to the mother-child relationship—that is, she had no legal standing. This was the case even if, as in *Curiale v. Reagan*,[10] a 1990 California case, it was clear that an informal understanding had been reached that both women would mother the child and that the partner who was not the biological mother had previously provided considerable financial support to the child.

In a related case, *McGuffin v. Overton*,[11] in 1995 a Michigan court gave custody of a child to the biological father, even though the biological mother specifically dictated in her will that her female partner (who had lived with the child for eight years) and not the father be given custody. The court decided that, according to Michigan law, the lesbian partner met none of the five criteria by which a third party could have standing.

An early turning point involved a New York case in 1995.[12] The family court did not support the guardianship petition of a white woman on the basis of her lesbian relationship with the male infant's then-deceased African American mother, who had died in the hospital after giving birth to her only child. However the court did not bar her petition. According to her lawyer, since the child was sickly and the white woman had been taking good care of him, the court found that the child's best interests would be served by his remaining with the petitioner. This occurred even though the African American woman's former mother-in-law and estranged husband (who was not the biological father) were suing for guardianship.

However, over time, courts increasingly began to consider lesbian partners worthy of parental rights, provided that they could demonstrate that they had been in a "parentlike" relationship with the child or that they were parents who were "psychological"[13] or "de facto."[14] In the case of *V.C. v. M.J.B.*,[15] the New Jersey Supreme Court outlined specifically the criteria that had to be met in that state to establish "psychological" parentage. The criteria were as follows: (1) the legal parent consented to and fostered a relationship between the third party and the child; (2) the third party lived with the child; (3) the third party must have performed parental functions to a significant degree; and, most importantly, (4) a parent-child bond was forged.

Between 1990 and 1999 (based only on this handful of cases under review), courts concluded that lesbian partners had legal standing only 30 percent of the time. However, between 2000 and 2009, courts granted parental privileges to lesbian partners 54 percent of the time. In cases where they didn't, courts increasingly recognized that lesbian partners could in theory have certain parental rights as "de facto" parents.[16]

However, biased decisions still exist—some as recent as 2009. A "third party" can function as a "parent" and still not be awarded any rights, such as visitation.

For example, in the 2009 Missouri case of *Leslea Diane White v. Elizabeth Michelle White*,[17] a court ruled on behalf of a biological mother who conceived two children via artificial insemination, saying that her lesbian partner of eight years had no standing even though the children lived part of the time with the partner. The court's ruling stated (rather paradoxically) that "even assuming for the sake of argument that the mother did stand in loco parentis to the former partner's child while the mother and the former partner lived together, the status terminated when they separated and would have deprived the mother of standing to bring her action." (Ironically, this court should have referred to the mother whom they were depriving of all rights as the "third party," but they do not; instead, they refer to her as the "mother" and then deny her any standing.)

In New York in 2009 (*Debra H. v. Janice R.*), an appellate court also dismissed a lesbian partner as merely a third party even though she had a parental relationship with the child: "Although the record indicates that petitioner served as a loving and caring parental figure during the first 2 1/2 years of the child's life, she never legally adopted the child." What was unique about this case was that the two women, the petitioner and defendant, had actually obtained a civil union in Vermont a few years earlier. The nonbiological "third party" mother argued, in essence, gender discrimination. This case was appealed to the highest court in New York State, the Court of Appeals.[18] In 2010 the court found that Debra H. had standing to seek custody and visitation of the child on the grounds of "comity." In other words, the state recognized another state's civil union.

In 2009 the Delaware Supreme Court overturned an appellate ruling in favor of a lesbian partner, arguing that state law was clear on the matter of who can legitimately be considered a parent. In *Lacey M. Smith v. Charlene M. Gordon*,[19] the two women had decided to adopt a child from Kazakhstan after many attempts on the part of both to conceive via in vitro fertilization. However, Kazakhstan does not allow its citizens to be adopted by lesbian couples, so only one of the parents could officially adopt the child. Despite her demonstrated efforts to conceive a child with the adoptive mother and the fact that she had even traveled to Kazakhstan with her, the nonadoptive partner lost all claim to parental rights.

But at the end of 2009 in Vermont, a completely opposite decision[20] was rendered. A lesbian couple had been married there in 2000 in a civil union, but the biological mother changed her mind about being a lesbian and became a Christian evangelical. When the two women split up, the Supreme Courts of Virginia and Vermont granted the biological mother custody but also gave her partner liberal visitation rights because she had been acting as a co-parent. The courts deliberately treated the case as if it were a custody dispute between a heterosexual couple. The biological mother then fled the jurisdiction and refused to allow court-ordered visitation to take place—at which point Judge William Cohen ordered sole custody to the "third party" parent, saying that this was the only way to ensure equal access to the child.

FETAL POLITICS: IN VITRO FERTILIZATION, TURKEY-BASTER INSEMINATION, AND SURROGACY

In 1884 Dr. William Pancoast, an American physician, treated a married couple for sterility by using the sperm of a medical student to fertilize the wife, who was etherized and unconscious! A successful pregnancy resulted. Dr. Pancoast told the husband, but not the wife, of the artificial insemination. The husband was pleased. The action was supported by the medical profession, as four out of every five men in New York City were, at the time, afflicted with venereal disease.[21]

Today, artificial insemination and fertility treatments are booming industries. For people who are gay, straight, single, or in relationships, these treatments are an option if they have money.

In vitro fertilization is the fertilization of egg and sperm outside the womb—literally "in glass." This technique can allow a woman to give birth successfully, even if her fallopian tubes are blocked.[22] Once an egg has been fertilized outside a woman's body, it is possible to relocate and "house" the fetus in another womb or ultimately in a test tube.

A surrogate mother could be hired for gestation alone. A married or wealthy-enough genetic mother, for reasons of health or personal preference, could still have a genetic child without having to experience pregnancy or childbirth. A woman could experience pregnancy and give birth to her husband's (and another woman's) genetic child.

This procedure raises but does not answer exceedingly complex questions. For example, is a child conceived "in glass" the property of the genetic mother, the gestational mother, the adoptive social mother—or no woman at all? What if a test-tube embryo is "orphaned" long before birth by the death of its genetic parents? Who has the power of life or death over such an embryo?[23]

SURROGATE MOTHERS FOR HIRE: 1981–1990

The popularity of surrogate motherhood is based on women's economic poverty, male genetic narcissism, an increase in sterility among older women, and the profit motive of lawyers, physicians, and other "middlemen." Wealthy white married couples, as well as single individuals, who are straight or gay can now bypass the scrutiny of an adoption agency in their pursuit of a "blond, blue-eyed, and college-educated womb" for hire. According to Mary Kay Blakeley,

> Surrogate babies, remember, are brought to us by the same professionals who gave us the concept of "illegitimate babies"—that is, a baby is only as real as the father's identity. The issue of surrogate mothers, as it turns around in my mind, is not the issue at all. Racism is the issue, and why thousands of babies come to be unsuitable. Ownership is the issue, and the conceit of patriarchal genetics. Barren women are the issue, and why some women must come to feel an excruciating sense of failure because they cannot bear a child. Saving a marriage is the issue, and why some marriages might not be worth saving for the cost of a child. And guilt and money, and how women earn both, are the issues that need honest attention.[24]

The surrogate-mother industry raises more questions than anyone can currently answer. For example, can a surrogate mother keep her genetic baby if she changes her mind after giving birth? Can she sell a baby to a couple who operate a child brothel? What happens if a surrogate mother subsequently discovers she can have no more children of her own—would she be entitled to visitation or custody of the child she sold? What would happen if a couple rented a woman's womb and then divorced? Who would be the child's legal and financial custodian?[25]

There is actually a case that illustrates how many things can go wrong when a fertile man with an infertile wife turns to a surrogate mother. In 1982 Judy Stiver agreed to bear Alexander Malahoff's genetic child for ten thousand dollars. Malahoff also paid a lawyer five thousand dollars for "arranging" Judy Stiver's services. In January 1983 Mrs. Stiver gave birth to a microcephalic, brain-damaged boy who suffered from a severe infection.

Malahoff was present at the delivery, as was Judy's husband, Ray Stiver. (Only Mrs. Malahoff, the legal mother-to-be, wasn't there.) Malahoff signed the birth certificate. However, according to hospital physicians, Malahoff then refused to allow the administration of lifesaving treatment to "his" child. "Let the baby die and have another one for me," Judy Stiver alleged he said. The physicians performed surgery.[26]

Amazingly the newborn's blood type bore no relation to Alexander Malahoff's. The boy was the genetic child of Judy and Ray Stiver! Malahoff withheld the agreed-upon ten thousand dollars, renounced all custodial rights and obligations, and proceeded to sue the Stivers for breach of contract. In turn, the Stivers sued their inseminating physician, whose orders they had followed precisely.

Suppose Malahoff had rejected his obligations to a defective child and Judy's husband had done the same? Whose child would he have been? Suppose the newborn had died after Malahoff had forbidden any lifesaving treatment? Could Malahoff be prosecuted for murder if it had been discovered that the child was not "his" to kill? (Could he still be prosecuted for murder if the child *was* his to kill?) Suppose Malahoff had taken custody of a healthy child and years later discovered that the child wasn't genetically his? Could Malahoff have successfully sued the Stivers for fraud or for back child support?

I have written about the New Jersey Baby M case elsewhere. Please see chapter 14, as well as my book *Sacred Bond: The Legacy of Baby M.*[27]

SURROGATE MOTHERS FOR HIRE: 1990–2009

Due to the corporatization of biblical surrogacy, the new reproductive technologies, contemporary society's acceptance of untraditional family arrangements, and the vagaries of human nature, custody cases involving surrogate births can be incredibly complex. In two-thirds of the twelve cases I reviewed, the surrogate mother who gave birth to the child sued for custody. She lost 75 percent of the time.

The twelve surrogacy cases I reviewed ran the gamut from the biblical to the bizarre and futuristic. First, the case with a biblical twist: In a 1981 Wisconsin case,[28] an *actual* surrogate father—not artificial insemination—was used to conceive a child because the husband was infertile. When the husband and wife later divorced, the willfully cuckolded husband argued that he shouldn't have to pay child support since he had no genetic relationship to the child. He was nevertheless still deemed the child's legal father and ordered to pay child support.

Then there's the bizarre. In the 2009 New Jersey case of *A.G.R. v. S.H. and D.R.H.*,[29] a gay married couple used the sister of one of the men as the surrogate, gestational mother, although an anonymous egg donor had also been used. The other man provided the sperm. The three signed a gestational contract stipulating that custody would go to the two men. After being inseminated with the sperm of S.H., surrogate mother A.G.R. gave birth to twin girls in 2006. As in the case of Baby M, the surrogate mother then changed her mind about the contract. She actually hired Harold Cassidy, with whom I once worked on the Baby M case and who was Mary Beth Whitehead's lawyer. This time, however, the surrogate mother won. The judge used the Baby M decision as precedent for his ruling that, according to New Jersey law, any surrogacy contract is void and that therefore the birth mother must be the legal mother. The fact that the surrogate mother was not the genetic mother, as in the case of Baby M, was irrelevant, he argued. He wrote, "It also was the position of the Court that surrogacy as a whole is bad for women even if in any one particular case the surrogacy agreement is entirely satisfactorily [*sic*] to all parties involved."

Then there's the futuristic: In the 1998 California case of *In re Marriage of Buzzanca*,[30] the parents who wanted the baby used anonymous egg and sperm donors. The resulting embryo was implanted in a married woman who was not the egg donor—so there were six potential parents: the intended mother, the intended father, the sperm donor, the egg donor, the gestational mother, and the husband of the gestational mother. Just before the child was born, the intended mother and intended father divorced. The child was eventually given to the intended mother—who then sued her ex-husband for child support payments. The father claimed that since he had no genetic relationship to the child, he had no parental duties. A lower court agreed, stating that he was correct since the child was not a "child of the marriage." But the appellate court ruled against the husband, pointing out that if he were right, the child could potentially be left with no lawful parents at all—and this was not an acceptable outcome.

In custody cases involving surrogate births, judges always address one central question: Is the intent of the parties whose idea it was to have a baby by surrogacy the decisive factor in determining who should get custody and who has parental rights and responsibilities—or is intent irrelevant? In most cases the judges do not seem to address surrogacy itself as for or against public policy, nor do they usually factor in their views about the child's "best interest."

In the 1998 case of *Doe v. Doe*,[31] for instance, a Connecticut appeals court decided that the wife of a biological father who artificially inseminated a surrogate mother had no legal standing as a parent with respect to the child—even though it was she and her husband together who had decided to conceive a child in this way. In other words, intent was irrelevant.

On the other hand, in the landmark 1993 case of *Johnson v. Calvert*,[32] a California appeals court argued that a gestational surrogate mother had no legal relationship to the child she gave birth to because it was the demonstrated intent of the genetic parents to use the body of the surrogate mother to produce their child. The three had formerly signed a surrogacy contract to that effect. The court created an "intent test" to determine who the legal parents in a surrogacy case are and used that test to argue that the intended, genetic mother in the case was the legal mother as well.

California judges used the intent standard in three cases but rejected it in another case. In the 2003 case of *Robert B. v. Susan B.*,[33] judges deviated from the precedent set in their own state ten years earlier in *Johnson v. Calvert*, ruling that the intended mother had no legal standing with respect to the child because there was no genetic link between them—even though she would have been the egg donor had the fertility clinic not placed the wrong embryo in the surrogate's uterus. It's unclear why the court broke with precedent in this case.

In the two cases in which the surrogate mother won, it was she who had contributed the egg, and she was fighting against a custody challenge by the intended mother. But surrogate mothers sometimes lost even if they had a genetic link to the child.

Interestingly, in the two cases in which intended fathers tried to shirk their obligation to pay child support by claiming that they had no genetic link to the child, courts ruled against them and declared them legal fathers with parental duties. But when intended mothers petitioned for parental rights, courts ruled against them in all four cases and held that they were mere third parties because they had no genetic link. One might say that even here, egg donors, gestational mothers, and birthmothers had fewer rights than intended nonbiological and non–genetically related fathers did.

Some surrogacy cases raise another interesting question: What happens when there are two mothers who both have a *physical* claim to a child? This dilemma occurs when the gestational mother is not the egg donor and so is not the genetic mother, as happened in the 1993 case of *Johnson v. Calvert*. In ruling against the gestational surrogate mother and in favor of the genetic parents, the lower court stated specifically that it is the genetic component that counts in determining who the lawful parents are. In *Belsito v. Clark*,[34] a 1994 Ohio case, the court also ruled in favor of the genetic parents and against the gestational surrogate mother. The court felt that it had no choice but to rely on genetics as the determining factor because "intent" cannot be proven one way or the other.

Adoption of Matthew B.[35] in California in 1991 and the famous case of *Matter of Baby M* in New Jersey in 1988 were unique because the judges in those cases used a "best interest of the child" analysis in reaching their decisions.

In *Adoption of Matthew B.*, a surrogate mother tried to withdraw her consent to a stepparent adoption by the sperm donor's wife after she became pregnant. California law states that the donor whose sperm is used to artificially inseminate a woman other than the donor's wife is, as a matter of law, not the father of the child. Nevertheless, the judges ruled in favor of the sperm donor in this case and therefore against the surrogate mother. They pointed to the intent of the parties as documented in their surrogacy agreement. As an additional reason for ruling against the surrogate mother, the judges argued that it was in the best interest of the child to be adopted by the father's wife, because the child had lived and bonded with her since birth.

In the case of Baby M, the judges used the "best interest of the child" argument to restore but limit the parental rights of the birth mother to visitation, even though the New Jersey Supreme Court judges categorically rejected the intent test and said that surrogacy agreements are void and against public policy according to state law. In contrast, a California appeals court (in *Johnson v. Calvert*) went so far as to argue that the best interest standard is "repugnant" because it involves unnecessary government interference into people's private lives.

A MODEST PROPOSAL: A GENDER-NEUTRAL PRIMARY-CARETAKER PRESUMPTION

Mothers themselves often underestimate their own contribution and overestimate a father's involvement in child care. For example, a woman I'll call Marge consulted me. She was a psychiatrist and the mother of a two-year-old boy. Marge was convinced that her husband, Bob, would win custody. "He's an exceptionally good father," she said. In response to my questions, it became clear that although Bob actually did a lot less than Marge, he did more than he was "supposed" to do. Marge said,

> I breast-fed Sam until he was a year old. I fed him early in the morning, before I left for work. Bob would transport him to and from the child care I'd chosen. When I'd come home at night after seeing patients all day, Bob would proclaim how tired he was and would retire to the bedroom for a nap. I'd make dinner and clean up. I supervised Sam's diet, bought all his clothes, took him for checkups, cut his hair, nursed him when he was sick. On the weekends I'd do all the cooking, cleaning, laundry, and child care, and write the checks. Bob would read the newspapers, watch football, and nap. But Bob takes Sam out to dinner once, sometimes twice, a week. He shows Sam's picture to everyone. Bob says that everyone thinks he's the greatest father in the world.

Then Bob quit work. He announced that he was returning to graduate school and wanted Marge to move out of the house and to support him and Sam "for as long as necessary." In return, he'd allow Marge to see Sam two or three times a week. "He says he knows the law and can win in court," Marge said.

The experts would not conclude that Bob was suffering a premature midlife crisis or that he was a canny parasite; on the contrary, they might view Bob as a postfeminist father and Marge as a selfish career monster. If a father regularly performs one or two tasks (like taking Sam out for dinner and transporting him daily to and from child care), those tasks are valued more highly than the twenty tasks performed by a mother. Marge, of course, did everything else—including earn more money than Bob did.

Factoring in the role of the primary caretaker in custody disputes is a bit complicated. One the one hand, fathers who work outside the home say this disadvantages them unfairly because they have been doing what's required of them as fathers and that this should not be held against them. They have a point.

On the other hand, mothers who work outside the home and whose husbands are essentially unemployable or who refuse to work, say that just because a particular father "hangs out at home all day" does not mean that he is doing the shopping, cooking, doing the laundry, dressing the young children, doing homework with older children, arranging vacations, or arranging play dates. In short, just because someone is in the home does not necessarily mean that he is performing the tasks of a primary caretaker. Of course, this is true for mothers as well.

There are many fathers who are unemployable for a variety of reasons. These range from physical and mental illness to the nature of the economy. The fathers may also be Smother-Fathers. This means that they turn their children into their friends and allies and bond with them on the basis of being "against Mommy" and "against Mommy's rules." When such fathers fight for and win custody, often the children remain undisciplined or are far more devoted to Daddy's needs than to their own.

Nevertheless, factoring in who has actually done the primary caretaking tasks might help establish with whom the child may be most strongly bonded. As we have seen in chapter 4, there are at least twenty-five tasks that a functioning primary caretaker performs; they range from breast- or bottle-feeding, toilet-training, shopping and cooking, and taking care of a sick child to helping children with homework and organizing their birthday parties and play dates. In addition, the primary caretaker is the one who keeps the lists of what must be done. It is usually the mother who chooses, administers, and works alongside the nanny. Of course, some fathers do so as well.

Some judges do factor in primary caretaking, but most lawyers believe that this is rare, scattershot, and not anywhere as prevalent a consideration as is joint custody or allegations of parental alienation.

Nevertheless, in the 1986 Utah case of *Kathleen S. Pusey v. Robert O. Pusey*,[36] a court stated that it would rely on the primary-caretaker presumption because the "tender years presumption" was unconstitutionally gender biased. In 1988 in Vermont, an appeals court argued that great weight should be given to the primary-caretaker status unless the primary caretaker has been proven unfit.[37] This suggests that the burden of proof is on the nonprimary caretaker to show that he or she (usually he, of course) would be the better custodial parent. In 2001 in Ohio, a mother got an appeals court to agree with her that a parent's position as primary caretaker should be taken into consideration in making a best-interest determination.[38] Nevertheless, she lost custody because she had inappropriately obstructed her husband's parental rights during the marriage by moving with their children to Texas without warning.

In the 2003 Iowa case of *In re the Marriage of Connie Sue Boldt*,[39] the judges adopted the primary-caretaker presumption but gave primary physical custody to the father for that reason. It seems that the father took on this role at least in part because the mother suffered from severe depression and was even involuntarily admitted to a psychiatric treatment facility for more than a week after overdosing on prescription medication. And in 2007 in Iowa, an appeals court overturned an award of joint physical custody and gave the mother sole custody in large part because she was the primary caretaker.[40]

As some of the cases above illustrate, the primary-caretaker presumption does not always work in favor of the mother. Here's a particularly galling example: After an eight-year marriage in upstate New York, Rebecca gave birth to a daughter. For years she had been supporting her husband who had saddled her with enormous credit card debt. Her husband became "menacing" when she finally refused to give him any more money. That's when he "stole her ATM card" and "cleaned out her personal checking account."

Because her husband did not, could not, and refused to work, he "packaged himself as the primary parent" when all he really did was "sit around and be depressed." Hence, this father gained possession of the house and the earner and primary caretaker mother was ordered to pay child support. Apparently, both judges who had sat on her case had appeared as speakers at both a nearby and a national fathers' rights convention.

A number of lawyers and judges have argued that a "maternal presumption" might be far more consonant with a child's "best interest" than is the pro-father application of a gender-neutral standard or that of joint custody. These lawyers have argued that a "maternal presumption" would ensure the continuation of a child's "psychological" parenting and would also avoid the devastating combat of prolonged custodial litigation. In principle, this is true—but only if the mother has been the child's primary caretaker and the father has been, at best, her "sous-chef" or helper.

However, with so many mothers employed in the workforce and so many parents, both fathers and mothers, working at home or unemployed, exactly who the primary caretaker is might be hard to establish. In addition, while fathers may not be primary caretakers the way mothers are, a good father does parent in different but equally valuable ways and may become more active once the child is older.

Does this mean that we should custodially separate five- or ten-year-old children from their mothers? But why? Is her role now over? Traditionally, people have pointed out that fathers can better "introduce" a child to the larger world. But what if a mother is a physician, an architect, a lawyer, or a business executive with as many important life lessons to teach a child as a father can?

In *Beyond the Best Interests of the Child*, Drs. Joseph Goldstein, Anna Freud, and Albert J. Solnit make a strong argument on behalf of the psychological parent's right to custody. According to the authors, this "psychological parent" can be the child's biological or adoptive parent or any other "caring" adult. However, he or she cannot be "an absent, inactive adult, whatever his biological or legal relationship to the child may be."[41] Judge Rena K. Uviller specifically asks feminists to reevaluate the importance of a maternal custodial presumption: "For those of us dedicated to the elimination of rigidly dehumanizing sex-role assignments, it is disquieting to conclude that the maternal presumption should be defended and preserved. . . . The maternal preference, resting on the assumption that it has been the woman who has committed herself to care for home and children, should yield only to a showing that in fact it has been the father who has assumed that role during marriage."

If a father can prove that he and not the mother has devoted his time to domestic duties, that he and not she has compromised his work for the sake of family, then indeed he should prevail. This is not the same as determining who has been the "better" parent. If during her marriage a woman has devoted herself to child care at the expense of her economic and social independence, her past commitment should be reflected in custodial priority.[42]

Uviller's argument is not a biologically supremacist one. Nor does she claim that children belong to their mother by constitutional or natural right or only when they are of tender years. Uviller is challenging the belief that in a forced-choice situation, paternal custody—that is, economic stability and a "father figure"—is necessarily in a child's "best interest." Uviller suggests that a child's "best interest" consists of continued access to his or her primary caretaker or "psychological" parent.[43]

Attorney Lucy Katz, equally concerned with the reactionary erosion of the (nonexistent) "maternal presumption" in the name of feminism, suggests an outright "maternal preference" in contested custody cases. She also proposes a reconsideration of the "maternal presumption" on its merits (in terms of the psychological parent's importance to the child) as a way of reducing prolonged and injurious litigation and as a way of *encouraging* a noncustodial father's post-divorce involvement with his children:

> A maternal preference is not inconsistent with a greater parenting role for divorced fathers. There is no question that children need both parents, and that they and their fathers will thrive on closeness after the

divorce. This goal is ill-served by any system which places the mother under constant threat of losing custody; the closer the father comes, the greater the threat she perceives to her role as custodian. Nor is a maternal preference inconsistent with joint custody, when the parents can work with such an arrangement. A maternal preference may therefore actually strengthen the relationship between fathers and their children during and after dissolution of marriage.[44]

These lawyers were shocked by the depth of anti-mother bias among *feminist* lawyers and among judges, lawyers, fathers' rights activists, and legislators.[45] Helen Levine and Alma Estable have argued that in cases of contested custody we need to be

inequitable to ensure that we are just. The scales need to be weighted in favor of mothers. We do not advocate a return to the idea that "maternal instinct" makes women inherently better parents. Rather, we suggest that in custody disputes, the courts must systematically take into account the structural inequalities faced by women. It often takes a feminist framework for even well-seasoned activists to realize that "they've given fathers the children but they haven't given mothers the money." As Dr. Pauline Bart has noted: "Who among us does not know women who thought they had egalitarian relationships with men with whom they were co-parenting only to see it fall apart and the male sense of entitlement reemerge when they wanted to divorce?"[46]

Denise Nadeau said, "A feminism that denies the primacy of mothering denies the core of our power. The courts have taken a feminist demand, that fathers be more responsible for their child, and have turned it into a weapon against women. Our own theory must become clearer on why children should be with their mothers (when they are wanted) and why and how the qualities and value structure of mothering, when valued by this culture, can create healthier and saner human beings."[47]

Sara Ruddick noted that "those of us who live with the fathers of our children will eagerly welcome shared parenthood—for overwhelming practical as well as ideological reasons. But in our eagerness, we must not forget . . . that male presence can be harmful as well as beneficial. It does a woman no good to have the power of the Symbolic Father brought right into the nursery."[48]

We must at least begin to shift our sympathies toward mothers by *one inch* and view mothers as entitled to some of the *rights* that fathers already take for granted.

I am not saying that fathers should be barred from the family hearth. I am not saying that "good enough" fathers should be punished for the failings of unfit fathers. I am saying that a father's right to parent should never be obtained by separating a child from her primary caretaker—who is usually her mother. I join several pro-mother attorneys in suggesting that all things being equal, "any father who puts a child and his mother through the pain of a custody battle or who attempts to separate them from each other is, by definition, an unfit father."[49]

I suggested this more than a quarter century ago. However, from a judicial point of view, things have moved in an exactly opposite direction. We now have more female lawyers and female judges and more feminist male lawyers—but we have not obtained true justice for mothers economically or custodially.

What if a mother had been the primary caretaker but has been truly alienating the child from her "good enough" and nonviolent father? What if the mother has been the primary caretaker but has now descended into madness and the father, who has never been the primary caretaker, nevertheless now wants to rescue his child and introduce much-needed stability? These are precisely the kinds of decisions judges face every day. Therefore, I propose that, *all things being equal*, we replace the presumption of joint custody with that of a gender-neutral primary caretaker—and then continue to judge each case on its own individual merits.

•••••

In this second decade of the twenty-first century, what has changed for mothers looking for justice in their divorce and custody battles?

In the past, domestic violence was not even considered a crime. Now, it is and, however imperfectly, it is (or is supposed to be) factored into a custody decision. If domestic violence is documented, especially if a man has been arrested and a woman hospitalized, chances are such a man will not (or should not) get sole or joint custody. As we have seen, they still often do. In any case, a wife batterer will still get unsupervised visitation—no matter how badly he has battered his ex-wife and no matter how "bad" a personality he may have. Our legal system is not well equipped to stop a violent man with a bad personality who makes life hell for his own family but who poses no threat to the public.

Interestingly, in terms of spousal support, a traditional mother may fare well before a certain kind of judge. For example, a traditional judge, usually a man, who works in a small city or a suburb will order a respectable amount of spousal support for a woman whose lifework has been marriage and motherhood. He understands that, at fifty or sixty, she can hardly start her economic life over again. However, such a mother (as well as the mother of young children) will not fare as well before a progressive, female, big-city judge who expects every mother to "go out and get a job!" This kind of judge will award only a few years of spousal support. Realistically, if a woman has been out of the job market for ten, twenty, thirty, or forty years, the kinds of jobs she may find will only pay her a minimum wage. But the judge has a job—why can't every woman?

In truth, many judges who are career women, even if they themselves are mothers, do not really respect another woman's choice to be a full-time mother. They view women who do so as stubbornly naive and as "princess" parasites. These views affect a stay-at-home mother at trial adversely.

Thus, more than a quarter century later, awards of child support are still relatively modest and nonpayment of child support remains far too expensive for most mothers to litigate. True, the state now does garnish a father's wages but usually at very modest levels. If a father works off the books or is able to hide his earnings, that money is not available to his children of a former marriage. Increasingly, spousal support is granted for relatively short periods of time—the mothers of young children are ordered to "get a job, get a life." With some exceptions, marital assets are not divided fifty-fifty but remain a discretionary matter. After a ten- to forty-year marriage, some women might receive only 10 to 20 percent of the marital assets, if even that. Sometimes a good lawyer is able to arrange a better financial settlement out of court.

And, as we have seen, joint custody (or postdivorce patriarchy) is the preferred, automatic choice of many judges. This is often true whether or not male battering, child neglect, child abuse, or child sexual molestation has gone on. In fact, false allegations of parental alienation are taken very seriously; mothers who charge paternal incest usually lose custody and visitation. Those "protective" mothers who run away to protect their children are invariably captured and jailed—after which they lose not only custody but often visitation. Sometimes they are allowed brief and costly supervised visitation.

Thus, despite some of the advances noted above in the areas of gay and lesbian custody and in the area of domestic violence in general (not necessarily in relation to a custody battle), there have been relatively few real gains for mothers—or children—in custody battles. Certain things have gotten worse. Many family lawyers, family law professors, and some judges agree that this is true.

Most lawyers fight hard for their clients; some have hardened their hearts in order to do so and in order to absorb the inevitable injustices. Many hope for the best in each case but are in despair about a system that cannot be fixed. The lawyers describe having to appear before judges who are cruel, condescending, unpredictable, woman hating, too impatient, and very arrogant. The judges describe being reversed on appeal in ways that they do not understand; they also talk about being overwhelmed by cases and by having to spend countless hours on settling the petty problems of the wealthy instead of being able to focus on life-and-death matters among the poor. They also resent how angry and crazy so many litigants are.

Let us now turn to the mothers themselves, who are amazingly resilient and heroic despite their ordeals.

21

Mothers' Wisdom

....

Philosophical Perspectives
on Having and Losing Children

Most mothers do not view themselves as philosophers or heroes. However, what mothers have to say about the experience of mothering and about children probably constitutes the sum total of human wisdom on the subject. Such wisdom does not necessarily apply to how a mother interacts with a stranger. Such wisdom describes a mother's bond with her own child.

WHAT DID CUSTODIALLY CHALLENGED MOTHERS SAY ABOUT MOTHERING IN GENERAL?

Mother writers have described and theorized about their experiences of pregnancy, childbirth, and motherhood.[1] Custodially challenged mothers described being "connected" to their children in strong and intimate ways.

> **Ellie:** The mother-child bond is the most basic relationship there is. It's the first and most primary relationship. Most relationships in the world, except those we try to have with our ideals, change or end. Mothering is the only thing that is forever.
>
> **Anita:** Mothering comes from some kind of special woman place. Maybe it's an instinct. Something flows from inside you outward to your child. If a third person is present or com-

peting for my attention, this makes the flow I have with my child harder to maintain.

To what extent is maternal "connectedness" related to biological maternity or to the *experience* of mothering?

No one scientifically knows whether maternal bonding exists because women experience pregnancy, childbirth, and lactation or because all women, including biological mothers, have been socialized as potential mothers. Some theorists have exaggerated—while others have minimized—the importance of *biological* maternity per se.[2] The mothers I interviewed described their pregnancy experiences as powerful and as having long-lasting consequences.

> **Sally:** I began my life as a mother as soon as I became pregnant. I talked to my unborn child. I dreamt about her. I planned the next thirty years for both of us. By the time I went into labor, I felt I was going to meet the person I was closest to in the world.

Pregnancy, childbirth, and lactation are psychological as well as bodily experiences. As such, they seem to reinforce and extend the socializing of women into motherhood. Caroline Whitbeck observed that "a woman in labor experiences helplessness, and this experience more closely resembles the total helplessness of infants than any other experience a healthy adult is likely to have. . . . In being entirely caught up in one's bodily experience, the woman is like the infant. . . . Furthermore, in the last month of pregnancy, women not only experience some helplessness . . . but must also learn to take [care of] their own bodily functions in much the same way that it is necessary to take [care of] the newborn's."[3]

Biological mothers *know* they are the mothers of their children. They have no existential doubt about it.*

Many mothers remember childbirth and breast-feeding as specific and transcendent experiences—that is, as naturally religious events.

Neither men nor women remember clearly the act of being born, but women experience giving birth in an immediate way. Both men and women

---

* This may not be as true of mothers who were heavily drugged or unconscious during labor.

know about birth, think about it, and experience it as real, but they experience it differently. There is, in other words, such a thing as *reproductive consciousness*. By her labor, the woman confirms two very important things. One, obviously, is her knowledge that this child is in a concrete sense *her* child, the product of her labor, a *value* that her labor has created. The second is the experience of an integration with the actual continuity of her species.[4]

Mothers sometimes described their ties to a child in biological terms. Some mothers also described childbirth as an "active" part of their consciousness.

> **Helen:** A force larger than myself visited me during labor. That sense of being at one with God never left me. It sustained me during a violent marriage. It gave me the courage to leave it. Unfortunately it didn't prepare me to live without knowing whether my son is dead or alive.
>
> **Rose:** Nobody realizes that the umbilical cord does stretch beyond the door. Even though I was prevented from seeing my son, my mothering umbilical cord is alive for as long as I am. My child's umbilical cord was cut, not mine.
>
> **Judith:** The blood bond *is* the love bond.[5]

Long before any custodial challenge occurred, these mothers, like many mothers, felt endangered by the *public* indifference or hostility to such bio-religious feelings. This is what drove them even more deeply into private spaces.

> **Tracy:** I was mistreated by the doctors and nurses each time I gave birth. My husband seemed like a haven compared to that experience. He was a father figure to me. He just didn't want me to grow up. I had to. I was a mother.
>
> **Charlene:** Once I became pregnant, being married became very important to me. What if I ever became ill or died? Who else would my daughter have?

Mothers came to prefer private life as the best or only place to care for children. Idealized (white middle-class) mothering was accommodated only in private, male-subsidized families.

> **Adele:** I slept and ate when my children slept and ate. I became half child. My adult activities weren't as real as the dream I was living with my two children.

This maternal descent into preindustrial or seasonal rhythms was not perceived as naturally sacred. As mothers became more sensitively connected to their children, their public devaluation became more painful. Some mothers were driven into self-doubt by the absence of public recognition and support. Even the most loving or helpful of husbands couldn't prevent this from happening.

> **Winifred:** There's nothing less pleasant than walking into a school or hospital and being treated like an idiot. What can you really know, compared to social workers, teachers, and doctors? You're "only" a mother.
>
> **Phyllis:** Is it too dangerous to treat motherhood as too existentially grand an event [because] men don't become mothers? Should I [then] speak in a small voice about small things? The "cute" little baby clothes, the "darling" little baby? But to become a mother is to open the gates of your womb to admit life—and death—into the world. It is so significant an act, it is devalued. Falsely flattered. Lied about. Lived alone. A woman alone is a Mother. A Mother is a woman alone.[6]

Despite public hostility and private self-doubt, maternal experience was characterized by an altered and vivid perception of reality, by the daily remembrance of things past, and by an uneasy recognition that life and death are both close and far apart.

> **Ella Mae:** My canvases were love poems to my daughter. I found myself painting scenes of death as often as scenes of rebirth and life. I felt very close to both realities.
>
> **Nora:** Nothing in my life has ever surprised me so much as what happens to women when they have children. At the time I found it awful, or mostly awful, but now it seems to me as if my previous life had been a dim, flat, verbal thing. . . . My son interrupted that, and the way that interruption feels, still, is that he gave me the world.[7]

Mothers became emotionally complex and more mature. They encompassed opposites and were able to sustain profound ambivalence.

> **Ida:** I think only a mother could understand how strongly you can feel in two different directions. I mean, you can totally love your child all the time, but also feel that you never want to see the child again.
>
> **Ellie:** I've come to realize that my need to be free and away from my son is large, but is nowhere near as large as my need to be with him. They're contradictory feelings but they coexist.

Some mothers perceived motherhood as a very special learning experience.

> **Grace:** I learned how to love only after I became a mother. The growing love I feel for my children is different from anything I've ever felt for another adult.
>
> **Winifred:** I'd tell any woman who wants to know what it's like to be a mother to try walking around for a day and a night carrying an egg on her head—just to begin to get a feel for it. She'd see that she couldn't just take off. She'd learn that she'd have to be many people without losing her balance. It's actually a Zen exercise if you pay attention.
>
> **Phyllis:** Little ancestor, sweet baby! How you temper me, deepen me, like an ancient smithy working slowly. You—who need everything done for you—are the most powerful teacher I've ever known.[8]

WHAT HAPPENED TO MATERNAL "CONNECTEDNESS" UNDER CUSTODIAL SIEGE?

Under siege, mothers did not behave in "disconnected" ways toward their children. Even those mothers whose children rejected them did not necessarily experience such a traumatic separation as "final."

> **Gail:** My kids cross the street when they see me coming. It's the only way they can live with the guilt of leaving me. I'm

very, very angry. I'd take them back in a minute. I'm still their mother.

Norma: My teenagers don't want to see me very often. But I'm the only person who remembers everything about them. I have their baby pictures. I remember what they looked like when they were born. When they want to know about themselves, they'll have to come to me. I am the guardian of their history.

Under custodial siege, mothers desperately wanted their children's emotional support and loyalty. However, they were reluctant to "lean" on their children emotionally or to abdicate their disciplinary role in order to "win" a child over.

Janet: A custody struggle, in or out of court, gives a child an exaggerated sense of his own importance and power. This is bad. Maternal authority is the first thing to go. Your child will play one parent off against the other. If you give in to him in order to have him on your side, you're condemning him and yourself.

Mothers did not brainwash their children—that is, force them to commit psychological patricide. They lacked the requisite economic and emotional resources to underwrite a kidnapping or a brainwashing campaign. Mothers were also unwilling to hurt a child by telling him that "his father is dead" or "doesn't love him."

Beth: What kind of father tries to turn children against their own mother? What kind of father thinks his kids are better off *without* a mother? My husband knew I couldn't go for his jugular if it meant hurting the kids. If I "killed" their father as he was trying to "kill" me, how could I face my children afterwards?

As we have seen, when a custodially embattled father leaned on a child emotionally or engaged in an anti-mother brainwashing campaign, this was often experienced by the father and his children (and perceived by expert observers) as a long-overdue form of paternal "intimacy."

However, when a custodially embattled mother tried to ward off false ide-alizations of a father or to defend herself against her loss of maternal author-ity or credibility, this was experienced and perceived as "brainwashing."

When a mother "complained" to her children about the paternal non-payment of child support, lawyers, experts, judges, and neighbors viewed this as a savage denunciation of a child's father and as more destructive to a child's self-esteem than was his father's physical, economic, or psychologi-cal abandonment. Children refused to believe that fathers were withhold-ing child support "on purpose." Children got angry at their *mothers* for saying so.*

For two years I remained suspicious of the maternal reluctance to "fight dirty" or to "force a child to choose between her parents." Surely this was virtue by default. Most people, including mothers, aren't saints. Why didn't these mothers simply admit that they were unable to wage a pub-lic fight or that they didn't really want the burden of single motherhood? Why didn't they admit that physical and psychological nonviolence was their only means of "pacifying" already provoked and custodially violent husbands?

Because such reasons were not the only ones involved in how a mother chose to fight.

Maternal "connectedness" meant that a mother did not consciously use violent weapons against her child even in order to "win" custody.

> **Denise:** How could I ethically engage in an adversarial court battle, the win/lose type of situation that was against every-thing I believed in? How could I maintain my integrity in a way that wouldn't hurt my son or violate my feminist principles?
>
> **Sybil:** In fighting to keep our kids in a custody battle, we lose what we might call our motherhood. It's another, more painful version of trying to mother under patriarchy. This is too painful to face.

---

* Mystification of children, if it is in the service of fathers' rights, is always preferred to honesty.

WHY DID MATERNALLY "CONNECTED" WOMEN LOSE CUSTODY OF THEIR CHILDREN?

Custodially challenged mothers were heroic in their barefoot and unarmed fight for their children and in their refusal to adopt violent methods in order to "win."

A mother's emotional maturity functioned as a catch-22 against her. The maternal ability to experience emotional opposites, to love two people simultaneously, and to tolerate ambivalence creatively was, incredibly, taken as proof of maternal unfitness. ("Do you love your children or your lover? Your career or your child?" "How can you love this child when you yourself have admitted you want to run away?")

In a custody battle, anyone who was capable of strong and opposite emotions, capable of complex perceptions of emotional reality, or concerned with the nonviolent nurturance of a child lost custody of that child.

Few judges recognized maternal nonviolence as proof that a woman was the real mother of her child. Few judges viewed paternal domestic violence as "violent." Many such Solomons mistook a father's violent (dis)connection to his child for "love." The violent and "disconnected" paternal bond was judicially viewed as the "civilized" bond.

HOW DID MATERNAL CUSTODIAL VICTIMIZATION AFFECT WOMEN PHILOSOPHICALLY?

Many mothers tried to appreciate, in life-affirming ways, the practical or philosophical advantages of being forced to live apart from their children.

> **Adele:** We don't own our children. We only have the privilege of being alive and involved with them for a limited amount of time. When children become adults, they can choose never to see us again. My lease on mothering was more short-term than most. I could be a very bitter person. I was for awhile. I made a conscious choice not to poison my life. That is my strongest response to what happened.

> **Beth:** This custody struggle has changed me from an impulsive and unrealistic woman. The situation has kept my feet nailed to the wall. Now, before I do anything, I calculate what effect it really has on the kids and on me. This mis-

erable battle has actually made me more responsible and realistic.

In a sense, every custodially challenged mother was "radicalized"—that is, she became more informed about reality. This was a radical departure from her previous naïveté. No custodially challenged mother ever again confused her desire or *obligation* to mother with her *right* to mother, nor did anyone suffer her previously "normal" delusions of maternal omnipotence.

Ella Mae: Sitting in the courtroom, I began to fantasize that I was a mother lion protecting my cubs. I needed a fantasy this powerful to meditate on in a place where men had the legal right to separate a mother from her child. It took me years to regain my proper energy. I had to let this fantasy of myself as a mother lion go before I could forgive myself for losing my child.

Bettina: I always thought I could protect my kids from the whole world. I couldn't protect them from their father's kidnapping them. I can't protect them from poverty. What I *can* do is physically take care of them—if I'm allowed to. I can love them. I don't have the power to do more than this.

After a custody battle, no mother had any illusions about legal justice or legal protection. On the basis of what they knew, some mothers advised *other* mothers to steer clear of the courts in any way possible. A few mothers advised *other* mothers to "play dirty."

Josie: Please tell other mothers involved in custody struggles to give up being naive. Tell them they've got to go for the balls. We're outleagued emotionally and financially. We must play to win, not to show we're "better" than men. Our children are worth fighting for.

Helen: You can't depend on the legal system. You can't expect them to find your child. You have got to be your own detective. I respected the law my whole life. I can't anymore. Forget about the law. If the child is yours, take that child and go! Take him. Take your child and disappear. Forget about the law. There is none.

Being traumatized by injustice is not equivalent to understanding or fighting injustice. In order to survive, mothers used their newfound realpolitik in many ways. Some mothers became *less* ambitious, more cautious, and more secretive than they had been. They did not want to arouse the world's violence and indifference again. Some mothers redoubled their efforts to find and "connect" with a man for protection from (male) violence. Some mothers also reaffirmed the importance of marriage and traditional values for the same reason.

> **Belinda:** I would never, never commit adultery again, no matter what my [new] husband does. My baby is too precious to lose. Anyway, my husband rescued me. Without him I could never have survived losing my kids.
>
> **Sally:** When we fight with husbands, we're dealing with professional killers. They're trained as mental killers. You need a lot of ego strength. You must forget any feelings you have about your husband—like he's an honest man, he'd never do this or that. He will. I really needed another *man* to protect me from the first male killer. It was a big paradox.

Nearly a third (28 percent) of the mothers returned to school or embarked on careers. More than two-thirds attempted to become more self-loving and psychologically independent.

> **Dora:** For twenty years I sacrificed myself in a bad marriage. I was dying. I decided to live before it was too late and I was actually dead. I decided to be a model against suicide—and against obedience to tyranny—for my children's sake. I'm sixty-two years old now. The price of my freedom is very high. I'm willing to pay it. I have only one person in my life whom I can count on completely. It's myself.
>
> **Terry:** My strength lies in getting on with my own life. I also have a strong belief that the children whom I've loved and mothered will truly return to me.

About 40 percent of the mothers looked for "larger" explanations of reality in order to survive. Some expressed their custodial victimization in religious or psychological terms; others did so in verbally dramatic terms. Maureen described her husband as a "terrorist who, for three years, has aimed a gun at my heart." Miki and Angela described their custody battles as analogous to the battles of enslaved or racially despised peoples.

> **Miki:** I felt I was like a black person living under slavery or under the rules of South African apartheid. I had to carry identity papers with me at all times—proof that I had legal custody of my kids to show the police, in case my ex-husband ever challenged me in the street or in my apartment again. I felt I was living under military occupation. My judge was a racist. So was my ex-husband. I experienced losing my children as a form of racism.
>
> **Angela:** People say I'm crazy to compare the Nazi extermination of six million Jews with my situation. Maybe six million living women have not been exterminated or sterilized. Maybe ten thousand or ten million have. Whatever the number, people refuse to recognize that a mother who loses her kids the way I have has really been held hostage, tortured, and wiped out as a mother.

Rachel and Kate viewed their custodial victimization as part of the systemic victimization of women.

> **Rachel:** Taking a child away from his mother is a violent act of mother hatred. My ex-husband chopped my body in half. The judge helped him.
>
> **Kate:** All mothers are in an endangered political position whether they know it or not. If you were a resistance fighter during World War II, you'd make arrangements for your children in case you were caught or killed. These arrangements are almost impossible to make. But they're what you need in order to fight when everything's completely rigged against you.

Half the mothers (52 percent) did not even assert a sense of maternal entitlement verbally. They may have *felt* they deserved custody of their children, but they didn't say so.

Such mothers displayed no anger about losing a "right" they never had. Catherine MacKinnon has described a parallel sense of nonentitlement among women in her analysis of rape victims and the law: "Most women get the message that the law against rape [against fathers' rights] is virtually unenforceable as applied to them. Rape [fathers' rights] from women's point of view, is not prohibited; it is regulated."

Nearly half the mothers (47 percent) *verbally* expressed a mothers' rights position. The verbal expression of maternal rights was not correlated either with sexual preference or with political ideology.[9] What did a verbal expression of mothers' rights sound like?

> **Abigail:** We get pregnant. We experience physical and psychological changes. If we give birth to a healthy baby, why isn't that more important than a few drops of sperm? We bring the kids up. Isn't that as important as economically supporting them? What about those mothers who support the kids, too? Why don't mothers automatically have the right of way in a custody battle?
>
> **Alix:** How can a child be forcibly removed from a devoted and competent mother? There's one incredible explanation. It's because mothers are *women*. If mothers had any custody rights, *women* would already have equal rights.

Some mothers who verbally opposed *anyone's* having "rights" over children made similar statements. However in the same breath they insisted that mothers should never stand in the way of a father-child relationship and that all children need fathers. They perceived a difference between mothering and fathering—but one that they did not translate into any justification for maternal entitlement.

> **Sonia:** Parenting is a very delicate task. As long as men are trained to be selfish and domineering, they can't be trusted with children. They know this themselves. After men win custody, they toss the children right into another woman's lap. They won't take on the job themselves.
>
> **Maureen:** My husband did many good things for our children when they were small. Once we separated, he didn't care what he did to hurt his own children—as long as it hurt me and

weakened my relationship with them. He treated them as if they were extensions of me at the very time he was claiming that they "belonged" to him.

A traumatizing experience of injustice cannot politicize an isolated individual into a verbal assertion of her (nonexistent) "rights." Victims need an alternative vision of justice *plus* personal support in order to become politically assertive. Was there any correlation between being able to talk about mothers' rights and being supported during battle?

The twenty-one heterosexual mothers who expressed a mothers' rights position did so with very little personal or political support.[10] Only three (14 percent) of the heterosexual mothers sought any *political* support. Only one mother (Miki) received any.

Miki: A group of black women social workers came through for me. I was refused help by every male-run Asian American and black group I managed to contact.

Jessie: No feminist organization was willing to help me. They saw what happened to me as sexist, but they didn't know how to relate to it. The women I spoke to felt that fathers should have equal custodial rights. They didn't know how to support me without seeming to be against equality or against male participation in child care.

Emily: I'm a socialist. No one I knew politically wanted to handle this issue as a political issue. Some friends tried to put on a benefit for my legal expenses. It fell through.

Nine (20 percent) of the heterosexual advocates of mothers' rights were personally supported by male intimates. Of these, only a third expressed a mothers' rights position. This suggests that personal (male) support does not necessarily lead a woman into verbal assertions of maternal rights or into a political analysis of her experience.[11]

Half (50 percent) of the lesbian mothers did not seek any political support; they were isolated or too afraid to be publicly identified as lesbians. The other 50 percent both sought and received personal and political support.

Dorothy: A lot of lesbians sympathized with me and came to court. The community here tried to be helpful, but they actually thought that I couldn't win, that there was no point in fighting too hard. If it weren't for my lover, I would have had no contact with the community. I only had the energy to see my lawyer and go to work. I could never have arranged a benefit or gotten publicity.

Margo: I did all the work of keeping it together. Laura [the biological mother] was barely able to get up in the morning. She was seriously depressed. I helped our daughter lead an almost normal life. I also did all the political work. Actually I fought harder for that kid than she did. Maybe I had the strength and she didn't. She'd already lost her son.

Few women were able to defend themselves effectively in public battles. Fewer still were able to face the "whirlpool of cruelty" again on behalf of another woman victim.[12] Such principled and compassionate activity requires enormous psychological strength, ideological or religious conviction, and an economic and emotional base of some kind.

Ten mothers—17 percent of the maternally embattled population and 36 percent of the verbal advocates of mothers' rights—became pro-mother activists. All were feminists.

Seven of these activists had effectively fought their own battles. For example, they contacted social agencies, church groups, experts, and the media. After losing their battles, these ten advocates went on to counsel, support, or accompany to court other custodially embattled mothers. Two mothers formed a support group for themselves and for other victimized mothers. Two mothers went to law school to have a lawyer *they* could trust and to provide such a lawyer for other women. One mother joined a small crisis and counseling network for custodially embattled mothers, and a second mother created one such network.

There may actually be a high rate of altruistic activity among female victims. How many victims, male or female, ever become activists? How many victims, male or female, do so with as little support as these mothers had in their own battles?

By the twenty-first century, custodially challenged mothers were involved in writing books and pamphlets and launching websites. Now, many such mothers have created networks, attend support groups, hold conferences, and function as paid and unpaid divorce coaches for other mothers. Some mothers maintain websites that provide running time lines for their own cases—some have even been legally sued by their husbands for doing so. Some mother-run websites provide advice and helpful information. Some mothers hold and attend regional and national conferences and participate in demonstrations on behalf of custodially embattled and court-abused children.

WHAT AM I SAYING ABOUT MOTHERS?

All custodially challenged mothers "bonded" in nurturing and nonviolent ways to their children. Under siege, they remained *nonviolently* "connected" to their children. Mothers did not use violent or "disconnected" means to win custody of their children. After losing custody, these mothers saw or attempted to see their children regularly, even under difficult and humiliating circumstances. Remaining connected under the most adverse conditions is one measure of the optimistic resilience of the mother-child bond or social contract.

Adult women, including mothers, have been described as more "affiliative" and "attached" than men, as more "cooperative" than "competitive," and as preferring "intimate relationships" to "self-enhancement."[13]

This is only part of the larger truth. As we now know, adult women are as "competitive" with and "aggressive" toward *other women* as they are "cooperatively attached" to their "own" family men and children. Adult women rarely "affiliate" with or "nurture" other women or *their* children.[14] I have published a book on this very subject, entitled *Woman's Inhumanity to Woman*.

Nevertheless, Dr. Sara Ruddick's view of mothering as a "moral process" is a very useful concept. The fact that the human race is still here suggests that most mothers and female caretakers throughout evolution and recorded history have been physically nurturant and nonviolent to children in ways that have been "good enough." Despite the limitations and imperfections of individual mothers, and with all due respect to what men have also done to avert violence and save lives, Ruddick's description of mothers is fairly accurate. She said,

> I can think of no other situation in which someone with the resentments of social powerlessness, under enormous pressures of time and anger, faces a recalcitrant but helpless combatant with so much restraint. What is remarkable is that in a daily way mothers make so

much peace instead of fighting, and then when peace fails, conduct so many battles without resorting to violence. I don't want to trumpet a virtue but to point to a fact: that non-violence is a constitutive principle of maternal thinking, and that mothers honor it not in the breach, but in their daily practice, despite objective temptations to violence.[15]

Ruddick's maternal process is, at its best, concrete rather than abstract, subjective rather than objective, emotional rather than emotionless, flexible rather than dogmatic, and "whole" rather than compartmentalized. The maternal process is, at its best, both optimistic and pessimistic, both humble and grandiose. Once the maternal process is engaged, it is engaged continuously and in nurturing ways for life. Serious maternal disengagement or life-threatening violence is rare. Mothers do not often kill their children or go to war against them as a way of socializing them.[16]

The maternal process cannot "connect" to a large number of strangers. It cannot function in a world that is overly and impersonally organized. This doesn't mean that the maternal process is unsuited to the world at large. On the contrary. It suggests that the larger world, as presently constituted, may be unsuited to the nonviolent nurturance or preservation of life.

22

Mothers' Voices, Written on the Wind

. . . .

What Is a Custody Battle Really About?

Broud seldom stood face to face with Ayla. She was much taller than the tallest man in the clan, and Broud was not among the tallest. He barely reached her shoulders. She knew he didn't like looking up at her.

"As you know, I am your new leader," Broud started, "I will take Ayla as second woman to my hearth. I will not have [her son] living at my hearth." Ayla's head jerked up. "What does he mean? If I have to move to his hearth, my son comes with me." Children belonged with their mothers until they were grown. Why would Broud take Ayla, but refuse her son?

"Broud, you can't take Durc away from me. He's my son. Wherever a woman goes her children go with her." "Are you, woman, telling this leader what he can or cannot do? Every woman in the clan is mother to him. What difference does it make where he lives? He obviously doesn't care, he eats at everyone's hearth," Broud said. . . .

"You're going away," [Durc] accused [Ayla]. "You're all dressed and going away." "Yes, Durc, I'm going away. I have to go away." "Take me with you, Mama. Take me with you! Don't leave me!" "I can't take you with me, Durc. I love you, Durc. Never forget that, I love you."

The last thing Ayla heard as she disappeared behind the broken ridge was Durc's plaintive wail—

"Maama, Maaama, Maamaaa!"

—*Jean M. Auel,* The Clan of the Cave Bear

"A custody battle is *the* quintessential power struggle between men and women. It's about who controls a woman's mind and body. It's also about who gets to control the future. Children are the future."

"My husband loved me very much. He couldn't bear to lose me *and* our children, too. He fought to keep what he could."

"A custody battle is a reminder to women that our children are only on loan to us. We can lose children to death, and to insecure and angry fathers."

"Men think of children as the necessary chains to keep wives from flying away. If we fly away anyway, they transfer their needs to their children."

"Having to fight for custody is like being raped—only it's worse. It never stops. And there is no crisis intervention center for it."

"My husband was already jealous of how close I was to our kids. If I lived alone with them, he was afraid I'd get even closer. He did what he could to prevent that from happening."

"In a custody battle your children are blinded, turned into sleepwalkers. They do not see their mothers. They do not see her grieving. They do not understand her anger. They act as if she's crazy or as if 'nothing's wrong.' For me, losing custody was the way my husband had me legally sentenced to death. It was also his way of denying his part in my murder. After all, it was the judge's decision, not his."

"My ex-husband had a drinking problem. He needed our kids to help him look like he has a respectable life."

"In many ways a custody battle is a psychological war. The greatest danger lies in colluding with the enemy in self-doubt. I had to become a spiritual warrior to convince myself that I was a good mother. This personal conviction helped me endure."

WHAT TO DO WHEN A CUSTODY BATTLE INVADES YOUR LIFE

"First, take a deep breath and calm down. Save your strength for the long haul. Find out what all your options are. Find a therapist for some immediate support."

"Any mother involved in a custody struggle is the one who's on trial. You'll need people to hold your hand, to hold you, to take care of your kids, to cook a meal, to say 'I care.' You'll need people to keep telling you that you're sane and that you have rights. Find those people *now*."

"Never leave home without taking your kids with you—not if you're fighting over custody. Don't leave your kids behind to take a weekend vacation.

If you've just been beaten up and you're on your way to the hospital, you'd better take your kids along."

"You'll need to be on permanent good behavior in order to fight this fight. Your husband or someone will always be breathing down your neck spying on you and trying to make your life miserable."

"I allowed things to get very bad before I started to fight back. I would never have waited so long if I knew what I know now: that for me *not* fighting was worse than fighting."

"If you open up a power struggle with your husband, be prepared to learn how to win. Don't go on believing that your husband won't lie and manipulate to cheat you. He will. If he doesn't, his lawyer will. In order to win on their turf you've got to be as rotten as they are. Being fair means you're going to lose."

"Keep a record of how often your ex-husband visits and whether he's on time or late. Tape-record your phone conversations with him so you'll remember everything. Record any threats he makes to you. Record what he does with the kids. Do they come back unfed, unwashed, late? Are they suddenly critical or distant from you? That could be a sign of brainwashing."

"Organize your family photos into a 'Mom and Kids' showpiece album. Reconstruct a diary of what you did with and for your kids from your old calendars or appointment books. You'll have to prove that you're a good mother."

"No matter what happens, no matter what they say, never let any social worker or lawyer or judge or policeman make you doubt yourself or your self-worth."

"*Believe* that you're stronger than you think you are. Become very assertive about getting what you need from others, but depend only on yourself. You have the most to lose and the most to gain."

"Once you're married and a mother, it's too late to think about how to win a custody battle. The time to think about whether and how you should become a mother is long before you're pregnant and definitely before you marry."

"Read the marriage contract. Talk to previously married or still married mothers who are living in poverty or who have lost custody of their children. Maybe it's more realistic *not* to have children at all—or to have them through woman-controlled anonymous artificial insemination. But the state can still take your child away if you forge a check, work as a prostitute, use dope, sell dope, kill your violent husband in self-defense, or refuse to do whatever your state welfare worker wants you to do—if you're economically dependent on the state. If your own *mother* doesn't like how you're raising your child, she can call in the state against you. This happened to me. I won. But I never sleep easy."

"Consider adopting a child as a single mother. I know a number of women lawyers who have chosen this route. And don't marry or partner up. Not with a man, not with a woman."

ON HIRING A LAWYER

"Get a copy of your legal bill of rights. Refer to it when you're talking to your lawyer. Interview more than one lawyer. Be prepared to leave a lawyer who doesn't treat you well and to sue him or her for legal malpractice."

"Once you're involved in the court system, you must ask your lawyer's advice about everything. You can't start a new job or love affair without first weighing the legal consequences involved. You must assume that everything you do can and will be used against you."

"Your lawyer isn't God. He or she is your employee. Don't let your lawyer pressure you into anything 'temporarily' that you wouldn't want permanently."

"Talk to other women who've been through custody battles. Find a lawyer who's experienced in *custody* battles, not just in matters of divorce."

"Don't let your lawyer convince you that joint custody is the 'answer.' It isn't. My ex-husband wanted to be the one who'd live with our kids in the house or, failing that, he wanted the judge to order that the house be sold. Then, once the cash from the sale of the house ran out, and I really had to struggle economically, that's when my ex stopped paying child support. He told the kids that 'he didn't have to pay because they lived with him half the time.' The kids had a much higher standard of living with him than with me. Gradually, they began to live with him full time. Then he moved two thousand miles away to take a very well-paying job. I still have joint custody. I just can't afford to take my ex back to court or to travel four thousand miles a week in order to exercise my joint custody decree."

"It's important to find a good woman lawyer. Treat her with more respect than women usually treat each other. Don't expect her to be your friend. Expect her to treat you with respect and to use the law vigorously and creatively on your behalf."

ON LAWSUITS

"A man can sue for damages if someone alienates his wife's affections or if he loses her services. He can also sue for damages if he loses his penis or his mind in an industrial accident or as a result of a robber's chasing him down the block. How much money would a jury award him as compensation for such losses? Why should a mother who loses her children get any less compensation? She should really get a lot more."

"Why can't kids sue their father if he refuses to visit them at all? The money could pay for a house-husband, a male babysitter or a shrink."

"Any mother who is alienated from the affections of her own child should sue whoever did this for a lot of money. No mother should be deprived of this most fundamental right of nature. Money is the only language men understand."

"A father should be sued for damages if he says he's going to visit but doesn't show up at the last minute. He should pay for a babysitter to replace him. If his irresponsibility causes a mother to lose her job or her mental health, he should be responsible for her lost wages. His kids should sue him for losing the services of their mother and for a diminished standard of living."

"We need a law that prevents a judge from routinely awarding visitation or joint or sole custody to an incestuous or physically violent father. Non-payment of child support is also a form of child abuse. It should be treated as a criminal act and not buried in family court."

"Gender-neutral no-fault divorce has been used to impoverish and disenfranchise mothers and children. A gender-neutral primary-caretaker presumption can probably be used against mothers too. Do we really want to forget that women, not men, are pregnant for nine months; that women, not men, go into labor; that women, not men, can and do breast-feed; and that women, not men, are socialized from childhood into motherhood? A primary caretaker is not synonymous with a stay-at-home mother, nor should such a presumption be used to further ghettoize women as breeders and caretakers of children."

"Feminists have to think twice before they deem a contract between a mother surrogate and a sperm donor to be more sacred than the natural bond between a mother and child. A woman's right to biological motherhood is as important as her right to contractual motherhood and to abortion."

WHAT TO TELL YOUR CHILDREN

"In a custody battle, children challenge maternal authority right away. Don't let them do this. Remind them that you're still their mother, even if you're fighting with their father."

"If one parent is blatantly destructive to the children, it's the job of the other parent to say so, loud and clear. I don't believe that cover-ups are good for children."

"If the state takes you away from your kids, tell them that you love them and always will. Tell them that you'll always be their mother. Tell them you'll be out looking for them as soon as you can. Tell them whatever happens, it's not their fault."

"I kept quiet for too long. I didn't believe it was right to involve kids in private adult matters. But my kids needed to hear my point of view *too*. They needed to know that I loved them *too* and would fight for them. They also needed to know that I would keep loving them no matter what happened."

"My children really wanted to leave me. I fought this for a long time. I should have let them go. They already had my love. They couldn't have their father's love if they lived with me."

ON CHILD KIDNAPPING

"If your child is kidnapped by his father, don't be surprised if you lose your job and have a nervous breakdown. I did. Don't be surprised by how much money it takes to keep looking for your child. Don't be surprised if you never see your child again. I never have."

"After your child has been kidnapped, be prepared to become your own detective. Don't put your faith in some detached person who's doing it only for the money and who doesn't know your child or your husband. Plan your own strategy. Think of your lawyer and your detective as *your* assistants."

"One day I met a woman who had kidnapped her kids. She asked me if I was ready to spend the rest of my life under a false name. *I wasn't.* She asked me if I was sure my kids would come with me. *I wasn't.* For six months I contemplated kidnapping them. I didn't want my kids to lead an abnormal life. They'd already suffered through a divorce and a custody battle. How could I subject them and myself to an underground life? *I couldn't.*"

"As a mother, you owe it to yourself and your child to kidnap her away from a violent father. Kidnapping a child is very risky. You have to cut all your ties so that no one can trace you. You have to keep a low profile. You have to be willing to lead a secret and isolated life. You have to learn whom to trust with what information. But how can a mother live with herself knowing that her child is being seriously abused? You are the most important person in your child's life. No one else will save her but you."

"Why don't they put the *fathers'* pictures on the milk cartons? Kidnapping is a 90 percent male crime, but it's the mothers who get caught. I think it's important for a mother to really think twice before she runs away. Chances are she will be caught and never allowed to see her children again. I decided not to run that risk. Why should I sacrifice myself and my hard-won identity so totally? Is it my fault that society seems to agree that a father who rapes his daughter is OK but a mother who leaves her husband and runs away to protect her child is *not* OK?"

"My daughter and I are allowed to live together—as long as I let her father see her. It's very painful to watch her being destroyed, but I have no choice. My child's blood is not on my head. It's on everybody else's head who looked the other way and refused to help us. It's definitely on her father's head."

"If your husband threatens to kidnap your child, go to court immediately and get temporary custody. Get an order of protection and demand that his visitation be supervised by the court. Demand that he get some counseling. Get a judge to spell out to your husband that he can't move out of state with your child even if you're not divorced. Make sure you have your husband's credit card numbers and the names and addresses of his employer, relatives, and friends. Make sure you have recent photos of your child and his or her fingerprints."

A MOTHER-OUTLAW TALKS ABOUT KIDNAPPING HER CHILDREN LONG AGO

"Think of it this way: you're a secret agent going into 'deep cover.' You're completely untrained. In fact, you've been carefully *trained* to uphold men's laws. A lady is someone who can't stand being disliked even by her enemies! How many ladies can live an outlaw's life?

"Remember: you're a secret agent but you have no contact person and no escape route. You can never tell anyone who you really are (or were) or what you're doing. You're totally on your own. No one can help you. If they do, they're putting themselves in jeopardy.

"In the 1960s, when I decided to take my children underground, away from their father who played kinky games with his daughter, I wondered if there was an underground railway for mothers, something like the slaves had as they headed north. I also wondered if the antiwar movement would see me as a draft dodger of sorts and help me escape to Canada and start a new life there. I discovered that there was absolutely no political movement or sanctuary for mothers. To the best of my knowledge, there still isn't anything like this today.

"I once read a novel about a man who wanted to disappear. What he did was fake his own death. I thought about trying that, but I didn't know how to fake a death. In a sense, it was easy for me as a woman to drop out of sight and start a new life. No one expected me to have a long work history. All I had to say was that I was never married or that my husband had abandoned us. Today, it might be easier to buy false ID than it was years ago. I'm told that people do this on street corners in big cities. Also, there are open ads for false IDs in *Soldier of Fortune* magazine.

"If you can't lie, don't run away. An outlaw has to lie, almost endlessly and to everyone, about very small and very large things. You actually have to enjoy the process of fictionalizing your life. I never would have thought I was this kind of person. I made up lots of stories. For example, I'd say that my mom was an eccentric, that she'd insisted on giving birth to me at home and then refused to have my birth registered! I'd act real passionate and outraged that my mom would pull such a stunt on me.

"I never tried to get on public assistance. First, the money wasn't that good. But you can't tell a welfare investigator that you're breaking the law. You also need a birth certificate and a Social Security number. They'll ask you for the name and address of your children's father. They'll want to track him. You can make up a man's name and a false place of birth. But they'll check it out. Then, if it doesn't check out, they may check *you* out.

"I learned that you can't afford to trust *anyone*, at least not a professional. I never told a lawyer or a physician or a school teacher what my true situation was. Professionals have too much to lose to take any great risks for you. In fact, no outlaw can afford to trust anyone who could be pressured or blackmailed into divulging her whereabouts. How many people do you know who are that strong?

"I learned to expect very little from anyone. I learned not to be surprised if people didn't do what they promised. I even learned to *mistrust* anyone who went out of her way to help me. This could be an emotional setup. Such a person may ultimately turn you in or drop you for the same reasons she went overboard for you in the first place. Maybe she herself lost custody and both wants to help you *and* see you hurt just like she was. Maybe she's an incest victim herself and needs to attack and appease her own father through you and your child.

"Based on my own experiences, I might trust a particular individual, man or woman . . . but I'd keep far away from ideologicals. They're more interested in principles than in real people. In my case, I couldn't trust my parents, but my sister and one of my friends both came through for me. Over a twenty-year period, I told three different boyfriends what I was doing. Each man was very supportive and never blabbed, even after we broke up.

"It's a mistake not to fight for your children as hard as you can. As mothers, we must protect our children—even if it means breaking the law. I decided that one man, my ex-husband, did not have the right to 'care' for my children in a destructive and pathological way. Certainly not because some other man—a judge—said it was OK.

"In a sense, any mother who saves her children from being abused is like a woman trying to save all living creatures from nuclear madness. It's part of the same battle."

A CHILD, NOW A GROWN MAN OF FORTY, TALKS ABOUT LOSING HIS MOTHER IN A CUSTODY BATTLE LONG AGO

"I was two and a half years old when my father got custody of me. I have no memory of living with my mother. I do recall sitting under the table, which I wasn't allowed to do, and asking about my mother, saying that I wanted to see her.

"I remember the house we lived in as dark and badly lit. I remember my friends' houses as much brighter. Early on, I acquired the skill of being 'adopted' for a few hours at a time by other people's mothers. I think this shows resourcefulness on my part.

"I didn't want to believe that my mother had left me. I remember pretending that I had a young mother like everyone else did, instead of a grandmother. I fantasized a mother who came to see me once or twice a week instead of once a year.

"My mother was permitted to come to the house once a year at Christmas. In the morning I always received many lavish gifts from my grandmother and my father. In the afternoon my mother came, bearing less lavish but carefully chosen gifts. I was always glad to see her. I don't remember feeling angry toward her.

"My grandmother never left my mother alone with me. My mother would have to talk to her while she was trying to talk to me. My father would also be in the room, watching and listening. It was an odd and embarrassing situation.

"My father was happy enough to have me around. He was great to play games with. But he was also a spoiled and only child who expected hot meals prepared for him at odd hours. When he was impatient or angry, it was tough to be around him. He was arrogant and very selfish.

"I don't remember how he was to my mother. When I knew him, he had a terrible temper. Maybe my mother couldn't bear living with him anymore, not even to keep her child—to keep me.

"As I got older, my grandmother wasn't strong enough to control or amuse me. I know this hurt her a lot. Having a child at home is what kept my grandmother alive. She literally died the day I left home. I refuse to take any responsibility for her death, but it was a powerful event.

"In college, friends always complained about how their mothers wouldn't let go of them. The most obvious cases were some Jewish friends from New York. They were my favorite people. My very oldest and dearest friend, Robert, is a Jew from New York whose mother called him every Sunday night, saying the most inane things. And then Robert's voice would be reduced to this little puppy laughter, and the rest of the people in our house would say, 'Ah, it's Robert's mother. . . .'

"Soon after I started college, my mother invited me to her home for the first time. It seems that my father's family were the wealthy ones. My mother was a poor farm girl. My father had eloped with her against his mother's wishes. It seems she was pregnant. It was easy for them to get rid of her once I was born.

"My mother remarried when I was about five. She went on to have three other sons. Had we been neighbors, I would have been a part of it. I met these other children. I'm fond of them, but we're not close. Maybe it's just plain jealousy. They got all my mother's love. I see them regularly, once or twice a year.

"My father remarried and got divorced again. Then he retired early. He lives on his inheritance in the same house we both grew up in. He sits home alone in the shadows. I see him regularly, about once a year.

"My mother is this short woman who seems very healthy. She has good skin color. She wears earth-colored clothes and smiles easily. It recently occurred to me that it would be nice having her nearby. If she were close—I mean geographically—then we could talk to each other whenever one of us felt like it.

"Not having my mother is the trauma of my life. It's a loss that never ends. I have never lived with a woman—even with one that I loved. That's the most painful part of my legacy: my fear of getting too close to anyone.

"My mother always invites me over on the holidays. Thankfully she doesn't insist that I come. She knows how painful holidays are for me. She knows I don't like being there, at her house."

i knew you before you had a mother,
when you were newt-like, swimming,
a horrible brain in water.
i knew you when your connections
belonged only to yourself,
when you had no history
to hook on to,
barnacle,
when you had no sustenance of metal
when you had no beat to travel
when you stayed in the same
place, treading the question;
i knew you when you were all
eyes and a cocktail,
blank as the sky of a mind,
a root,
neither ground nor placental;
not yet
red with the cut nor astonished
by pain, one terrible eye
open in the center of your head
to night, turning and the stars
blinked like a cat. we swam
in the last trickle of champagne
before we knew breastmilk—we

shared the night of the closet,
the parasitic
closing on our thumbprint,
we were smudged in a yellow book.
son, we were oak without
mouth, uncut, we were
brave without memory
                    —Toi Derricotte, "In Knowledge of Young Boys"

23

What to Expect When You're Expecting a Divorce

·············

An Interview with Divorce Lawyer Susan L. Bender

Susan L. Bender is a distinguished Manhattan matrimonial attorney who has practiced law for nearly thirty years. She is a trial lawyer's trial lawyer. This means that people come to her when all other options—and lawyers—have been thoroughly exhausted or rejected. Bender is not in the business of losing cases. And yet she is known for being both ethical and experienced. Bender represents both women and men.

Bender is a past president of the Women's Bar Association of the State of New York; currently, she is the chair of the Matrimonial Committee of the Association of the Bar of the City of New York, a fellow of the American College of Family Trial Lawyers, and a fellow of the American Academy of Matrimonial Lawyers. Over the years, Bender has been appointed to various commissions by former Chief Judge Judith S. Kaye, and former Presiding Judge of the First Department Betty Weinberg Ellerin. Her firm, Bender Rosenthal Isaacs & Richter LLP, has been ranked as a number-one matrimonial firm in the city many times in leading magazines.

I thought Susan L. Bender would be the perfect lawyer to consult with on behalf of my readers. And so, in the fall of 2010, we sat down together. I asked her about what a woman needs to know when she consults a divorce lawyer—what to expect when you're expecting a divorce—and I asked her about some other burning topics of the day. Here is an edited transcript of our discussion.

PC: What are the things that every woman needs to know when she consults a divorce lawyer?

SLB: A woman going through a divorce or a custody battle has to become the person she may not have been trained to be or may not have wanted to be. The law is based on facts, and she must have those facts available to her. Let me give you an example. A soccer mom came into my office. Although she was a college graduate, she had decided not to work after her children were born. She was a home-maker-spouse. Her husband, an investment banker, commuted to work every day from their suburban home. He left early and came home late at night. All of the bank accounts and portfolio statements were in his name. One morning, when the children were college age, he left and never returned to her. He used the family savings to buy a co-op for himself and his girlfriend in the city. My soccer mom client was left with no funds of her own, no funds she could access to pay her bills, and no money to retain an attorney.

Let me give you another example. A woman gives up her career and raises her children. She is married ten years, and after ten years the marriage falls apart. This woman might say to me, "I'm now forty years old. I don't have the same financial prospects I had in my twenties. In order for me to able to live in the same manner that I lived in during the marriage, I need lifetime spousal support or until I get married again because I can't go back, I'll never again be twenty-five years old and able to start my career track all over again." I will say to her, "You're right; there's no way you can turn the clock back. But you are not going to get support for life in most jurisdictions in this country. If there are no marital assets to divide, then you're going to get a limited amount of support for a limited number of years." What she wants and what she needs will be very different from what the law is going to provide to her. So she has to pay an attorney to get the best that the law can provide, knowing in advance that it won't be enough.

PC: What's the next thing a woman should know?

SLB: She must understand what the role of her attorney is and how enormous the costs associated with a lawsuit are. Her attorney will lead her through the litigation or mediation process. He or she is not her therapist or her emotional confidant. Her attorney cannot right any of the wrongs she suffered during her marriage. Her attorney can only help her resolve the dissolution of her marriage and resolve the financial and custodial issues in her case. She must understand that she cannot nor should she depend on her attorney for emotional support. When she picks up the phone or e-mails her attorney, she will be billed for that time.

PC: How should a woman prepare for her first visit with her lawyer?

SLB: When a woman consults a lawyer, she should already have a plan for herself and her children in mind. She should also have the information about the family finances in hand. She must think ahead, anticipate the problems she will encounter from her husband so that her lawyer will be able to prepare for those problems. She must discuss with her lawyer how to protect her children, how to protect herself, where she and her children will live after the divorce. She needs to think about how she is going to pay for her lawyers and how she will pay for her and the children's expenses. She needs to think logically without her feelings interfering. But many women walk into the lawyer's office expecting the lawyer to have the solutions to their problems. Many women do not have an understanding of what the family expenses are. Some women don't know where the checkbook is, whether the bills of the family are paid online, or whose names are on the checking accounts, savings accounts, or other accounts. They are often blindsided when their husbands cut off their ability to use the credit cards and bar their access to the bank accounts. It is shocking how many women, young women, educated women, permit themselves to be so vulnerable. Without this information, the lawyer will not have the ability to protect his or her client.

PC: Many women still see men as their protectors.

SLB: And if they continue to believe that their husbands are their protectors, they will be disadvantaged. The woman litigant must pull her head out of the sand. She must review her financial statements, tax returns, credit card statements, and financial portfolios with her lawyers. She is instrumental in helping her lawyer decide what is best for her and her children. I have a woman right now who is a Wharton

MBA graduate. She naively depended on her husband to manage the expenses of the family. She never questioned him. She never looked at a credit card statement, never looked at a bank statement, never questioned the expenses, and was shocked to learn that her husband was a gambler and the family was living on credit cards. When she came to me, their co-op apartment was in foreclosure and the IRS had liens on their accounts. What was her excuse for being so naive?

PC: What else must a divorcing woman know?

SLB: Hard as it may be at a difficult time, a woman must understand the law and the legal process before she walks into a lawyer's office. Information about the laws of her state and the judicial process are available online. She must familiarize herself with the child support, spousal maintenance, and the distribution of marital property laws in her state. She must have an understanding of what "marital property" is and therefore to what she is entitled. And she absolutely must learn what the laws regarding custody are and about what the biases of the judges, the law guardians, and the forensic psychologists are.

The client also needs to know that their case could take years to be resolved because of the pretrial process of discovery, the trial process itself, and the post-trial process. A long and frustrating delay doesn't necessarily mean the judge is doing anything wrong. They have a lot of cases. And then, after the judge issues the decision, there's always the right to take an appeal, and the appellate process could take up to two more years. So it could be four to five years before there is any absolute resolution of an issue. So clients don't get instant justice. There's nothing about the justice system that's instantaneous. Resolutions take years to work themselves through.

PC: So you're saying that at a moment of grave crisis one has to become a realist?

SLB: I am saying exactly that.

PC: What kind of additional economic knowledge must a woman have?

SLB: A woman must learn to understand her tax returns. She must have a very clear understanding of her medical insurance coverage, and what the "out of network" expenses are. She must understand her family's predivorce expenses and must understand and learn how to prepare a budget for herself and her children. She must understand the expenses that she and her children will incur during the lawsuit and postdivorce. She must understand that to her lawyer, law is a *business*, and the more she depends on her lawyer, the more time the lawyer must devote to a case, the greater the legal fees will be.

PC: What's the first thing a divorcing woman should do?

SLB: I often tell women that they should remove personal property to which they are emotionally attached from their home. A man understands that he can manipulate a woman's feelings by undermining her emotional security. He will deprive her of those "things" which have meaning to her. He may also change her routine and interfere with her habits without any advance notice. He will try to pull the rug out from under her life. I also tell women to find the financial records in the marital residence and make copies. If there is a family computer, I tell her to download copies of financial records and statements. I tell a woman to check their credit cards so they know the amount of their available credit. I also tell her to determine whether their debt is current.

PC: An example?

SLB: I have a case where my client discovered that her husband had removed her jewelry, her memorabilia—the children's baby pictures and her grandmother's wedding band. Without her knowledge, he canceled her credit cards. So when she went to the gas station to fill up her car with gas, her credit card was declined. He even canceled her credit at the local grocery store without telling her. Of course, the computer was wiped clean and there was not a single bill in the house. She didn't even have the cab money to come to my office. I finally persuaded her husband's attorney to turn over funds to her.

JOINT CUSTODY

PC: Is joint custody always the presumption?

SLB: Joint custody is the unspoken presumption. Even though most jurisdictions have not legislatively created a *prima facie* right to joint custody, the judges are actually treating cases as if there were a presumption of joint custody. Fifteen years ago the question the judges would ask was "Who is the better custodial parent?" Now the judges ask, "What's wrong with you that you don't want the father to have joint custody?" The burden has shifted in a very draconian way against the primary caretaker, who is usually the woman.

There are two basic forms of custody: (1) residential custody, which is where the children primarily live; and (2) decision making, which is who has the authority to make decisions for the children. The courts often mix it up by giving one parent primary residential custody and the other parent decision-making authority over the major issues in a child's life, such as health and education. The parents are therefore in a constant tug of war. Political correctness has poisoned the custody wars. I wouldn't say that joint custody is always the presumption; I would say that it is a rebuttable presumption, which means that the primary caretaker has the burden of proving to the court that she is the better parent.

PC: Why has this happened?

SLB: Mothers are in the workplace. Mothers are judges, attorneys, physicians, businesswomen—with children at home. This workplace dynamic has influenced custody decisions. I also think that working mothers resent stay-at-home mothers.

PC: Give me an example of joint decision making at its worst.

SLB: A court has awarded parents joint decision-making authority over the choice of the mental health professional. The child's mental health professional identifies the father as the problem. The father then determines that this child can no longer work with this therapist or any therapist who identifies the father as the problem. The result is that the child is prevented from obtaining the benefit of being in the care of a therapist. This is one example of the ordinary, everyday, bread-and-butter problem with joint decision making. Recently I had a case where a six-year-old fell and broke his finger in three places while he was in his father's care. The father did not bring the child to a doctor. He merely gave the child Tylenol. The child spent the entire weekend in excruciating pain. The mother was on the phone trying to get the father to take the child to the doctor. But as they had joint decision making and the father refused, the mother did not have the authority to go to the father's home with a police officer to get the child and take him to the doctor. On Sunday the child returns to her and she takes him to the doctor. The child has one screwed-up finger, not to mention the pain he suffered all weekend.

PC: Could the mother take this back to court?

SLB: She did. We took it back to court and the judge said, "We had a nineteen-day custody trial. I made my decision and I will not revisit this case. It's just a finger. Live with it."

REPRESENTING A BATTERED WOMAN

PC: What is it like to represent a battered woman?

SLB: Battered women are difficult clients to represent. Most attorneys are not adequately trained to represent a battered woman. By definition, a battered woman was never in a position of power vis-à-vis her spouse. She may resent her attorney for getting for her what she was unable to get for herself, or she may implode her own case to ensure she remains the victim.

PC: Can you give us an example of how a battered woman might sabotage her own case?

SLB: I represented a woman who was battered. There were three children involved. As we were walking into the courtroom for the custody trial she said, "Susan, there's something I forgot to tell you. I tried to slit my wrists last night." Then she showed me her wrists and I saw wounds. What was she telling me? She was telling me that she was about to sabotage the case when she got on the witness stand—or that she would be unable to withstand the pressure of cross-examination. So I settled the custody dispute, which was unfortunate because the children ended up being jointly parented by the batterer.

PC: Was she relieved when you told her you would do this?

SLB: Yes. I read her signals correctly.

PC: Will a battered woman who has a career also sabotage herself and/or turn on her lawyer?

SLB: I'll give you an example of a battered woman who has a professional career. She is a dentist. She earned a very good living during the marriage and was the chief bread winner. Her husband did not have a professional career. He earned a modest income. He battered her on many occasions during the marriage, but she did nothing to protect herself. After one terrible incident, the husband left the apartment. I told her that she had to obtain an order prohibiting him from returning to the marital home. "No, no, I don't want to." The day before he was coming back to the marital residence she calls me and says, "*Now* I want to bring on the application." I said, "The judge is not going to believe you now. You waited all this time. You should have brought on the application after the incident occurred, not a month later." Because of the delay and the timing of the application, the judge believed that my client had another agenda. The court granted the stay-away order on condition that my client pay for the husband's living accommodations and for his counsel fees. Of course, my client blamed me for the judge's decision. She fired me, sued me, and reported me to the professional disciplinary committee. And, by the way, she's living with her batterer again.

PC: Do some battered women have unrealistic expectations?

SLB: Some battered women believe that as a consequence of being battered, they are entitled to "restitution." One woman who consulted with me believed she was entitled to relocate from this jurisdiction to another jurisdiction with the party's child on the theory that she'd been battered and that the father should not have a relationship with the child. She believed that she was entitled to a greater allocation of the assets and to a greater award of spousal support. But that is not the law.

PC: With whom did she discuss these expectations?

SLB: She came to see me after having consulted with a number of attorneys. I told her that she would not be able to relocate with her child because she was battered, nor would she be entitled to a greater share of the marital assets because he was a batterer.

PC: What would you say to a battered mother?

SLB: "Dear Woman: The legal system cannot eradicate or erase the pain you and your children suffered at the hands of your batterer. The courts permit a batterer to have a parental relationship with his children. While you may be awarded an order of protection, you will not likely be able to relocate to another jurisdiction with your children. You cannot expect to receive a greater share of the marital assets because you've suffered."

PC: If the batterer is in jail or has a prison record, would that change anything?

SLB: Probably not. The courts often require that the children visit the batterer in jail.

PC: If a mother or father is concerned that the other parent is mentally ill or is abusing or neglecting the child, but they have a joint-custody arrangement, and they come into court with documentation of some kind that shows this, why won't they get an immediate resolution?

SLB: It simply won't happen. The legal system is a big frustration for the litigants. First, you have to assume that the person making the accusation, the accuser, has reliable evidence, which could be in the form of documents, e-mails, medical decisions, pictures of the child's body if there's abuse. The burden of proof is on the party making the accusation. If they don't have sufficient facts, they will not prevail. If they do have enough facts to start an investigation, most jurisdictions in the country have various agencies that will investigate abuse and neglect cases. A judge can order the investigation, or in many cases a party can go directly to the agencies and file an abuse or neglect report.

PC: How long does that take?

SLB: The agencies generally respond fairly quickly. It depends upon the accusation and the state. It could take days, weeks, or months. In the meantime, unless the agency or court terminates visitation because they feel they have enough evidence, visitation will continue during the investigation process.

PC: Would this be different if the accuser went directly to the district attorney and filed a criminal complaint?

SLB: Most states have overlapping agencies. It will all wind up in the same place no matter what.

PC: So there's no way of speeding this up? Could a district attorney's office assign an abuse case a different priority than a matrimonial court would?

SLB: The answer depends upon the jurisdiction. If you're talking about physical abuse, the district attorney and the agencies will act immediately. If you're talking about psychological abuse, damage that's not visible, then it could take weeks, months, years, or never. Unfortunately, the court system does not dispense justice like a vitamin pill.

PC: Some men are so dangerous that their wives believe it is safer to stay married. Do you ever advise women to stay married?

SLB: I never advise a woman who was battered to remain living with the batterer. But I may advise women to stay married for economic reasons. I may advise women to stay married so that they can keep an eye on their children. The question is: How bearable is this for these children?

PC: That's like a nineteenth-century solution.

SLB: In some cases there is no other solution.

BRAINWASHING AND PARENTAL ALIENATION

PC: If it can be proved that a father has brainwashed a child against his mother, what will the court do?

SLB: When it is proved that one parent willfully interfered with the children's relationship with another parent by denigrating, undermining, minimizing, or chastising the other parent in front of the children or to the children, the courts may limit that parent's access time with the children. Because the courts rarely grant supervised visitation, the brainwasher will continue to have the time to continue alienating or brainwashing the children. It is a nightmare and a hell that has no walls, no ceiling, no floor—it is a black hole for these women. Most courts do not have a system of triage in place to protect the children from their brainwashing, alienating parent. Often by the time the court catches up to the problem, the damage is irreparable.

I want to raise a point on the alienation issue. Today, the alienators are able to enlist their children as collaborators. Fathers may have their computer-savvy children break into their mother's private e-mail communications and forward those e-mails to him. The children are asked to load spyware programs onto their mother's computer to enable them and the father to read the mother's e-mail communications, which includes her communications with her attorneys. GPS devices are, with the help of the children, installed on cars so that the father can stalk and track the mother by sitting at his computer. I've had cases where the children have helped the father install gadgets on the home telephone lines [that] record the conversations of the mother.

PC: What would you say to a mother who sees her child being alienated against her, and she may have to wait years before the court does anything about it, at which point the alienation may be a fait accompli, a done deal?

SLB: The allegations must be presented in a written application. The judge may or may not appoint an independent forensic psychologist to analyze the family, and, if so, that could take months. There is no concrete, reliable objective testing to determine if there has been "alienation."

PC: What would you advise a parent to do when he or she first notices signs of parental alienation?

SLB: That parent must report this behavior to a mental health professional and must immediately go to court and file a written application in order for the court to intervene. There is no guarantee that these efforts of the rejected parent will result in court intervention or the intervention of a mental health professional to stop the alienation.

PC: You mentioned that there are some programs that attempt to deprogram alienated children. Have you gotten any feedback from rejected parents about them?

SLB: These two programs are in their very early stages, and it's too soon to tell. Also the number of people involved has been so small that there's no conclusion at this moment.

CHILD SEXUAL ABUSE ALLEGATIONS

PC: What would you tell a woman who has a very good reason to believe that her young daughter or son is being sexually abused by her husband?

SLB: My advice to my client is "make no accusation unless you are sure of it. If you do make an accusation and you don't have the right facts or can't prove it, you'll lose your child, who will likely at some point become your husband's tool and/or 'wife.'" When I represent people with resources, I send them for professional help. But not all mental health professionals believe incest exists. Some believe that mothers making such accusations are unstable and only using it as litigation strategy. The right professional must be engaged.

PC: Do you send the child with the mother?

SLB: No. I send the mother. I let the mental health professional make the assessment.

PC: Would you give such a mother a choice between seeing a pediatrician and a mental health professional?

SLB: It depends upon what she's telling me.

PC: Have you had bad experiences in this area?

SLB: Too many.

GAY AND LESBIAN CUSTODY

PC: What should a lesbian or homosexual client know in addition to your general advice?

SLB: There are three issues that we must discuss: custody, visitation, and child support. In most jurisdictions, the biological parent has the absolute right to parent her child if the "de facto parent" or the "biological stranger" has not also adopted the child. If the nonbiological parent has not adopted the child, then she has virtually no rights to remain a parent if the parties dissolve their relationship. She might not have the right to visit with the child, talk to the child, or have any relationship with her child during the child's minority. However, if the nonbiological parent has adopted the child, then she and the biological mother are equally entitled to custody. Both parents have equal standing to seek custody and visitation, and both are obligated to pay support. My advice to the lesbian client with respect to her child therefore depends on whether there has been a second parent adoption. As I just noted, in addition to the custody issues, there are child support issues. Both issues depend on whether there has been a second parent adoption.

PC: Deborah H. is a high profile case [that] set a precedent for gay custody rights in New York State. It got resolved in 2010. Tell me about it.

SLB: It's a complicated resolution. The Court of Appeals, which is the highest court in New York State, determined that it's up to the legislature to pass appropriate legislation in order to permit a nonbiological parent who has not adopted the child to have visitation. Right now the case in New York State, Alison D., prohibits the nonbiological parent who has not adopted the child from having anything to do with the child once the biological parent determines that the nonbiological parent cannot have any involvement with the child.

What happened in the Deborah H. case is that Deborah H. attempted to convince the Court of Appeals that their decision in Alison D. should be overturned on the theory of estoppel. "Estoppel" essentially means that Janice R. cannot come to the court and say that Deborah H. was not an involved parent because she was involved in the child's life in dozens of ways. The Court of Appeals determined that Deborah H.'s equitable estoppel argument was not valid because the New York State legislature had not drafted a statute [that] expanded parental rights to a nonbiological parent.

In other words, Deborah H. argued, "Yes, I am not a biological parent; that's true. And yes, Janice refused to permit the adoption to go through; that's true. However, I acted like the parent of this child in every way. Therefore, Janice R. should be 'estopped' or prevented from arguing that I am not a parent and have no parental rights."

The Court of Appeals denied Deborah H.'s estoppel argument but determined something completely different, which was that because Debora H. and Janice R. had gone to Vermont before the child was born and had a civil union there, and the civil union extends parenting rights to both parents—it had to award parental rights to Deborah H. under the "theory of comity." (This means that one state is bound to recognize the laws of another American state.) But what's most important is that the New York State Court of Appeals has clearly determined once and for all that it will not extend parenting rights to a nonbiological parent (without a prior marriage or civil union) until the New York State legislature passes legislation extending rights to nonbiological parents.

In other words, they lost the equitable estoppel argument but won the comity argument. They won the lesser of two arguments.

PC: So how will this particular case in New York State affect other same-sex couples who are having custody battles?

SLB: If the same-sex couple who is engaged in a custody battle had previously been either married or had a civil union that accorded parental rights before the child was born, then this state is going to recognize the relationship and give parenting rights to the nonbiological parent with a second parent adoption.

If, however, the parties had not obtained a civil union that accorded parental rights or married in another state, and if there wasn't a second parent adoption, that same-sex couple will be relegated to the laws of Allison D., and Allison D. says if the nonbiological parent has not adopted the child, then she has no standing to have visitation.

PC: Even if, as in the case of Deborah H., there was not only a parenting history but there was payment of child support?

SLB: Correct.

ETHICS

PC: What should clients understand about how lawyers relate to judges outside of the courtroom?

SLB: Lawyers and judges belong to the same professional associations and attend the same educational seminars. They might even conduct educational seminars together. Their children might attend the same schools. Clients wrongly believe that this means that there are "deals" made between the lawyers and the judges or that the judges will determine a case based on his or her relationship with the lawyer. This is simply not true. Of course there are corrupt judges and corrupt lawyers. But our system of justice is based on an adversarial system. The lawyers are adversaries representing their clients. The judges are finders of fact and determine the law. Most of us know the boundaries of our relationships, and very few of us violate those boundaries.

PC: Have you had lawyers as clients?

SLB: I have had lawyers as clients, and most of the time I've either fired them or they've fired me. They are virtually impossible to represent, because they understand all the ins and outs of the law, and they want us to use every single in and every single out, which is not possible. They are very difficult to represent.

PC: Can you give me an example?

SLB: I had a client from a prominent law firm, and he wanted me to serve subpoenas on just about every financial entity with which the parties had a relationship, which, in my judgment, was abusive because we had the information from another source. The client also was asking me to make an application on his behalf with respect to custody, which I believed was excessive, not realistic, would not be awarded by the court, and would have an adverse impact on his case. So when I explained to him that the road that he wanted me to take would adversely affect him financially as well as in the custody dispute, our relationship came to a mutual end. He continued to represent himself pro se. It's likely that no other lawyer would take his case.

PC: What area of law was he in?

SLB: He was a commercial attorney. He went to a hostile commercial-litigation mode, which is very different than the litigation mode in matrimonial law.

PC: Do you have another example of a lawyer?

SLB: During the course of representing another lawyer, I discovered that he was dipping into his escrow account for purposes other than what the account enabled him to do. I advised him that based on this information I could no longer represent him, because it put me in an ethical quandary. I knew that if I disclosed this information and released the records to the other side, my client would probably be subject at some point to disciplinary proceedings, so I obviously did not want to disclose that material. I told him that I did not feel comfortable in that ethical quandary, so he got himself a different attorney.

PC: Do you have a female-lawyer story?

SLB: I represented one female lawyer in a visitation case, and she was a litigator. And I usually tell my clients before we go to court how to dress appropriately, but I did not tell this client what to wear because she was a litigator and I just assumed that she knew what to do. So we get to court and she was wearing a skirt that was inappropriately short, and a top that was inappropriately tight and low-cut, and the impression she gave the judge was not the positive impression I was hoping she would give. When I admonished her for the clothing that she wore and suggested that she wear something else, she made accusations against me, and I decided that it was no longer feasible for me to represent this client.

REPRESENTING MALE CLIENTS

PC: What do you tell your male clients?

SLB: There are three categories of male clients. The first category is the male client who performed the traditional role in the family. He is the primary wage earner and the weekend father. I tell this male client that it is likely he will continue to be the primary supporter of the family for a period of time until the assets are distributed to his wife and until his ex-wife becomes employed in a meaningful way. I also tell him that if he wants to change his role from that of a weekend father, he should change that role slowly to give the children time to adjust to the changes in their lives as a result of the divorce.

The second category is the male client who shared the parenting role. He may have also shared the role of the wage earner. I tell this male client that it is likely these two roles will continue.

The third category is the male client whose goal is scorched earth. He wants to undermine the children's relationship with the mother. Or his goal is to immediately become the parent he never was, without any adjustment time for the children. His goal may be to impoverish his wife, the mother of his children. I show that male client the door. I will not represent him.

The biases that once existed against men as parents are not as apparent as they were in the past. It is now not unusual to have a male client who was the primary caretaker and who was not the primary earner.

One of my clients gave up his tenured position at a college in order to take care of the children and the parties' real estate because his wife's earning potential was much more than his. The wife was able to climb the corporate ladder and, in so doing, became involved with another man. She wanted out of the marriage, custody of the children, and exclusive possession of the real estate. My client wanted to continue as the primary custodial parent; he wanted his share of the marital assets. He wanted child support and spousal support. The mother is fighting hard to obtain sole custody, even though she is the one who left the marriage and who was never the primary caretaker.

PC: Can you describe the strategies you use when you represent men?

SLB: With respect to representing men, let's assume that the father has not been actively engaged in the child's life. So the strategy would be to provide for an expanded access schedule for the father to expand more and more over time. It might start with every other weekend to every other weekend and a couple of dinners, to sixty-forty time, and then to fifty-fifty time. It may be that the father does not have the skills to be a parent. So the advice that the father will often get is to hire someone to teach him parenting skills. They go to therapists; they go to parenting coordinators; they go to social workers. So the strategy is often to start out with as much as the court will award and expand that over time. Keep in mind that the prevailing wind in this country is for joint custody. That is the default position of most courts throughout the country.

PC: What are the issues that most concern your male clients?

SLB: In 2010, the main issue is that male clients want joint custody. They want to have as much decision-making authority, as much time as possible. Some seek joint custody in order to avoid their child-support obligations, to destroy their ex-wives, or because they have been genuinely involved fathers.

Another major issue is alienation. There are parents who are being trained in parental alienation through the Internet. I've represented both men and women where alienation is the key issue in the case.

The Internet has opened up an entire new field of problems because parents can become self-taught in terms of how to become an alienating parent and thus how to get custody. The fathers' rights groups have websites on how to prepare a custody battle, on how to become an involved parent. The parties have become far more educated than they were twenty years ago. They often come to the lawyers having already prepared the case in their own mind.

The websites for the mothers' groups are not as sophisticated as the websites for the fathers' rights groups. And remember that it's very difficult to be in the defensive position as opposed to the offensive position when it comes to custody. For example, the noninvolved parent can easily be instructed on how to become involved.

PC: In that case, one could argue that the prospect of divorce has finally made them see the light.

SLB: If the noninvolved parent is really coming in peace, the parents always have the choice to collaborate. But I'm talking about wholesale warfare. We're taking about fathers who are in the scorched-earth mode, not in collaboration mode. As I've said, the defensive position is very difficult position for the custodially challenged mother to be in.

Resources

....

There are very few free, high-quality, or fully vetted resources out there for custodially embattled mothers. However, there is certainly more available now than there was twenty-five years ago. Let's begin with the books.

BOOKS

Many custodially embattled mothers have written, published, and circulated their memoirs. Although they are essentially the works of laypeople, these accounts are, nevertheless, both beautifully and carefully written. Some are available online. In addition, lawyers and authors who were formerly embattled mothers or have an interest in this subject have published blistering indictments of the injustices they or others have faced. I cannot list all these works, but allow me to list just a few:

Grieco, Helen, Rachel Allen, and Jennifer Friedlin, eds. *Disorder in the Courts: Mothers and Their Allies Take On the Family Law System*. California NOW published this work in 2004 as an e-book. It is available at California NOW's online store (http://www.canowstore.org/store/merchant.mvc). I wrote the introduction to this work.

Hannah, Mo Therese, and Barry Goldstein. *Domestic Violence, Abuse, and Child Custody: Legal Strategies and Policy Issues*. Kingston, NJ: Civic Research Institute, 2010.

Juillon, Jeanne. *Long Way Home: The Odyssey of a Lesbian Mother and Her Children*. San Francisco: Cleis Press, 1985.

Lawrence, Candida. *Reeling and Writhing*. Aspen, CO: MacMurray & Beck, Inc., 1994.

Neustein, Amy, and Michael Lesher. *From Madness to Mutiny: Why Mothers Are Running from the Family Courts—and What Can Be Done About It*. Lebanon, NH: Northeastern University Press, 2005.

Paradise, Jan. "Substantiation of Sexual Abuse Charges When Parents Dispute Custody or Visitation." *Pediatrics* 81, no. 6 (June 1988).

Pearson, Jessica, and Nancy Thoennes. "Summary of Findings from the Sexual Abuse Allegations Project." In *Sexual Abuse Allegations in Custody and Visitation Cases: A Resource Book for Judges and Court Personnel*, edited by E. B. Nicholson and J. Bulkley. Washington, DC: American Bar Association, 1988.

Rubin, Margery. *What Your Divorce Lawyer May Not Tell You: The 125 Questions Every Woman Should Ask*. New York: Fireside, 2009.

Stark, Evan. *Coercive Control: How Men Entrap Women in Personal Life*. New York: Oxford University Press, 2007.

Winner, Karen. *Divorced from Justice: The Abuse of Women and Children by Divorce Lawyers and Judges*. New York: HarperCollins, 1996.

Zorza, Joan, ed. *Domestic Violence Report*. Kingston, NJ: Civic Research Institute. http://www.civicresearchinstitute.com/.

WEBSITES

At the beginning of the twenty-first century, custodially embattled mothers started launching websites about their struggles, and they continue to do so today. Some mothers document their own cases, while other website creators document ongoing public cases and some give mothers advice. Some of the stories are horrifying but are, alas, common. Here are some important websites to view:

http://mothers-of-valor.org/

http://www.thehostagechild.com/

http://www.thelizlibrary.org/

http://www.valeriecarlton.com/

http://www.valetteclark.com/

FILMS

Early in the twenty-first century, Garland Waller directed two videos: *Small Justice: Little Justice in America's Family Courts* (2001) and *Debating Richard Gardner* (2006). She interviewed Gardner himself at length and provides a devastating portrait of a dangerous man who nevertheless managed to con the entire court system about alleged parental alienation. See chapter 20 for more on this tragedy.

ORGANIZATIONS

The following organizations are not necessarily geared to the needs of each individual custodially embattled mother. Some educate lawyers and judges about domestic violence. Some are concerned with gender equality issues. A few are concerned with "protective" mothers and raped children or with the needs of immigrant women and prisoners. Most are large advocacy organizations that may or may not be able to make reliable individual referrals. Again, I want readers to at least have a starting point.

American Bar Association Center on Children and the Law

740 15th Street, NW
Washington, DC 20005
Phone: (202) 662-1720 or (800) 285-2221
Fax: (202) 662-1755
Website: http://www.americanbar.org/groups/child_law.html
E-mail: ctrchildlaw@abanet.org

American Professional Society on the Abuse of Children (APSAC)

350 Poplar Avenue
Elmhurst, IL 60126
Phone: (630) 941-1235 or (877) 402-7722
Fax: (630) 359-4274
Website: http://www.apsac.org/
E-mail: apsac@apsac.org

Battered Women's Justice Project

1801 Nicollet Ave South, Suite 102
Minneapolis, MN 55403
Phone: (612) 824-8768 or (800) 903-0111, ext. 1
Fax: (612) 824-8965
Website: http://www.bwjp.org/bwjp_home.aspx

California Protective Parents Association

PO Box 15284
Sacramento, CA 95851-0284
Phone: (866) 874-9815
Website: http://www.protectiveparents.com/
E-mail: cppa001@aol.com

The Center for Survivor Agency and Justice (Erika Sussman)

2001 S Street NW, Suite 400
Washington, DC 20009
Phone: (202) 552-8304
Fax: (202) 543-5626
Website: http://www.csaj.org/

Custody Preparation for Moms

Website: http://www.custodyprepformoms.org/index.php

Justice for Children

2600 Southwest Freeway, Suite 806
Houston, TX 77098
Phone: (713) 225-4357 or (800) 733-0059
Fax: (713) 225-2818
Website: http://www.justiceforchildren.org/default.asp

Legal Resource Center on Violence Against Women (LRC)

6930 Carroll Avenue
Takoma Park, MD 20912-4423
Phone: (301) 270-1550
Survivor hotline: (800) 556-4053
Fax: (301) 270-7272
Website: http://www.lrcvaw.org/
E-mail: lrc@lrcvaw.org

National Clearinghouse for the Defense of Battered Women

125 South 9th Street, Suite 302
Philadelphia, PA 19107
Phone: (215) 351-0010 or (800) 903-0111 ext. 3
Website: http://www.ncdbw.org/

National Coalition Against Domestic Violence (NCADV)

1120 Lincoln Street, Suite 1603
Denver, CO 80203
Phone: (303) 839-1852
Website: http://www.ncadv.org/
E-mail: mainoffice@ncadv.org

The National Crime Victim Bar Association

2000 M Street NW, Suite 480
Washington, DC 20036
Phone: (202) 467-8701
Lawyer referral line: (800) FYI-CALL (394-2255)
Website: http://www.victimbar.org/vb/Main.aspx
E-mail: victimbar@ncvc.org

Office on Violence Against Women (OVW)

145 N Street, NE, Suite 10W.121
Washington, DC 20530
Phone: (202) 307-6026
Fax: (202) 305-2589
Website: http://www.ovw.usdoj.gov/

Rights for Mothers

Website: http://rightsformothers.com/

Violence Against Women Online Resources (VAWOR)

Website: http://www.vaw.umn.edu/

WomensLaw.org

Website: http://womenslaw.org/

Notes

. . . .

New Introduction to the 2011 Lawrence Hill Books Edition

1. These reports on gender bias have been published by the state supreme courts of Florida, Maryland, Massachusetts, Michigan, Minnesota, Nevada, New Jersey, New York, Rhode Island, and Washington. These reports explore the different ways in which men and women are discriminated against in terms of custody. However, the fact that fathers have been discriminated against does not change the overall picture of women's greater custodial vulnerability, nor does it change the effect on children of losing a mother who has, in all probability, been their primary caretaker.

2. "In His Own Words: Dr. Lee Salk Speaking for Babies," *People*, March 11, 1974. Quoted by Sheila Moran in "Courts and Custody: A Break for Fathers?," *New York Post*, November 22, 1975. This case is known as *Salk v. Salk*, NY 393, 2nd 841 (1975).

3. Janet R. Johnston, Marsha Kline, Jeanne M. Tschann, "Ongoing Post-Divorce Conflict in Families Contesting Custody: Do Joint Custody and Frequent Access Help?," *American Journal of Orthopsychiatry* 59 (1989), 576–592.

4. Jennifer E. McIntosh, "Enduring Conflict in Parental Separation: Pathways of Impact on Child Development," *Journal of Family Studies* 9, 63 (April 2003).

5. Joan B. Kelly, "Children's Living Arrangements Following Separation and Divorce: Insights from Empirical and Clinical Research," *Family Process* 46, no. 1 (2006).

6. The website of the Association for Children for Enforcement of Support, accessed March 17, 2010, http://www.childsupport-aces.com.

7. The website of the National Coalition for Family Justice, accessed March 17, 2010, http://www.ncfj.org/.

8. Mo Therese Hannah, PhD, and Barry Goldstein, JD, *Domestic Violence, Abuse, and Child Custody: Legal Strategies and Policy Issues* (Kingston, NJ: Civic Research Institute, 2010).

9. Margery Rubin, *What Your Divorce Lawyer May Not Tell You: The 125 Questions Every Woman Should Ask* (New York: Fireside, 2009).

10. Lurie can be reached at divorcecoach@msn.com.

11. The website of the National Family Court Watch Project, accessed March 17, 2010, http://www.nationalfamilycourtwatchproject.org.

1. A Historical Overview

1. In 1861 the slave Harriet Brent Jacobs published her autobiography. See *Incidents in the Life of a Slave Girl* (Boston: 1861; reprint ed., New York: Harcourt Brace Jovanovich, 1973). Reprinted with new introduction and notes by Walter Teller.

2. Dorothy Sterling, ed., *We Are Your Sisters: Black Women in the Nineteenth Century* (New York: W. W. Norton, 1984), and Jacqueline Jones, *Labor of Love, Labor of Sorrow: Black Women, Work, and the Family from Slavery to the Present* (New York: Basic Books, 1985). Both discuss and cite many examples of white men's sexual harassment and rape of black slave women and of the jealousy, powerlessness, and cruelty of many white wives toward black slave women.

    For accounts of slave life also see Mary Boykin Chestnut, *A Diary from Dixie*, ed. Ben Ames Williams (Cambridge, MA: Harvard University Press, 1980); Eugene D. Genovese, *Roll Jordan Roll: The World the Slaves Made* (New York: Random House, 1974); Paula Giddings, *When and Where I Enter: The Impact of Black Women on Race and Sex in America* (New York: William Morrow, 1984); Mattie Griffiths, *Autobiography of a Female Slave* (Redfield, NY, 1857; reprint ed., Miami: Mnemosyne Press, 1969); Herbert C. Gutman, *The Black Family in Slavery and Freedom, 1750–1925* (New York: Pantheon, 1976); Gloria T. Hull, Patricia Bell Scott, and Barbara Smith, eds., *All the Women Are White, All the Blacks Are Men, but Some of Us Are Brave: Black Women's Studies* (Old Westbury, NY: Feminist Press, 1982); Frances A. Kemble, *Journal of a Residence on a Georgian Plantation in 1838–1839* (London: Longman, Green, 1863); Suzanne Lebsock, *The Free Women of Petersburg: Status and Culture in a Southern Town, 1784–1860* (New York: W. W. Norton, 1984); Leslie Howard Owens, *This Species of Property: Slave Life and Culture in the Old South* (New York: Oxford University Press, 1980); Dorothy Sterling, ed., *The Trouble They Seen: Black People Tell the Story of Reconstruction* (New York: Doubleday, 1976).

3. Jacobs, *Incidents*. Jacobs describes the facts and accompanying emotions of her seven years' separation from both her children. She revealed herself *once*, to her seven-year-old daughter (after a five-year separation), on the eve of Louisa's

("Ellen's") departure north. "'Ellen, my dear child, I am your mother.' She drew back a little, and looked at me; I folded her to [my] heart. 'You really *are* my mother?' . . . She wept, and I did not check her tears. Perhaps she would never again have a chance to pour her tears into a mother's bosom. All night she nestled in my arms. Once, when I thought she was asleep, I kissed her forehead softly, and she said, 'I am not asleep, dear mother. . . . Mother, I will never tell.' And she never did."

Harriet also had one very emotional "interview" with her son Joseph when he was twelve, after a seven-year separation and on the eve of her own escape to the North. Joseph never revealed his mother's whereabouts either.

Sterling, in *We Are Your Sisters*, recounts a number of extremely painful first-person accounts of the separation of slave mothers, slave children, and slave families. Here are two descriptions; the first is by an anonymous ex-slave.

O, dat was a terrible time! All de slaves be in de field, plowin', hoein', and singin' in de boilin' sun. Old Marse, he comes through de field with a man call de speculator. Dey walked round just lookin'. All de darkies know what dis mean. Dey didn't dare look up, just work right on. Den de speculator he see who he want. He talk to old Marse, den dey slaps de handcuffs on him and take him away to de cotton country. . . . When darkies went to dinner de ole nigger mammy she ask where am such and such. None of de others want to tell her. But when she see dem look down to de ground she just say: "De speculator, de speculator." Den de tears roll down her cheeks, cause maybe it her son or husband and she knows she never see 'em again.

This second description was written in 1858 by ex-slave Emma Brown of Petersburg, Virginia.

It was durin' cottin chopping time dat year, a day I'll never forgit, when the speculataws bought me. Ma come home from de fiel' 'bout haf after leven dat day an cooked a good dinner, I hopin her. O, I never has forgot dat last dinner wid my folks: bout de middle of the even' up rid my young master an' two strange white mens. Dey hitch dere hosses an' cum in de house. Den one o'de strangers said, "Get yo clothes, Mary: We has bought you from Mr. Shorter." I c'menced cryin' an' beggin' Mr. Shorter to not let 'em take me away. But he say, "Yes Mary, I has sole yer, an' yer must go wid em."

Den dese strange mens drive off wid me, me hollerin' at de top' my voice an' callin my ma! Den dem speculataws begin to sing loud—jes to drown out my hollerin. We passed de very filed whar paw an' all my fokes wuz wuckin, an' I calt out as loud an' as long as I could see 'em, "Good-bye Ma! Good-bye Ma!" But she never heard me. I ain't never seed nor heared tell o' ma an' pa, an' bruthers, an' susters from dat day to dis.

4. Mattie Griffiths, *Autobiography of a Female Slave* (1857; reprint ed., Miami: Mnemosyne Press, 1969). Mattie Griffiths's *Autobiography of a Female Slave* was written after emancipation; she doesn't recount a fugitive life, only her life as a slave. It is priceless and similar in style to Harriet Brent Jacobs's *Incidents in the Life of a Slave Girl*.

5. This article is cited by Dorothy Sterling in *We Are Your Sisters*. Jacobs wrote it in response to an article by Julia Taylor, the wife of ex-president Taylor, who claimed that "slaves were not sold away from their families, except under 'peculiar circumstances.'"

6. Griffiths, *Autobiography*.

7. Jacobs, *Incidents*.

8. Jacobs arrived in Philadelphia in 1842. Throughout *Incidents in the Life of a Slave Girl*, Jacobs, like Mattie Griffiths and other women writers of the era, is very romantic about womanly virtue, God, marriage, motherhood, children, and loving, *lawful* family relationships. Jacobs remains deeply "ashamed" of her illegal love affair with Sawyer.

9. This story and all direct quotes for it are contained in Elizabeth Parsons Ware Packard's work, *Modern Persecution, or Insane Asylums Unveiled, as Demonstrated by the Report of the Investigating Committee of the Legislature of Illinois* (New York: Pelletreau & Raynor, 1873), or in its second volume, *Modern Persecution, or Married Woman's Liabilities, as Demonstrated by the Action of the Illinois Legislature* (Hartford, CT: Case, Lockwood & Brainard, 1873). I wrote about this extraordinary American hero in *Women and Madness* (New York: Four Walls Eight Windows, 1997). From 1864 on, Mrs. Elizabeth Packard supported herself by writing, publishing, and selling twenty-eight thousand copies of the account of her persecution. Packard also went on to lobby state legislatures on behalf of mental patients. In 1867 the Illinois legislature passed her Personal Liberty Bill, granting certain legal rights to all imprisoned mental patients and to those accused of insanity. She also lobbied for the rights of married women. Where is the Hollywood film about her? I long to see one.

10. People, ex rel Uriel M. Rhoades, Sophia Rhoades v. George Humphreys, county judge of Cayuga County, Cayuga General Term (June 1, 1857). New York State Supreme Court, Johnson, T. T. Strong and Smith, Justices. This decision overturned a previous one that granted Sophia custody of the "tender" child.

It is important to remember that throughout the eighteenth and nineteenth centuries in America, judicial decisions were based on English common law.

Some American judges were as conservative as (or more conservative than) the most conservative of English jurists; others attempted to Americanize (democratize) the English common law. Some judges attempted to use the law on behalf of children; others bowed, with enormous regret, to the need to enforce laws that were clearly cruel to mothers and not in their children's "best interest." According to Jamil S. Zinaildin in "The Emergence of a Modern American Family Law: Child Custody, Adoption, and the Courts, 1796–1851," *Northwestern University Law Review*, vol. 73, no. 6, (1979),

> The nineteenth-century English judge adopted a patriarchal paradigm of family relations and applied it to the law with such force and vigor that it had the effect of creating new paternal rights, the existence of which had only been vaguely hinted at by previous judges. . . . During the first part of the nineteenth century, many American courts declared an increasing independence from precedent, especially British precedent. . . . Not all American jurists, however, were willing to make an abrupt break with the past. Moreover, European laws and decisions were often powerful forces in shaping American legal thought. Highly influential figures such as Supreme Court Justice Story and New York's Chancellor Kent supported their views of modern law by citing the rulings in contemporary English cases.

Rather than cite a string of illustrative lawsuits by name only, I would like to describe two cases from the 1830s and 1840s. In 1834 in Massachusetts, Mrs. Samuel Thacher left her "cruel and intemperate" husband. She and her three-year-old daughter returned to her parents. The judge ordered the child into paternal custody, saying that "the Court 'ought not to sanction an unjustified and unauthorized [marital] separation, by now ordering the child into the mother's possession. In general, the father is by law clearly entitled to the custody of the child.'" (Commonwealth v. Briggs, Chief Justice Shaw, Massachusetts, Supreme Judicial Court 73 Mass. [16 Pick] 203 [1834].)

Between 1840 and 1842 a more notorious case occurred. In 1835 Eliza Anna Mercein married John Barry, a widower with four daughters. Eliza described her husband as a man of irascible temper and a domineering and vindictive spirit. He was unfeeling, harsh, tyrannical, and cruel. In 1838 John returned to his native Nova Scotia after his business failed. He asked Eliza to move to Nova Scotia and to have her father establish him in business there. She refused. John said he would force her to go by taking their three-year-old son. The boy was surrendered. John then demanded possession of their nineteen-month-old daughter. At first Eliza was allowed to keep her "tender" daughter. Then Justice Bronson of New York overturned the decision that granted her (and her wealthy father) temporary custody. He wrote that "Mrs. Barry cannot expect to deprive a father of his children. The husband may be at fault in relation to his conjugal duties [and may still have] paramount right to custody, which no court is at liberty to disregard. By the law of the land, the claims of the father are superior to those of the mother. Ordered accordingly."

Bronson ends his decision in sarcasm. "It is possible that our laws relating to the rights and duties of husband and wife have not kept pace with (the) progress of civilization. It may be best that the wife should be at liberty to desert her husband at pleasure and take the children of the marriage with her. . . . I will however venture the remark, even at the hazard of being thought out of fashion, that human laws cannot be very far out of the way when they are in accordance with the law of God." (Mercein ex rel. Barry, 25 Wendell [NY] 64 [1840]: 3 Hill NY 399 [1842].)

11. There is an eerie parallel between Mrs. Packard's house arrest and confinement to her bedroom and that of Mrs. Charles (Catherine) Dickens in England during the 1850s and 1860s. According to Phyllis Rose, in her book *Parallel Lives: Five Victorian Marriages* (New York: Knopf, 1983),

> Mrs. Charles Dickens had given birth to ten children in sixteen years of marriage, and [also had] miscarriages. Almost always pregnant or caring for an infant, she was exhausted. If Catherine would commit adultery, [Dickens] could be free of her. But that was preposterous. Immobile conventional Catherine would never do anything so daring. . . . The first gesture [Dickens] devised to express outwardly the separation from Catherine that existed in his [already adulterous life] was to [ask] the servant at Tavistock House to arrange for separate bedrooms for himself and his wife. Mrs. Dickens was to have the bedroom which they had formerly shared. His dressing room was to be turned into a bedroom for himself. The connection between the two rooms was to be walled up and covered over with bookshelves. He was to have a new iron bedstand. Who was being walled up?

12. Ibid. Rose notes that

> Catherine felt she had been wronged and hoped that posterity would vindicate her. Near the end of her life, she gave the letters which Charles Dickens had written to her in the course of their life together to her daughter Kate. . . . It took George Bernard Shaw, whom she consulted on the matter, to convince Kate to save [her mother's letters] and donate them to the British Museum. It took Shaw to get her to

see that a case could be made for her mother. For Kate was an old-fashioned romantic, and she liked the story of a great man mismated and dragged down by an inferior woman. Shaw did not. He argued that the sentimental sympathy of the nineteenth century with the man of genius tied to a commonplace wife had been rudely upset by a writer named Ibsen. He predicted that posterity would sympathize more with the woman sacrificed to her husband's uxoriousness to the extent of being made to bear ten children in sixteen years than with the man whose grievance only amounted to the fact "that she was not a female Charles Dickens."

Countess Sophie Tolstoy was also married to a much-beloved novelist. She was as conservative as Catherine Dickens, although far more energetic and efficient. Nevertheless, she was also "rejected" by her children, especially by her eldest daughter, who, like Dickens's children, preferred their charismatic father. Sophie wrote in her *Diaries,*

> Everyone, [Tolstoy] as well as the children who follow him like a flock of sheep—have come to think of me as a *scourge*. [Masha and Tanya] have embraced Tolstoy's philosophy and become distant to me. After throwing on me the whole responsibility of the children and their education, household duties, money matters, and all the other material things, they come along, and with a cold, officious, and pious expression, tell me to give a horse to a peasant, or some money. God! I am so tired of all this life and the struggle and suffering! How deep is the unconscious hatred of even one's nearest people, and how great their selfishness.

This information is contained in Anne Edwards, *Sonya: Life of Countess Tolstoy* (New York: Simon and Schuster, 1981), and in Sophie's diaries of 1886, reprinted in Mary Jane Moffat and Charlotte Painter, eds., *Revelations: Diaries of Women* (New York: Vintage Books, 1975).

13. Packard, *Modern Persecution, or Married Woman's Liabilities.* A bill concerning the economic and property rights of married women was passed in Illinois in 1872. It did not deal with custody issues. Women obtained the legal right to property and an equal (male) court-decided right to their children in Kansas in 1859, in Massachusetts in 1869, in Oregon in 1880, and in Pennsylvania in 1895. Peggy A. Rabkin discussed this in *Fathers to Daughters: The Legal Foundation of Female Emancipation* (Westport, CT: Greenwood Press, 1980).

14. Packard, *Modern Persecution, or Married Woman's Liabilities.*

15. This speech is fictionalized. It is based on the following accounts: that of the Phelps story contained in Katharine Anthony's biography of Susan B. Anthony, entitled *Susan B. Anthony: Her Personal History and Her Era* (New York: Doubleday, 1954); that given by Lois W. Banner in *Elizabeth Cady Stanton: A Radical for Women's Rights* (Boston: Little, Brown, 1980); that given by Alice Felt Tyler in *Freedom's Ferment: Phases of American Social History to 1860* (New York: Harper/Torch, 1944); and Rheta Childe Dorr's work on Susan B. Anthony, which was published in 1928 and is now out of print.

16. According to Katharine Anthony in *Susan B. Anthony*, Susan B. Anthony first placed Mrs. Phelps with Abby Hopper Gibbons, daughter of the Quaker philanthropist Isaac Hopper, and then with Elizabeth F. Ellet, author of *The Women of the American Revolution*.

17. Anthony's "reverence" for the abolitionists Phillips and Garrison is quoted by Katharine Anthony in *Susan B. Anthony*, where their letter to her also appears.

18. This quote is taken from Alice Felt Tyler's *Freedom's Ferment*, 459–460. The source for Tyler's anecdote is a book on Susan B. Anthony by Rheta Childe Dorr, *What Eight Million Women Want* (Boston: Small, Maynard, 1910). It was first called to my attention in 1981 by historian Miriam Schneir and again by playwright Mary Vasiliades. Katharine Anthony quoted the following in her biography from a letter written by Susan B. Anthony to Phillips and Garrison: "Trust me, that I ignore all law to help the slave, so will I ignore it all to protect an enslaved woman."

19. This anecdote appears in several places, including Michael Grossberg's article, "Who Gets the Child? Custody, Guardianship, and the Role of a Judicial Patriarchy in Nineteenth Century America," *Feminist Studies* 9, no. 2 (Summer 1983).

20. Elizabeth Cady Stanton, "Speech to the McFarland-Richardson Protest Meeting" (May 1869). Reprinted in Ellen C. Dubois, ed., *Elizabeth Cady Stanton, Susan B. Anthony: Correspondence, Writings, Speeches* (New York: Schocken, 1981). Susan B. Anthony and Elizabeth Cady Stanton both argued for custodial rights on behalf of married women, and both saw analogies between slavery for black people and legal marriage for women. See Dubois, *Elizabeth Cady Stanton*.

21. While some American judges sometimes allowed a nonadulterous mother *temporary* custody of her children—especially if her father was wealthy and her husband was flagrantly abusive—custody was temporary, and decisions like this were rare. For example, in 1809 in South Carolina, Mr. Prather deserted his wife for his mistress. In what was regarded as a highly "radical" decision, the judge allowed Mrs. Prather to keep her young infant "temporarily," with the clear understanding that she would return the child to his father. (Prather v. Prather [S.C. 1809], 4 Deseau., 33, 34, 44.) See Grossberg, "Who Gets the Child?," 471.

More characteristic of how most judges decided is the following one. In 1813 in Pennsylvania, a judge allowed Barbara Lee to keep her two young daughters "temporarily." Barbara had been beaten and deserted by her adulterous husband. For years she was her family's sole economic provider. However, Barbara had begun living with a Mr. Addicks *before* she obtained her divorce. (She subsequently married him.) By law, Barbara Lee could not marry a man she had lived with in adultery, as a "paramour," during the lifetime of her former husband. In 1816 the court ordered the girls back into their father's custody. The judge "could not allow two potential wives to be reared by a mother who thought a marital vow could be so easily broken. At present, [the girls] may not reflect upon it, but soon they will, and when they inquire why it was that they were separated from their mother, they will be taught, as far as our opinion can teach them that in good fortune or bad, sickness or in health, in happiness or in misery, the marriage contract, unless dissolved by the law of the country, is sacred and inviolable." (Commonwealth v. Addicks, S. Binn S20 [PA 1813]: 2 Serge and Rawle, 174 [PA 1816].)

In 1854 Mrs. Lindsay sought custody of her daughter. She claimed that her husband's cruelty and lack of financial support drove her to seek asylum with another man. Her petition was denied by the Georgia Supreme Court, which claimed that

> there may be no difference in the sins of the man and the woman who violate the laws of chastity, but in the opinion of society it is otherwise. When a man commits adultery he isn't excluded from associating with "decent people." . . . The frail female is reduced to "utter and irredeemable ruin, where her associations are with the Vulgar, the Vile and the Depraved. If her children be with her, their characters must be, more or less, influenced and formed by the circumstances which surround them." (Lindsay v. Lindsay. 14 Ga 657 [1854]; see also Matter of Viele, 44 How. Pr. 14 [1872].)

As late as 1884 in New York an unmarried or separated "adulteress" and petty thief "lost her children, was forbidden from visiting them, and evidently not even told where they were." In re Diss. Debar, 3 N.Y.S. (1889). Cited by Douglas R. Rendleman, "Parens Patriae: From Chancery to the Juvenile Court," *South Carolina Law Review* 23 (1971).

22. "Sergeant Talfourd's Argument for the British Infants' Custody Act," *Hansard's Parliamentary Debates* 39 (1837). This act became law in 1839. Talfourd reviews a number of cases in which virtuous mothers were abused and abandoned by adulterous and profligate husbands—who also removed their children. The cases read like Gothic tales of horror. For example,

In 1836, in England, Mr. Greenhill lived in "open adultery." Mrs. Greenhill returned to her parents with her three daughters, all under five. She asked the court's permission "to continue bestowing upon her children the same personal care and attention which they had hitherto received from her, and which was necessary to their welfare; she further stated that she would consent even to relinquish the custody and control of her children, if she might be assured of permission to give them her personal care and attention during their tender years." The court refused her request. First, Mrs. Greenhill was not a good enough "Christian" wife; she remained unwilling to "forgive" her husband. Second, the children belonged to their father by law—and were so remanded into his custody. (*The King Against Henrietta Lavinia Greenhill,* Lord Chief Justice Derman presiding. 4 Adolphus and Ellis, King's Bench Reports 624 [1836].)

23. My account of Frances "Fanny" Wright is primarily based on Cecilia Morris Eckhardt's work, *Fanny Wright: Rebel in America* (Cambridge, MA: Harvard University Press, 1984).

24. Eckhardt, *Fanny Wright.* It is important to remember that under common law in England and America (and under equivalent laws in all countries), husbands were legally entitled to their wives' dowries, inheritance, and earnings. Common law made it illegal for married women to contract, sue, or collect debts without their husbands' consent. Women married to untrustworthy husbands could not engage in business without encountering enormous obstacles. (They were denied credit.)

25. Ibid.

26. My account of George Sand is based on the following: Curtis Cate's biography, *George Sand: A Biography* (Boston: Houghton Mifflin, 1975); George Sand, *The Intimate Journal,* trans. Marie Jenney Howe (reprint ed., Chicago: Academy Press, Cassandra Editions, 1977); George Sand, *My Life,* trans. Don Hofstadter (reprint ed., New York: Harper/Colophon, 1979); and George Sand, *Winter in Majorca,* trans. Marie Jenney Howe (reprint ed., Chicago: Academy Press, Cassandra Editions, 1978).

27. Norton's writings can be found in Erna Olafson Hellerstein, Leslie Parker Hume, and Karen M. Offen, eds., Estelle B. Freedman, Barbara Charlesworth Gelpi, and Marilyn Yalom, assoc. eds., *Victorian Women: A Documentary Account of Women's Lives in Nineteenth-Century England, France, and the United States* (Palo Alto, CA: Stanford University Press, 1981).

28. Joan Perkin, *Women and Marriage in Nineteenth-Century England* (London: Routledge, 1989), 26–28.

29. Barbara Caine, *English Feminism, 1780–1980* (New York: Oxford University Press, 1997), 67.
30. Perkin, *Women and Marriage.*
31. L. G. Mitchell, *Lord Melbourne, 1779–1848* (New York: Oxford University Press, 1997), 221–223.
32. Ibid.
33. David I. Kertzer and Marzio Barbagli, eds., *Family Life in the Long Nineteenth Century, 1789–1913: The History of the European Family: Volume 2* (New Haven, CT: Yale University Press, 2002), 125–126.
34. Mary Mark Ockerbloom, ed., "Caroline Norton (1808–1877)," *A Celebration of Women Writers*, accessed March 12, 2010, http://digital.library.upenn.edu /women/norton/nc-biography.html.
35. Lawrence Stone, *Road to Divorce: England, 1530–1987* (New York: Oxford University Press, 1990), 178.
36. Mark Ockerbloom, ed., "Caroline Norton."
37. Perkin, *Women and Marriage.*
38. At this time in America, Victoria C. Woodhull and Elizabeth Cady Stanton were publishing their views on voluntary motherhood, women's suffrage, and "free love." In 1873 the infamous Comstock Laws were passed in America, prohibiting the advocacy of birth control. Margaret Sanger would later be forced to leave America for England because of these laws.
39. In re Besant, Chancery Division, vol. XI, 508–522.
40. Ibid.
41. Ibid. There are other cases of prominent English (male) atheists losing custody of their children. In 1817 the poet Percy Bysshe Shelley, who had previously abandoned his wife and children, was denied custody of the children after their mother's death. According to the English court, Shelley "avowed himself an atheist; he had written and published a work in which he blasphemously derided the truth of the Christian revelation and denied the existence of a God as creator of the universe." Shelley was considered morally unfit to parent. The maternal *grandfather*, Mr. Westbrooke, who presumably believed in God, assumed custody of his grandchildren. (Shelley v. Westbrooke, Jacob Chancery Reports 226 [1817].)
42. William Shakespeare, *A Midsummer Night's Dream*, in *The Complete Works of William Shakespeare* (London: Abby Library, 1977). The Indian child is only the dramatic "excuse" for a domestic quarrel among immortals.
43. The Christian king's right to his genetic children symbolized and maintained patriarchal order. It ensured every man his legal and obedient heir and every heir his rightful inheritance. The medieval Arthurian legends are essentially about the importance of father-owned and father-controlled children. The natural relationship between a queen and her child must be sacrificed for the sake

of Christian patriarchal order. Arthur's father, Uther Pendragon, "mates" with the Lady Igraine to beget his "once and future King." He demands that Igraine give the newborn Arthur away at birth, which she obediently does. "When the lady [Igraine] was delivered, the king commanded two knights and two ladies to take the child, bound in a cloth of gold. . . . So the child was delivered unto Merlin, and so he bore it forth to Ector, and made an holy man to christen him, and named him Arthur; and so Sir Ector's wife nourished him with her own pap." Sir Thomas Malory, *La Morte d'Arthur* (New York: Everyman, 1967). See also Marion Zimmer Bradley's excellent popular retelling of the Arthurian myths in *The Mists of Avalon.*

While it is true that mothers of all classes routinely gave their children "away" to wet nurses, governesses, and tutors, it was not always done at birth or in a way that denied the mother all access to her child—if she wanted it. The mother-surrogates were usually social inferiors and employees rather than another woman of the mother's own station, as Sir Ector's wife was.

44. Joseph Dahmus, *Seven Medieval Queens* (New York: Doubleday, 1972).

45. Elizabeth Jenkins, in her biography of *Elizabeth the Great* (New York: Berkley Medallion, 1958), notes that "apart from (two indirect) instances there is no record of Elizabeth having uttered her mother's name. But with this determined silence, there went a marked kindness toward her mother's connections. In her kindness to these, she paid a mute tribute where she could not speak."

In the sixteenth century King Henry VIII married, divorced, imprisoned, or beheaded queen after queen in his obsessive search for a male heir. His first wife, the pious Catherine of Aragon, refused to agree to a divorce. Henry separated her from Mary, their only child, for five years. Despite this enforced separation and despite the humiliation of house arrest, Queen Catherine continued to refuse to consent to a divorce. How could she? At stake were Mary's legitimacy and Catherine's own religious beliefs. See Nora Loft, *The King's Pleasure* (London: Coronet Books, 1969).

46. Lady Ann Roos eventually gave birth to another son, retained custody of Ignoto, moved to Ireland, and was duly divorced "in the ecclesiastical court" for adultery. Her children, John and Charles Manners, were subsequently declared "illegitimate" by an act of Parliament. See Antonia Fraser, *The Weaker Vessel* (New York: Knopf, 1984).

47. In 1796 when Sophie/Catherine the Great died, a sealed envelope of her memoirs was discovered; it was addressed as follows: "To his Imperial Highness the Czarevich and Grand Duke Paul, my dearly loved son." Her memoirs were suppressed because she admits that her son and royal heir had "no Romanov blood"—that is, he was an illegitimate child. My information about Catherine the Great of Russia is contained in *The Memoirs of Catherine the Great*, trans. Moura Budberg, ed. Dominique Maroger (London: Hamish Hamilton, 1955).

The volume is as extraordinary as it is little known.

48. Catherine the Great, *Memoirs*.
49. Ibid. Count Sergei Saltikov is considered the father of Sophie/Catherine's son Paul I for several reasons. Maroger notes that

> everything: the Empress's suspicion, Saltikov's cautiousness, the speed with which Saltikov is removed as soon as the child is born (but not beforehand so as not to endanger Catherine's health), the Grand Duke's attitude, that of the Empress who snatches the new-born child from Catherine, everything seems to indicate that Catherine's entourage had no doubt whatsoever that Saltikov was the father of the child. The secret had to be closely guarded as in these circumstances the heir to the throne was no longer of the blood of the Romanovs. It is surprising that Catherine should have half-revealed it in memoirs which were essentially destined for her son and her grandson, Alexander.

50. Ibid.
51. Catherine's memoirs give us a glimpse into the kind of power a queen (like the Empress Elizabeth) could exercise if she had no king and if her heir (in this case, her nephew) were insane and incompetent.
52. Sophie/Catherine is never clear about what her role is in her husband's assassination or about whether she knew beforehand of the plans to assassinate Peter. There was one other contender for the throne: a four-year-old boy named Ivan. In the 1740s the Empress Elizabeth "dethroned" him, separated him from his mother, and had him imprisoned for the rest of his life. Sophie/Catherine met him once; she described him as "stammering" and as "insulting" to her. She probably had him murdered after she assumed the throne.
53. Catherine the Great, *Memoirs*. In her private writings and letters (some of which are reprinted together with her memoirs), the Empress Catherine, a devotee of the French Enlightenment, envisions the emancipation of the serfs and mourns the existence of "slavery" and the "high infant mortality" among the peasants. She reminds herself to avoid "flatterers," to be "kind, gentle, accessible, and liberal-minded," and to "behave so that the kind love you, the evil fear you, and all respect you."
54. Rendleman, "Parens Patriae."
55. Ann Jones, *Women Who Kill* (New York: Holt, Rinehart, and Winston, 1980). Jones notes that the colonial lawmakers fell back upon English common law, which defined the murder of a husband or master as petit treason. Since the husband was "lord" of the wife, the common law said her killing him was treachery comparable to murdering the king, though on a lesser scale. A Virginia judge defined the gravity of the crime: "Other offenses are injurious to

Private Persons only, but this is a Public Mischief, and often strikes at the Root of all Civil Government."

56. Lorena S. Walsh, "Child Custody in the Early Chesapeake: A Case Study" (paper presented at the Berkshire Conference in Women's History, Poughkeepsie, New York, 1981). Walsh notes that the law in seventeenth-century Maryland condemned mulatto offspring to be sold for thirty-one years of servitude. In some ways unwed mothers had more rights over their children than did married mothers. Walsh cites some examples of unwed maternal rights to wages of an apprenticed child, even when the natural father sought the nonlegitimated child for his own economic purpose.

In *Women Who Kill*, Ann Jones notes that "when Eve Sewell, a free white woman, bore a child in 1790 by a black slave, under Maryland law her white husband received an automatic divorce and both she and her child were sold into slavery."

57. Jones, *Women Who Kill*.

58. Walsh, "Child Custody." Rape was also a serious colonial offense. Unwed pregnant girls who were neither servants nor paupers who claimed that their pregnancies were the result of rape were sometimes *formally interrogated* in the throes of childbirth. If they stuck to their story of rape, could name the father, and were believed, the father was then ordered to support his child. According to Ellen Fitzpatrick, in 1686 Elizabeth Emerson of New England accused Thomas Swan of raping and impregnating her. She was "examined" during childbirth, and her charges were confirmed. "The child was a year old before a Salem court settled the case in the Emersons' favor. Swan was ordered to pay ten shillings six pence per week in child support. But the Emersons were back in court shortly after the child's second birthday. They had yet to receive any money from Swan. Instead, the reluctant father had offered molasses, lumber, a cow, and other goods which the Emersons complained were 'useless and frivolous things which will afford said Child no maintenance.'" (Ellen Fitzpatrick, "Childbirth and an Unwed Mother in 17th Century New England," *Signs* 8, no. 4 [Summer 1983].)

59. In colonial America, both men and women were punished for fornication and adultery by economic fines, public whipping, imprisonment, or death by hanging. Needless to say, women were far more vulnerable than men were to the consequences of such crimes.

In Nathaniel Hawthorne's 1850 version of Puritan New England as seen in *The Scarlet Letter*, Hester Prynne was imprisoned and forced to wear the scarlet letter *A*—for "adulteress"—over her heart forever. Hester refuses to name Dimmesdale as her daughter's father. He is also Hester's pastor and a prominent member of the community. Hester is allowed to keep her daughter, Pearl, "as a way of saving her from becoming a witch." Hester's ostracism is total and lifelong. Crowds reject her or follow her. Children jeer at her. If Hester "entered a church, trusting to share the Sabbath smile of the Universal Father, it was often her mishap to find herself the text of the discourse. . . . Another peculiar torture was felt in the gaze of a new eye. When strangers looked curiously at the scarlet letter—and none ever failed to do so—they branded it afresh into Hester's soul. The spot never grew callous; it seemed on the contrary to grow more sensitive with daily torture." When Pearl is three years old, the town magistrates decide to remove her from her mother's "un-Christian custody." Hester now threatens Dimmesdale with exposure. He persuades the magistrates to allow Hester the solace and rights of natural motherhood (Nathaniel Hawthorne, *The Scarlet Letter* [1850; New York: Bantam, 1965]).

60. Jones, *Women Who Kill*, notes that just about the same time that Hanna Piggin and Abiel Converse were hanged in Northampton, Massachusetts, for concealing the birth of a bastard or for infanticide, six male leaders of Shays's Rebellion, convicted in the same jurisdiction of treason and sentenced to hang, were pardoned. Still others, guilty of far more brutal crimes, got off with light sentences. When Robert Thompson was convicted of assault in the same Northampton jurisdiction, he was whipped twenty stripes, set on the gallows for one hour, whipped nineteen more stripes, jailed for one year, and ordered to pay costs. He had beaten up his wife, Agnes Thompson, and "dug out both her eyes with his thumbs and a stick so she is entirely blind."

   In the 1860s Elizabeth Cady Stanton referred to one "Hester Vaughan," then "under sentence of death for the alleged crime of infanticide, which could not be proved against her [and who] has dragged the weary days of a whole year away in the solitude and gloom of a Pennsylvania prison, while he who betrayed her walks this green earth in freedom" (Dubois, *Elizabeth Cady Stanton*).

   Also see Nicole Hahn Rafter, *Partial Justice: Women in State Prisons, 1800–1935* (Boston: Northeastern University Press, 1985).

61. Walsh, "Child Custody." The Watts children were lucky; they had a maternal grandfather who petitioned for their custody. It took three years of persistent effort before he obtained it.

62. Marcus Wilson Jernigan, *The Laboring and Dependent Classes in Colonial America, 1607–1783* (New York: Frederick Ungar, 1960), 157. Cited by Rendleman, "Parens Patriae."

63. Walsh, "Child Custody," also notes that colonial widows who did not remarry attempted to have their children released from bondage to a cruel master.

64. Ibid. In her study of colonial custody in Maryland, Walsh concludes that the "preferred custodial solution" was to grant custody to the "closest surviving and nurturing kin," a decision that "strongly reinforced the rights of the natural mother and also encouraged strong kin networks."

Perhaps such widows, if they remained unmarried, were in the unusual position of being single women of property. As such, they may have been vulnerable to accusations of witchcraft for just this reason, just as their married, abused, and property-less female counterparts were vulnerable to similar accusations for another set of reasons. See chapter 11 for a discussion of this.

65. Jones, *Women Who Kill.*

66. Nancy F. Cott, "Eighteenth-Century Family and Social Life Revealed in Massachusetts Divorce Records," in Nancy F. Cott and Elizabeth H. Pleck, eds., *A Heritage of Her Own: Toward a New Social History of American Women* (New York: Touchstone Books/Simon & Schuster, 1980), notes that between 1692 and 1786 women clung to married status longer than men did, even when aware of their spouses' wrongs. Aggrieved wives waited a longer time before suing for divorce than aggrieved husbands did. On the average, wives waited almost five years, while husbands petitioned after only two and a half years.

67. There are always many exceptions to any rule, including that of fathers' rights. A close reading of some of these judicial exceptions reveals that an "intemperate" and wealthy father's custodial petition failed only when *his* own father, the paternal grandfather, refused to back him. Instead he backed his wife (or his dead wife's equally wealthy family). The best example of this is the case known as *Wellesley v. Wellesley* or *The Wellesley Children v. Duke of Beaufort*, 2 Russell Chancery Reports, I., 1827. Cited by Grace Abbott, *The Child and the State* (Westport, CT: Greenwood Press, 1938).

68. Nichols v. Giles, 2 Root 461 (Conn. 1796), cited by Zinaildin, "Emergence." There are other cases in which a wealthy maternal grandfather was granted custody of a grandchild. For example, in 1816 John Waldron petitioned for custody of his daughter, Margaret Eliza. He claimed that his father-in-law, Andrew McGowan, had "improperly restrained" her. Waldron also claimed that McGowan had on numerous occasions "repulsed" his attempts to visit his wife and child. McGowan described Waldron as "insolvent" and unable to pay "trifling debts" and as a man who had to "live with his mother." Waldron was Margaret's father. His mother was offering to help him economically. Nevertheless, the court denied Waldron's petition. Andrew McGowan was a "very affluent [man], and abundantly able to maintain his grand-daughter [who] would most probably receive the greater part of the property of her grandparents, on their death" (In re Waldron 13 Johns, 418–419, New York [1816], cited by Zinaildin, "Emergence").

69. Exparte Crouse, 4 Whart. (9 Penn. 1839). Earlier, in 1810, when the child was not charged with "immorality" but her parents were, the state acted as the child's superior guardian. However, it did not establish any precedent in so doing. In 1810 Levi Nutt of Pennsylvania petitioned the court for custody of his

daughter. Nutt had no property or income. He also "cursed in front of his wife and daughter."

"Mrs. Nutt was also of a 'disgusting character.' She frequently 'kept house for Amos Howell,' a tavernkeeper who had separated from his wife. There is every reason to believe they lived in constant habits of adultery. The virtue and innocence of the child, a girl named Acha, 'could not be trusted with safety' in 'either party's custody. . . . The father has a right to custody of his children' but Acha will be placed with a relative 'where her mind and morals [were] in the least danger of being corrupted'" (Commonwealth v. Nutt, I Bro 143 [Philadelphia County 1810], cited by Zinaildin, "Emergence").

Rendleman, "Parens Patriae," explains the state's misuse and misinterpretation of *parens patriae* as a way of controlling, punishing, and profiting from the poor without developing a guilty conscience and without having to find better or more costly programs to rehabilitate the impoverished. According to Rendleman, "The Latin phrase 'parens patriae' had acquired meaning over a long period of time and was sensibly applied between private parties, usually where property or guardianship was an issue. The Crouse [court used this phrase] to justify the state statutory schemes to part poor or incompetent parents from their children."

Rendleman also observes the following (here he quotes from Norval Morris and Gordon Hawkins's *The Honest Politician's Guide to Crime Control*):

> The juvenile court emerged from what was a legal misinterpretation of the *parens patriae* concept. This concept was developed for quite different purposes—property and wardship—and had nothing to do with what juvenile courts do now. Though we keep on practicing *parens patriae,* we might as well burn incense. Historical idiosyncrasies gave us a doubtful assumption of power over children. With the quasi-legal concept of *parens patriae* to brace it, this assumption of power blended well with the earlier humanitarian traditions in churches and other charitable organizations regarding child care and child-saving. The juvenile court is thus the product of paternal error and maternal generosity, which is not [the] usual genesis of illegitimacy.

70. Ackley v. Tinker, 26 Kansas 485 (1881), cited by Zinaildin, "Emergence."
71. Harrison v. Gilbert, 71 Conn. 724, 43A 190 (1899), cited by Zinaildin, "Emergence." The last sentence is Zinaildin's comment on the case.

Strictly speaking, the state was not legally involved in human slavery. Rendleman, "Parens Patriae," notes that "the practice of breaking up families by sale [slavery] was a private enterprise." The state was neither a buyer nor a seller and not an integral party to the transaction. The state, however, was intimately involved in the economic benefits or savings of child apprenticeships.

72. Sterling, *We Are Your Sisters*. Child savers also became anti-Irish in the 1840s after mass Irish immigration to America.

73. Most contemporary historians have been forced to focus on the parental mistreatment of *poor* nineteenth-century children. Fewer records were kept charting the parental mistreatment of middle- or upper-class children. Private and state organizations began to keep records of child abuse only after the Civil War. Even then, such records are more suggestive than comprehensive.

In 1821 Sir William Blackstone in his *Commentaries on the Laws of England* (8th ed., 1821), noted that "the rich indeed are left at their own option, whether they will breed up their children to be ornaments or disgraces to their family."

74. According to Charles Loring Brace, founder of the Children's Aid Society of New York,

> As Christian men, we cannot look upon this great multitude of unhappy, deserted and degraded boys and girls without feeling our responsibility to God for them. The class increases; immigration is pouring in its multitudes . . . of helpless foreigners who crowd into the tenements in the Russian, Polish, Bohemian, Hungarian, and Italian quarters of our city. . . . They must be taught our language. They must be trained to be clean, obedient to authority, industrious and truthful, and must be instructed in the elements of an English education.
>
> These boys and girls, it should be remembered, will soon form the great lower class of our city. They will influence elections; they may shape the policy of the city; they will assuredly, if unreclaimed, poison society all around them. They will help to form the great multitude of robbers, thieves, and vagrants, who are now such a burden upon the law-respecting community.

These words are taken from a series of circulars written in the 1820s by Brace. See Charles Loring Brace, "The Children's Aid Society of New York: Its History, Plans and Results," in Anthony Platt, ed., *History of Child-Saving in the United States* (1893; reprint ed., Montclair, NY: Patterson Smith, 1971). Brace also described the overwhelming and serious problems faced by impoverished children.

75. Robert S. Pickert, *House of Refuge: Origins of Juvenile Reform in New York State, 1815–1857* (Syracuse, NY: Syracuse University Press, 1969).

76. The boy was beaten to death as Russian prisoners are under the knout. It was shown that the father had continued his brutal conduct for months. The man was sentenced to be hanged, but he applied for a new trial on a technicality.

A new trial was granted, conditioned on his pleading guilty, as the jury had coupled a recommendation of mercy with their verdict. He was then sentenced to imprisonment for life (Oscar L. Dudley, "Saving the Children: Sixteen Years' Work among the Dependent Youth of Chicago," in Platt, *History of Child-Saving*).

For other accounts of abused, impoverished children, see Pickert, *House of Refuge*; Brace, "Children's Aid Society"; Rendleman, "Parens Patriae"; Zinaildin, "Emergence"; and Anne B. Richardson, "The Massachusetts System for Caring for State Minor Wards," in Platt, *History of Child-Saving*.

77. For example, in 1833 in South Carolina (In re Kottman), a judge awarded an adolescent male to the kind mother-surrogate who took him in and reared him after his father beat him savagely. The judges made no legal ruling in this case *against* a father's right to custody.

In 1846 in Tennessee (Ward v. Roper), a judge awarded a child to her maternal grandparents who had raised her and refused custody to her paternally appointed guardian. The "ties" to her maternal grandmother "should not be broken."

In 1851 in Pennsylvania (Gilkeson v. Gilkeson), a judge awarded custody to a girl's paternal aunt and uncle who had been acting as her adoptive parents for six years. The father's claim was dismissed.

In 1881 in Kansas (Chapsky v. Wood), a father's custodial claim was dismissed in favor of the child's preexisting live-in relationship with her maternal aunt, who was "like a mother to her."

Such exceptional cases must be contrasted with the cases I've referred to in which moral or economically solvent mothers, such as Fanny Wright, Elizabeth Packard, Abby McFarland, and others, were denied custody of their own children when custody was contested by an immoral and economically solvent father.

78. An 1810 case illustrates my point: A widowed biological mother was forced to apprentice her daughter "in upper Canada." Later, the child returned to Massachusetts with her master, William Hamilton. The child's now remarried mother petitioned the court for her daughter's return. However, since the mother was remarried, she "ceased to have any power of controlling her own actions," and her new husband was under no legal obligation to provide for the girl. Without any precedent, the court cautioned the mother not to "molest, interrupt or disturb" her daughter "in respect to her residence in the family of said Hamilton" (Commonwealth v. Hamilton, 6 Mass. 273 [1810], cited by Zinaildin, "Emergence").

In certain cases throughout the nineteenth century, some widowed biological mothers who could afford a lawsuit were judicially found to be entitled to the services or wages of their children. For example, see *Osborn v. Allen* (26,

New Jersey Law Reports, 388 [1857]). This was not true if a father was alive or if the mother was seen as "immoral."

79. Grossberg, "Who Gets the Child?" See also Elisabeth Badinter, *Mother Love: Myth and Reality* (New York: Macmillan, 1981).

80. Barbara Hobson studied prostitutes in Victorian Boston. She cites proof of discrepancies in treatment of males and females brought into court on charges of immoral behavior. Greater numbers of females were found guilty, and, upon sentencing, a larger proportion was imprisoned. Men were often fined. Women were overwhelmingly accused of moral turpitude and were tried for offenses against the public order more often than they were charged with crimes against persons or property. Impoverished, deviant women suffered more than their more well-to-do sisters in the criminal world. (Barbara Hobson, "Sex in the Marketplace: Prostitution in an American Victorian City, Boston, 1820–1880" [PhD dissertation, Boston University, 1981], cited by Barbara M. Brenzel, *Daughters of the State: A Social Portrait of the First Reform School for Girls in North America, 1856–1905* [Cambridge, MA: MIT Press, 1983].)

Ann Jones, in *Women Who Kill*, documents this same point for colonial, Victorian, and contemporary women in America.

81. Brenzel, *Daughters of the State*. Rendleman, "Parens Patriae," also notes the anti-Catholic, anti-Irish, and anti-immigrant biases of nineteenth-century "child saving." He notes the O'Connell case (1870), which on appeal returned a Catholic child to a Catholic home. "Justice Redfield commented after O'Connell that a Catholic 'child cannot be torn from home and immured in a Protestant prison, for ten or more years, and trained in what he regards as a heretical and deadly faith, to the destruction of his own soul.' The O'Connell decision did not stop this practice."

82. Brenzel, *Daughters of the State*.

83. Ibid.

84. Ibid., quoting the "14th Annual Report regarding Lancaster, to the Board of State Charities," Public Document 20 (1869). Later in the century, when factories required cheap female labor, Lancaster inmates were trained accordingly—despite the continued probability of sexual harassment and rape on the job. Perhaps Lancaster (and its many counterparts) really tried to "save" as many individual girls as possible—given that their poverty rendered them and their mothers so vulnerable to male sexual aggression and exploitation.

85. "According to Dr. Walter E. Fernald of Massachusetts, one strong indicator of feeble-mindedness in young girls was sexual activity: imbeciles of both sexes show active sexual propensities and perversions at an early age" ([an unpublished record of Dr. Walter E. Fernald, The Walter E. Fernald State School, 1910], cited by Brenzel, *Daughters of the State*).

86. Brenzel, *Daughters of the State.*
87. Grossberg, "Who Gets the Child?"

2. A Contemporary Overview

1. In re Abdullah, 80 Ill. App. 3d. 1144, 400 N.E. 2d. 1063 (1980). In re Abdullah, 85 Ill. 2d. 300, 423 N.E. 2d. 915 (1981). The *Abdullah* decision is contained and discussed in *The Family Advocate* (1981) in an article by attorney Michael Minton, entitled "Should a Divorced Mother Lose Custody Because She Has a Lover?" Mr. Minton is Mrs. Jarrett's attorney. The *Abdullah* decision was reversed three years later due to the result of mounting pressure. When the Abdullahs' child was six years old, he was legally "adoptable."

2. Minton, "Should a Divorced Mother." The dissenting judge in the *Abdullah* decision concluded the following:

    We acquiesced in depriving a woman of the custody of her children. . . . We held that the fact of open and notorious cohabitation alone made it in the best interests of the children that they live with their father. In this case, however (Abdullah), the majority holds that the unrebutted murder of the child's mother . . . is insufficient to justify dispensing with the murderer's consent before the child may be placed for adoption. In other words, cohabitation [with no tangible evidence that her conduct harmed the children in any way] may justify losing custody of children, but the murder of one's wife, the mother of the child, will not.

3. It is important to realize that judicial decisions are interpreted differently by both lawyers and judges depending upon the state, the time, and the case. It is also important to realize that custody remains an open matter until a child reaches his or her majority. Thus decisions are sometimes appealed endlessly; private custodial arrangements are appealed for the first time in courts years later; judicial custodial decisions are also modified by the parents and children involved on a daily basis.

    The fact that such decisions as I cite here can happen even *once* in contemporary America is important. The effect they have on each mother involved and on any other mother who hears about it is important. What it tells us about judicial practice is important. Please see chapter 13 for a discussion of judicial trends in general.

4. "Natural Parent Entitled to Custody Absent 'Extraordinary Circumstances,'" *Family Law Reporter* 9 (August 16, 1983).

5. Ibid.

6. Landaverde v. Home. Reported in *Family Law Reporter* (August 16, 1983).

7. In re Marriage of Gould, 112 Wisc. 2d 674, 333 N.W. 2d 733 (March 1983). This decision was reversed on appeal, 342 N.W. 2d 426 (Wisc. S.C., 1984). I am indebted to Nancy Polikoff's discussion of this case in her review of case law, "Gender and Child-Custody Determinations: Exploding the Myths," in *Families, Politics and Public Policy: A Feminist Dialogue on Women and the State*, ed. Irene Diamond (New York: Longman, 1983).

    Please see chapter 13 for a discussion of the judicial and legislative devaluation of mothers in terms of the levels of child support set by the state ("welfare") and the levels of child support set by individual judges.

8. Porter v. Porter, 21A N.W. 2d 235 (N. D. 1979). The comments are Nancy Polikoff's from "Gender and Child-Custody Determinations."

9. Dempsey v. Dempsey, 95 Mich. App. 285, 292 N. W., 2d 549 (1980); 409 Mich. 495, 296 N. W: 2d 813 (1980). Quoted by Nancy Polikoff, "Why Are Mothers Losing? A Brief Analysis of Criteria Used in Child Custody Determinations," *Women's Rights Law Reporter* 7, no. 3 (Spring 1982).

10. Gulyas v. Gulyas, 75 Mich. App. 138, 254 N.W. 2d 818 (1977). According to Nancy Polikoff's review of the Gulyas case ("Why Are Mothers Losing?"),

    > There was no evidence that the father spent any more time with his child than her mother did. The record offered no factual support for an implicit finding that the mother's career, and not the father's, interfered with the giving of love, affection, and guidance to the child.
    >
    > It should be noted that the child in *Gulyas* has resided with her mother for over one and a half years during the marital separation, but the father had snatched her in New York four months before the hearing. As a result, the judge gave the father an edge on the factor of continuity.

11. Simmons v. Simmons, 223 Kansas 639, 576 P. 2d 598 (1978).

12. In re the Marriage of Milovich, 105 Ill. App. 3d 596, 434 N.E. 2d. 811 (1982).

13. Judge Duran's decision was discussed in the *National Law Journal* on September 26, 1983. His opinion is partly paraphrased. Margaret Gaines (Mrs. Raoul Bezou) appealed this decision. Judge Duran's decision was upheld on June 28, 1983. (A. Raoul Bezou v. Margaret Gaines, wife of A. Raoul Bezou, Court of Appeal of Louisiana [June 28, 1983].)

14. Tina Fishman was originally awarded legal custody of Riva in Indiana. She then lived with Riva for seven years in Illinois, where her order was recognized as valid. Ted Fishman moved to California after the original Indiana custody order. Riva visited and was detained by him in California. Tina was a member of the Revolutionary Communist Party. Its members—American citizens—demonstrated in Washington to protest the state visit of the Communist

Chinese Premier. Tina was arrested, indicted, and acquitted for exercising her civil rights.

15. In re the Marriage of Fishman, Superior Court of the State of California, #255665. Commissioner Browning had spearheaded the government investigations of the Revolutionary Union (forerunner of the Revolutionary Communist Party) in the early 1970s. As the U.S. attorney in San Francisco, he had also presided over Patricia Hearst's trial.

16. Leslie Guevarra, *San Francisco Examiner*, quoting Judge Ragan (June 24, 1983).

17. Communication from Tina Fishman's defense committee.

18. Anon. v. Anon., reported in the *New York Law Journal* (July 20, 1981). This mother is convicted by her own hand. The diary allows or forces her to convict herself.

19. Roxanne Pulitzer lost her appeal of the custody decision in April 1984. Herbert sharply curtailed her visitation (during a subsequent period of "intimacy") when she asked for an increase in alimony in December 1984. The judge denied Roxanne's request for thirty-eight thousand dollars in legal fees, cutting it back to twenty-six thousand in March 1985. "The judge was apparently unimpressed by Roxanne's claims that her $160 earnings as an aerobics instructor can't cover her monthly expenses of $2,740." I obtained this information from coverage in the *New York Times*, *New York Post*, and *Miami Herald*.

 The Pulitzer appeal is *Pulitzer v. Pulitzer*, 449 Southern Reporter, 2nd Series 370 (May 24, 1984).

 In the early 1970s, Yoko Ono lost her daughter to "kidnapping" custody because she committed adultery and moved in with her future husband, John Lennon. Quite by accident, years later, I found myself interviewing a psychiatrist who had been part of that kidnapping conspiracy. He justified his actions, these many years later, by saying, "Yoko Ono was too ambitious. She was going to leave her first husband with nothing. She was moving into the big time and was going to get everything: Why should she also have his child?"

20. The *Pulitzer v. Pulitzer* decision was reported in the *New York Post* in 1983; her appeal was reported on April 19, 1984.

21. Simmons v. Simmons, 223 Kan. 639, 576, P. 2d 589 (1978); Blonsky v. Blonsky, 84 Ill. App. 3d 810, 405 N.E. 2d 112 (1980). Stewart v. Stewart, 430S. 2d, 189, La. App. 2 Cir. (1983). Krabel v. Krabel, 12/18/81, summarized in 8 *FLR* 2249, v. 8,#18; Ryan v. Ryan, Mo. Ct. App. E. Dist., 5/17/83, summarized in 9 *FLR* 2489; Cleeton v. Cleeton, 6 *FLR* 2577; Stephenson v. Stephenson, La. Sup. Ct. 9/28/81, 7 *FLR* 2774.

22. Bunim v. Bunim, 273 App Div 861, 76, N.Y.S. 2nd 456 (February 10, 1948).

23. Grimditch v. Grimditch, 71 Ariz. 198, 225 P.2d. 489 (1950).

24. Ibid. In Maryland in 1967, a remarried Mr. Miller sued his ex-wife for sole custody of their three children on the ground that she had verbally "confessed" to a

two-month adulterous affair. The ex–Mrs. Miller was allowed to retain custody because, in the presiding judge's opinion, "there had been a true repentance of the illicit relationship. When the mother realized that her relationship with the children was jeopardized by this one affair, she broke off relations and has not seen the man. . . . [Since the divorce the mother] has not had improper relations with a subsequent admirer. . . . [The children] seemed to have good training in school, church and home, for much of which the mother was responsible." Miller v. Miller, 228 *Atlantic Reporter*, 2nd Series (April 8, 1967), 311–312.

25. Blain v. Blain, Ark. 346, 168, S.W. 2nd, 807 (1943).
26. Blackburn v. Blackburn, 249 Ga. 689, 292 S. E. 2d., 821 (1982). Blackburn v. Blackburn, 168 Ga. App. 66, 308 S.E. 2d., 19 (1983).
27. Judge Hawkins's and Kathleen Blackburn's comments were quoted by Katie Wood in the *Florida Times Union* (September 7, 1983). There is another case similar to the Blackburn case (Palmore v. Sidoti, Fl. Ct. App. 2nd District [1982]). According to *Off Our Backs* (June 1984),

> Melanie Sidoti, who is now six, went to live with her mother when the Sidotis divorced in 1980. Two years later a Florida court of law decided to protect Melanie from the "social stigmatization that was sure to follow" from continuing to live with her mother and her mother's husband, Clarence Palmore. The judge awarded custody of Melanie to her father, a white man who had remarried a white woman. This April 26, the Supreme Court unanimously struck down that ruling.
>
> What was not decided, however, was the outcome of the custody battle. One day after the Supreme Court decision, Anthony Sidoti, who now lives in Texas, was able to obtain a temporary restraining order from judge Tom McDonald, Jr., forbidding Palmore to remove Melanie from her father's custody. *In These Times* reported in mid-May that the action would give Sidoti "a few more weeks to come up with a tactic to try to win Melanie permanently."
>
> Linda Sidoti Palmore put in an emergency request to Chief Justice Burger asking him to block the Texas court's attempt to interfere in the case. Burger ignored the request, though he did return the case to Florida rather than wait until May 20, when the Supreme Court ruling would normally take effect.

28. Schuster v. Schuster, No. D-36863 (Washington Sup. Ct. King Cty., December 22, 1972). Isaacson v. Isaacson, D-36867 (Washington Sup. Ct. King Cty., December 22, 1972).
    In *Schuster, Isaacson*, and, for example, in *People v. Brown* (1973), a judge allowed a lesbian mother to keep her child under certain conditions—or

decided that lesbianism per se was not relevant to a determination of parental fitness. Cited by D. R. A. Basile, "Lesbian Mothers I," *Women's Rights Law Reporter* 2, no. 2 (December 1974).

The first recorded lesbian mother case was *Nadler v. Superior Court Cal.* (1967). The mother lost on the grounds of her lesbianism at the trial level and upon appeal.

29. In re Matthews (California, 1975), reported by Donna J. Hitchens and Barbara E. Price, "Trial Strategy in Lesbian Mother Custody Cases," *Golden Gate Review* 9 (1979), 451–479.

30. In re Tammy F., I Civ. No. 32648 (Cal. 1st App. Dist., Div. 2, August 21, 1973). In re Deanna P., No. 10447-J (Sup. Ct. Sonoma Cty., July 12, 1973).

Ms. Driber and Ms. Koop, two lesbian mothers, were living together with their children. Ms. Driber was awarded custody of her three children. Ms. Koop, tried on the same day by a different judge, lost custody of two of her three children, although all three stated that they wanted to live with their mother. The other two were sent to live with their father, but when they ran away several times, Ms. Koop filed for custody, claiming that their behavior constituted a change in circumstance. The judge denied the request and ordered the children to be placed in a juvenile home when they said that they would not return to their father. They were later given into the custody of their married half-sister. The judge ultimately decided that the children should remain in the "neutral" home of the half-sister because it would not be in the children's "best interests" to live with their mother.

Driber v. Driber, No. 220748, Wash. Super. Ct., Pierce County (September 7, 1973), and In re Koop, nos. 28218 and 28219 (Wash. Superior Court, Pierce County, Juvenile Dept., February 6, 1976), cited in "Lesbian Mother Custody Cases," an unpublished paper by Robin G. Burdulis.

31. This California case is a "closed case." It was reported to me by San Francisco attorney Donna Hitchens, who was the director of the Lesbian Rights Project in 1983.

32. Ann Jones makes this point and presents many cases of battered women's mistreatment by the law. Also see Susan Schechter, *Women and Male Violence: The Visions and Struggles of the Battered Women's Movement* (Cambridge, MA: South End Press, 1982).

33. Jones, *Women Who Kill.*

34. Jones is quoting the first detective assigned to the case, "Jerry Piering, a Catholic father of six," one of the jurors, and many, many reporters.

For a good book on the Alice Crimmins case, see Kenneth Gross, *The Alice Crimmins Case* (New York: Knopf, 1975). See also People v. Crimmins, 33 A.D. 2d. 793 307 N.Y.S. 2d. 81 (1969); People v. Crimmins, 26 N.Y. 2d. 319, 310 N.Y. S. 2d. 300 (1970); People v. Crimmins, 41 A. D. 2d. 933, 343 N.Y.S. 2d. 203 (1973);

People v. Crimmins, 48 A.D. 2d. 663, 367 N.Y.S. 2d. 532 (1975); People v. Crimmins, 381 N.Y.S. 2d. 1, 343 N.E. 2d. 719 (1975).

35. Jones, *Women Who Kill.*
36. Ibid.
37. I quote from Euripides' *Medea*, in *The Complete Greek Tragedies*, trans. Rex Warner, introduction by Richard Lattimore (University of Chicago Press, 1955), as well as Robinson Jeffers's play, *Medea* (New York: Samuel French, 1948).
38. Here Medea embodies the patriarchal "good girl" who must leave her parents and her homeland, never to return, to live in her husband's house and bear her husband's children.
39. Marrying Creon's daughter Glauce confers Corinthian citizenship upon Jason. By renouncing Medea but asking her to stay on, he is "demoting" her to the position of hetaera—a legal prostitute/male companion. As such, Medea would have no rights whatsoever to dwell within the city without being "kept"—and complying with every whim of her "keeper."

    A legal prostitute cannot be employed anywhere, by anyone, for any reason; she cannot trade in the marketplace or take advantage of the considerable state benefits afforded to citizens. Jason's offer to make "some provisions" for a legal prostitute, or to keep her sons, is a reasonable offer by Greek ("civilized") standards. The offer outrages Medea.
40. Euripides, *Medea.*
41. In Jeffers's play, *Medea*, Medea refuses to let Jason bury her sons. She says, "You would betray even the little bodies: / coin them for silver. / Sell them for power."
42. Ibid. Euripides's *Medea* says,

    Let no one think me a weak one, feeble-spirited,
    A stay-at-home, but rather just the opposite,
    One who can hurt my enemies and help my friends;
    For the lives of such persons are most remembered.

43. Jeffers, *Medea.*
44. Ibid.
45. Euripides, *Medea.* If she does not kill her "enemies," then she is not the "barbarian" Medea but some other woman, a humbled Greek woman perhaps.
46. Jeffers, *Medea.*
47. Euripides, *Medea.*
48. According to Barbara G. Walker's quoting of Briffault and Herodotus, "Mycenaean Demeter made a god of the sacrificial victim Pelops by resurrecting him from her magic cauldron. The same regenerative magic was performed by Demeter's Colchian counterpart Medea, who came into Hellenic myth as a mortal queen, but who was an eponymous Crone Mother of the Medes. Her

name meant 'wisdom.' She was known as an all-healer; our word medicine descended from her." Barbara G. Walker, *The Crone: Woman of Age, Wisdom, and Power* (New York: Harper & Row, 1985).

49. Medea's murder of her brother (also her king-consort) constitutes the murder of a sacred blood tie. It is not a ceremonial murder. It is done for "love" of Jason, not as part of a preordained religious ritual. As such, it is a profound betrayal of Medea's own self, of her religion, family, and homeland. This betrayal dooms Medea.

50. Euripides first presented and won a prize for *Medea* in 431 BCE in Athens. His audience was long familiar with the figure and with the clash of cultures the play represents.

In classical Greece and Rome, fathers, not mothers, had the legal right to commit infanticide.

3. What Is a "Fit" Mother or Father?
An "Unfit" Mother or Father? Who Decides?

1. Judith Arcana, *Every Mother's Son* (New York: Doubleday-Anchor, 1983).
2. Ibid.
3. The biblical Abraham didn't ask his wife Sarah for permission to sacrifice their son Isaac. See my book *About Men* for a discussion of this in contemporary terms (New York: Simon & Schuster, 1978; Bantam, 1980; Harcourt Brace, 1989).
4. We forget that Oedipus's father, Laius, ordered his newborn son placed on a mountaintop to die. We do not remember Oedipus's mother, Jocasta, as the "good" mother who saved her son. We remember her as the "bad" mother who, many years later, married him. In the twentieth century, Laius was actually popularized, psychoanalytically, as his *son's* victim. Few experts theorized about the "Laiusian" complex among fathers.
5. Philippe Arriès, *Centuries of Childhood: A Social History of Family Life* (New York: Knopf, 1962); Badinter, *Mother Love*; David Bakan, *Slaughter of the Innocents: A Study of the Battered Child Phenomenon* (Boston: Beacon Press, 1971); Ruth H. Bloch, "American Feminine Ideals in Transition: The Rise of the Moral Mother, 1785–1815," *Feminist Studies* 4 (June 1978), and "Untangling the Roots of Modern Sex Roles," *Signs* 4 (Winter 1978); Cott and Pleck, eds., *Heritage*; Ann Dally, *Inventing Motherhood: The Consequences of an Ideal Childhood* (New York: Schocken Books, 1981); Carl Degler, *At Odds: Women and the Family in America from the Revolution to the Present* (New York: Oxford University Press, 1980); Lloyd de Mause, ed., *The History of Childhood* (New York: Harper & Row, 1974); John Demos, *Entertaining Satan* (New York: Oxford University Press, 1982); Alice Miller, *For Your Own Good: Hidden Cruelty in Child-Rearing*

and the Roots of Violence (New York: Farrar, Straus & Giroux, 1983); Morton Schatzman, *Soul Murder: Persecution in the Family* (New York: Random House, 1983); Abigail Stewart, David G. Winter, and David A. Jones, "Coding Categories for the Study of Child-Rearing from Historical Sources," *Journal of Interdisciplinary History* 5 (Spring 1975).

6. Miller, *For Your Own Good.*

7. Demos, *Entertaining Satan.*

8. Degler, *At Odds.*

9. Bloch, "American Feminine Ideals." Badinter suggests that too many children died in infancy, that colonialist European countries wanted their native populations to survive, and that mothers were viewed as crucial to this effort.

10. Jean-Jacques Rousseau as quoted by Badinter, *Mother Love.* Badinter also notes the economic and ideological advantages involved in persuading large numbers of women to concentrate on (unpaid) child care rather than on employment and single motherhood.

11. Dr. Daniel G. M. Schreber has been used as an example of an exceedingly popular and influential nineteenth-century scientific father whose harsh "regimes" probably led to his own son's insanity and, in psychoanalyst Wilhelm Reich's and Alice Miller's opinions, also led to the twentieth-century "obedience" of the German masses to charismatic fascism. See Badinter, *Mother Love*; Dally, *Inventing Motherhood*; and Schatzman, *Soul Murder.*

12. Dally reviews Schreber's twentieth-century English counterpart, Dr. Truby King. King recommended "a scheme of rigidly regular four-hour feedings. No baby was to be fed until the clock struck, no matter how much he cried. Most particularly, they were not to be fed at night. They had to learn to sleep at the proper times and not be allowed to manipulate and dominate their mothers by their demands. Regularity of bowel movements was important and he advised pot-training from the age of two months, aided by enemas if the baby did not perform."

13. Ibid. I have drawn on Dally's review of D. W. Winnicott, R. Spitz, and J. Bowlby.

14. Ibid. Dally notes that such beliefs made it unnecessary for the British government to provide tax-supported child care. Nor was private industry pressured to provide on-site child care or other benefits for its parent-employees.

15. In the late nineteenth century, the most "moral" of full-time middle-class wives and mothers were probably plagued by maternal guilt. In 1887 Charlena Anderson wrote to her husband that her

> daily round of household chores [was] overwhelming and difficult to organize. She recognized that a mother could not adequately care for the children and maintain a house at the same time. If only she had "relief from the time-consuming details of housekeeping," she wrote her husband in 1887, so that she might spend more time with the children. "Every

night when I go to bed my heart sinks at the thought of opportunities lost for drawing out some faculty or doing just a little toward it, for directing them into better habits, or for having some pleasant impressions upon minds." (Charlena Anderson [1887], quoted by Degler, *At Odds*.)

16. See Barbara Ehrenreich and Deidre English, *For Her Own Good* (New York: Doubleday-Anchor, 1978). The authors analyze the ultimately destructive influence exerted over mothers by nineteenth- and twentieth-century experts in obstetrics and gynecology. Tempting promises were made to mothers in this area also.

17. Donald Winnicott, quoted by Dally, *Inventing Motherhood*.

18. I am thinking about Sigmund Freud's Oedipal theory and its widespread acceptance by other experts and ordinary people (Sigmund Freud, *The Basic Writings of Sigmund Freud*, trans. and ed. A. A. Brill [New York: Modern Library, 1938], and *Moses and Monotheism* [New York: Random House Vintage Books, 1939]). See my book *About Men* and Judith Arcana's *Our Mothers' Daughters* (Oakland, CA: Shameless Hussy Press, 1980) for some interpretations of why Freud and so many other child development experts remained silent about—or denied—the existence of tyrannical, incestuous, or cruelly absent fathers.

19. Louise Armstrong, *The Home Front: Notes from the Family War Zone* (New York: McGraw-Hill, 1983); Judith Lewis Herman, *Father-Daughter Incest* (Cambridge, MA: Harvard University Press, 1981); Ann Jackowitz, "Anna O./ Bertha Peppenheim and Me," in *Between Women: Biographers, Novelists, Critics, Teachers, and Artists Write About Their Work on Women*, eds. Carol Ascher, Louise De Salvo, and Sara Ruddick (Boston: Beacon Press, 1984); Jeffrey Moussaieff Masson, *The Assault on Truth: Freud's Suppression of the Seduction Theory* (New York: Farrar, Straus & Giroux, 1984); Florence Rush, *The Best-Kept Secret: The Sexual Abuse of Children* (Englewood Cliffs, NJ: Prentice-Hall, 1980).

20. Compared to what? To past nonreports on child abuse? Child-abuse data are based on official reports, not on studies of incidence. Reports are not filed in each state equally, nor do they always indicate the severity and kind of abuse involved. Reports do not always indicate the abuser's sex, nor do they define "abuse" in psychologically complex ways.

21. Naomi Feigelson Chase, *A Child Is Being Beaten: Violence Against Children, an American Tragedy* (New York: Holt, Rinehart, & Winston, 1975).

22. Leontine Young, *Wednesday's Children: A Study of Child Neglect and Abuse* (New York: McGraw-Hill, 1964), cited by Chase, *A Child Is Being Beaten*.

23. Chase, *A Child Is Being Beaten*.

24. David G. Gil, ed., *Violence Against Children: Physical Child Abuse in the United States* (New York: AMS Press, 1978).

25. Gil's composite of "serious" child abusers, based on 6,110 cases, had the following characteristics: (1) were younger than twenty-five, (2) had appeared before

in family courts, (3) had been in foster care, (4) had an annual income of less than thirty-five hundred dollars, and/or (5) were single mothers.

26. Chase, *A Child Is Being Beaten.*

27. This study was done by Drs. Byron Egelund, Ellen Farber, et al. I did not read the study itself—only the newspaper coverage of the study. My point here was not to analyze the study's methodology but to rely on newspaper accounts, the way most people do, to draw certain emotional conclusions. If I have in any way misrepresented or drawn the wrong conclusions about this study, I apologize (*New York Times*, December 20, 1983).

28. If our state fathers pay attention to such a study, it is doubtful they will triple the welfare levels and expand support services to single mothers in order that they can "nurture" well.

    I interviewed ten unfit mothers for this chapter. Eight mothers called me in response to an ad for "mothers who were involved in custody battles." Some mothers responded to the ad because they wanted sympathy and advice on how to deal with state bureaucrats and relatives. Two mothers were referred to me by colleagues. Three mothers were black; one was Hispanic; six were white.

    Of the ten, 80 percent were teenage mothers; 60 percent were unwed; 80 percent were very poor. No mother was economically supported by her child's father or by her own parents. Most mothers were, in fact, *persecuted* by their own families and by the state when they were children and when they gave birth to children. Ninety percent of these mothers did not starve, beat, torture, abandon, or try to kill their child or children. They were, however, unable to provide emotional care and an adequate level of economic care. Two mothers (20 percent) were, in my clinical opinion, suffering from mental illness.

    Most of these mothers could, in my opinion, have been helped to assume more responsibility for their children. Certainly they could have maintained regular contact with them. This would have required massive infusions of emotional, economic, and educational support. This particular group of unfit mothers had no truly vicious or callously sadistic member. Another group might have such mothers.

    These unfit mothers did not present themselves as unjustly accused—only as unjustly punished. I would not want to be the child victim of any one of these mothers. However, they are unfit, not inhuman. They are not fire-breathing dragons.

29. In 1979 Lenore E. Walker (*The Battered Woman* [New York: Harper & Row, 1979]) estimated that 50 percent of all married women in America were or would be battered in marriage. In 1980 Drs. Murray A. Straus, Richard J. Gelles, and Suzanne K. Steinmetz (*Behind Closed Doors: Violence in the American Family* [New York: Doubleday-Anchor, 1980]) estimated a domestic violence rate of 50 to 60 percent based on a 28-percent *reported* rate. In 1980 Irene

Frieze ("Causes and Consequences of Marital Rape" [paper presented at the American Psychological Association meeting, Montreal, Canada, September 1980]) reported that 34 percent of geographically selected women reported "some marital violence."

In 1982 Dr. Diana E. H. Russell (*Rape in Marriage* [New York: Macmillan, 1982]) reported that "21 percent of her [randomly selected] 644 women who had ever been married reported being subjected to physical violence by a husband at some time in their lives." Dr. Russell explained the discrepancy between her own estimate and Dr. Frieze's estimate as a function of Frieze's "much broader definition of marital violence." She also noted that Walker's estimate was extrapolated from a battered female population.

In 1983 the National Center of Child Abuse and Neglect reported that "the number of women beaten yearly by their husbands ranges from two to six million." Of 18,000 incidents of domestic violence *reported* in 1983, women were the victims 86 percent of the time (*New York Times*, December 11, 1983). This study was based on reported cases in New Jersey from January to September 1983 (reported in the *New York Times*, October 5, 1983).

In 1984 Dr. Louie Andrews ("Family Violence in the Florida Panhandle," *Ms.* magazine [March 1984]) found that "one in six wives [surveyed] say their husbands force them to have intercourse against their wills. One in eight say their husbands physically abuse them or threaten them with weapons. One out of 23 wives surveyed were threatened with guns by their husbands. One in 66 had the guns actually fired at them." These findings are extrapolated from a survey of four hundred married women who *did not* fit the classic description of the isolated, abused wife. The incidence of wife battering and abuse may actually be higher among more isolated wives. The original survey was conducted by Drs. Louie Andrews and Diane Patrick.

30. Mildred D. Pagelow conducted a study of three hundred six battered mothers between 1976 and 1980. Of the mothers in her study, 76 percent reported that their children were present at the beatings. One-third of all the children were victims of parental violence as well; half of them were beaten in conjunction with their mothers, half of them separately. Mildred D. Pagelow, "Children in Violent Families," in *Young Children and Their Families,* eds. Shirley Hill and B. J. Barnes (Boston: Lexington Books, 1982). See also Mildred D. Pagelow, "Violence in Families: Is There an Intergenerational Transmission?" (paper prepared for a meeting of the Society for the Study of Social Problems, 1982).

A 1980 study of hyperactive and socially deviant boys reemphasizes the correlation between a child's disruptive behavior and wife or child abuse. The researchers found a high rate of psychiatric disorders among the fathers of boys who exhibited antisocial conduct. Boys who were unusually aggressive tended to have fathers who were alcoholic, antisocial, and physically abusive to their wives (Mark A. Steward, C. Susan DeBlois, and Claudette Cummings, "Psychiatric Disorder in the Parents of Hyperactive Boys and Those with Conduct Disorders," *Journal of Child Psychology and Psychiatry* 21 [1980]).

According to Elaine Hilberman's 1977 study of battered wives, "half of the women we studied reported violence between their parents (usually the father assaulting the mother)." Elaine Hilberman, "Overview: The Wife-Beater's Wife Reconsidered," *American Journal of Psychiatry* 137 (November 1980): 11.

31. See chapters 9 and 14. Armstrong, *The Home Front*; Kathleen Brady, *Kiss Daddy Goodnight: A Speak Out on Incest* (New York: Hawthorn, 1978); Herman, *Father-Daughter Incest*; Mary Haneman Lystad, "Sexual Abuse in the Home: A Review of the Literature," *International Journal of Family Psychiatry, 1982: The Urban and Social Change Review* 15, no. 2 (1982). U.S. Department of Health and Human Services, *Sexual Abuse of Children* (Washington, DC: Government Printing Office, 1980); Masson, *The Assault on Truth*; Rush, *The Best-Kept Secret*; William Stacey and Anson Shupe, *The Family Secret: Domestic Violence in America* (Boston: Beacon Press, 1983); Walker, *The Battered Woman*.

32. Russell, *Rape in Marriage*, and "Incest: An Unpublished Study of Incidence," 1983. Russell's random sample survey of women for her study of marital rape also asked about childhood sexual abuse. Her findings were published in 1986. (Personal communication, 1983.) Incest includes stepfathers within the home.

33. Dr. Mary Rimsza, quoted in the *New York Times* (April 4, 1984). It is unclear whether Rimsza is talking about incest plus a variety of other sexual crimes against children, committed by older brothers, uncles, schoolteachers, and others.

34. Dr. David Finkelhor, quoted in *Newsweek* (May 14, 1984).

35. David Finkelhor, "Current Information on the Nature and Scope of Child Sexual Abuse," *The Future of Children* 4, no. 2 (1994).

36. "Child Sexual Abuse," U.S. Department of Veterans Affairs website, accessed March 12, 2010, http://www.ptsd.va.gov/public/pages/child-sexual-abuse.asp.

37. Mothers sometimes "confess" to child abuse in order to keep the family intact or in the false belief that they will receive lighter sentences than men. When it is clear that a father has abused his child, church and state experts still wonder if the mother isn't "really" to blame—for marrying such a man in the first place, for allowing him to abuse his children, for not seeking help, and for not leaving him sooner.

When a mother flees a domestically violent father, she is immediately punished by the state's imposition of (welfare or minimum wage) poverty and then blamed for impoverishing her children.

38. Sara Ruddick, "Preservative Love and Military Destruction: Some Reflections on Mothering and Peace," in *Mothering: Essays in Feminist Theory*, ed. Joyce Treblicot (Totowa, NJ: Rowman and Allanheld, 1984).

39. Paul L. Adams, Judith R. Milner, and Nancy A. Schrepf, *Fatherless Children* (New York: John Wiley & Sons, 1984); N. D. Coletta, "The Impact of Divorce: Father Absence or Poverty?" *Journal of Divorce* 3, no. 1 (1979): 27–36; M. E. Lamb, ed., *The Role of the Father in Child Development* (New York: John Wiley & Sons, 1976); David B. Lynn, *The Father: His Role in Child Development* (Belmont, CA: Wadsworth, 1974); J. O. Wisdom, "The Role of the Father in the Minds of Parents, in Psychoanalytic Theory and in the Life of the Infant," *International Review of Psycho-Analysis* 3 (1976): 231–239; E. Herzog and C. E. Sudia, "Fatherless Homes: A Review of Research," *Children* 15, 5 (September-October 1968), 177–182.

40. Adams, Milner, and Schrepf, *Fatherless Children*.

41. Often these researchers have observed or studied what fathers experimentally (not actually) *do* with their children, what fathers *think* they do, and what fathers say they would *like* to do.

42. For reviews of this research, see Adams, Milner, and Schrepf, *Fatherless Children*; Grace Baruch and Rosalind Barnett, *Life Patterns* (New York: McGraw-Hill, 1983); S. W. Leonard, "How First Time Fathers Feel Toward Their Newborn," *American Journal of Maternal Child Nursing* (November-December 1976); Robert MacTurk, P. Nettelbladt, N. Uddenberg, and I. Englesson, "Father-Child Relationship: Background Factors in the Father," *Acta Psychiatrica Scandinavia* 61 (1980); Frank Pederson and Joseph Pleck, eds. *Men's New Roles in the Family: Housework and Child Care*, Institute for Social Research (1976); and V. Reiber, "Is the Nurturing Role Natural to Fathers?," *American Journal of Maternal Child Nursing* (December 1976).

43. One study estimated that fathers spent from 37.7 seconds to 10 minutes and 26 seconds daily with infants (F. Rebelsky and C. Hanks, "Fathers' Verbal Interaction with Infants in the First Three Months of Life," *Child Development* [1971]).

    Another 1974 study estimated that fathers spent between fifteen and twenty minutes a day with one-year-olds and sixteen minutes daily with children between the ages of six and sixteen (P. L. Ban and M. Lewis, "Mothers and Fathers, Girls and Boys: Attachment Behavior in the One-Year-Old," *Merrill-Palmer Quarterly* [July 1974]).

    A 1976 study found that fathers spent fifteen minutes a day feeding their babies, compared to mothers who spent one and a half hours a day doing so. Nearly half these fathers had never changed the baby's diapers (I. Rendina and J. D. Dickerschand, "Father Involvement with First-Born Infants," *Family Coordinator* [October 1976], cited by Letty Cottin Pogrebin, *Family Politics* [New York: McGraw-Hill, 1983]).

44. There are always exceptions to this rule. Such exceptional men are probably capable of doing many more domestic and infant-related chores than most men

currently perform. However, even exceptional men who perform 50 percent of all domestic and infant-rearing chores are not the same as mothers. They remain (socialized) men, who therefore experience the same things differently than (socialized) women do.

45. Adams, Milner, and Schrepf, *Fatherless Children*.

46. K. E. Walker, "Time Spent in Household Work by Homemakers," *Family Economic Review* (1969), and "Time Spent by Husbands in Household Work," *Family Economics Review* (1970); M. Meissner, et al., "No Exit for Wives: Sexual Division of Labor and the Cumulation of Household Demands," *Canadian Review of Sociology and Anthropology* 12 (1975); K. Walker and M. Woods, *Time Use: A Measure of Household Production of Family Goods and Services,* Center for the Family, American Home Economics Association (1976); J. Robinson, *How Americans Use Time: A Social Psychological Analysis* (New York: Praeger, 1977); S. F. Berk, ed., *Women and Household Labor* (Beverly Hills, CA: Sage, 1980), cited by Pogrebin, *Family Politics*.

47. Drs. Philip Blumstein and Pepper Schwartz, *American Couples* (New York: Morrow, 1983).

48. As I have noted, contemporary sons tend to remain silent about their fathers in public—*especially* if their fathers have been abusive. Many daughters who achieve public voices remember their fathers as far more encouraging and "maternal" than their mothers. It is hard for them—and for us—to remember that paternally nurtured daughters who become women of "male" achievement have been the exception and not the rule.

   Most mothers and fathers do not and cannot nurture their daughters or their sons into public intellectual achievement. This is usually a privilege of class—not of gender. It is also true that most mothers do not "like" daughters to achieve like men and do little to psychologically nurture them. Dr. Ann Oakley describes a fairly common twentieth-century "memory" of a patient "maternal" father and an angry "masculine" mother in *Taking It Like a Woman: A Personal History* (New York: Random House, 1984).

49. Please see what I've written about the destructive quality of the mother-daughter "bond" and about the lack of or circumscribed nature of maternal nurturance for daughters in *Women and Madness*; in *Women, Money and Power* (New York: William Morrow, 1976); in *With Child* (New York: Lippincott-Crowell, 1979); and in the latest edition of *Woman's Inhumanity to Woman* (Chicago: Lawrence Hill Books, 2009). Please see what I've written about the mother-son bond in *About Men* (New York: Simon & Schuster, 1978).

50. Drs. Joseph Goldstein, Anna Freud, and Albert J. Solnit, *Beyond the Best Interests of the Child,* new edition with epilogue (New York: Macmillan, The Free Press, 1979). They note that

children may also be deeply attached to parents with impoverished or unstable personalities . . . where the tie is to adults who are "unfit" as parents, unbroken closeness to them, especially identification with them, may cease to be a benefit and become a threat. In extreme cases this necessitates state interference. . . . [However,] whatever beneficial qualities a psychological parent may be lacking, he offers the child the chance to become a wanted and needed member within a family structure; ordinarily this cannot happen even in the institutions where care, safety and stimulation may be provided, but where the individual child has no psychological parents.

51. Miller, *For Your Own Good.*
52. See chapter 4 for this list. More than one and a half years after I chose these chores, the Supreme Court in West Virginia chose the performance of such "chores" as the way to "identify" the primary and psychological parent in a custody contest. See chapter 14 for a discussion of the 1981 West Virginia case known as *Garska v. McCoy.*

4. Do "Good Enough" Mothers Still Lose Custody of Their Children in North America Today?

1. It is hard to chart an "increase" in a previously unstudied area. The following studies all attempt to do so in different ways, for different reasons, using different kinds of basic materials, and with different degrees of methodological success. From one point of view, Lenore J. Weitzman and Ruth B. Dixon have published the most comprehensive and methodologically generalizable study to date (Lenore J. Weitzman and Ruth B. Dixon, "The Economics of Divorce," *UCLA Law Review* 28 [1981]).

   From another point of view, Nancy D. Polikoff has published the most comprehensive analysis of case law. Polikoff's article is an excellent description of anti-mother judicial trends in contested custody, based on case law (Polikoff, "Gender and Child-Custody Determinations").

   From yet another point of view are three separate studies by psychologists from which we can *infer* some kind of increase in paternal custody. The studies were done by Dr. Deborah Anna Luepnitz, *Child Custody: A Study of Families After Divorce* (Lexington, MA: Lexington Books–D.C. Heath, 1982); Patricia Pascowicz, *Absentee Mothers* (Totowa, NJ: Allanheld Universe, 1982); and James R. Turner, "Divorced Fathers Who Win Contested Custody of Their Children: An Exploratory Study," *American Journal of Orthopsychiatry* 54, no. 3 (July 1984). I read this last study long after I completed my own. In Turner's words, his study is "preliminary" and not "statistically significant." As we shall see, I think his two major motivational patterns among fathers are true, although my interpretation of what a "close" relationship with a child means to such fathers may not be as "positive" as Turner's is.

A number of other studies also exist regarding an increase in paternal custody when custody is contested. Each is limited methodologically or to a specific geographical region. Based on a study of one New York judge's custodial decisions over a five-year period during the 1970s, in sixty to seventy cases Michael Wheeler found an increase in paternal custody (M. L. Wheeler, *Divided Children: A Legal Guide for Divorcing Parents* [New York: Norton, 1980]). Betty Blair reported an increase in judicial paternal custody decisions in Michigan between 1972 and 1974—this increase was based on the recommendations made by court referees to judges in three Michigan counties (Betty Blair, *Detroit News*, March 16, 1976). Dennis K. Orthner and Ken Lewis suggested an increase in judicial paternal custody in Minnesota based on a survey (Dennis K. Orthner and Ken Lewis, "Evidence of Single Father Competence in Child Rearing," *Family Law Quarterly* 8 [1970]). M. Ricke, quoted by Blair, reported an increase in paternal custody judicially in the state of Washington, based on a study of three counties, between 1972 and 1974. The Legal Aid Society of Alameda County, California, reported that of thirteen contested custodial trials in 1979, five (38 percent) resulted in paternal custody (Adele Hendrickson, attorney, Family Law Unit, Oakland, California).

Since the mid-1970s, lawyers have *observed* (rather than studied) an increase in the number of divorcing fathers who threaten, fight, and win custody battles in court. For example, attorneys Laurie Woods and Joanne Schulman of the National Center for Women and Family Law; Nancy Polikoff of the Women's Legal Defense Fund in Washington, D.C.; and Donna Hitchens of what was then the Lesbian Rights Project (now the National Center for Lesbian Rights) in San Francisco, California, have observed such an increase in general and among domestically violent fathers in particular. Fathers' rights lawyers, such as Edward Winter Jr., Maurice K. Franks, and Ken Lewis, have also observed such an increase.

2. Weitzman and Dixon, "The Economics of Divorce." This study found that 33 percent of the fathers who fought for custody in 1968 and 37 percent of the fathers who fought for custody in 1972 won custody. This is the most comprehensive and methodologically generalizable study done to date.

3. Ibid., 1181, 1245; Ruth Sanders, "Child Support and Alimony," U.S. Bureau of Census, 1983; Nan D. Hunter, "Women and Child Support," in *Families, Politics and Public Policy: A Feminist Dialogue on Women and the State*, Irene Diamond, ed. (New York: Longman, 1983).

4. Polikoff, "Why Are Mothers Losing?" and "Gender and Child-Custody Determinations."

5. Group for the Advancement of Psychiatry, *Divorce, Child Custody and the Family* (New York: Mental Health Materials Center, 1980). This work estimates that, as of 1976, a half million fathers had custody of their children.

   Weitzman and Dixon, "The Economics of Divorce," estimate that thirty thousand fathers won sole custody and ten thousand fathers won joint custody each year in the United States.

   Patricia Hoff of the American Bar Association Section of Family Law, quoted in the *New York Times*, January 20, 1981.

6. Privately coerced "agreements" to paternal custody remain statistically unstudied. Several researchers, in passing, do note that "more" mothers seem to be "agreeing" to paternal custody.

7. Gil, *Violence Against Children*. In 1984 Republican Senator Arlen Specter of Pennsylvania also estimated that one hundred thousand cases a year are parental kidnappings. Specter was then the chairman of the Senate Subcommittee on Juvenile Justice.

8. Richard J. Gelles, "Parental Child Snatching: A Preliminary Estimate of the National Incidence," *Journal of Marriage and the Family* (August 1984): 735. Gelles did not analyze these data as a function of parental gender. In personal communication, he noted that the majority of parental child kidnappings were "probably" carried out by fathers.

9. I am using Weitzman and Dixon's extrapolated estimate of 40,000 cases of paternal custody *each year* beginning in 1977 as a stable and continuous (rather than an increasing) number. I am also arbitrarily using a paternal kidnapping rate of 200,000 each year—less than Gelles's estimate of 459,000 to 751,000 but more than Gill's estimate of 100,000 to 125,000 annually.

10. Imprisoned mothers, most of whom are women of color, always lose their children when they are arrested.

11. M. Hetherington, M. Cos, and R. Cox, "Divorcing Fathers," *Family Coordinator* (October 1976), and M. Hetherington, et al., "Play and Social Interaction in Children Following Divorce," *Journal of Social Issues* 35, 4 (1979): 26–49; Deborah Luepnitz, "Children of Divorce: A Review of the Psychological Literature," *Law and Human Behavior* 2 (1978): 167–179; Judith Wallerstein and Joan Kelly, *Surviving the Breakup: How Children and Parents Cope with Divorce* (New York: Basic Books, 1980).

12. Kelen Gersick, "Father by Choice: Divorced Men Who Received Custody of Their Children," in *Divorce and Separation*, eds. G. Levinger and O. Moles (New York: Basic Books, 1979); K. Rosenthal and H. Keshet, *Fathers Without Partners* (Totowa, NJ: Rowman and Littlefield, 1981); Judith Greif, "Fathers, Children and Joint Custody," *American Journal of Orthopsychiatry* (1979): 311–319; M.

Roman and W. Haddad, *The Disposable Parent* (New York: Holt, Rinehart & Winston, 1978).

13. Luepnitz, *Child Custody.*

14. Pascowicz, *Absentee Mothers.* Sixty-one percent of her mothers were "intimidated" or coerced by their husbands, physically, psychologically, and/or economically. (They lost outright in court, were rejected by their children, or were economically impoverished. Four percent were forced to relinquish custody by their second husbands.)

15. Turner, "Divorced Fathers."

16. I am purposely concentrating on parents rather than on children in this particular study.

17. Twenty mothers had such materials.

18. Each mother had from one to five children; each marriage lasted from two to twenty years. At the time of our interviews, these mothers ranged in age from twenty-one to sixty.

19. Maternal education ranged from noncompleted high school to completed graduate and medical school.

20. As noted in *Women, Money and Power*, "Unlike businessmen, wives and mothers cannot convert skills and time into experience that 'counts' in some (other) job—nor can they convert their labor into liquid capital. Mothers are not automatically promoted to other positions after they have completed the job of child raising. ('Dropping out' of the job market to have children usually means a permanent crippling of direct moneymaking capabilities.)" Phyllis Chesler and Emily Jane Goodman, *Women, Money and Power* (New York: Morrow, 1976; Bantam, 1978).

21. This list is similar to what the Supreme Court of West Virginia specified as the tasks of a primary caregiver in 1981. See chapter 13. This list does not include what a wife does for a husband. For example, mothers also wrote checks, balanced the checkbook, and budgeted money. They listened to their husbands' problems; they shopped, cooked, and cleaned for their husbands and guests. A number of mothers also worked as bookkeepers, secretaries, nurses, and receptionists in their husbands' offices.

22. Accurate information about fathering was hard to elicit. Traditional mothers are not used to evaluating men in terms of child care. They are not used to saying "bad" things—not even about ex-husbands. Mothers found it difficult to describe what their ex-husbands did, exactly, in terms of child care, without fearing they were being "unfair" or "biased."

23. Jules Henry, *Culture Against Men* (New York: Random House, 1965), describes the American phenomenon of the father as an "imp of fun," who, instead of allowing the children to share his activities, shares the children's. Some Peer-Buddies also involved children in adult activities.

24. I independently interviewed nine additional Smother-Fathers. See chapter 8 for a discussion of this. All Smother-Fathers in this study won custody—despite the fact that a strong judicial bias presumably exists against fathers competing with mothers for the "maternal" role.

25. Only 15 percent of the heterosexual mothers—compared to 52 percent of the heterosexual fathers—remarried or had a grandmother or a live-in lover who was willing to provide child care. Unfortunately a mother's heterosexual remarriage didn't always work to her custodial advantage. A lesbian's remarrying never worked to maternal custodial advantage.

26. Once they won custody, an almost equal number of fathers moved away without being prevented from doing so.

27. Barbara Bode, "Background Facts on Child Support Enforcement" (Washington, DC: Children's Foundation, 1982). Also see Nan D. Hunter, "Women and Child Support," in *Families, Politics and Public Policy: A Feminist Dialogue on Women and the State*, Irene Diamond, ed. (New York: Longman, 1983).

   In 1984 the Internal Revenue Service published the results of its "experiment" to attach unpaid child support payments from *tax refunds* due the fathers. It discontinued this approach after it was clear that such targeted fathers then refused to comply with filing their income tax returns (David Burnham, "Diverting Refund to Child Support Raises Tax Cheating, Study Finds," *New York Times*, June 7, 1984).

   In 1985 a study subsidized by the Social Security Administration and the Federal Office of Child Support Enforcement was published. According to *New York Times* reporter Andree Brooks,

   > "One of our most shocking findings," said Dr. Ron Haskins, Associate Director of the Bush Institute, "was that middle-class fathers feel at greater liberty not to pay a substantial amount either because the courts never insisted or the collection agencies never took their family situations seriously. . . . Census figures show that the average male wage earner made $24,120 in 1984." . . .

   > The study found that a national formula was only a partial answer. Dr. Haskins, commenting on the much-discussed problem of delinquency in payments, said that in his own view if these fathers were going to pay their fair share the amount should be withheld from the father's paycheck from the start, instead of waiting for him to fall behind in payments.

   > The study suggested that middle-income fathers should provide more support for the custodial mother in nontraditional ways, such as setting aside a night or two a week to babysit (if they live nearby) or helping her get special job training.

Low-income noncustodial fathers, the study found, seem to be far more involved in the daily lives of their children and the mother than most middle-income absentee fathers. (Andree Brooks, *New York Times*, February 22, 1985.)

28. Sanders, "Child Support and Alimony." The economic vulnerability and degradation of American mothers and children is truly shocking. Everyone "knows" that stay-at-home mothers are unsalaried, receive no social security or pensions for housework or mothering, and are horrendously underpaid by state welfare departments. Everyone also knows that salaried fathers earn at least twice as much as salaried mothers.

5. The "Sexual" Mother

1. When husbands are impotent or sexually inept and insist on marital celibacy, it is wives whom they blame. When a father who wants custody is sexually celibate, he is seen as "pure" rather than as "disturbed." Celibacy presumably entails more suffering for a man than a woman.
2. Leo Tolstoy, *Anna Karenina*, trans. Rosemary Edmund (New York: Penguin, 1979).

6. The "Uppity" Mother

1. In 1983 Leslie Silko, the poet and writer who was one of only a few women awarded a grant from the MacArthur Foundation, said, "I paid and paid and paid in my personal life for not being more conventional. The very qualities that got me the award made me lose custody of my younger son. Society makes it real hard for a woman to excel in the ways rewarded by the MacArthur Foundation" (quoted in the *Village Voice*, December 7, 1983).

7. The Lesbian Mother

1. Ellen Lewin, "Lesbianism and Motherhood: Implications for Child Custody," *Human Organization* 40, no. 1 (1980).
2. Martha Kirkpatrick, "Lesbian Mother Families," *Psychiatric Annals* 12, no. 9 (September 1982); Mildred I. Pagelow, "Heterosexual and Lesbian Single Mothers: A Comparison of Problems, Coping and Solutions," *Journal of Homosexuality* 5, no. 3 (Spring 1980). Lesbian and nonlesbian mothers differ in this way: The nonlesbian mothers have a greater desire to remarry. Otherwise, lesbian and nonlesbian mothers seem to have similar childhoods and parenting histories and similar attitudes toward marriage, divorce, sex roles, and sex education.

See my book *Women and Madness* for a discussion of the psychological similarities between heterosexual and lesbian women in general.

3. Perhaps single men do not want to be responsible for another man's children and do not want to live through a prolonged custody battle. Perhaps lesbian mothers and lesbian nonmothers are more interested in creating or supporting a woman-centered family life than heterosexual men are.

4. Homosexual fathers are also custodially persecuted. However, they are rarely the primary parents that lesbian mothers are. If they *are*, judges see that as doubly "abnormal." If they're *not*, their claim to children is often seen as nonexistent. Homosexual fathers face overwhelming judicial fears about homosexual paternal incest from the same judges who deny the existence of far more widespread paternal incest on the part of heterosexual fathers.

5. This belief holds fast despite the overwhelming reality that most lesbians and homosexuals come from heterosexual families and despite expert observations that the children of lesbian and homosexual parents tend to become heterosexual. See Richard Green, "Children of Homosexuals Seem Headed Straight," *Psychology Today* (November 1978); Richard Green, "Sexual Identity of 37 Children Raised by Homosexual or Transsexual Parents," *American Journal Psychology* 692 (1978); Martha Kirkpatrick, MD, Ronald Roy, MD, and Catherine Smith, "A New Look at Lesbian Mothers," *Human Behavior* 5, no. 8 (August 1976).

6. Townsend v. Townsend, I Fam. L. Rep. p. 2830, Ohio Court Common Pleas (October 21, 1975), cited in *Mom's Apple Pie*, the Lesbian Mothers National Defense Fund Newsletter (June 1975).

Larraine Townsend lost custody of her three children in March 1975. In this newsletter, the tone of judicial disgust is very clear.

> Judge Albert Carais, a retired judge who heard the case by special assignment, said that if Larraine had indicated that she would abandon Lesbianism while the children were young, "the court might have been tempted to experiment" with giving her custody. He said that there was no doubt that Larraine and Vicky "intend to continue the relationship they began. They intend to live together. They intend to engage in Lesbianism. . . . I would think for the sake of the children, a Lesbian would abandon the practice. . . . Orgasm means more to them than children or anything else."
>
> Larraine was denied custody because her Lesbianism was "clearly to the neglect of supervision of the children" (no apparent nexus), the father was denied custody because he ignored the children for ten months and, at one point, attempted suicide in the mother's presence.

The children were instead awarded to the 65 year old paternal grand-mother, who neither asked for the children nor testified in court. (Cited by Burdulis, "Lesbian Mother Custody Cases.")

In *Spence v. Durham*, a lesbian mother was allowed to keep her child on the grounds that she was no longer involved in lesbian activity; in *Mitchell v. Mitchell*, a California court allowed a lesbian mother to keep her child on the condition that she not associate with her lover (both cited by E. Carrington Boggan, Marilyn G. Haft, Charles Lister, and John P. Rupp, in *The Rights of Gay People* [Toronto: Clarke, Irwin & Co., 1975]).

In 1981 a custodially embattled lesbian mother was judicially castigated for *acting* on her lesbian impulses. If she would control herself and give up her lover, the court said, it "would" or "might" allow her to keep her children. This mother didn't lose her children because she was a lesbian—but because she *behaved* like a lesbian. Jacobson v. Jacobson, 314 N.W. 2d 78, 8 *FLR* 2154, N.D. (1981).

7. Nearly a third of the lesbian mothers were married to men who tried to bully them into bed with another woman. Lesbian sexual activity is a popular porno-graphic theme. The reasons for this are complex and may also involve hetero-sexual women's "prurient" interest in other women. Please see my book *About Men* for a discussion of pornography.

8. They may project this self-hatred outward—and condemn it in other lesbians and homosexuals.

9. See chapters 7, 10, and 11 for Cecily's story.

8. The Mother Married to a Violent Man

1. Mothers also harbor equally intense and murderous feelings toward their ex-husbands. However, they hide or minimize such feelings—even to themselves. I don't think mothers are allowed to express such emotions. Fathers are.

2. Nora Ephron, in her novel *Heartburn* (New York: Knopf, 1982), describes a potentially smothering father in a bitterly humorous way: "[He's the kind of man] who goes through the whole business [of pregnancy and childbirth] under the delusion that it's as much his experience as it is yours. All this starts in Lamaze classes, where your husband ends up thinking he's pregnant, and let me tell you he's not. It's not his body, it's not his labor, it's not his pain—it's yours, and does any man give you credit or respect for it? No. They're too busy getting in on the act, holding their stop watches and telling you when to breathe and when to push. . . . Beware of men who cry. It's true that men who cry are sensitive to and in touch with their feelings, but the only feelings they tend to be sensitive to and in touch with are their own."

3. I asked Beth to listen to my taped interview with Eric. Here are some of her comments:

> Eric reminds me of Simon. They are both desperate to have their kids constantly engaged with them. By not setting any rules, limits, structures for his kids, Eric forces them to stay engaged with him at all times. Daddy says, "I'll let you stay up late"—which really means "I don't want to let go of you and experience the emptiness"—"if you promise not to be tired in the morning."
>
> Eric doesn't let his kids learn to control themselves or to tolerate frustration because if they were self-controlling, self-generating people, then he could not be all-controlling and all-central. It really does make Eric crazy (irrational, impulsive, out of control, emotionally violent) if he's separated from them. All this has less to do with the welfare of his children and more to do with his needing them to supply the missing center of his own life. In order to "have" his kids—hell, even hurt them—by separating them from their mother totally, by keeping them up late, by letting them eat junk food, by kidnapping them.
>
> Eric puts his ex-wife down because she wants an adult "private" life. He says she's cold and uncaring because she sets limits and provides structure. Eric is worse than the "clutchiest" of mothers. His poor kids! He thinks that playing with them is a form of child care. His kids already know that they have to stay attached to Daddy to keep Daddy from falling apart. If Daddy falls apart, so will they.

4. In my study, daughters were either unimportant, less important, or important only as "cute little mothers." Smother-Fathers (with one exception) did not seem to encourage their daughters to achieve anything beyond domestic subservience. For example, according to Catherine, her husband "Thomas prefers the boys to the girl. I feel he sees me in my daughter and mistrusts her. She tries very hard to please him. She baked him a cake for Christmas. He never thanked her for it. He didn't give her a Christmas present. But Thomas refuses to cover her tuition if she switches colleges to live closer to me."

According to Miki, "My daughter treats her father just like I used to. She agrees with him, flatters him, keeps her eyes down a lot. He treats her like he treated me: as stubborn, but stupid. Maybe she's also learned to behave in self-demeaning ways by watching me do it. She certainly doesn't identify with me as a woman or an abused wife. Maybe she thinks she can escape her father's violence if she completely gives me up and tries very hard to please him."

Maureen battled against her children's brainwashing. She said, "My sons have never seen any physical warmth between their father and mother. Now that we're battling, all they see is physical violence: kidnapping, beating, banging on doors. They see him beating me down economically too. How will my sons relate to women? Like their father related to me?"

5. See chapter 13 for a more extensive discussion of how judges handle incestuous fathers. During the course of writing the first edition of this book, I interviewed three additional mothers after I had closed my study, each of whom lost custody of her daughter to an incestuous father. All three were recommended by psychiatrists who had interviewed them and their daughters. One of these mothers said, "My daughter is six. I think she's going crazy. I'm allowed to see her every other weekend. I don't know which of us is in worse shape. I've exhausted all my economic resources. By the time I begin another legal action, my daughter will be permanently destroyed. How can one trust a legal system that would do this in the first place?"

6. In my core population (chapter 4) both custodial and noncustodial fathers and mothers "legally" and "illegally" kidnapped or rekidnapped children. I have counted all such incidents. With one exception, the custodial fathers who "legally" kidnapped their children did so before the divorce was final. Like noncustodial or "illegal" paternal kidnappers, they took children on "sprees," cutting all contact with their ex-wives. Twelve percent of the noncustodial mothers and 23 percent of the noncustodial fathers kidnapped their children. In general, half the paternal kidnappings were "legal"; half were not. See chapter 13 for an additional discussion of parental kidnapping.

7. Judges take fathers' accusations of maternal interference with parental visitation far more seriously than they take similar accusations by mothers. Also, fathers are less frightened by maternal threats than mothers are of paternal threats to sue or kidnap.

Judges did economically penalize mothers for presumably interfering with paternal *visitation*. For example, Sally was perpetually victimized by her ex-husband's lateness. After two years of having all her plans disrupted by his late arrivals or returns, she "put her foot down." When he arrived two hours late, Sally told him to wait an hour until the family finished dinner. She said, "He had a screaming episode. He hurled rocks at my window. He went to court and actually got a judge to fine me five hundred dollars for holding the children for three hours when they judicially belonged to him. I was devastated." Please see chapter 13 for similar examples.

8. In the 1981 Australian film *Smash Palace*, we see a kidnapper-father unable to emotionally handle his daughter's sudden fever without panicking and becoming enraged. Jack Olson, *Have You Seen My Son* (New York: Atheneum, 1982);

Joy Fielding, *Kiss Mommy Goodbye* (New York: Doubleday, 1981); Bonnie Lee Black, *Somewhere Child* (New York: Viking Press, 1981); and Norma Fox Mazer, *Taking Terri Mueller* (New York: Avon Books, 1981) all describe the "spree" phenomenon, the paternal refusal to talk about the mother left behind, the paternal lying about a mother's "being dead" or not "loving" the kidnapped child anyway, and the paternal phenomenon of exaggerated domestic and emotional dependence on a kidnapped child, coupled with paranoia about the rest of the world.

9. See John Edward Gill, *Stolen Children: How and Why Parents Kidnap Their Kids—and What to Do About It* (New York: Seaview Books, 1981).

10. Ibid. Gill cites the case of a kidnapped, brainwashed, and apprehended child who was unwilling to be taken back. This girl was taken by her father when she was three. When she was recovered, she was about five. She'd grown to know her father's girlfriend as her mother and when the natural mother confronted her, she didn't know what to think. She'd been calling the girlfriend "Mommy."

> "It took her a few days to realize and remember who her mother was. She was told her natural mother had died in an automobile accident and that she would now have the girlfriend as her mother. The child accepted this." How did she adjust? "'It took her grandmother,' Cerone said. 'Her father had never said anything about her grandmother, so she knew she could trust her grandmother. It was sad. When she was first recovered, she called for "Mommy" but it was for her surrogate mother. . . .' 'A man in Tennessee told his girls their mother didn't love them and didn't want them. We've had a lot of them say the other parent is dead. That's *much* more damaging than an actual recovery.'"

11. See chapter 13 for a discussion of this.

12. This information is based on a private detective's report. The investigation turned up correspondence between Johnson and various fathers' rights activists around the country. One activist offered Johnson the babysitting services of his second wife if Johnson would help him kidnap his children. I read the photocopied correspondence at the National Center for Women and Family Law in 1981 and 1982.

13. Demeter, *Legal Kidnapping*.

14. One maternal kidnapper rekidnapped her child back from Europe. Her husband was psychiatrically imprisoned by his own family and died shortly thereafter. No one from the family ever pursued her. One maternal kidnapper who lost custody and was prevented from all access to her children, both physically and psychologically, kidnapped them in 1970 when they were ten and twelve years old. She was never pursued or found.

15. Rachel's husband did find her with the assistance of the FBI—in the mid-1970s, before the FBI was legally empowered to do this.

9. Paternal Brainwashing

1. Dr. John C. Clark, Dr. Stanley H. Cath, Dr. Robert Jay Lifton, and Dr. Margaret T. Singer all have studied brainwashing in prisoner-of-war camps and/or among cults.
2. Chesler, *About Men.*
3. Arcana, *Every Mother's Son.*
4. Gill, *Stolen Children.* Please see chapter 21 for a discussion of mother rejection as a function of paternal alienation and kidnapping. Also in my own study and in this chapter, there are many examples of kidnapped children rejecting their mothers. Thirty-seven percent of all battling fathers in my study kidnapped their children. Sixty-two percent were physically abusive to the mothers of their children.
5. Demeter, *Legal Kidnapping.*
6. It is important to note that *none* of these economically forceful fathers engaged in long-term or "spree"-like kidnappings. Only two of these fathers engaged in short-term-kidnapping skirmishes. Four fathers physically prevented maternal visitation by legally moving far away after obtaining courtroom custody.
7. One previously absent and economically superior father allowed himself to be used by his daughter against her mother—although he didn't really want her. Ida said,

> Bernie left us when Kim was five. He never visited. Sometimes, he called or sent a gift. When Kim turned eight, *she* began to use Bernie's existence as a weapon against me. She threatened to move out whenever I wanted her to clean her room. Bernie would tell her "that he'd buy her clothes and let her do whatever she wanted."
>
> When Kim was ten, she insisted on spending the summer with Bernie and his wife. I had to secretly beg him to take her. When Kim returned she was real unhappy about how we lived compared to how her father lived. She kept asking about why we split up. I tried to explain about his violence. "If he's so violent, why does his other wife stay with him?" Kim is fourteen now. I think she'll go back and forth between us in her mind, comparing us, putting me into competition with Bernie for a long time.
>
> I can't say he's brainwashed her. It's a cultural setup. All Bernie had to do was have a penis and keep his distance.

8. Gill, *Stolen Children*, quotes a mother whose children were "indoctrinated" against her: "'You could call it brainwashing, I guess,' the mother, Elena Hoffman, thirty-one, said. 'It wasn't anything you could notice directly. But every now or then my son would say something like, "Mommy likes her work more than me," or "Why do you have to use the typewriter when I'm here?" I think he'd been taught to say that by his father, who worked on a ranch and lived with a woman who stayed home,' [Hoffman] said. 'In fact, my son even complained once that I wasn't doing enough housework. He'd found dirty dishes in the sink.'"

9. Paternal grandmothers made up 39 percent of all mother competitors.

10. One of these Smother-Fathers was also assisted by a virulent paternal grandmother for a limited period of time.

11. A number of autobiographies and biographies describe the competitive role of paternal grandmothers. For example, Black, *Somewhere Child*, describes the paternal grandmother who assisted her husband in kidnapping and initially brainwashing their daughter:

> "Let me teach you how to cook," Jim's mother said soon after I moved in.
>
> "Thank you," I said, as tactfully as I could, "but I already know how. I've been cooking for my family since my mother went back to work when I was eleven." I didn't add that I'd been studying cookbooks religiously for years. She seemed insulted. "Well, Jimmy likes things done a certain way. *My way.*" She showed me how she prepared asparagus, "one of Jimmy's favorites," by boiling it in a large potful of water for twenty minutes, then pouring all the water down the drain, burning some butter in a frying pan until it was black, stirring in some breadcrumbs, and pouring this all over the platter of soggy spears.
>
> "I think I would do it a little differently," I said after she finished her demonstration.
>
> She left the kitchen then without a word, but when Jim came home from work she complained to him that I was "pigheaded," "ungrateful," "insolent," and "stubborn."

12. Barbara Goldsmith, *Little Gloria . . . Happy at Last* (New York: Knopf, 1980), describes a maternal grandmother, paternal aunt, and maternally hired governess who fought a widowed mother for custody. Mother Gloria's own fortune-seeking mother, the maternal grandmother, testified that her daughter pursued a "gay life" and treated her granddaughter "like an orphan." Gertrude Whitney, the paternal aunt, said she was appalled at little Gloria's "terror" of her own mother. Gertrude Whitney won custody. Goldsmith wrote,

"[A lawyer] told several associates that Gertrude Whitney was everything she accused Gloria of being: she loved to travel and had left her children for months at a time while she pursued her own life; she was extravagant, she liked to drink alcohol, she'd had many lovers and there were rumors of lesbian relationships. But there were essential differences which protected Gertrude Whitney: Gloria led her life in print while Gertrude's was shrouded in a secrecy purchased by her vast wealth. And at twenty-nine, Gloria could not disguise her sexuality while Gertrude at fifty-nine seemed the quintessential conservative, austere widow."

13. Mary Zenorini Silverzweig, *The Other Mother* (New York: Harper & Row, 1982). Mary uses everyone's real name in her account of this brainwashing and custody battle—except for the biological mother.

14. I also tried to interview Mary and Stanley Silverzweig, but the interview never worked out. I felt I knew more than I wanted to know once Mary's book was published. After our interview, Roberta agreed to joint custody of her two youngest daughters on the eve of her third or fourth separate court date. Her eldest daughter still refused to see her.

15. Goldsmith, *Little Gloria*, depicts a child who is terrified of her mother, a child who physically runs away from her mother screaming "I hate you . . . don't kill me" and who cannot identify her mother's photograph in court and claims she never loved her anyway.

Goldsmith theorizes that little Gloria's Nurse Keislish (along with others) somehow convinced her charge that her mother would kidnap her—just like the Lindbergh child. According to Goldsmith, two physicians examined little Gloria. They concluded that she had "been poisoned against her mother." Their testimony didn't persuade the judge to remove little Gloria from those who had "poisoned" her.

In 1985 Gloria Vanderbilt published *Once Upon A Time: A True Story* (New York: Knopf, 1985). She describes how she was coerced into the "game" of betraying her mother. Despite this and the fact that Gloria's mother led a socialite's life, Gloria still needed, longed for, and romanticized her socially and legally absent but psychologically present mother. She describes maternal visitation after the custody trial in this way:

Then Aunt Gertrude said something in her graceful way, and—to my horror—my mother reached out to take my hand. I was torn apart not knowing what it meant or what exactly was going on or what I was supposed to do. No one had ever said this might happen—no one ever said that my mother might reach over and take my hand into the beauty of hers. I left my hand there, dumped on the cushion, as if it were a dead thing. I kept staring at Aunt Gertrude's hat, holding my eyes onto it, as if something about it would tell me something and give me a clue as to what I should do and what to expect next. But no answer came.

So there we all sat . . . my mother, on the other side, her veiled beauty now turned from me. I sat in the middle, half wanting to throw myself into her arms, half wanting to yank my hand away from hers so fast and hard that it would tear her soft fingers off into mine—for then she would belong to me forever!

16. Gill, *Stolen Children.*
17. Glenn Collins, "The Psychology of the Cult Experience," *New York Times,* March 15, 1982. Dr. Clark and Dr. Stanley Cath are based in Boston. They have treated former members of the Unification Church, the International Society for Krishna Consciousness, Scientology, the Way International, The Divine Light Mission, the Children of God, the Church of Bible-Understanding, and others.
18. These letters were long, single spaced, and handwritten in a very neat script. I read five such letters. Similar letters arrived weekly for at least a year.

10. The "Voluntarily" Noncustodial Mother

1. Charlotte Perkins Gilman, *The Living Charlotte Perkins Gilman: An Autobiography* (New York: Arno, 1972). In 1892 Gilman wrote a story entitled "The Unnatural Mother." The fictional mother is condemned for her willingness to sacrifice her child's life in order to save an entire community. The child and the villagers survive. The mother and her husband die. After her death, the mother is still condemned as "unnatural."
2. Ibid. Gilman's story has a happy ending. In her old age, when she was ill and dying, her daughter and her co-mother, Grace Channing, came together to nurse her and love her in California.
3. "Self-realization" included leaving an abusive marriage; accepting a meaningful job, often in another city, state, or country; continuing to work at an artistic career; or "giving up" the losing battle of single motherhood with still existing career ambitions. Pascowicz, *Absentee Mothers,* first used the term *self-realization* to describe one of the motives involved in maternal noncustodial status.
4. I interviewed ten noncustodial fathers who had never battled for custody. I found them through newspaper ads and through professional and personal referrals.
5. Luepnitz, *Child Custody,* found that sole (and joint) custodial fathers were "very welcome at school functions" and were treated as "heroes" for being able to work and simultaneously raise a child.

6. Alice Walker's heroine Meridian, in the novel of the same name, does locate herself historically. Her historical perspective only leads to more guilt and a greater sense of deviance.

> Meridian knew that enslaved women had been made miserable by the sale of their children, that they had laid down their lives, gladly, for their children, that the daughters of these enslaved women had thought their greatest blessing from "Freedom" was that it meant they could keep their children. And what had Meridian Hill done with *her* precious child? She had given him away. She thought of her mother as being worthy of this maternal history, and of herself as belonging to an unworthy minority, for which there was no precedent and of which she was, as far as she knew, the only member. (Alice Walker, *Meridian* [New York: Harcourt Brace Jovanovich, 1976].)

7. Some fathers like to integrate themselves into their teenage sons' activities as a way of "rebelling" against mothers. See previous chapters for a discussion of the "Imp of Fun," Peer-Buddy, and Smother-Father styles of parenting.

8. For those fathers who did not wish to remarry or who did not wish to "share" their children with a *woman*, such "help" was perceived as a potential problem. My point is that fathers had this option; mothers did not.

9. There are exceptions to this rule. Some mothers were "helped" by boyfriends or second husbands. Some fathers were unable to get anyone to "take over" for them. I interviewed only *one* blue-collar widower who single-handedly reared his six-year-old twins after their mother's death. He didn't remarry. He rarely dated. He started bringing his children to work with him when necessary. Ultimately, he insisted on working part-time.

10. Luepnitz, *Child Custody*.

11. This is not necessarily my view of all fathers, nor are all fathers deserving of this view. It is, however, one of the major unspoken reasons that noncustodial mothers are instinctively condemned. See what I have written on the subject of father-child violence in *About Men* and in other chapters of this book.

12. Pascowicz, *Absentee Mothers*.

13. Pascowicz, *Absentee Mothers*, notes that "married life is best enjoyed by the childfree; studies indicate that the most content people are married couples with no children. This supports [her] assertion that a portion of the anger displayed toward absentee mothers results from repressed resentment among custodial parents that they must bear the burdens of childrearing while absentee mothers go free."

11. The Price of Battle

1. The Bull of Innocent VIII, reprinted in Heinrich Kramer and Jacobus Sprenger *Malleus Maleficarum*, trans. Montague Summers (London: Arrow Books, 1928).
2. Miki and Nora are discussed in chapter 6; Adele is discussed in chapter 9.
3. For example, Catherine, Lucy, and Josie are discussed in chapter 5; Ella Mae, Jessie, Miki, and Nora in chapter 6; Rachel in chapter 8; and Carrie and Marta in chapter 12. Nora is also discussed in chapters 2 and 8.
4. See chapters 8 and 13.
5. Please see my book *Women and Madness* for a discussion of this. Also note my discussion of the study that demonstrated that clinical experts routinely perceive normal women as "unhealthy" adults (Inge Broverman et al., "Sex Role Stereotypes and Clinical Judgments of Mental Health," *Journal of Consulting and Clinical Psychology* 34, [1970]).
6. Elizabeth Packard is discussed in chapter 1 and in *Women and Madness*. Nora is discussed in chapters 2 and 6.
7. Demeter, *Legal Kidnapping*.
8. See chapter 13 for a discussion of Brigette and Arlene. Neither mother is part of my formal group.
9. See chapter 13 for a discussion of Brigette. Also see Armstrong, *The Home Front*, and Sarah Begus and Pamela Armstrong, "Daddy's Right," in *Families, Politics and Public Policy*, for a fuller discussion of the role of experts in blaming the mother for paternal incest.
10. Armstrong, *The Home Front*, noted, "It is more, not less, serious to do severe harm to those toward whom you stand in a relationship of trust—than to do similar harm to a stranger."
11. For a long time, such mothers behave like incestuously abused children who can't name what is happening to them. When they do, they aren't believed. They sometimes don't believe themselves. All female victims of paternal domestic violence become self-destructive (and blame their mothers) more readily than they blame their fathers or become "other" destructive.
12. Sonia Johnson, *From Housewife to Heretic* (New York: Doubleday-Anchor, 1982), describes a confrontation with her husband, Rick:

> Back at his office, [Rick] asked me calmly, in a detached sort of way, which two of our four children I wanted to keep.... There in his office, his face an expressionless mask, he pointed out coolly that the agreement I had signed (!) divvied up the kids equally between us, and that he wouldn't mind getting me in court (*and here his voice got ugly, and*

I saw such astonishing hatred in his face I felt faint), because if he ever did, he would show me a thing or two. He would make me wish I had kept quietly to our "agreement."

13. Black, *Somewhere Child.*
14. Gill, *Stolen Children*, has many examples of how woman friends betray or are not supportive to the mother of a paternally kidnapped child.
15. Of the fathers, 44 percent of those with high incomes, 7 percent of those with midrange incomes, and none of those with low incomes paid alimony. See table 2, page 77.
16. See chapter 4.
17. See chapter 21 for a discussion of maternal heroism and nonviolence under siege.
18. We may remember that Anna Karenina was profoundly "indifferent" to her newborn daughter. Being without her son, she knew how easily she could lose her daughter. Karenina's way of "denying" or "expressing" this blow to her body consisted of drug addiction and, ultimately, suicide.
19. Pascowicz, *Absentee Mothers*, finds that this was most pronounced among mothers who lost custody in court and then among those who were physically or financially "intimidated" into relinquishing custody.

    Pascowicz notes that forty of her one hundred respondents (40 percent) led "happy well adjusted lives" after becoming noncustodial mothers. "Not that they have not experienced sadness . . . but they coped [with it] with or without support."
20. It is psychologically dangerous to "gloss over" a genuine loss. Jane Brody, in the *New York Times*, January 17, 1984, summarized the research on victims done by Dr. Linda S. Perlofl; Dr. Ronnie Janoff-Bulman and Dr. Irene Hanson Frieze; Dr. Shelley E. Taylor; and Dr. Camille B. Wortman. Brody notes that "sometimes, victims may adopt a falsely optimistic attitude solely for social reasons, since a person who continually bemoans his fate is not likely to be popular with other people. But while keeping one's emotional distress within manageable limits may be seen as a sign of a good adjustment, letting out one's feelings of deep distress appears more therapeutic. Thus, taking the disaster 'very well' may be thwarting recovery."
21. Of the (smaller number of) lesbian mothers, 71 percent cohabited with mates during or immediately after their custody loss—compared to 17 percent of the heterosexual mothers.
22. Pascowicz, *Absentee Mothers*, also found that more husbands than wives remarried after a custody struggle—and that they did so more rapidly. Pascowicz found that 9 percent of her maternal respondents and 20 percent of their ex-husbands remarried within a year, and 50 percent of her mothers eventually remarried.

It is important to note that my maternal population all reported battling against their will. Pascowicz claims that 40 percent of her population either "wanted" or "accepted" custody losses because of emotional incapacity or creative ambitions.

23. It is important to remember that nearly half—twenty-nine fathers—did not reproduce or did not say they would. One of these fathers died, and one father's subsequent reproductive activity is unknown—inasmuch as he disappeared with his child.

24. Of the fertile, custodially "triumphant" fathers, 33 percent genetically reproduced themselves again, and 14 percent said they still wanted to have children. Of the "winning" fathers, 12 percent were infertile or had infertile wives; 12 percent were Smother-Fathers.

25. Remember, we are talking about a small number of fathers—eighteen to be exact, 13 percent of whom had infertility problems and of whom 13 percent were Smother-Fathers.

26. Forty-three (72 percent) of the mothers were still of childbearing age when they ended their initial fights for custody. They were between the ages of twenty-one and thirty-nine. I interviewed these mothers anywhere from two to seventeen years after they had fought for custody. Eighteen (40 percent) lost custody two to five years prior to the interview; eighteen (40 percent) lost custody six to ten years prior to the interview. Seven mothers (16 percent) lost custody eleven to fourteen years prior to the interview; two (4 percent) lost custody fifteen to seventeen years prior to the interview. Seventeen mothers (28 percent) were forty or more at the end of their initial fight. Their ages ranged from forty to forty-eight. They did not view themselves as capable of biological reproduction.

27. Pascowicz, *Absentee Mothers*, notes that 50 percent of these mothers said they had made a conscious "decision" not to have any more children. Eighty-five percent had none. Again, it is important to note that her population is somewhat different from mine. Forty percent of her interviewees did not lose custody legally or through violent intimidation.

28. Alice Walker's heroine Meridian, in the novel *Meridian*, gives her child up for adoption "with a light heart" because she wants him—and herself—to live and have good lives. "But she had not anticipated the nightmares that began to trouble her sleep. Nightmares of the child, Rundi, calling to her, crying, suffering unbearable deprivations because she was not there, yet she knew it was just the opposite: Because she was not there he needn't worry, ever, about being deprived. Of his life, for instance. She felt deeply that what she'd done was the only thing, and was right, but that did not seem to matter. On some deeper level than she had anticipated or had even been aware of, she felt condemned, consigned to penitence, for life."

12. The Mother-Lawyer Relationship

1. Of the forty-three mothers who retained lawyers, thirty-eight were able or willing to describe or "rate" their lawyers afterward. Altogether ten women lawyers and twenty-eight male lawyers were described or rated. Some mothers hired more than one lawyer. I counted a mother's description of only one lawyer: either the one she had the strongest feelings about, whether they were positive or negative, or her last lawyer.

2. In terms of lawyers' sexism, in 1979 Weitzman and Dixon, "The Economics of Divorce," studied the conditions under which the "maternal preference" broke down. They asked lawyers to predict the factors that influence judges in custody battles. Lawyers ranked maternal "sexual promiscuity" as the third most important factor after maternal physical and psychological neglect of children. They didn't mention fathers' "sexual promiscuity" at all. This may be a measure of lawyers' accurate perception of judicial sexism. It may also be a measure of lawyers' preordained complicity with such sexism.

3. See chapter 13 for a discussion of this.

4. Luepnitz, *Child Custody*.

5. This was true at the time of publication of the first edition of *Mothers on Trial*. However, poor people were and still are entitled to "free" counsel if they are accused of murder, rape, robbery, and other crimes.

6. There are exceptions to this rule. However, in a woman- and mother-hating culture and a man- and father-idealizing culture, few people are absolutely "equal" in their pro-mother and pro-father sentiments or are genuinely capable of treating their clients equally, regardless of gender. For a variety of reasons, this is true of feminist, nonfeminist, and anti-feminist lawyers.

7. Luepnitz, *Child Custody*.

8. Eleanor Kuykendall, "Breaking the Double Binds," *Language and Style* 13 (1980).

9. Nontraditional or too-assertive female clients have another kind of "problem" with male or female lawyers.

10. Sharon is not officially part of the study reported in chapter 4.

11. How different are these expectations from those held by nineteenth-century judges in England and America, who custodially condemned wives who were unwilling to forgive their husbands' past cruelties or unwilling to drop their divorce action as "un-Christian," as proof that they were no longer the Victorian angel at home?

13. The Mother-Judge and Father-Judge Relationships

1. See Polikoff, "Gender and Child-Custody Determinations," for a description of what is available and/or accessible to the public.

2. Seventy-eight percent of the women lawyers reported that they were "treated disadvantageously" by judges in the courtroom because of their sex. House-wives involved in personal-injury suits received smaller awards because these awards are "unfairly skewed" to earning potential, and homemakers are unpaid for their labor. Divorced women are forced into "deepening cycles of poverty" because of awards of insufficient child and spousal support—which is not even enforced. Police, judges, and probation officers all failed to enforce New Jersey's 1982 Prevention of Domestic Violence Act, aimed at wife beating.

   This study was commissioned by New Jersey Chief Justice Robert N. Wilentz and coordinated by Attorney Lynn Hecht Schafran, chair of the National Judicial Education Program to Promote Equality for Women and Men in the Courts. (This program is a project of the National Organization for Women's Legal Defense and Education Fund.)

3. *Off Our Backs* (May 1982).

4. See chapters 1 and 2. Also see Mary Dunlap, "Toward a Recognition of a Right to Be Sexual," *Women's Rights Law Reporter* 7, no. 3 (Spring 1982). She gives several examples of rulings against female sexuality, including the case of a sixty-seven-year-old woman being ejected from her nursing home in 1979 because of her sexual activity (Wagner v. Sheltz, Connecticut [1979]). Mary Dunlap, "Where the Person Ends, Does the Government Begin? An Explora-tion of Present Controversies Concerning the 'Right to Privacy,'" *Lincoln Law Review* 12, no. 47 (1981): 54–63.

5. According to Judge Rena K. Uviller,

   > Unfortunately, the "best interest of the child" formulation, while high-toned and well intended, is devoid of substance. A "child's best interest" comprises any and all of the deciding judge's child rearing prejudices. These may range from the need for religious training to the respective virtues and pitfalls of permissiveness and authority. A "child's best interests" may involve a judicial preference for living in the country as opposed to the city, as in *Shaw v. Shaw*, where the court noted disapprovingly that the mother lives "in an apartment complex" whereas the father lives "in a rural community with an environment of the minor child concerned." (Rena K. Uviller, "Father's Rights and Feminism: The Maternal Presumption Revisited," *Harvard Women's Law Journal* 1, 1 [1978]: 107–130.)

6. In the *People v. Sinclair* (95 N.Y. Supp 861 [1905]), a five-year-old boy was awarded to his mother when he was three. Two years later, the judge considered him "old enough" to do without his mother and "ready for paternal custody."

In *Jenkins v. Jenkins* (173 Wis. 592, 181 NW 826 [1921]), a mother was awarded custody of her three-year-old. He was still judicially considered "tender." However, on appeal, the judge decided that the mother could not retain custody of her "older" sons, who were five and eight.

In *Butler v. Butler* (222 Alabama 684 [1931]), the judge determined that "older children, even if they were forcibly prevented from remaining with [their] mother, are now happily adjusted in the household of two paternal aunts. They can remain there. A four-year-old girl, however, still needs her mother."

In *Tuter v. Tuter* (Springfield Court of Appeals, Missouri 120 S.W. [October 2, 1938]), a judge decided that "older children can remain with [their] father in [an] environment hostile to mother, but that the younger child must be returned to mother."

7. Interviews with Lillian Kozak, then chair of the Committee on Domestic Relations for NOW–New York State, 1981–1984.

8. Women are rarely rewarded for "following orders." Their reward consists of avoiding the punishment meted out to women who "disobey orders." I noted this in 1976 in *Women, Money and Power*.

9. Kersten Salk v. Lee Salk, 393 NY 2nd 841 (October 28, 1975). Even though Dr. Salk had a very busy career, the court "[considered] it more important to ascertain the quality, rather than the quantity of time a parent devotes to his or her children, in determining the best interest of the child."

10. Kersten Salk, unpublished paper, 1976.

11. Polikoff is commenting on *Neis v. Neis*, 599 P. 2d 305 (Kan., App. 1979).

12. Van Dyke v. Van Dyke, 48 Or. App. 965, 618, P. 2d, 465 (1980). Commented on by Nancy Polikoff, "Why Are Mothers Losing?"

13. Polikoff, "Gender and Child-Custody Determinations," commenting on *Porter v. Porter*, 274 N.W. 2d 235 (N. D. 1979).

14. Garska v. McCoy, 278 S.E. 2nd 357, 361 W. Va. (1981). The case itself concerns Gwendolyn McCoy, a young unwed mother who, at the age of fifteen, was impregnated by her mother's boarder, Michael Garska. Garska did not see or support McCoy after the birth of Jonathan. In order for Jonathan to become eligible for medical coverage, his grandparents agreed to adopt him. At this point, Garska began sending fifteen dollars a week and moved for custody.

The trial level court which awarded Garska sole custody found that he "is more intelligent than the natural mother," is "better able to provide financial support and maintenance than the natural mother," "has a somewhat better command of the English language than the natural mother," and "has a better appearance and demeanor than the natural mother."

The Supreme Court reversed this decision. Nancy Polikoff (in "Gender and Child-Custody Determinations") notes that this case "developed a standard which preserves sex neutrality, encourages paternal involvement in child rearing, and guarantees that the child's bond with the parent providing daily care and nurturance will be maintained." Unfortunately, this "primary caretaker" presumption may apply only to young children. Once a child is "older," custody determination may not have to take past primary care into account.

15. Communication to the now-dissolved National Center for Women and Family Law.

16. In re Herbert A.D. v. Charlene D., reported in *New York Law Journal* (September 3, 1981).

17. Ibid. In 1983 in California, a custodial mother's "interference" with paternal visitation was "proper grounds for change of custody" (In re Wood, 9 *FLR* 2414; Cal. Ct. App. 5th Dist. [April 15, 1983]).

18. Ledsome v. Ledsome, 51 LW 2591, 9 *FLR* 2331 (West Virginia Ct. of App., August 11, 1983).

19. Joye v. Schechter, 460 NYS 2d 992, 9 FLR 2384 (New York Family Ct., April 15, 1983). Note that this judge holds the *mother* responsible for both implementing a court order and for persuading her child to "love" her father.

20. Daghir v. Daghir, 441 N.Y.S. 2d494 (N.Y. App. Div., 2d Dept., 1981); N.Y. 439 N.E. 2nd 324. Frances Daghir Coughlin's appeal of this decision was also unsuccessful.

21. Some judges have allowed mothers to move away. For example, see Auge v. Auge, 61 L.W. 2768 Minn. Sup. Ct., (June 30, 1983); Klein v. Klein 93 A. D. 2d 807, 460 N.Y.S. 2d 607, *FLR* 2049 (April 4, 1983). These are exceptions to the rule.

22. Louden v. Olpin, App. 173 Cal. Rptr. 447 (May 14, 1981; June 24, 1981).

23. Thomas Grubiscich, "Unwed Father Wins Custody of Daughter," *Washington Post*, August 13, 1980.

24. Ibid.

25. See Schechter, *Women and Male Violence*.

26. Armstrong, *The Home Front*.

27. Schechter, *Women and Male Violence*.

28. Ibid.

29. Harriet Berne fled Rochester, New York, with her two sons. Family judge Bruce Wettman ordered eleven-year-old Scott Berne and his seven-year-old brother to return from Texas to their father, who had been awarded custody of the boys after the divorce. The boys wanted to live with their mother. Ms. Berne was so distraught by losing her sons that she attempted suicide shortly after her sons were removed. (*Family Law Reporter* [Summer 1981].)

In December 1980, the Federal Parental Kidnapping Prevention Act was signed into law.

30. It is my initial impression, which was gained through the National Center for Women and Family Law, that Mimi "J." preferred that her case not be publicized by name. I honored her request. There was, however, media coverage of her case in the Washington-based feminist newspaper *Off Our Backs*. The name of the judge is known.

31. This information is contained in Brigette's unpublished "Chronology of Events."

32. The mental health profession has to date or until very recently been resistant to take reports of incest seriously or *blame* the fathers for it. They tend to blame the mothers for paternal incest. In 1984 Dr. Deborah Luepnitz, a researcher and child analyst who worked with me on sections of this book, suddenly shared the following information with me:

> Before 1983 and our work together, I never "noticed" how the mothers of paternal incest victims were scapegoated in family therapy and in incest therapy. I remember a recent case I was involved in, in which a mother lost custody of her daughter when the mother's boyfriend was jailed for raping a woman. The 16-year-old daughter was then placed in the custody of her natural father, a "respectable" Naval officer. In the course of therapy, it was discovered that the natural father had sexually molested the girl several years beforehand.
>
> The father said he felt "badly" about what had happened, but "relieved" that they were finally discussing it and that "it's all taken care of now." He proceeded to request that the girl come and live with him—although the daughter stated that he was still fondling her as recently as last year.
>
> Meanwhile, the mother is targeted from every side. The attitude of professionals and counselors is, "Imagine what kind of *mother* that woman must be! First she marries a child molester, and then her boyfriend is a rapist!"

33. The report was prepared by Arlene White with the assistance of many involved professionals and groups. It was on file with the now-dissolved National Center for Women and Family Law.

34. I knew that when adult women reported incestuous assaults they were disbelieved or viewed as neurotic or psychotic. Mental health experts have accused female victims of "imagining" paternal sexual molestation, of "seducing" their fathers, and of secretly "wanting" (what never happened) to happen anyway.

    I knew that female victims were usually blamed for their victimization. I didn't know that incestuous fathers, with the help of psychiatrists, psychologists, and judges, were actually getting custody of their daughters.

Feminist researchers and writers such as Louise Armstrong, Kathleen Brady, Judith Herman, Florence Rush, and Diana Russell—to name only a few—have been writing about this since the early 1970s. A scandal erupted when Jeffrey Moussaieff Masson in *The Assault on Truth* added his voice to this growing body of literature.

35. Tom Vesey, "Claims Children Are Molested. Mother Defies Custody Terms," *Washington Post*, March 24, 1984.

36. Armstrong, *The Home Front*.

14. Court-Enabled Incest in the 1980s and 1990s

1. Beginning in 1993, or several years after Linda's case, this lawyer was reproved in public for "having failed to perform legal services competently"; in 1996 she failed an exam; in 1997 she "failed to comply with Rule #955; in addition, she was cited for having failed to pay bar membership fees, for failing to notify the pertinent parties that she had been suspended, for failing to file a required affidavit with the Supreme Court; and for also violating a condition of her probation—which finally led to her disbarment."

17. The International Custody Situation

1. Two anonymous informants from the Fingo and Mtoko tribes. Quoted by Kate McCalman, "We Carry a Heavy Load: Report of a Survey Carried Out by the Zimbabwe Women's Bureau," December 1981, distributed by the United Nations.

2. Liang Heng and Judith Shapiro, *Son of the Revolution* (New York: Alfred A. Knopf, 1983).

3. Alec Samuels, "*Kramer vs. Kramer* in England," *Solicitor's Journal* 125 (July 10, 1981): 470.

4. For example, Samuels, "*Kramer vs. Kramer*," describes *Owen v. Owen* (1974), 4 *Family Law* 13; *B. v. B.* (1975), 119 *Sol. Journal* 610; *Hutchinson v. Hutchinson* (1978), 8 *Family Law* 140; and *T. v. T.* (1974).

5. Dr. Martin Richards, "Post-Divorce Arrangements for Children: A Psychological Perspective" (unpublished paper, 1981). Richards, in personal communication (1983), confirmed that there is enormous prejudice against lesbian and homosexual parents and that more mothers are "agreeing" to paternal custody than in the past. Like most researchers in America, Richards failed to take into account that most mothers who "agree" to paternal custody have essentially been forced into it. He did note that the vast majority of custody battles are fought by relatively wealthy parents who can afford both the initial trial and a series of appeals.

6. Norma Steele, quoted in *Gay News,* London, January 26, 1978. Steele is a member of Black Women for Wages for Housework, a London-based group. An extraordinary film made in the 1960s, *Tears for Cathy*, depicts how the English welfare state drives a white father away from his family, denies housing and employment to the abandoned mother and children, and then takes the children away from their impoverished and state-debilitated mother.

7. "Judge Orders Boy, 11, to Live with Father He Hates and Hasn't Seen for Four Years," *The Daily Mail,* January 24, 2010, accessed March 11, 2010, http://www .dailymail.co.uk/news/article-1245603/Judge-orders-boy-11-live-father-hates -seen-years.html.

8. Christopher L. Blakesley, "Child Custody and Parental Authority in France and Louisiana," *Boston College International and Comparative Law Review* 4, no. 2 (Fall 1981), stated, "Notwithstanding the de facto maternal preference that developed, the concept of 'paternal power' continued to have an impact under the [Napoleonic] Code, as the father maintained his power of control over the children, even when the court did not award custody to him."

    As Blakesley shows, mothers in northern and western Europe may retain custody of their children, unless they are judged "morally" or "maternally" unfit— that is, adulterous; sexually active after divorce; a lesbian; relatively impoverished; a "career" woman; an atheist; "unstable;" alcoholic; or mentally ill.

9. I met Ellen Cahill at a feminist conference in Salzburg, Austria. We corresponded, and she answered my questions about custody for many European countries, especially France, Holland, and Ireland. Cahill ran a consulting agency, "Les Resources," in Bordeaux, France.

10. Dallemagne v. Dallemagne (In re D.D.), 440 F. Supp. 2d 1283 (M.D. Fla., 2006).

11. In an interview given to the Canadian journalist Jacqueline Schwartz.

12. Haris Livas, "Breaking the Mold: An Interview with Margaret Papandreou," *Ana: Athens News Agency* 62 (March 28, 1983).

    According to the revised Greek civil code, mutual agreement between husband and wife has legally supplanted a man's traditional right to rule his family legally. However, alimony and child support are not automatic or fixed. The Synergazomena Gynekia Somatia (Common Front of Women's Associations) has been organizing to protect both the lives and the rights of divorcing women. The Synergazomena proposed that in some situations, divorced women should receive a percentage of their ex-husbands' pension or another form of compensation. My respondent, Ellen J. Cahill, gave me this information.

13. Virginia Visani, who lives in Milan, Italy, provided me with several examples of "notorious" custody battles in Italy. For example, a ten-year-old girl had been living with her mother for five years, from the time her parents separated. The separation agreement contained a clause allowing the mother and daughter to

keep living in the marital home in Salerno. The mother could no longer afford the rent and moved to a cheaper apartment in a nearby village. In 1981 the father demanded that the girl be turned over to him. The girl threatened to kill herself if she had to leave her mother. After many exhausting meetings, the girl was finally allowed to remain with her mother.

14. Cecilia Onfelt writes, edits a feminist magazine, and works in a shelter for battered women. I interviewed her in New York. She also responded to my questions about custody.

15. Ann Manager, "Custody for Unwed Father," *San Francisco Chronicle,* May 25, 1980.

16. Joshua Rhett Miller, "Custody Battle Keeps Arizona Mom and Daughter Stuck in Bahrain," Fox News, June 16, 2010.

17. United States v. Amer, 1998 U.S. App. LEXIS 22299 (2d Cir. N.Y., March 26, 1998).

18. Betty Mahmoody, *Not Without My Daughter* (New York: St. Martin's, 1988).

19. Nadine Claire is an Algerian feminist who was interviewed by the English feminist magazine *Trouble and Strife.* The interview was reprinted in *Off Our Backs,* March 1985.

20. Under Communist totalitarianism, women as *mothers* have no special place. Women as *workers* are at best, part of middle management. According to Roxanne Witke, the biographer of Chiang-Ch'ing, Mao's imprisoned widow, and member of the infamous "Gang of Four," Chiang-Ch'ing's real crime was having too much power—for a woman. Her misuse of power is another matter. She also supported the entrance of too many other women into visible positions in "middle management" (Roxanne Witke, personal interview).

21. Liang's mother "said that her Section Head sometimes used crude language and liked to criticize people, that he should give his housekeeper a bed to sleep on instead of making her sleep on the floor, and that sometimes when it came time to give raises, the leaders didn't listen to the masses' opinions" (Liang Heng and Judith Shapiro, *Son of the Revolution* [New York: Knopf, 1983]).

22. Ibid. According to Amanda Bennett in the *Wall Street Journal* on July 6, 1983, and Bernard Nossiter in the *New York Times* on July 23, 1983, the Chinese state attempted to limit population growth by punishing premarital or extramarital sex, by legalizing abortion and contraception, and by encouraging "late" marriage. By the mid-1970s, the state had to restrict every legally married couple to only one child. The results were an increase in female infanticide.

    The Chinese government did not deny the problem and was in fact attempting to grapple with it. On July 23, 1983, despite some protest, the United Nations Fund for Population Activities awarded China and India joint prizes for their family planning programs.

23. I first met Dr. Kiyomi Kawano in Copenhagen in 1980. She is a Japanese-born and Tokyo-based feminist psychotherapist and the translator of *Women and Madness* into Japanese.

24. Keiko's "case" was reported in Diana Russell and Nicole Van de Ven, eds., *Crimes Against Women: Proceedings of the International Tribunal* (Millbrae, California: Les Femmes, 1976); new edition with introduction by Charlotte Bunch (Millbrae, California: Frog in the Well, 1984).

25. Lynn Bennett, "Tradition and Change in the Legal Status of Nepalese Women," in *The Status of Women in Nepal* 1, part 2 (New York: United Nations, 1978). According to Bennett, Nepalese mothers are entitled to custody of children under the age of five. Mothers may retain custody of children until they are sixteen if they do not remarry—and if the father doesn't want custody.

26. Daniel Haile, "Law and the Status of Women in Ethiopia" (Addis Ababa, Ethiopia: African Training and Research Centre for Women, 1980).

27. Dr. J. O. Debo Akande, "Law and the Status of Women in Nigeria" (Nigeria: Economic Commission for Africa, African Training Center for Women, 1979).

    In *The Joys of Motherhood*, Nigerian novelist Buchi Emecheta dramatizes the effects of modernization on her rural hero, Nnu Ego. Her husband has taken another wife; he has also refused to give her any money to feed their children. (Buchi Emecheta, *The Joys of Motherhood* [New York: George Braziller, 1979].)

28. Greene, interview with the author.

29. *Mozambique: Women, the Law and Agrarian Reform* (New York: United Nations, 1980). This report noted that "women's productive and reproductive potential, at least in patrilineal societies, was [controlled and] regulated by the practice of brideprice. Once brideprice was paid by the husband's to the wife's lineage, all children born of the union belonged to the husband's lineage, whether or not he was the biological father. When brideprice was not given or was only partially paid, the children belonged to the lineage of the mother's father. Since the husband's family had bought both the woman's services and her fertility, she was from that date onward expected to obey and serve her husband's lineage."

30. Ibid.

31. Luisa Valenzuela is the author of *Strange Things Happen Here* (New York: Harcourt Brace Jovanovich, 1979). She also noted that "children who were born in jail to tortured mothers were given to unknown people. Some children left behind when their parents were arrested, were put in parks. Sometimes they'd be wearing a sign: 'I'm a Lost Child. Take me with you.' Children were given away at airports. Some were simply taken by military officials who needed to adopt."

32. Dr. Saffieti, a Brazilian sociologist, responded to my specific queries about custody.

33. Greene, interview with the author.
34. Catherine Mallon, "Joshua Williams Memorial Essay 1973: A Critical Examination of Judicial Interpretation of a Child's Best Interest in Inter-Parental Custody Disputes in New Zealand," *Otago Law Review* 3 (August 1974): 191–204.
35. It is important to note that some mothers do *have privileges*—not rights—as a function of their national, family, and class origin, as well as their race, skin color, caste, and good fortune.

18. The Fathers' Supremacist Movement from the 1980s to 2010

1. Charles Metz, *Divorce and Custody for Men* (New York: Doubleday, 1968).
2. George Gilder, *Sexual Suicide* (New York: Quadrangle, 1973).
3. Daniel Amneus, *Back to Patriarchy* (New York: Arlington House, 1979). Amneus and Metz both are cited by Polikoff, "Gender and Child-Custody Determinations" and "Why Are Mothers Losing?"
4. William K. Stevens, "A Congress of Men Asks Equality for Both Sexes," *New York Times*, June 15, 1981. The NCM also "resolved" to "extend sexual equality to men and women."
5. John Rossler, president, and Dr. Robert Fay, consultant, Equal Rights for Fatherhood, New York State. *Contributions of the Homemaker*, organization pamphlet (October 21, 1981). I have chosen one of several propositions fashioned by Dr. Fay and endorsed by Rossler for the organization.
6. This suit was ultimately denied. Similar class-action lawsuits on behalf of fathers have been attempted before and since in at least ten American states. Equal Rights for Fathers of Alaska v. Superior Court Judges, U.S. District Court, No. A82-008 CIV, reported in 8 FLR 2702 (February 9, 1982).
7. Gerald A. Silver and Myrna Silver, *Weekend Fathers* (Los Angeles: Stratford Press, 1981).
8. Maurice K. Franks, *Winning Custody: A No-Holds-Barred Guide for Fathers* (Englewood Cliffs, NJ: Prentice-Hall, 1983). Maurice Franks's book is accompanied by a lawyer-geared brochure outlining seventy-five "special custody-winning strategies to enable you to handle the ever-increasing demand for child custody by fathers."
9. As reprinted in *Marriage and Divorce Today* 9 (September 12, 1983): 6. The NCM "resolved" that children must be assured of "frequent and continuing contact" with both parents and that the Federal Parental Kidnapping Act should be enforced regardless of the custodial status of the parent's sex. It also "resolved" to "support all efforts to replace the adversarial system of custody litigation by a system of mediation; to 'support' the education of fathers in birth and parenting and [the] increased participation by fathers in their children's lives."

10. Susan Dominus, "The Fathers' Crusade," *New York Times Magazine*, May 8, 2005, accessed March 15, 2010, http://www.nytimes.com/2005/05/08/magazine /08FATHERS.html?pagewanted=all.

11. Dominus, "The Fathers' Crusade."

12. Kathryn Joyce, "Men's Rights Groups Have Become Frighteningly Effective," *Slate*, November 5, 2009, accessed March 15, 2010, http://www.doublex.com /section/news-politics/mens-rights-groups-have-become-frighteningly-effective.

13. Joyce, "Men's Rights Groups."

14. Richard Collier and Sally Sheldon, "Unfamiliar Territory," *Guardian*, November 1, 2006, accessed March 15, 2010, http://www.guardian.co.uk/society/2006 /nov/01/childrensservices.guardiansocietysupplement1.

15. Collier and Sheldon, "Unfamiliar Territory."

16. Dominus, "The Fathers' Crusade."

17. "Mission Statement," the website of the American Coalition for Fathers and Children, accessed March 15, 2010, http://acfc.convio.net/site/PageServer?page name=MissionStatement.

18. Dominus, "The Fathers' Crusade."

19. Joyce, "Men's Rights Groups."

20. Michael Flood, "What's Wrong with Fathers' Rights?," in *Men Speak Out: Views on Gender, Sex, and Power*, ed. Shira Tarrant (New York: Routledge, 2007).

21. Joyce, "Men's Rights Groups."

22. This quote is taken from what two activists said on a program aired on National Public Radio early in 1983. They also said that "a man doesn't know the meaning of viciousness in comparison with a woman. If a man's got *his* opponent on the ground, he'll back off. A woman won't. A female-dominated society [is to blame] for many of today's social problems. [Think of] Indira Gandi, Golda Meir, and even the infamous Bitch of Buchenwald, who committed atrocities as head of a Nazi concentration camp. Every time a woman's been in that kind of position of power, it ain't been good!"

23. The "right-wing" demand for fathers' rights is somewhat analogous to the demand for white rights in a racist society. Indeed, those whites who are not privileged by class feel discriminated against when efforts to redress racial or sexual discrimination succeed, even in token ways.

24. Pogrebin, *Family Politics*.

19. Contemporary Legal Trends, Part I

1. Beck v. Beck, New Jersey, Supreme Court, Docket #A-76; 86 N.J. 480, 432 A 2d 63 (1981); 173 N.J. Super. 33 App. Div. (1980).

2. Strictly speaking, the Supreme Court reversed the Appellate decision by *upholding* the right of the trial-court judge to mandate joint custody. The Supreme

Court concluded that it did not retain jurisdiction in this matter and that since two years had elapsed since the original joint custody decree, a new trial-court hearing should take place.

The appellate court had noted that Mrs. Beck was a "more than adequate mother," that Mr. Beck had not been an "involved parent," and that he used his "custodial time" to play golf and "utilized the services of the maternal grandmother" in his stead. The trial-court judge relied on expert testimony that insisted that, although Mr. Beck enjoyed liberal *visitation*, joint custody would be "better" for an uninvolved father than is visitation. "Visitation for all its liberality is not the same thing. . . . It's just entertainment time."

The Supreme Court did note that other experts counseled against joint custody in this *particular* case and that both children did not want joint custody. Although required to do so by the New Jersey Statutes Annotated, the trial judge did not, as previously indicated, interview the children to determine their preference as to custody before arriving at his June 12, 1979, disposition of the matter. And, even after he did interview the two girls during the proceedings which followed the entry of the June 12 judgment, he failed to give to their clear preference the "due weight" required by that statute. It appears that he summarily brushed aside their wishes with the comment that "they may not fully understand" the alternating custody plan he had imposed. "But children are not pawns to be maneuvered and molded into agreement with an arbitrarily produced way of life which they strongly oppose and which neither parent had sought."

3. Luepnitz, private interview, 1984.
4. Luepnitz's custodial and joint custodial fathers *do* describe becoming less "authoritarian" and more "relaxed" in their single fathering style. None of her fathers passed along child-care responsibilities to girlfriends, mothers, or wives.
5. Polikoff, "Gender and Child-Custody Determinations."
6. Laurie Woods, personal interviews, 1981–1984.
7. Paul L. Adams, Judith R. Milner, and Nancy A. Schrepf, *Fatherless Children* (New York: John Wiley and Sons, 1984). Also see chapters 8, 9, and 13.

   Dr. Judith Herman, author of *Father-Daughter Incest* and a psychiatrist and psychotherapist, has also testified as an expert witness on behalf of sexually abused children whose incestuous fathers were fighting for their custody. Her testimony rarely "carries the day." See chapter 13.
8. Justice Vincent R. Balletta Jr., "A View from the Bench: Joint Custody Revisited—Who Will be Given Custody of the Children?," *Family Law Review* 15 (March 1983): 1.

   Carol S. Bruch, a family law professor at the University of California, Davis, and a 1983 consultant to California's law revision commission, saw "a knee-jerk reaction on joint custody. In one recent case, a judge took a nursing infant and said, "'Two weeks with the mother, two weeks with the father.' Now that's insanity." Professor Bruch was quoted by Georgia Dullea, "Wide Changes in Family Life Are Altering Family Law," *New York Times* (February 7, 1983).

9. Luepnitz, private communication, 1984.

10. M. Roman and W. Haddad, *The Disposable Parent: The Case for Joint Custody* (New York: Holt, Reinhart, & Winston, 1978).

11. J. Greif, "Fathers, Children, and Joint Custody," *American Journal of Orthopsychiatry* 49 (1979).

12. Joanne Schulman, "The Truth About Joint Custody: Some Current Myths Exposed," *The Woman's Advocate*, newsletter of the National Center on Women and Family Law, no. 2 (June 1982), and personal communication.

    Susan B. Steinman, Steven Zemmelman, and Thomas M. Knoblauch, "A Study of Parents Who Sought Joint Custody Following Divorce: Who Reaches Agreement and Sustains Joint Custody and Who Returns to Court," *Journal of the American Academy of Child Psychiatry* (1985): 554, 558.

13. Steinman, Zemmelman, and Knoblauch, "Study of Parents."

14. Elizabeth J. Kates, "Debunking Bauserman on Joint versus Sole Custody," The Liz Library, accessed March 12, 2010, http://www.thelizlibrary.org/liz/joint_custody_studies.html.

15. Ibid.

16. Martin Halla, "The Effect of Joint Custody on Marriage and Divorce," The Institute for the Study of Labor (IZA), July 2009.

17. "Study: Joint Custody Best for Kids After Divorce," *USA Today*, accessed March 12, 2010, http://www.usatoday.com/news/health/child/2002-03-25-joint-custody.htm.

18. Laurie Woods, "Mediation: A Backlash to Women's Progress on Family Law Issues in the Courts and Legislatures," National Center on Women and Family Law (1985). Woods notes further that

> in divorce or family law mediation there is no process by which the dependent spouse can verify the extent of the assets or attempt to discover hidden assets of the propertied spouse. The parties are not informed of their legal rights and have no rules or precedents to guide them as to what is equitable or reasonable under the circumstances. The parties deal directly with each other without an independent advocate who can deal with the issues without the emotional baggage burdening the parties. Thus the parties are susceptible to giving away rights out of guilt, domination, intimidation, lack of resources or coercion. Settlements may be agreed upon, but not equitable. Settlements may be agreed upon, but not enforceable. Only those items which both

parties wish to put on the table are settled. And not all issues are foreseen by the parties. There is no guarantee of confidentiality of communications made either to the mediator or in the mediation sessions. Accordingly, the parties may use the statements made in mediation as admissions in a later court proceeding. In many jurisdictions mediators made recommendations to the court but can not be cross-examined with respect to their recommendations. Lay mediation is, in the words of one commentator, "(a) self-determined process between two uninformed spouses guided by a neutral person unfamiliar with the legal rights of the parties, operating without standards or rules which may produce an unenforceable agreement."

It is not a concidence that, just when state legislators were passing strong laws with respect to battery, marital property, and child support enforcement and when the U.S. Congress and U.S. Supreme Court were acting for the first time in history on family law issues, we had a movement to exclude those issues from the courts. It is no coincidence, that as battered women were gaining increased access to the courts through pro se civil procedures or increased arrests, we had a movement that would exclude those cases from the jurisdiction of the civil and criminal courts. Nor is it a coincidence that as standards and enforcement were beginning to be developed by the legal system in the areas of child and spousal support, mediation—which offered no enforcement—was being pushed. "Only the legal system has the power to remove the batterer from the home, to arrest when necessary, to enforce the terms of any decree if a new assault occurs, to discover hidden assets, to prevent dissipation of assets, and to enforce support orders. Only the legislatures and courts can create, develop, expand, and enforce women's rights. Mediation offers no protection, no deterrence, no enforcement, and no opportunity to expand women's rights."

19. Penelope E. Bryan, "Killing Us Softly: Divorce Mediation and the Politics of Power," *Buffalo Law Review* 40 (1992): 441–523.
20. David Finkelhor, "Current Information on the Nature and Scope of Child Sexual Abuse," *The Future of Children* 4 (1994), 31–53; "Child Sexual Abuse," United States Department of Veterans Affairs, accessed March 12, 2010, http://www.ptsd.va.gov/public/pages/child-sexual-abuse.asp.
21. Merrilyn McDonald, "The Myth of Epidemic False Allegations of Sexual Abuse in Divorce Cases," *Court Review* (Spring 1998), 12–19.
22. People v. Amine Baba-Ali, 179 A.D.2d 725 (2d Dept. 1992).
23. In re Nassau Count Dept. of Social Services o/b/o Erika K., 176 A.D.2d 326 (2d Dept. 1991).
24. McClelland v. McClelland, 231 Ill. App. 3d 214 (Ill. App. Ct., 1st Dist., 1st Div'n 1992).

25. In re A.V., 849 S.W. 2d 393 (Ct. App. Tx., 2d Dist., Fort Worth 1993).

26. People v. Yolande, 274 Ill. App. 3d 208 (Ill. App. Ct., 1st Dist., 3rd Div'n 1995).

27. In re P.A., 144 Cal. App. 4th 1339 (Ct. App. Cal., 2d App. Dist., Div'n 3 2006).

28. In re Brynn UU, 220 A.D.2d 830 (3d Dept. 1995).

29. Hale v. Hale, 2006 Tex. App. LEXIS 747 (Ct. App. Tx., 4th Dist., San Antonio, 2006).

30. Carol S. Bruch, "Parental Alienation Syndrome and Alienated Children—Getting It Wrong in Child Custody Cases," *Family Law Quarterly* 35, no. 527 (Fall 2001).

31. Ibid.

32. In 1992 Gardner wrote these views in "True and False Accusations of Child Sex Abuse," which was published by *Creative Therapeutics*.

33. See N.K. v. M.K. (2007); People v. Fortin (2001); Snyder v. Cedar (2009).

34. Arizona Coalition Against Domestic Violence (2003); Massachusetts Supreme Judicial Court (1990); Meier (2003); Silverman et al. (2004).

20. Contemporary Legal Trends, Part II

1. An experienced lawyer randomly chose these cases for me.

2. In re K.F., 437 N.W.2d 559.

3. Wetzel v. Wetzel, 715 S.W.2d 387 (Tex. App. Dalls 1986).

4. Denise R. v. Arizona Department of Economic Security, 221 Ariz. 92; 210 P.3d 1263; 2009 Ariz. App.

5. C.S.B. v. State Dep't of Human Res., 2009 Ala. Civ. App. LEXIS 95 (Ala. Civ. App. Apr. 3, 2009).

6. In re the Marriage of Birdsall, 197 Cal. App.3d 1024, 243 Cal.Rptr. 287 (Cal. Ct.App.1988).

7. Blew v. Verta, 420 Pa. Super. 528.

8. Teegarden v. Teegarden, 642 N.E.2d 1007, 1008 (Ind. Ct. App. 1994).

9. In re Marriage of Wicklund, 84 Wn. App. 763, 770, 932 P.2d 652 (1996).

10. Curiale v. Reagan, 222 Cal. App. 3d 1597, 272 Cal. Rptr. 520.

11. McGuffin v. Overton, 214 Mich. App. 95, 542 N.W. 2d 288 (1995).

12. Matter of Guardianship of Astonn H., 167 Misc. 2d 840; 635 N.Y.S. 2d 418.

13. V.C. v. M.J.B., 163 N.J. 200, 748 A. 2d 539, 80 A.L.R. 5th 663 (2000).

14. C.E.W. v. D.E.W., 2004 ME 43, 845 A. 2d 1146 (Me. 2004).

15. V.C. v. M.J.B., 319 N.J. Super. 103, 725 A. 2d 13 (App. Div. 1999).

16. Smith v. Jones, 69 Mass. App. Ct. 400, 868 N.E. 2d 629 (2007). B.F. v. T.D., 194 S.W. 3d 310 (Ky. 2006).

17. Leslea Diane White, individually and as next friend for C.E.W. and Z.A.W., Appellants v. Elizabeth Michelle White, n/k/a Elizabeth Michelle Crowe, respondent, No. 69580 (Mo. App. W.D., June 23, 2009).

18. Debra H. v. Janice R., 877 N.Y.S. 2d 259 (N.Y. App. Div. 2009).

19. Lacey M. Smith v. Charlene M. Gordon, 968 A.2d 1; 2009 Del.

20. Miller-Jenkins v. Miller-Jenkins (VT 78 2006); 180 Vt. 441; 912 A. 2d 951 (Vt. 2006).

21. Robert Francoeur, *Utopian Motherhood: New Trends in Human Reproduction* (New York: Doubleday, 1970).

22. This is the way Drs. Patrick Steptoe and Robert Edwards engineered "test-tube" baby Louise Brown's birth on July 25, 1978.

23. This happened in Australia when a South American couple died without heirs, leaving two fertilized embryos behind in a Melbourne hospital. Physicians have asked "an ethics committee for advice on whether a surrogate mother should give birth to them so that they can grow up and claim their multi-million dollar fortune" (*New York Post,* June 18, 1984).

24. Mary Kay Blakely, "Surrogate Mothers: For Whom Are They Working?" *Ms.* magazine (March 1983).

25. Reluctance to part with a newborn child is not surprising. In September 1981, a surrogate mother, Elizabeth Kane, said of the child she bore for a Kentucky couple, "If I had the opportunity to hold him again, I would have to turn it down because I couldn't trust myself" ("And She's a Mom in Mourning," *New York Post,* September 8, 1981).

    The same year, surrogate mother Denise Thrane was forced into a custody battle in California for the child she was still bearing. During her pregnancy, Thrane had decided to retain the child she had originally conceived for another couple. ("Whose Baby Is It, Anyway?," *Newsweek,* April 6, 1981).

26. Ivor Peterson, *New York Times,* February 6, 1983. Malahoff has since denied that he refused to allow lifesaving procedures to be administered.

27. Phyllis Chesler, *Sacred Bond: The Legacy of Baby M.* (Times Books: New York, 1988).

28. L.M.S. v. S.L.S., 105 Wis. 2d 118, 312 N.W. 2d 853 (Ct. App. 1981).

29. A.G.R. v. S.H. and D.R.H., Superior Court of New Jersey, Docket #FD-09-1838-07.

30. In re Marriage of Buzzanca, 61 Cal. App. 4th 1410, 72 Cal. Rptr. 2d 280, 77 A.L.R. 5th 775 (4th Dist. 1998).

31. Doe v. Doe, 244 Conn. 403, 710 A. 2d 1297 (1998).

32. Johnson v. Calvert, 5 Cal. 4th 84, 19 Cal. Rptr. 2d 494, 851 P. 2d 776 (1993).

33. Robert B. v. Susan B., 109 Cal. App. 4th 1109, 135 Cal. Rptr. 2d 785 (6th Dist. 2003).

34. Belsito v. Clark, 67 Ohio Misc. 2d 54, 644 N.E. 2d 760 (C.P. 1994).

35. Adoption of Matthew B., 232 Cal. App. 1239, 284 Cal. Rptr. 18 (1st Dist. 1991).

36. Kathleen S. Pusey v. Robert O. Pusey, 728 P. 2d 117 (Utah 1986).

37. Peter Q. Harris v. Bonnie L. Harris, 546 A. 2d 208 (Ver. 1988).

38. Jason B. Marsh v. Penny V. Marsh, Ohio App. LEXIS 3348 (Ohio App. 2001).
39. In re the Marriage of Connie Sue Boldt and Kevin Scott Boldt, 2003 Iowa App., LEXIS 1129 (Iowa App. 2003).
40. In re the Marriage of Lyle Martin Hansen and Delores Lorene Hansen, 733 N.W. 2d 683 (Iowa 2007).
41. Joseph Goldstein, Anna Freud, and Albert J. Solnit, *Beyond the Best Interests of the Child* (London: The Free Press, 1979).
42. Rena K. Uviller, "Fathers' Rights and Feminism: The Maternal Presumption Revisited," *Harvard Women's Law Journal* 1, no. 1 (1978): 107–130.
43. Uviller is not saying that children need their "psychological" parent only during infancy or until they can reach less "tender" ages. Under the American and European "tender years" tradition, children automatically reverted back to their fathers' custody at any one of several arbitrary ages between five and thirteen. Those who conceived of and fought for the "tender years" presumption sincerely believed that access to maternal (or female) tenderness was in the child's "best interest." The presumption itself was used to maximize the amount of time that children could be assured of access to their mothers— *without* eroding the principle of father rule and father right.
44. Lucy Katz, "The Maternal Preference and the Psychological Parent: Suggestions for Allocating the Burden of Proof in Custody Litigation," *Connecticut Bar Journal* 53 (1979): 343–348.
45. Many feminist lawyers are more concerned with "equal" rights, even for unequals, and for fathers' rights as opposed to mothers' rights. Three pro-mother lawyers (a minority among feminist lawyers to date) have interpreted this in different ways.

> **Lucille:** Feminist lawyers for fathers' rights seem compelled to offer men an incentive or reward for remaining involved with mothers and children. I don't understand why else feminists would be emotionally invested in fathers' custodial rights at all when there's so much undone for mothers. Is this their way of personally working out their feminism, their careers, or their heterosexuality?
>
> **Barbara:** Some feminists for fathers' rights are so male-identified they don't like to behave like mothers in their office or in the courtroom. They either have no children, or if they do, they don't parent themselves. They see biological reproduction as messy or as a woman's own responsibility. Just like the department of welfare does.
>
> **Peggy:** Feminists for fathers' rights are mainly interested in getting publicity and money. Fathers' rights is more dramatic, sexier, better-paying than trying to get child support enforced for a mother who has no money.

Reading the proposals of the pro-mother lawyers was a great pleasure. It is always a pleasure for me, as a psychologist, to contemplate the ways in which human reason remains nobly and creatively at the disposal of human emotions: necessarily subjective, not objective.

46. Helen Levine and Alma Estable, "The Power Politics of Motherhood," and occasional papers. Unpublished Canadian manuscript (1983), Carlton School of Social Work.

The last sentence is a quote from Pauline Bart's review of Nancy Chodorow, *The Reproduction of Mothering* in *Off Our Backs,* January 1981.

47. Denise Nadeau, mother and theorist, unpublished communication.

48. Ruddick, "Maternal Thinking."

49. Private interviews, 1981–1984.

21. Mother's Wisdom

1. Alta, *Momma: A Start on All the Untold Stories* (New York: Times Change Press, 1984); Arcana, *Every Mother's Son*; Virginia Barber and Merrill Maguire Skaggs, *The Mother Person* (Indianapolis: Bobbs-Merrill, 1975); J. Bernard, *Self-Portrait of a Family* (Boston: Beacon Press, 1978), *The Future of Motherhood* (New York: Dial, 1974), and *Women, Wives and Mothers* (Chicago: Aldine, 1975); Phyllis Chesler, *With Child* (New York: Thomas Y. Crowell, 1979; Berkeley, 1981); Nancy Chodorow, *The Reproduction of Mothering* (Berkeley: University of California Press, 1978); Toi Derricott, "In Knowledge of Young Boys" in *The Empress of the Death House* (Detroit: Lotus, 1978); Dorothy Dinnerstein, *The Mermaid and the Minotaur* (New York: Harper & Row, 1976); Jean Bethke Elshtain, "Feminist Discourse and Its Discontents: Language Power and Meaning"and "Antigone's Daughters: Reflections on Female Identity and the State," in Diamond, ed., *Families, Politics and Public Policy: A Feminist Dialogue on Women and the State*; Oriana Fallaci, *Letter to a Child Never Born* (New York: Simon & Schuster, 1976); Joan Goulianos, ed., *By a Woman Writ: Literature from Six Centuries By and About Women* (Indianapolis: Bobbs-Merrill, 1973); Joanne Haggerty, *Daughters of the Moon* (New York: Bobbs-Merrill, 1971); G. E. Hanscombe and J. Forster, *Rocking the Cradle: Lesbian Mothers—A Challenge in Family Living* (Boston: Alyson Publications, 1982); Gladys Hindmarch, *A Birth Account* (Vancouver: New Star Books, 1976); Brigitte Jordan, *Birth in Four Cultures: A Cross-Cultural Investigation of Childbirth in Yucatan, Holland, Sweden and the United States* (St. Albans, VT: Eden Press Women's Publications, 1978); Eleanor H. Kuykendall, "Toward an Ethic of Nurturance: Luce Irigaray on Mothering and Power," in *Mothering: Essays in Feminist Theory,* Joyce Treblicot, ed. (Totowa, N.J: Rowman & Allanheld, 1984); Jane Lazarre, *The Mother Knot* (New York: Dell, 1976); Angela Barron McBride, *The Growth*

and Development of Mothers (New York: Harper & Row Perennial Library, 1973); Tillie Olsen, *Silences* (New York: Delacorte Press—Seymour Lawrence, 1978); Alicia Ostriker, "The Mother/Child Papers," *Feminist Studies* (1978); Shirley L. Radl, *Mothers Day Is Over* (New York: Warner Books, 1973), and *How to Be a Mother and a Person Too* (New York: Rawson-Wade, 1979); Adrienne Rich, *Of Woman Born: Motherhood as Experience and Institution* (New York: W. W. Norton, 1976); Ruddick, "Maternal Thinking" and "Preservative Love and Military Destruction: Some Reflections on Mothering and Peace," in Joyce Treblicot, ed., *Mothering: Essays on Feminist Theory* (Totowa, NJ: Rowman & Allanheld, 1984); Jain Nyborg Sherrand, *Mother Warrior Pilgrim: A Personal Chronicle* (Kansas City: Andrews and McMeel, 1980); Caroline Whitbeck, "The Maternal Instinct," in Treblicot, *Mothering.*

2. Feminist theorists are, understandably, very concerned with patriarchy's use of biological differences as a way of keeping women, including mothers, economically dependent or impoverished. Some feminist theorists are also concerned with minimizing women's unique biological role in relation to children in order to persuade men to assume domestic and "maternal" responsibilities at home.

   It is important to remember that women *can* and do perform "male" activities. Women have been denied proper training—and wages—for doing so because of presumed biological differences.

3. Whitbeck, "The Maternal Instinct" (1972) and "Afterward" (1982) in Treblicot, *Mothering.*

4. Mary O'Brien, "Feminist Theory and Dialectical Logic," in *Feminist Theory: A Criticism of Ideology*, Nannerl O'Keohane, Michelle Rosaldo, and Barbara C. Gelpi, eds. (University of Chicago Press, 1981, 1982). I don't know whether biological mothers are significantly different from adoptive mothers in either their experience or their practice of motherhood. They may or must have differences in feeling and perception. However, both biological and adoptive mothers have been socialized as women; both have experienced daughterhood; both have experienced being mothers under similar patriarchal conditions.

5. Arcana, *Our Mothers' Daughters.*

6. Chesler, *With Child.*

7. Nora Bartlett, "An Excerpt from My Unpublished Writing," in Michelle Wandor, ed., *On Gender and Writing* (Boston: Pandora Press, 1983).

8. Chesler, *With Child.*

9. Nearly half of the heterosexual mothers (46 percent) and 50 percent of the lesbian mothers verbally expressed a mothers' rights view, while 30 percent of the heterosexual mothers and 43 percent of the lesbian mothers identified themselves as feminists at the time of the interview.

10. All custodially embattled mothers experienced maternal "connectedness."

Both maternally assertive and nonassertive heterosexual mothers had achieved the same average education and had mothered for the same average number of years. None of the maternally assertive mothers ever won in court; nearly a third (27 percent) of the *nonassertive* mothers did at first. Perhaps an initial courtroom victory confused mothers about the existence of their rights or about the willingness of the law to protect them from subsequent paternal harassment. Perhaps those mothers who were able to settle privately, as 20 percent of the *assertive* mothers had, were already "clear" about their natural maternal rights and the nonexistence of their maternal legal rights; perhaps, as we have seen, they were also married to less violent husbands.

11. It is important to realize that the numbers involved here are relatively small and that no statistical significance is involved.

12. This excellent phrase belongs to John Demos, author of *Entertaining Satan*.

13. Some recent feminist theorists have described women and men as "similar"; other theorists have described women and men as profoundly "different." The majority of these studies of women (and men) have been psychological rather than political or historical, rather than theoretical or experimental, rather than based on field studies of the real lives of adult women. They are also written from the point of view of white, Western, middle-class, educated, married, or heterosexual women. This is not meant as a criticism. It is a description of the unspoken or unacknowledged angle of vision.

14. Sitting in the same playground and engaging in parallel comothering are not ways of maternally nurturing another woman or her child, although the company is always appreciated. Taking over the care of a blood daughter or blood sister's child is more common among the impoverished or the racially marginalized. However, it is a *familial* form of affiliation. It is sometimes, but not always, a form of female-female competition within the same blood family.

15. Ruddick, "Maternal Thinking."

16. I am not saying that practicing mothers don't have breaking points or are not entitled to sabbaticals as well as assistance and support. They are. I am saying that few practicing mothers voluntarily leave their children for long or in "disconnected" ways if they do. Mothers remain "connected" to their children for life.

Index

. . . .